THE STRUGGLE OVER THE SOUL OF ECONOMICS

THE STRUGGLE OVER THE SOUL OF ECONOMICS

INSTITUTIONALIST AND NEOCLASSICAL

ECONOMISTS IN AMERICA

BETWEEN THE WARS

Yuval P. Yonay

PRINCETON UNIVERSITY PRESS   PRINCETON, NEW JERSEY

Copyright © 1998 by Princeton University Press
Published by Princeton University Press, 41 William Street,
Princeton, New Jersey 08540
In the United Kingdom: Princeton University Press,
Chichester, West Sussex
All Rights Reserved

Library of Congress Cataloging-in-Publication Data
Yonay, Yuval P., 1958–
The struggle over the soul of economics : institutionalist
and neoclassical economists in America between the wars /
Yuval P. Yonay
p.   cm.
Includes bibliographical references and index.
ISBN 0-691-03419-2 (cl : alk. paper)
1. Institutional economics—History—20th century.
2. Neoclassical school of economics—History—20th century.
3. Economics—United States—History—20th century. I. Title.
HB99.5.Y66   1998
330.1—dc21   97-42954   CIP

This book has been composed in Sabon

Princeton University Press books are printed
on acid-free paper and meet the guidelines
for permanence and durability of the Committee
on Production Guidelines for Book Longevity
of the Council on Library Resources

http//:pup.princeton.edu

Printed in the United States of America

10   9   8   7   6   5   4   3   2   1

TO MY PARENTS

Haim and Haviva Yonay ———————————————————

WHO TAUGHT ME THE IMPORTANCE OF LOVE,

SOCIAL RESPONSIBILITY, AND KNOWLEDGE

AND IN MEMORY OF MY GRANDPARENTS,

ISAAC AND ALTA YONAY AND SIMCHA

AND TZINA BAR-SHALOM, WHO BEQUEATHED

US THE APPRECIATION OF THESE NOBLE VALUES

Contents

Acknowledgments   xi

One
Introduction: A Sociological Interpretation of the Modern
History of Economics   3

Overview   3
A Textbook Version of the History of Economics   7
The Construction of Scientific Knowledge   14
Accounts of Scientific Development: The Actor-Network
  Analysis   20
The Goals of This Study   24

Two
The Neoclassical Era (1870–1914) from a Different Angle   29

The Economics of Marshall and His Students   30
The Economic Rebels and the Establishment of the
  American Economic Association   35
Conclusions: Economists in the Forefront of Social Reform   46

Three
Reconstructing the History of Institutionalism   49

The Rise of Institutionalism (1890–1914)   50
The Sway of Institutionalism during the Interwar Period   53
The Institutionalist Contributions to Economics   60
Is There an Institutionalist Doctrine?   65
The "Old-Fashioned" Neoclassical School and
  Institutionalism   70
Conclusions: A Prospering, Mighty, and Fertile School   75

Four
The Struggle over the Meaning of Science   77

The Institutionalist Attack   80
The Neoclassicist Counterattack   87
The Evaluation and Perception of Theory   89
Conclusions: Contesting Perceptions of an Economic Science   94

Five
Bringing People and Institutions Back In: The Struggle over the
Scope of Economics   100

Exorcising the Economic Man: The Institutionalist
  Critique   101
Rearranging the Boundaries of Economics: The Neoclassical
  Defense   106
Social Institutions as Allies   110
Conclusions: Changing Concepts of Human Nature   112

Six
The Free Market on Trial: The Struggle over the Gap between
Reality and Theory   115

Making Money and Making Goods: Nonmonetary Evaluation
  of Welfare   118
Lack of Knowledge and Its Implications   122
Competition as a Source of Waste   124
The Missing Dimension: Power Disparity and Labor Relations   128
Conclusions: Economic Realities and Economic Models   130

Seven
The Struggle over Social Relevance and the Place of Values   136

Institutionalists: Overpriced Value Theory   137
Institutionalists: Promises and Alleged Successes   140
The Neoclassical Attack: Doubting the Institutionalist Strategy   143
The Neoclassical Defense: Theory Is the Key to Powerful
  Policies   147
The Scientific Study of Value: Should Economics Be an
  Ethical Science?   150
Conclusions: The Coupling of Validity and Relevance   157

Eight
Evolution or Revolution? The Struggle over the History
of the Discipline   163

A "Revolutionary" Stigma: The Neoclassical Attack on
  Institutionalism   165
Institutionalists as the Guardians of Tradition   168
Recruitment of Unorthodox Authorities   175
Conclusions: How to Be Both Traditional and Innovative   177

Nine
Epilogue: The Fall of Institutionalism and the Rise of Modern
Economics   184

The Rise of Mathematical Economics   185
The Mathematical Economics-Econometrics Alliance   187
Keynes, Keynesianism, and the Transformation of Economics   190
The Old and the New Economics   193

Ten
Conclusions: The Evolution of Economic Analysis 196
   *The Translation of Mute Objects: How to Explain Economic
     Knowledge?* 199
   Economics as an Open Network: Did Economics Progress? 211
   Pride without Arrogance: What Is a Good Science? 218

Notes 223

Bibliography 251

Index 279

Acknowledgments

THE understanding, patience, and support of my family, many good friends, teachers, colleagues, and institutions made it possible to successfully finish the writing and publishing of this manuscript. It all started with my dissertation at Northwestern University, for which I owe a great deal to my dissertation committee. Allan Schnaiberg, the chair of the committee, spent dozens of hours listening to my problems and offering valuable advice. His constant interest and enthusiasm kept motivating my research and writing all along. The confidence and encouragement of Art Stinchcombe were no less valuable in keeping me moving, and his scrutinizing criticism raised the quality of my research. Bernie Beck's office often served as the testing-ground for my arguments, and his insightful comments helped me to clarify my ideas and elaborate on their implications. Howie Becker was responsible both for keeping me on the terrain of common sense and for exposing me to the Latourian framework in which this work is heavily immersed. Finally, the broad knowledge of Joel Mokyr prevented some embarrassing mistakes in my work and helped me to reach valuable sources I had ignored. Together the committee members are largely responsible for my success, although all of them let me go my own way. Their confidence in me and their endless willingness to help me whenever I needed were priceless.

After my dissertation had been completed I enjoyed postdoctoral fellowships at the Edelstein Center for the History and Philosophy of Science and Medicine at the Hebrew University in Jerusalem and at the Institute for Advanced Study in Princeton. I would like to greatly thank these institutions and the Center for the Sociology of Innovation at the École des Mines de Paris for financial support during the time I revised my dissertation and improved it toward publication. Many colleagues and friends with whom I discussed my project in these years contributed to its betterment from a dissertation to a "real book." During my stay at the Edelstein Center I benefited from conversations with Michael Ben-Chaim, Yoav Ben-Dov, Yaron Ezrahi, Michael Head, and Alon Kadish from the Hebrew University, and Yehuda Elkana from Tel Aviv University. In Princeton I was lucky to hear comments and helpful suggestions from Steve Cole, Paul Dimaggio, Frank Dobbin, Otniel Dror, Clifford Geertz, Alan Gilbert, Walter Jackson, Larry Lauden, Jim Rule, Robert Wade, Michael Walzer, and Norton Wise. Michel Callon, Marianne De Laet, and Karin Knorr-Cetina must be specially mentioned for "straightening me out" and correcting my understanding of the actor-network analysis. My term at the Institute also enabled me to meet Albert Hirschman, one of the heroes of the story I tell in this book. This unique opportunity allowed me to benefit from his generosity and incisive wisdom and to enrich my understanding of the changes in the economic profession on which I am writing here. In Paris I was able to test my command of the actor-network analysis on its native soil (with results that still leave some room for improvement) in conversations with Bas de Laat, Bruno Latour, Alexander Mallard, and Ivan Tchalakov.

I owe special thanks to many economists who discussed with me current problems in economics and its past. Although I cannot list them all, I must mention Robert Gordon who let me sit in his macroeconomic course and revealed to me many of the secrets of macroeconomics, past and present. Charles Calomiris's critical views were also important in understanding the history of macroeconomics before this field was officially christened. My friends Elchanan Ben-Porath, Yitzhak Gilboa, and Yossef Spiegel served as a kind audience and allowed me to "test" my arguments on economists, at the same time that they exposed me to novel developments in game theory and industrial organization. I also thank Jonathan Hughes, who informed me on the recent trends in economic history; Morton Kamien, who shared with me his thoughts on the mathematization of economics; Don Patinkin, who listened to my arguments and shared with me his findings and ideas concerning the emergence of Keynesian economics; and Jacob Mincer, who told me his memories and thoughts on the changes in economics in the postwar years. It is a special pleasure for me to warmly express my gratitude to Marc Perelman, who spent many hours with me in his nice house, commented on my work, and offered more insights into the processes that had taken economics to its current place. One of the nicest things about academia is the willingness of many people to help even when they have no duty to do so. In addition to the people mentioned so far I have to mention Professor Granovetter, who was then at SUNY, and who gave me important advice in an early stage of my project. Yehuda Shenhav from Tel Aviv University also offered insightful comment that helped me to organize my thoughts toward the end of the project.

A special gratitude I owe to the referees of the manuscript, Michael Bernstein and Arjo Klamer, who read the whole work twice and made numerous suggestions on how to make it better. The finished product is no doubt much better than the original due to their painstaking reading and thoughtful comments. I wish to thank also my editors at Princeton University Press—Peter Dougherty, Bill Laznovsky, and their associates—for their patience and help, and especially for the enthusiasm Peter showed toward my work.

As important as intellectual stimulation is, the spiritual help of loyal and supporting friends is even more crucial for the success of such a project. It is impossible to mention all of the friends who accompanied me along the way but some deserve special acknowledgment: Gil Amrami, Ilan ben-Ami and Debbie London, Adi Ben-Ari, Nitza Berkovitch, Avi Cordova, Eli and Ula Goldstein, David Gordon, Won Kim, Vered Kraus, Marianne De Laet, Giddy Landan, Ronen Raz, Horacio Rotestein, Allan Schnaiberg, Head Sela, Sharon Sheehan, Haya Stier, Richard Steiner, Ilan Talmud, Nurit Tzafrir, Amnon Walman, Adam Weinberg. But most of all I would like to thank Yvonne Newsome and Nati and Linda Urieli who supported me during the hard hours of churning the dissertation out. Without them this book would have never been completed.

I would like to make one more personal note here. As I was preparing the final draft of this book I learned that Thomas Kuhn passed away. I have never met Mr. Kuhn and I know nothing about him personally, but his book *The Structure of Scientific Revolutions* has had an immense influence on my thinking. I first read it when I was an undergraduate student and it fascinated me ever since. As can be seen in the following pages, I disagree with many of the things Kuhn said, but his classic book is still full of insightful observations that make it perennially illuminating regardless of one's theoretical approach.

THE STRUGGLE OVER THE SOUL OF ECONOMICS

One

Introduction: A Sociological Interpretation of the Modern History of Economics

The Purely analytic scientist becomes so accustomed to seeing matter as a demonstration of certain verifiable or falsifiable principles that he lives at one remove from it. Between him and the real world springs the law, the explanation, the necessity to categorize. Everything Midas turned to gold, everything this kind of scientist touches turns to its function in his analysis. . . . The Complexity of the modern sciences is such that specialization is essential; not only in the interest of scientific or industrial efficiency, but in the nature of the mind's capacity. The scholar in many fields is extinct; not because the desire to be such a scholar is extinct, but because the *fields* are too many, and too complex.

   (John Fowles, *Aristos* 9:33–34)

Overview

This book analyzes a struggle between two schools of economics in the period between the world wars. The two schools are the neoclassical school, which emerged at the last third of the nineteenth century, and the institutionalist one,[1] which had started with the works of Veblen and Commons at the end of the nineteenth century and had enjoyed a short period of prosperity in the interwar period before rapidly declining after the Second World War. Current historians of economic thought usually ignore the institutionalists or consider their movement to be an ephemeral and inconsequential episode in the history of economics. My story, however, reveals that the rise of the institutionalist school was an important chapter in the history of economics and has had lingering effects on the practice of economics to the present.

By analyzing in detail the neoclassical-institutionalist conflict, I wish to achieve three goals. First, I hope to expose a forgotten chapter in the history of economics. Historians of the period commonly assume that pre-Keynesian economists were strong supporters of *laissez-faire* policies, who continued to oppose fiercely any intervention of the state in the man-

agement of the economy, despite the protracted Great Depression. It is
commonly argued that it was the Great Depression which proved the
inadequacy of neoclassical theory, and that it was Keynes who managed
to find a better theory (e.g., Lekachman 1966; Heilbroner 1972, chap. 8;
Hall 1989; Blaug 1990b). As we will see in chapter 2, this presumed gap
between pre-Keynesian neoclassical economics on one hand, and Keynesianism on the other hand is grossly distorted. But my focus is on another
aspect of pre-Keynesian economics, which is completely missing or seriously distorted in many works on economic thought during the first half
of the twentieth century.

This study shows that the institutionalist economists, who were quite
numerous at the time, strongly attacked that economic theory which proscribed state intervention. Marshall and his students had already criticized the notion of *laissez-faire,* but the institutionalists went much farther. The support of most American economists in intervention *preceded*
the Great Depression.[2] The experience of a managed economy during
World War I strengthened the belief of many economists that coordination and planning could increase economic productivity.[3] The fact that
many of the American economists in the interwar period espoused institutionalism may change our conception of the intellectual history that led to
the New Deal and to the emergence of the American welfare state. At the
same time it makes problematic some phenomena which have looked
"natural" so far. These include the support of many economists for later
conservative economic policies and the highly abstract nature of economic science after the Second World War. The current so-called "neoclassical school" cannot be conceived of as the natural outgrowth of the
prewar Marshallian neoclassical school. From certain perspectives these
"neoclassical" schools appear more antagonistic to each other than
Marshallian neoclassicism and the institutionalist school that fought over
the discipline before the Second World War.

Important as these historical theses are, I hope that this analysis of
interwar conflicts in economics has important implications for a broader
set of theoretical issues concerning the nature of scientific practice and the
forces behind changes in scientific knowledge. My second goal in this
work is to use the case of the struggle between institutionalism and neoclassical economics to demonstrate the merits of the constructivist approach in the sociology of science, and especially the actor-network analysis of Bruno Latour, for understanding the nature of scientific practice in
economics. Although I am not suggesting here an explanation of the
changes in economics, the story I tell is relevant to models of "progress"
in scientific knowledge. In economics as in other fields, historians and
methodologists have used Kuhnian and Lakatosian perspectives to make
sense of the history of their field. These reconstructions of history, I will

show, are based on selective reading of the history and on arbitrary definitions of the boundaries of economics. Furthermore, they impose obsolete conceptions of science on the practice of economists and use value judgments instead of impartial analysis of the history. Although the constructivists are conscious of the fact that no historical account is free of biases, they seek to explain the development of science *not* on the basis of what present-day practitioners consider "good science." I will argue that my constructivist account is more compatible with the full history of economics and that it avoids many of the problems that Kuhnian and Lakatosian accounts have met.

Instead of explaining change solely by the accumulation of problematic anomalies (Kuhn), or by the exhaustion of the ability of a research program to generate innovations (Lakatos), the cause of change implicit in Latour's scheme is conflict and negotiation among various players, economists and noneconomists alike. The neoclassical-institutionalist struggle is a good illustration of this. The rise of institutionalism after World War I could indeed be attributed either to anomalies which made it difficult to accept neoclassical theory, or to the depletion of new, interesting things to say from that perspective. The constructivist view, however, would not deem these explanations sufficient. It would inquire as to (1) why certain phenomena were *perceived* anomalies by *some*, but not all, economists, (2) why certain anomalies were *considered* important enough for *some* economists to invalidate neoclassical economics, and (3) why *some* economists stopped believing in the potential of neoclassical economics to yield more important findings. The answers to questions of this sort are to be found in the beliefs of individual scientists, the negotiations among them, and their capabilities to mobilize various resources and to forge alliances to promote their opinions. This view *does* admit the cardinal role of cognitive factors in decisions scientists make, but it reminds us that cognitive factors—such as contradictions between theory and empirical findings ("anomalies"), the validity of evidence of various sorts, or the priority of different standards—are mediated through and realized in social, hence contingent, processes. The same cognitive principles and ideals can be actualized by various practitioners in *different* ways. The question, then, is *whose* perspective is more powerful, and *which* direction gains enough momentum to sweep the majority of the discipline. The answers to these questions cannot be deduced from the cognitive factors alone: they must be sought after in the social relations among practitioners.

For historians and methodologists of economics, this book offers a new way to look at the history of their discipline. For the wider audience of students of science the book provides an application of the constructivist approach to the description of a broad historical process, which encompassed a whole discipline and several decades. This is the third goal of the book. Most constructivist research has been preoccupied so far with analyses of practices in single laboratories (e.g., Latour and Woolgar 1979), with the tactics and strategies of individuals or small teams (e.g., Latour 1988a; 1988b), and with similar "micro" studies. This "bias" is not accidental. The constructivist approach is suspicious of "macro" concepts such as "disciplines," "paradigms," and "research programs." It is more interested in exposing the dynamics of scientific practice by thick descriptions of how concrete scientists use instruments, handle materials, communicate with each other, and negotiate with non-scientists (see Pickering 1992a).

Entities, such as "neoclassical economics," "institutionalism," "Cambridge school," and so forth, are indeed not objects that stand independently of human action and interaction. The decision to lump together a large number of economists, whose works are diverse and heterogeneous, is always somewhat arbitrary and disputable. The boundaries of such entities often, if not always, change over time. It is not unusual that the "schools" are "created" only after their members had disappeared. Similarly, bitter enemies, who conceived of their views as diametrically opposed to each other, can be pigeonholed as peers of the same camp by later-day practitioners. All these facts renders my decision to interpret the struggle between a "neoclassical school" and an "institutionalist school" more than a bit suspicious. Many sociologists would prefer my story to revolve around a concrete group of economists or a specific moment in the history of economics.

And yet, categorization of individuals into paradigms and mapping the terrain of disciplines are important practices both for practicing scientists and for historians who wish to present a coherent reading of history. Various labels were used by the interwar economists themselves, as we will see in chapter 3, and the current historiography of economics is replete with references to neoclassical, institutionalist, historicist, and many other schools. This might be the cause for much of the confusion among historians and economists concerning the works of individual practitioners and the relations among them. Nonetheless, I thought it would be easier for current readers to follow the historical story if I use the common ambiguous labels. I do so with utmost care. The next two chapters tell the history of neoclassical economics and institutionalism—mostly in the United States but with unavoidable digressions to its British sources of influence—as I see it. This narrative, I hope, will dispel much of the confusion caused by the conventional nomenclature. But I have to warn the reader again: when I use the terms "neoclassical economics" and "institutionalism" I do not refer to two clear-cut camps of economists. The terms are used to illuminate the variety of views of economists in regard to the nature of their field. Some economists stood closer to what one can call the institutionalist pole, while others occupied the space near the neoclassical one. But each economist stood in a unique position of his or her own, and many were somewhere between these two poles.

The next sections provide a background for each of the main goals and a summary of my arguments. First, the conventional history of economics is presented and its Kuhnian and Lakatosian reconstructions are critically examined. The following section presents the constructivist approach in the sociology of science in general, while the fourth section concentrates on the actor-network analysis and on how scientific changes are explained by that specific variant of the constructivist approach. Finally, the last section takes us back to interwar economics and previews the neoclassical-institutionalist struggle, which will be described in detail in chapters 4 to 8.

A Textbook Version of the History of Economics

The history of economics as commonly presented in economics introductory textbooks, or as told by historians of economic thought, is quite straightforward (Mirowski 1994, 68). First, Adam Smith (1723–90) created the new science of economics. His *The Wealth of Nations*, published in 1776, is considered to be the cornerstone of the discipline, and, combined with the works of David Ricardo (1772–1823), Thomas Malthus (1766–1834), and others, constitutes classical economics.[4] In the 1870s this tradition was elaborated on by the introduction of marginal calculus by several scholars simultaneously: William Jevons (1835–82) in England, Carl Menger (1840–1921) in Austria, Léon Walras (1834–1910) in France, and, a bit later, John Bates Clark (1847–1938) in the United States. Menger's work laid the foundations for the Austrian School, and Walras's work is the basis for the Lausanne school, where Walras and his successor, Vilfredo Pareto (1848–1923), taught. The new marginal economics, systematized and organized by Alfred Marshall (1842–1924), continued to entertain the basic assumptions of hedonism and rationality, held by the classical tradition. And like the classical tradition, it supported *laissez-faire* policy of government nonintervention. Hence, it became known as *neo*classical economics.[5]

This theory had dominated the discipline until the Great Depression challenged its maxims and threatened its preeminence, if not the very existence of the discipline itself. Fortunately, John Maynard Keynes (1883–1946) appeared with a solution to the paradox of the Great Depression and saved the discipline. Post–World War II economics saw the synthesis of Keynesian and neoclassical teachings and the application of mathematical and statistical tools to this "neoclassical-Keynesian synthesis."[6] This development, it is argued, led economic theory to its heights, and made it the most developed social science. Later writers added a new chapter: the so-called failure of economics in the 1970s—they argue—led many to doubt the Keynesian Revolution, and the neoclassical approach has found new supporters in what some call "the new classical economics." The current situation is depicted as a struggle between Keynesians (or neo-Keynesians) and new classicist theories (monetarism, rational expectations, real business cycle), which is a new chapter in the development of the theory, which had started with Adam Smith, and progressed continuously through the works of Ricardo, Marshall, and Keynes. All these economists are thus presented as links in a chain. Each one of them built on the theory of his immediate predecessor, corrected some of his or her mistakes, and endowed to his successors theory in a better shape (cf. Leijonhufvud 1976, 67–68). Each theory is replaced by a more powerful one, and economic knowledge grows and improves with each generation of economists.

The textbook version of the history of economics was used as a basis for Kuhnian and Lakatosian historiographies. Historians of economics have debated whether the development of the discipline was achieved through neoclassical and Keynesian revolutions, according to the Kuhnian model, or through a gradual succession of degenerating research programs by progressive ones, according to the Lakatosian model. I will argue that both views are seriously inadequate and misleading. They reconstruct the history to fit the models, ignore important episodes and ideas that played significant roles in the history, and leave unanswered deep conceptual problems. In what follows I discuss the Kuhnian and the Lakatosian applications offered so far and the problems with these applications.

Kuhn's main idea is that scientists in each field share the same paradigm. A paradigm is an exemplar of how to work in the field. It is usually based on a major success in the past and is acquired by practitioners during their professional socialization. The paradigm defines for practitioners what is worthwhile investigating, what methods are valid, and what kinds of solutions are acceptable. Most of the time, Kuhn claims, scientists accumulate more knowledge and solve puzzles within the framework of such a paradigm. This is what he calls "normal science." But alongside the accumulation of knowledge, anomalies accumulate as well. Scientists find more and more phenomena and problems which cannot be explained or solved by the theories and methods of the existing paradigm. With the accumulation of such problems, more and more scientists feel uneasy. This is when revolutions are bound to happen. A revolution means that a new paradigm is adopted, which allows scientists to solve the most disturbing anomalies. This involves a profound shift of

research focuses and styles of work. Older practitioners often find it difficult to make the change and the revolution is carried primarily by
younger scientists.[7] Kuhn's work has contradictory interpretations. Relativist philosophers and sociologists of science interpreted the idea of revolutions as negating the idea of progress (e.g., Barnes 1982; see discussion
in Laudan 1990). Kuhn himself, however, was not comfortable with such
an interpretation and in his later work sought to preserve the notion of
progress.[8]

During the 1960s and 1970s, Kuhn's model was much in vogue. It also
appealed to social scientists despite Kuhn's explicit statement that social
science had not yet reached the stage of paradigmatic science (Baumberger 1977). Kuhn's model was employed by sociologists (e.g., Wiley
1979), psychologists (e.g., Weimer and Palermo 1973), political science
(Almond, 1966, 875), and others. Many historians of economics joined
that trend and reinterpreted the history of economics as a succession of
paradigms (e.g., Blaug 1975: 410–11; Redman 1991, chaps. 7–9). I will
present only a brief summary of this reading.[9]

The rise of classical economics following Adam Smith's *The Wealth
of Nations* is presented in this historiography as the moment of transition
from a *pre*-paradigmatic stage to the stage of *"mature science."* During
the pre-paradigmatic stage, there is no single paradigm to guide the
work of scientists. Individual scientists work according to their whims
and intuitions. Then one of the scientists makes a discovery, or suggests
an explanation that impresses many fellow workers and becomes an exemplar for future work. *The Wealth of Nations* was such a momentous
achievement. It was the first time that someone offered a comprehensive
framework to analyze economic problems of various kinds. Smith's successors adopted his framework and worked on problems which developed out of it.

The rise of *neo*classical economics has several properties which resem-
ble Kuhn's model of revolutions (e.g., Bronfenbrenner 1971; De Vroey
1975). First, it introduced marginalist calculus as a standardized method
of economic analysis. Second, it changed the focus of economists from
macro-questions of national income to micro-analysis of firms and consumers (Birken 1988). Third, there is some evidence that there was a "crisis" in economics in the 1860s. The fact that marginal economics was
suggested simultaneously by three economists appears as a reaction to
this crisis. That marginalist analysis was actually suggested much earlier
by Thünen (1783–1850), Gossen (1810–58), Cournot (1801–77), and
others only corroborates the Kuhnian model, which includes the appearance of forerunners before a revolution takes place.[10]

Not all historians of economics agree that economics experienced a
revolution in the end of the nineteenth century. Stigler (1973) admitted,
for example, that marginalism was part of economic teaching, but he

insisted that very few economists actually employed it in their research (cf. Howey 1973, 35). Other historians emphasized that Walras, Jevons, Marshall, J. B. Clark, and Menger held widely different views on methodology, the scope of economics, human behavior, economic policies, and more, thus rendering the notion of one "marginalist paradigm" inaccurate and misleading (Blaug 1973, Coats 1973, 38; Jaffé 1976). The disagreement about the dating of the supposed revolution poses another problem.[11] Finally, it is argued that some of the pioneer "revolutionaries," including Marshall and Menger, actually claimed that they merely refined earlier teachings (Blaug 1973, 11).

While there are problems with the Kuhnian view of neoclassical economics, the case of Keynesian economics seems, at least on the face of it, much less problematic. If revolutions occurred in economics, it is widely accepted, the emergence of Keynesian economics must be regarded among them (Blaug 1975, 411–12). Keynes, it is commonly argued, combined the two branches of economics, price theory and monetary economics, which had been practiced separately (Harcourt 1987, 6). He demolished Say's Law, which supposedly dominated economic thought from early in the nineteenth century, and showed that the market may reach equilibrium below full employment. The so-called Keynesian revolution, it is almost universally assumed, revived macroeconomics and provided it with new concepts and tools (Stanfield 1974). Saving and consumption propensities, multiplier, effective demand, liquidity trap, and liquidity preference were all introduced to the economic discourse by Keynes and have become common terms since then. Expectations and other psychological factors have been given a bigger role in Keynes's theory (Shackle 1967). Investment has replaced savings as the crucial variable in accounting for growth and development. Keynes "legalized" state intervention in the economy and undermined the doctrine of *laissez-faire,* which, the Kuhnians say, had dominated economic doctrines until then. Deficit budgets, an anathema prior to Keynes, became a common tool of economic policy. Frugality which until then had been regarded by economists as a virtue, suddenly became a vice.

Coats, who is among those who argue that the rise of Keynesianism "possessed many of the characteristics associated with Kuhn's 'scientific revolutions,'" adds the sociological aspects of a revolution. "There were," he says, "unrecognized precursors of Keynes, a growing concern about the inadequacy of existing theory, and a change of psychological outlook on the part of many economists virtually amounting to a 'conversion experience.'" In accordance with the Kuhnian model, "the revolution was led by a band of youngsters who encountered fierce resistance from their elders." And, also compatible with Kuhn, "within a remarkably short time the new paradigm had won an almost complete victory"

(1969, 293). Seers writes that many economists "resisted changes in the syllabus to accommodate Keynesian economics and even appointment of Keynesians to economics faculty" (quoted in Routh 1975, 25; cf. Galbraith 1987, 238; Backhouse 1985, 333; J. M. Clark 1947, 1).

In spite of these apparently convincing facts, there are many who contend that Keynesian economics did not break so much from the old neoclassical theory. This line is usually carried by critics of orthodox economists, for whom the reform of the economic thought by Keynes was not sufficiently off the beaten track. Routh, for instance, maintains that Keynes continued to employ the same deductive reasoning and abstract analyses of neoclassicists (1975, 286–93). Interestingly, this view is shared by those who support the Keynesian teaching but perceive it as continuation of the past (e.g., D. F. Gordon 1965). Oser writes that the Keynesian system "arose out of the neoclassical, or marginalist, school, and Keynes himself was steeped in the Marshallian tradition." "Although Keynes sharply criticized certain aspects of neoclassical economics," Oser explains, "he used many of its postulates and methods. His system was based on a subjective, psychological approach, and it was permeated with marginalist concepts, including static equilibrium economics" (1970, 390; cf. Deane 1978). Canterbery tries to synthesize the conflicting views concerning Keynes by arguing that "Keynes' theory was not as revolutionary *as it appeared*, which is not the same as saying that it was not revolutionary" (1976, 140; italics in original).[12]

Keynes was not an unknown or a peripheral economist. On the contrary, he stood in the center of the establishment: a son of a prominent neoclassical economist, a pupil of Marshall, and an acquaintance of powerful officials at the Cambridge administration, the Treasury, and the business community. Moreover, when *The General Theory* was published, Keynes held the most prestigious chair in political economy, the one at Cambridge, and edited the most circulated professional outlet, *The Economic Journal*. Keynes's contemporaries listened very carefully to anything that he uttered. His earlier book, *Treatise on Money* (pub. 1930), already received a great deal of attention, and when economists heard that *The General Theory*, which they had already been awaiting for several months, was finally published, they lined up in bookstores to get a copy (Tobin in Breit and Spencer 1986; S. Weintraub 1988, 41; Samuelson 1966, 4:1517).

Other historians, who emphasized the continuity of Keynes and his predecessors, used this continuity to support a Lakatosian view of the history of economics as progressing not through revolutions but through gradual shifts from "degenerating scientific research programmes" to "progressive" ones. The notion of "scientific research program" (SRP) resembles Kuhn's notion of "paradigm" but carries other implications. A scientific research program is composed of a "hard core" which is surrounded by a "protective belt." The hard core includes fundamental axioms which are based on metaphysical beliefs and are taken as given. Research is done by constructing theories to reconcile the hard core with observations of the real world. Researchers follow the "positive heuristic"—the principles derived from the hard core that dictate what should be studied and the ways it should be done—and observe the "negative heuristic"—the research topics, and methods precluded by the logic of the hard core. The theories are called "a protective belt" because their manipulation enables scientists to retain their hard-core beliefs. According to Lakatos, a hard core cannot be refuted. If it is abandoned eventually it is *not* because of a "crisis" caused by accumulation of anomalies. The reason is rather that scientists move from "degenerating SRPs"—programs that construct theories only to explain ad-hoc facts which are *already* known—to "progressive SRPs"—programs that lead to the discovery of new facts. Lakatos says very little on the process of change itself, but historians of economics tend to interpret such a transition as a smooth and gradual transformation in contrast to the extreme change implied by the concept of a revolution (e.g., Blaug 1994; Backhouse 1994c).[13]

The Lakatosian historians admit that economics has been changed during the 1930s but perceive this change in a different manner. Mark Blaug, the leader of this approach, argues that the idea of a "Keynesian Revolution" is based on a "Walt Disney version of interwar economics": "No American economist," he says, "advocated [the neoclassical] policy of wage cutting" between 1929 and 1936. On the contrary, "the leaders of the American profession strongly supported a ["Keynesian"] programme of public works and specifically attacked the shibboleth of a balanced budget." Hence, he continues, there is no need to resort to the notion of a Keynesian Revolution which creates an "image of a whole generation of economists dumbfounded by the persistence of the Great Depression, unwilling to entertain the obvious remedies of expansionary fiscal and monetary policy . . . and finally, in despair, abandoning their old beliefs in an instant conversion to the new paradigm" (1975, 414–15; see also id. 1990a, chap. 4; Backhouse 1985, 275–76; Weir 1989, 55; Lee 1989). Blaug thus suggests that "the history of a science is more fruitfully conceived, not as a steady progress punctured every few hundred years by a scientific revolution, but as succession of progressive research programmes constantly superseding one another with theories of ever-increasing empirical content" (1975, 409–10).[14]

The Lakatosian view has its own problems. Blaug ignores all too easily many manifestations of resistance to Keynesian innovations. His argument that economists "were united in respect of practical measures for dealing with the depression, but utterly disunited in respect of the theory that lay behind these policy conclusions" (ibid., 415), is at least exaggerated, if not altogether wrong. J. R. Davis's seminal research (1971; see also Barber 1985) shows, indeed, that the support of public work and deficit budget was much wider than one could expect based on the "Walt Disney version." But that there was some resistance is hardly disputed.[15]

In the late 1970s, the Lakatosian view became popular among historians and methodologists of economics and constituted the "orthodoxy" in the field (Redman 1991, 142–4; Hausman 1992, 87; Backhouse 1994c, 173). Recent debates have been concerned with examining various theories or research traditions to examine whether they have followed the methodology of SRPs. The results were mixed; some have argued that economics passed the test successfully; others have claimed that it failed. In a conference dedicated to Lakatosian methodology held in Capri in October 1989, most participants viewed the Lakatosian framework with suspicion or even with unabashed objection. According to Blaug, the veteran Lakatosian, twenty-five out of the thirty-seven participants were inclined to abandon the Lakatosian approach altogether because they found the concept of a scientific research program too vague and were unable to agree on the contents of hard cores (Blaug 1991, 500; see also Backhouse 1994c, 176–77; Hands 1993).[16] More important, the attempts to apply the Lakatosian explanation to changes in economics failed to show unequivocally that winning SRPs, however defined, had excess empirical content. Blaug tries to save the Lakatosian model by listing a series of improvements in economic theory and concludes that "there has been much theoretical progress in twentieth-century economics. There has also been some empirical progress which, however limited, is perhaps enough to refute the extreme pessimists" (1994, 121).

In Blaug's view the constructivist positions of McCloskey and Weintraub imply that there is no real progress in economics (Blaug 1994, 130); that is why he calls them "pessimists." But the constructivist approach in general, and the Latourian actor-network analysis that I will present below in particular, do not imply anything of this sort. The opposite is true: for Latour, it is the very nature of science that it constantly produces "new agencies and hybrids" (1987). The fact that science progresses does not mean that we must choose between Kuhnian and Lakatosian models. As we will see below, there are other possibilities to perceive such progress.

When Blaug brought the Lakatosian framework into economics, he claimed that "certain puzzles about the Keynesian Revolution dissolve when it is viewed through Lakatosian spectacles" (1975, 415). I believe that many puzzles which have remained thereafter dissolve when they are viewed through "constructivist spectacles." The constructivist sociology of science, I suggest, can account for the revolutionary *image* of some episodes in the history of science, including economics, and to the contrary *image* of other episodes. Moreover, it helps us understand why the same episodes may appear both as revolutionary and as traditional. It also helps us understand why the evaluations of "progressiveness" of SRPs are never conclusive. In general, it provides us with a framework in which we can incorporate all the elements of the history of economic thought, not only those that the current mainstream has selected as "significant." And it is a framework which shows that many enduring problems with which historians of economics have grappled for many years are constructed only by artificial conceptualizations that problematize natural aspects of scientific practice.

My effort in this direction is not the first such effort. In the Capri conference in October 1989, the Lakatosian reconstructions were challenged by two prominent sociologists of science, Harry Collins and Karin Knorr-Cetina, and by a reputable philosopher of science, Nancy Cartwright. Apparently the other participants were "not really comfortable with the reconceptualization these individuals offered about the enterprise of economic science" (Weintraub 1991a, 101) and chose to ignore it and not publish it in the conference proceedings (De Marchi and Blaug 1991). The omitted papers were later published in *History of Political Economy*, but most economists seem to have paid little attention. As Weintraub notes, "there are not many historians of economics who have an interest in the sociology of the economics profession" (1991b, 9). Weintraub's own book (1991b) is one of the very few attempts to apply the views of Collins, Knorr-Cetina, and other sociologists of science to specific episodes in the history of economics, and I hope that this book helps to attract more attention of economists to views which are seriously considered and discussed by sociologists, historians, and philosophers of other sciences.

The Construction of Scientific Knowledge[17]

Scientific knowledge, as any other kind of knowledge, is produced by human beings working together. Philosophers have debated for centuries the possibilities of the human mind to know Nature. Sociologists have added to this the recognition that the human mind is a social mind (Amann and Knorr-Cetina 1989; Knorr-Cetina 1980, 1991). The language in which we think, the concepts we use, the principles of logic we apply—all our basic tools of thinking are acquired and shaped in a long process of interaction with other people. Furthermore, whatever the possibilities of knowing are in theory, the outcomes of scientific inquiries depend on the practices of research and on the social process that accompany the production of scientific knowledge. "The world is out there," Rorty admits, "but descriptions of the world are not"; they are human-made (1989, 5). The constructivist approach has not originated, however, in philosophical reflections and is not directly related to any school in philosophy (cf. Fuller 1990). It is rooted in historical studies and observations of working scientists that show how scientific knowledge is actually constructed.

The essence of constructivism is the attempt to study science "as it is" (Latour and Woolgar 1979; cf. Klamer 1990, 27).[18] Its advocates have refused to accept conventions that privileged science and set themselves to watch scientists working in their laboratories, to listen to their conversations, and to follow rigorously the historical development of machines, methods, theories, and inventions (Collins 1991a). It is somewhat ironic, but not a coincidence, that this "positivistic" approach yielded results that challenged traditional positivism.[19] Constructivists have drawn attention to the fact that the content of scientific knowledge is being shaped in a complex social process. This applies to their own findings, a fact which is often brought as a "proof" of self-refutation. The constructivists do not deny that their findings are as shaky, *or as stable*, as the findings of other empirical scientists (Latour 1988a, 266n; McCloskey 1994b, chap. 15; McCloskey 1995, 1322).[20] Constructivists do not say that empirical findings are valueless but rather that their value, their meaning, is not given; it has to be negotiated among competent scientists (i.e., persons who are regarded competent by their peers) who hold different interpretations. The empirical findings are therefore contingent, which is by no means tantamount to saying that they are of no importance (Smith 1993).

Those who are familiar with the growing tradition of the rhetoric of economics would undoubtedly identify the similarity between that tradition and constructivism. McCloskey, Klamer, and their fellow rhetoricians refuse—like the constructivists—to take what economists say about how they practice economics at face value (McCloskey 1985, 1988a, 1988b, 1990a, 1990b, 1994a, 1994b; Klamer 1987, 1990; Klamer et al. 1988). Like constructivists, they think one should go and see how economists actually persuade each other (McCloskey 1994a; see also Lind 1992, 1993).[21] If science works well and reaches some goals (a matter for another discussion), it is because of that unseen know-how gathered on the job and not due to the official rules one learns in school.

Both the constructivists and the rhetoricians of economics are accused of being sheer relativists who oppose the use of empirical evidence in science. McCloskey (1994b) labors to dispel this charge and, like the constructivist sociologists of science, claims that empirical evidence is crucial in science, but its meaning is never objectively given (Latour 1987; see also Smith 1988). Roy Weintraub—a constructivist influenced mainly by Stanley Fish's approach to literary texts—insists that constructivism "does not mean that anything goes" (1989, 488). Texts, like empirical findings, can be interpreted in many different ways, but texts, like empirical evidence, limit the range of possible interpretations (on Fish, see Hoover 1994, 290). Defending the traditional view that perceives the outcome of experiments and observations as unproblematic runs against what we know on the practices of scientists. It is *self-refuting* to defend the value of empirical research and, at the same time, to deny the empirical findings of constructivists![22]

The finding that knowledge is socially constructed was mistakenly interpreted as meaning that knowledge is determined by interests external to the scientific practice, such as political and ideological beliefs, religious convictions, egoistic pursuits of fame or power, and so forth.[23] To prevent this mistake, some constructivists have recently cut the word "social" out of "social constructivism"; they prefer to be called "constructivists" rather than "social constructivists" to avoid the erroneous identification as sheer externalists and to emphasize that "there seems no warrant for assigning causal priority to the social in understanding scientific practice and culture" (Pickering 1992a, 14). This step is not intended "to deny that science is constitutively 'social'" (ibid.). It is intended only to underline that scientific knowledge is the result of dialectical relations among social, institutional, conceptual, material, and other elements of science in various combinations. The old debate between internalists and externalists (Shapin 1982; 1992) in the study of science is obsolete, because the elements of the outside world do not appear as "purely internal" or "purely external." "Internal" factors—what is a fact, how the validity of a fact has to be established and reaffirmed, the priority of various logical requirements—are themselves the result of negotiation and resource mobilization in the "external" world (Johnson [a.k.a. Latour] 1987).

Shapin and Schaffer's study (1985) of the conflict between Hobbes and Boyle over what constitutes a valid way of knowing is one of the best demonstrations of the constructed nature of scientific knowledge. Boyle promoted experiments as the only reliable method of determining the truth. He conducted his experiments in public and argued that the agreement of all viewers validated the outcomes and safeguarded against idiosyncratic errors and perceptual deceptions. Hobbes, in contrast, believed in the more traditional view that the only valid knowledge was the knowledge based on infallible mathematical proofs. Experiments, he believed, were not reliable because our senses often misled us. Amidst the seventeenth century, both positions were considered viable, and only due to Boyle's victory—a victory contingent on the specific social circumstances of seventeenth-century England—experimentalism has become so pervasive and "reliable" in modern science. Shapin and Schaffer describe the rise of experimental ideology that has become a core belief of almost all disciplines.

Economics, in which frequent references to the scientific method of Boyle are abundant, is among the few fields in which the Hobbesian approach still takes precedence over Boyle's experimentalism. According to several surveys, empirical papers in professional literature are much less frequent in economics than any other discipline (McCloskey 1994b, 172). Theoretical papers that use no empirical evidence are considered more prestigious and empirical tests are devised based on theoretical considerations. *From the constructivist perspective, this feature of economics is no reason for alarm.* One of the findings of the laboratory studies of constructivists is the large heterogeneity of science (Watson-Verran and Turnbull 1995). Karin Knorr-Cetina (1991), for example, had documented the emergence of epistemic cultures in different fields. Epistemic culture is composed of know-how techniques, rules of thumb, and other informal, practical guidelines for how to do various things; "untidy goings-on" in Knorr-Cetina's language. The emphasis here is on the "disunity of science": there are different cultures, because each field has its own history, its own dynamic of personal relations, *and* its own subject matter. We cannot make a distinction between a unified scientific method and different contexts, because the core of science, its epistemic foundations, are themselves constituted by the context (ibid., 107). From this point of view, Dudley-Evans's finding (1993) that economics articles constitute a different genre than scientific papers in biology is not surprising; each field, not only economics, has its own "genre." The constructivist emphasis on the diversity of sciences dissolves the traditionally made distinction between natural and social sciences. Both the so-called "natural sciences" and "social sciences" are conglomerates of various practices that differ enormously. The desire of many economists to imitate the physicists and their pride that their science is the most similar to physics are therefore based on an utter misunderstanding of what science is (Mirowski 1994, 55).[24]

The recognition of the contingency and plurality of science led constructivists to the "principle of symmetry."[25] According to this principle students of science should treat in the same fashion scientific theories that have triumphed and those that have lost and disappeared. Traditional interpreters of the history of science have tended to explain victories of scientific approaches by their superior quality. They problematize only the resistance to theories which have later been recognized as better. The assumption is that no explanation is needed for the reception of Newtonian mechanics, because rational actors would naturally prefer it given the evidence available at the time of Newton. In contrast, the constructivist approach treats all scientific theories in the same manner, regardless of their eventual destiny (cf. Weintraub 1991b, 5–6). The goal is not to show how "good" theories win, but to document how the view of what is "good" is being constituted and then used to resolve debates about Nature.

The traditional view takes the position of the winner and interprets history from the winner's perspective (Weintraub 1991b, 5). Whoever wins is the right winner. This is why this approach produces Whig histories, which are, as McCloskey says, "too easy" (1994b, 90; see also her comment on p. 103; Mirowski 1994, 65). Of course, all historians are familiar with cases in which a scientist who had appeared as a winner in the beginning was later declared wrong. There are also numerous cases of "losers" who were crowned as "winners" many years after their works had been rejected. The Whig historians simply dodge the problem such cases pose by taking the position of the *last* winner. They explain her previous defeat as caused by social—that is, "unscientific"—causes and celebrate her eventual victory as the triumph of reason. The constructivist approach, in contrast, does not perceive history as a "Greek tragedy," to use Elkana's potent image (1981). We cannot assume that what has happened was the only way it could have happened.

The critics of constructivism accuse it of undermining the noble quest for truth that has guided scientists for centuries. If the sanctity of the Scientific Method is challenged, they imply, the most invidious and preposterous theories, such as Nazism or astrology, would claim the same social recognition and public support that science receives today. This critique is based on a deep misunderstanding of constructivism.[26] Constructivism does not seek to challenge the validity of science nor to challenge its methods. On the contrary, it opts for symmetric treatment because of its *deference* toward science and its recognition that philosophers and methodologists cannot legislate for scientists (Callon and Latour 1992). Saying that truth-claims are contingent does not mean that everything goes, nor does it mean that any two views are equally plausible. There can be bad and good arguments (Smith 1988; Gerrard 1993; McCloskey 1994a). But when two camps of scientists make opposite claims, there is no outside arbitrator who can determine which camp is right. If a group of researchers—trained and socially recognized as competent—accept in good faith a certain theory as convincing, we, as outsiders, must assume that it is a reasonable theory.[27]

The criticism of constructivism might be based on the realist notion that there is one truth against which scientific theories should be measured. A certain theory might be either true or wrong, and if it is true, than all rival theories are wrong (Mäki 1995). The constructivist approach is different. It does not deny that some claims are true and others are false, but it highlights the fact that at the frontier of science the known evidence usually gives rise to more than one reasonable theory, that is, a theory that competent practitioners deem reasonable in light of the known evidence. Maybe there is one superior method—the philosopher's stone or the holy grail—to rule which theory is the correct one, but unfortunately we are offered contradicting "philosopher's stones." How can we decide which one is the "true" one? This is decided only by the negotiation, alliances, and rhetoric of "stone merchants," as illustrated, for example, by the historical study of Shapin and Schaffer and by the empirical studies of Knorr-Cetina, studies that show that what scientists have perceived as the ideals of science have varied across disciplines, times, and places (cf. McCloskey 1995, 1320–21).

In an attempt to save Popperian/Lakatosian methodology of economics, Backhouse (1994) argues that empirical progress as evident in predicting novel facts should still be considered a universal principle of methodology. This defense fails to grasp the nature of the constructivist critique. Constructivists would have no argument with either the positive observations that many scientists pay attention to successful predictions, or with a normative argument that they should. Successful predictions, neat explanations, and practical utility are evidently very persuasive in science, which may account for the victory of approaches that *appear* to perform these tasks. But unlike other approaches, the constructivist approach calls attention to the fact that "success," "neatness," and "usefulness" are not given by Nature but constructed in a process of negotiation and conflict. Moreover, the question of what relative weights should successful predictions, neatness, and usefulness be assigned is not answered by traditional methodology. Indeed, it is answered differently by various communities of scientists.

Unlike the traditional views of science, the constructivist approach does not entail that all sciences work well. For positivists, if a scientific field is shown to have failed, it is immediately excluded from the domain of science. There is no such thing as "bad science." For an extreme relativist, no scientific project is better than others, nor is it better than nonscientific enterprises of knowledge production. The constructivist approach is different. It acknowledges the unique features of scientific practices that *might* endow its products unique qualities. But the actual outcomes depend on many factors and vary substantially from one field to another. The constructivists themselves, *as outsider observers of science*, are not interested in evaluating the sciences they study. This is not because such evaluation is unimportant. From their perspective, evaluation is an integral part of the practice of working scientists, who must make decisions concerning the direction of their field. The findings of historians and sociologists may influence such decisions, and historians and sociologists may express their own views concerning the direction the field they study should go. But constructivist accounts do not purport to entail clear conclusions about the suitability of various methods. It is compatible with all methods and approaches and refuses to deprive the status of science from a given practice because some powerful gatekeepers feel that its method are improper.

Accounts of Scientific Development: The Actor-Network Analysis

The constructivist approach emphasizes the diversity of science. This is an empirical finding, as well as a logical implication of the recognition that there is no absolute standard to judge scientific enterprises. This view can settle many barren and inconclusive debates among scientists and students of science. But at the same time it raises new questions. If many possibilities are open for scientific enterprises, how should we explain the options actually selected? Traditionally, students of science implied that the development of scientific knowledge is determined by the quality of contending theories and their use of the proper methods. The only thing that was left open for explanation was the tempo of science, that is, its rate of progress. This pace was explained by the degree of financial support and institutional freedom given to scientists. But if the question is what kind of theories are considered adequate and what scientific methods are used we need a new kind of conceptual framework. The actor-network approach (ANA) developed by Bruno Latour and Michel Callon offers us such a framework.[28]

The actor-network approach perceives scientists as involved in attempts to promote their own contributions and turn them into "black boxes"—that is, into knowledge which is accepted and used on a regular basis as a matter of fact. Scientists are involved in what Latour calls "trials of strength" at which their claims about the validity of their findings and the usefulness of their research have to withstand challenges made by competing colleagues. A successful trial means that an ongoing concern has incorporated the contribution into its institutional set of practices. It is not enough to be recognized as "valid" and then put aside. The new contribution has to become part of a larger apparatus which can be used regularly without any need to justify the use in order to become part of the ever-growing and ever-changing stock of knowledge. The contribution might be a theoretical principle which enters introductory textbooks or is referred to regularly in the reporting of experimental results (i.e., the "law of diminishing returns"). Or it might be a method of measuring a certain variable in order to test theories or for some practical reasons (price index, for instance, which is used both for comparing monetarist with Keynesian theories, and for deciding on pay raises and social security adjustment). The contribution might also be a part of a machine without which the machine cannot function properly. In short, any component that enters into the work of scientists, and which may be disputable, can become a "black box" *once an agreement has been reached.* In any case, the contribution has to become an *obligatory passage point* for some concerns, that is, something that cannot be dispensed with.[29]

In order to succeed in trials of strength, scientists, who compete among themselves, have to marshal various "allies" in order to harden their cases and make them more defensible. "Allies" can be anything that bears upon the strength of the contribution in question, including, of course, other scientists or people who support the contribution, either financially, or by bestowing their authority upon it, or simply by using it. But also included are various instruments and practices that embody the contribution and arguments that justify it. The authority of respected practitioners in the field, examples from neighboring fields or from other prestigious disciplines, the views of philosophers and methodologists—all can become part of the network that support the contribution. "Facts" are also allies, of course, and in most disciplines, they have a considerable weight. But facts do not speak for themselves! They need scientists as mouthpieces, and the scientists who summon them up must interpret them, convince others in their factuality, and explain how they support their arguments.[30] To achieve this they have to array the "facts" along with other allies, such as the interpretations of other famous scientists, other black boxes, or the way other established facts have been interpreted (Latour 1987, 94–104).

The idea is not that scientists are like crafty lawyers who do not care about "the Truth" and manipulate the facts to advance personal interests, as Latour is often, and mistakenly, interpreted. The point is that nobody knows what "the Truth" is before the trials of strength are concluded. Thus, scientists who believe that they have revealed a piece of "the Truth" must do their best to convince others. If we want to extend the metaphor of the court, we can think about it as a trial in court in which nobody (not even the plaintiff and the defendant!) knows what happened, and the role of lawyers is to present the best case for both sides; the jury—the scientific community in our case—has to decide on the basis of these presentations. As rhetoricians of law have noticed, one cannot separate between "substantive" arguments and "rhetorical" tricks. There is no argument without rhetoric. If a certain fact seems to be so unambiguously supportive of the other side, scientists often admit it and surrender, as happens occasionally in court. When they stick to their position in spite of this "obvious" fact, we, as observers from the sideline, cannot just say that they are pigheaded. After all, if it is not "obvious" for *them*, who are *we* to say that it is "obvious"?

Again, this approach is quite similar to the rhetoric of economics. Klamer, for example, presents economists as participating in conversations. They argue to persuade each other and, occasionally, to convince noneconomists. For that purpose they construct a variety of arguments; use analogies, metaphors, labels; reconstruct intellectual history; and make claims concerning the status of their arguments (Klamer 1987, 164). What Klamer calls "variety of arguments" is what Latour calls "allies." My use of the Latourian framework is partially due to my disciplinary training but also reflects my belief that it carries the rhetoric enterprise farther. McCloskey and Klamer deal with speech acts; what economists say and write. The sociology of science deals with what scientists *do*, and *where*—in which institutional and technical environments—they do it as well. The persuasiveness of claims depends not only on arguments, metaphors, analogies, and so forth; it also depends on financial resources, personal ties, and organizational skills. Whether McCloskey and Klamer would like to accept this, I am not sure. In any case, their defense on rhetoric is identical to the constructivist insistence that "facts do not speak for themselves." The relative weight of arguments versus practices and organization can be left for empirical study.[31]

All allies—facts, people, money, methodological principles, theories, instruments, machines, practices, organizations, and so forth—constitute a network which upholds and ratifies each element of it. It is difficult to undermine any single link of the network without undermining the others, and therefore the ability to connect a new element (method, theory, instrument, etc.) to a strong network is likely to ensure its success in ensuing trials of strength. If the new element is supported by many older elements that are already perceived as valid, it will be hard to dispute its own validity. It would be accepted by those who have accepted the whole network and become part of it. Such a success should not be interpreted, however, as a proof of the veracity of the new element. It is absolutely possible that the whole network is based on shaky foundations, but such a claim can be made only by other scientists and scholars who must base their claim on another network, stronger or weaker.

The concept of network overlaps in some degree institutional bodies such as disciplines, schools, paradigms, and research programs. An academic "school" is a group of scholars who make frequent use of each other's work. By using the conventions of their own group, its members convince each other, and if the network can mobilize enough resources (most importantly, money) it can be intellectually self-sufficient. But in order to convince outsiders they often have to connect their own school to other schools, other disciplines, or to cultural conventions of the society at large. A network is therefore wider and much more complex a unit than a school. A "paradigm," an exemplar of how to do research in a specific field (Kuhn 1970a) could be interpreted in the Latourian scheme as part of the network which many researchers try to get connected to. Unlike Kuhn however, the ANA does not assume that scientists necessarily use the "paradigm" in the same fashion, or that they mean the same thing when they refer to the underlying assumptions (cf. Gilbert and Mulkay 1984). Weintraub provides a fine example of this by showing us how "equilibrium" has been differently perceived even within the same group of early general equilibrium theorists (1991b, chap. 5).

Kuhnian historians have attempted to find boundaries among paradigms, as if there were some absolute boundaries independent of human agents. Yet researchers who study the histories of various disciplines, often come up with conflicting descriptions of the basics of paradigms, quarrel about when revolutions actually happened, and even find it difficult to categorize individual scholars and ideas. It is the same with "hard cores": "Attempting to apply Lakatos's view of the structure of research programs to economics creates unnecessary and unhelpful questions" (Hausman 1992, 88). It is not a surprise that those who have attempted to apply the Lakatosian model "have disagreed concerning what the hard core of neoclassical theory is" (Hausman 1992, 86; see further discussion, pp. 87–88; Backhouse 1994c, 176–77). Axel Leijonhufvud has noticed that "controversies may rage within as well as between research programmes" (1976, 66; see also Mäki 1994). Although he believes that the "first order of business" in the history of economics is to "characterize the essentials of the two contending programmes," he admits that "there is no—can be no—'canned programme' for how is it [sic] to be performed," and therefore attempts to do so would be controversial themselves (ibid., 69). Attempting to solve these difficulties, Mäki distinguishes between "antagonism" and "family quarrels." Antagonism is a dispute over "core assumptions," and family quarrels are disputes over "peripheral assumptions," apparently within the same camp (1994, 237). Mäki acknowledges the difficulty of deciding what is "core" and what is "peripheral" (ibid., 247; see also Blaug 1991), but he underestimates this difficulty. Any assumption can look either central or peripheral, depending on the social context in which the dispute is conducted.[32]

The ANA avoids the pitfalls involved in all the attempts to create indisputable and clear-cut maps of the discipline. Under the ANA we do not have to assume that all *so-called* neoclassical economists, for instance, shared the same metaphysical beliefs, an unlikely fact. It is enough to say that neoclassical economists often referred to similar allies—e.g., Alfred Marshall, supply and demand curves, or the "utility" of the consumer.

We also are not required to decide who is "in" and who is "out." It is absolutely conceivable that some scholars would make a more frequent use of the "neoclassical allies," that over time some elements of the "neoclassical network" would become more or less popular, or that some scholars would tie their works to more than one "hard core."[33] "Paradigms" and "hard cores" are not real objects "out there" that we, the students of science, have to reveal. The boundaries between them are shaped by negotiations and struggles of scientists who are involved in trials of strength, similar to the way "facts" are constructed (Dean 1979, 212). There is no one "correct" way to map a field and classify its practitioners. It is therefore fruitless to argue whether a certain practitioner "really" belongs to this or that paradigm, or whether a certain idea "really" constitutes a part of a certain paradigm or deviates from it.[34] The task of the historian or the sociologist is to locate the various *social* and *ideational* connections and follow how the practitioners themselves have defined the various schools and approaches. It is not our job to impose our perceptions on the history.

This was a brief summary of the constructivist approach and the actor-network analysis. It was meant to whet the interest of those who do not know about this approach, but it is obviously not enough to provide all its details and defend it against its many critics. I can only hope the readers would be interested enough to consult the works of constructivist sociologists in general,[35] and the works of the actor-network theorists in particular.[36]

The Goals of This Study

The struggle between institutionalists and neoclassical economists during the interwar period is an example of a competition between two networks vying for the same space and the same resources. In the situation analyzed in this book the struggle was over the question "What should economics be like?" This type of question often leads toward prolonged disagreements. When the destiny of a whole field is at stake, many people have an interest in the outcomes of the dispute. Furthermore, the question is too general and ambiguous to allow any side to easily compose an unassailable network, and therefore in many disciplines we find networks that have consolidated around different answers to similarly broad questions. Within each school the fundamental principles are taken for granted—as a black box—and used in the production of more black boxes. But at the same time at least some advocates of each school are preoccupied with a major "trial of strength" in which the whole structure of their black boxes—from the fundamental principles, assumptions, and methods to the most specific factual and theoretical propositions—is at stake. Some resources have to be devoted to this struggle over fundamentals. Nonetheless, and in contrary to what Kuhn and many others seem to believe, this is not necessarily a bad thing: as in economic competition, a rivalry between two (or more) scientific procedures may involve some waste, but it also constitutes a stimulus for the competitors to examine their "products" and improve them.

The competing methodologies of neoclassical economics and institutionalism were two black boxes that coexisted together and were employed simultaneously in producing further knowledge. But since the two camps fought over the same territory (i.e., nominations in economics departments, space in major journals, public attention) and made contradictory assertions, they had to channel at least some resources toward the continuing effort of asserting the validity and fruitfulness of their proposed methodologies. The bulk of this book is concerned with this controversy. We will see that economists promoted their methodological approaches by weaving and meshing together elements of many sorts, similar to the way scientists and engineers construct new facts or fabricate new machines. The proposed methodologies have to be "valid," they must fit the accepted "canon," they should be compatible with knowledge which is deemed sound, and they need to be regarded as useful and fruitful. Some of their properties might be less satisfactory than others. But as a whole, the approach has to be attractive enough relative to its competition in order to pass the trial of strength. Rivals are likely to challenge various elements of the arguments made in favor of the methodology and advocates must respond by mobilizing further allies, strengthening existing elements, and jettisoning weak allies that cannot be defended.

Given the unique subject matter of such trials of strength, the kinds of allies which are likely to be mobilized in such cases are quite different from the allies marshaled into concrete trials. I have identified five main types of allies which seem to me typical of conflicts over methodologies: (1) methodologies of prestigious disciplines, (2) theories from neighboring disciplines, (3) well-known features of the economy, (4) relevance to practical problems, and (5) respected authorities from the discipline's own past. Chapters 4 through 8 analyze how these allies were marshaled and employed by institutionalists and neoclassical economists in their conflict during the interwar years.

The analysis will employ another important concept that Callon and Latour brought into sociology, namely, translation. Borrowing from Michel Serres, Callon and Latour use the term to refer to the way actors take on themselves the task of speaking in the name of other entities (Callon and Latour 1981; Callon 1986; Latour 1987, 108–32). This is evident in the case of leaders of social groups who speak in the name of the group, thus defining its identity and interests. But, Callon and Latour maintain that this is also the case with scientists who speak in the name of Nature, which cannot speak for itself. It needs a mouthpiece, and scientists argue over the question who is the "authentic translator" who represents Nature most reliably (Latour 1987, 94–100). The same process of translation took place in the institutionalist-neoclassical struggle: various economists took on the task of speaking in the name of philosophical principles, recognized methods, theories, public interests, and the dead economists of the past, and interpreted for their colleagues what those mute entities meant for the question of "What should economics be like."

My goal is not to account for the outcome of the struggle but to analyze the case of inter-paradigmatic struggles and to identify some of their unique features. This limitation may disappoint many of the sociologists of science who will read this work, as well as some of the historians of economics who are interested in the social configurations that channeled the evolution of economics (Coats 1984). However, an account of outcomes requires the analyst to pay attention to *all* the components of the pertinent networks. In the case of economics that means that one has to study the businesspersons and government officials with whom economists were in touch, the positions economists held in government and corporations, the funds they were able to solicit, and the tools and the economic plans they constructed for their various clients. This is a project well beyond the capacity of this book. Although there are few sociological analyses of interwar economics, these are too few and two sporadic to be used as a basis for a comprehensive account of the developments in a field as rich and vast as economics, and in a period as eventful and fertile as the period between the world wars. I chose, therefore, to analyze scholastic and cognitive arguments only, and in this sense my study is not a full-blown ANA. What it does is to elucidate the structure of methodological controversies, and the logic of the actor-network approach serves this goal well.

A full sociological account must also take much more notice of the distinctions and disputes within each of the two camps of institutionalism and neoclassical economics. So far I have talked about institutionalists and neoclassical economists as if they belonged to two clear-cut groups with diametrically opposed views, incompatible methods, and unbridgeable approaches to economic problems. *This picture is very far from the truth* as we will see in the next chapters. It also contradicts our constructivist view of "paradigms"/"SRPs" presented earlier in this chapter. I nonetheless adopted these terms ("institutionalism" and "neoclassical economics") to simplify the presentation and make the main thesis comprehensible. Furthermore, contemporary economists were aware that there was a "fault line" within the discipline between what was often referred to as "orthodoxy" and a younger group challenging that orthodoxy. The latter was labeled differently by various writers, including "young economists," "recent thought," and even "institutionalism" (see chap. 3). Given this awareness by contemporary actors, and in order to keep this project manageable, I followed the traditional division into "institutionalism" and "neoclassical economics," but the readers are warned that our understanding of the development of economics would not be full until we investigate the divisions within each group.

The texts analyzed in this book are all the articles which were classified under the title "Methodology" (Category 1.1) in the *Index of Economic Articles, 1924–1939* (American Economic Association 1961, vol. 2). In contrast to Backhouse's statement that "before the 1970s the literature on economic methodology was very limited" (1994b, 1),[37] the interwar period was at least as prolific as the era after 1970, and the number of articles under the heading of "Methodology" was eighty-four. This was at a time in which there were only five general journals in economics in the U.S. and Britain and very few other minor journals. I augmented these materials by the essays in *The Trend of Economics*, a book edited by Rexford Tugwell (1924b) that included meta-theoretical essays of many promising young economists of the time, and that was frequently referred to by various writers during the interwar period. The importance of the book is indicated by the fact that eight out of its fifteen participants served later as presidents of the AEA, and at least four of them are considered among the most famous American economists ever (Wesley Mitchell, J. M. Clark, Frank Knight, and Paul Douglas). I also used primary and secondary sources of later years when those sources helped clarify the nature of the arguments of the contending parties.

The use of publicly published texts only has, of course, its limitations. But at the same time, it has "the advantage of being accessible, portable and static" (Backhouse et al., 1993, 17n). In order to dispel current misconceptions of interwar economics, which are based on an even more limited and biased selection of texts, the current analysis should be enough.

The interpretation of texts is not a straightforward practice. The way texts are understood depends on the readers and their prior knowledge and on the contexts in which the texts are read. As it was argued quite frequently recently, the very meaning of "meaning" is not clear; does "meaning" refer to what the author was trying to say? Is it the meaning ascribed to the texts by their intended or original readers? Or does each reader construct its own meaning of the text (Lavoie 1990a, 1990b; Gerrard 1993)? These fundamental questions are critical in any study based on the reading and analysis of texts.[38] Since these issues have been elaborated on by many writers, there is no need to repeat the arguments and I will simply state my position.

Nowhere I assume that my interpretation of the analyzed texts is objective and precise. My reading and analysis have been undoubtedly influenced by my motivation and in the context of establishing a general thesis about the history of economics. They were also influenced probably by my prior knowledge of sociology and economics and by my ideological inclinations and professional preferences as a sociologist. Yet my interpretation was done in good faith and offers—I believe—a plausible way to read these texts.[39] It is by no means a final interpretation, but, as McCloskey often argues, it is an invitation for a conversation. It is a suggestion of an interpretation that has not been voiced so far and which will hopefully engage those who disagree in a conversation over the proper interpretation.

Two

The Neoclassical Era (1870–1914) from a Different Angle

> Science is obviously seldom or never . . . a single monolithic
> and unified enterprise. . . . Often, viewing all fields together,
> [science] seems instead a rather ramshackle structure with
> little coherence among its various parts.
> (Thomas Kuhn, *The Structure of Scientific Revolutions*)

BECAUSE of the near-hegemony today of the modern neoclassical school, the written history of economics reflects neoclassical predilections and biases. Current historians of economics, who came of age in the post–World War II era, are more likely to focus on past economists who envisioned and contributed to lines of research which are practiced today by the vast majority of economists. It is not a reflection on their sincerity and professional integrity to expect them to judge rather negatively those approaches, such as institutionalism, that criticized and tried to block and replace those trends of thought which led to modern economics. It should therefore be emphasized from the very beginning that by speaking on the "biases" of modern historians, I have no intention of faulting their work.

However, we know today that there are many equally valid ways to tell the story of the past (White 1973, 1987; Gerrard 1993). Historians of science, who wish to say something about the contributions of past scientists, must use their own criteria of what is essential and what is good in the science they study. Hence, personal biases are inevitable. Our problem, as historians of economic thought, starts when virtually all of the practitioners in the field have similar biases and tell similar stories on the past. This may create a false impression that the conventional history, as told by those practitioners, is the only valid way to describe the past. Even though many of the stories told today by neoclassical historians are factually correct, their choices obscure important aspects of the past, including the nature, success, and fortune of institutional economics.

In order to understand the emergence of institutionalism, its message, and its struggle with neoclassical economics, one has to have a wider picture of the history of economics around the turn of the century. In this chapter I will present my interpretation of that history. Undoubtedly, the picture I will draw will have its own selective biases. But I hope it will complement pre-existing interpretations and contribute to an open and critical discussion of economics in the so-called "Neoclassical Era." My strategy follows Weintraub's attempt to understand historically the emergence and evolution of general equilibrium theory. Because history is "discursively rich, confused, and hardly ever convergent on any coherent perspective," Weintraub chose to emphasize the diversity of economic trends during the turbulent years of the 1930s (1991b, 10, 15–16). I made a similar choice and emphasized the pluralism of economic ideas between 1870 and the interwar period.

The following section deals with the approach of Alfred Marshall and other members of the Cambridge School which he established as the leading approach at that time. Following this I will cross the Ocean and discuss the group of economists in the United States, who rebelled against classical economics and founded the American Economic Association (AEA). The story I tell presents the neoclassical era in new colors: not as a refinement of classical theory but as a radical change in favor of economic reform, evolutionary images of human behavior and institutions, and empirical studies. This presentation differs from the current discourse on the continuity between classical and neoclassical economics by focusing on the broader philosophical and methodological beliefs that underlie economic reasoning. Most historians compared the treatment of concrete theoretical issues (e.g., the theory of value, the determination of wages, diminishing returns in production, etc.) and thus overlooked the *place* of those issues in the general outlooks of contemporary economists.[1] An emphasis on the larger philosophical framework would give us a better understanding of the emergence of institutionalism and its place in the history of economic thought.

The Economics of Marshall and His Students

For the traditional historiography of economics, the years between 1870 and 1933 are known as the "neoclassical era." The conventional textbook typically discusses the "marginalist revolution" of Jevons, Walras, and Menger, who introduced marginal utility as a key concept. Then, the story goes, Marshall synthesized the analysis of demand and supply—his famous scissors—and thus laid the foundations of economic teaching for the following half a century. One may easily get the impression that the main practice of contemporary economists was the application of marginal tools to specific situations and problems. This impression is grossly mistaken. Historicism, Marxism, and institutionalism were three other broad trends that emerged during the same "neoclassical era" and left their impact on all the economists of those days. But here I will show that even Marshall went far beyond marginalism.

That marginalism was not the core of economics during the neoclassical period we already know due to Stigler's extensive research and analysis. Stigler, the expert on the evolution of value theory, argued that "utility was not a part of the working equipment of economists during this period." To illustrate this, Stigler says that no article in the *American Economic Review* used marginal utility theory in 1940, while not less than fifteen (29% of all articles) did in 1970 (1973, 317–18).[2] Marginalist analysis gained, indeed, wide acceptance at the end of the nineteenth century and became part of the economic curriculum, but it was only *one* topic among many of equal importance. It did not become the basic tool of economists until after World War II. Until then one could have been a successful economist without mastering or even knowing much about marginal analysis.

Alfred Marshall (1842–1924) is recognized today as the quintessentially neoclassical economist who put the new marginalism in order, connected it with earlier teaching, and wrote the basic textbook that constituted the cornerstone of economic training worldwide. In the pantheon of economics, Marshall occupies a position similar to those held by Smith, Ricardo, Marx, and Keynes. His influence in England was huge. Niehans (1990, 246) says that at the time of his death, "British universities were completely Marshallian (see also Oser 1970, 235). Marshall's *Principles of Economics* (pub. 1890) dominated the teaching of economics (Niehans 1990, 246; cf. Rima 1977, 7) and was replaced as the most authoritative textbook only by Samuelson's *Economics: An Introductory Analysis* (pub. 1948). Present-day neoclassical economists treat Léon Walras as equal to Marshall in stature and influence. But this is a late development. The English-speaking economists at the last quarter of the nineteenth century knew about Walras but did not consider his work as important and fruitful as Marshall's.

The way Marshall is commonly presented and perceived is highly biased by the Kuhnian and Lakatosian reconstructions. The latter attempt to demonstrate the continuity from Marshall to modern neoclassical economics and, therefore, emphasize Marshall's contributions to marginal analysis—the famous scissors of supply and demand, the analysis of monopolies, the treatment of economies of scale, and so forth. Due to this bias relatively little attention has been given to evaluate Marshall's overall approach to economic science and to economic problems. In this section I will draw upon that part of the literature that does discuss

Marshall's foundational beliefs and on a few sections from his own book to shed light on the Marshall who is less known to most economists even though his existence has never been a secret.

Marshall wanted to "produce a balanced overall picture of the economic system with due weight given to historical and institutional factors" (O'Brien 1981, 63; Harcourt 1987, 5). The formative influences on Marshall included German idealism, Spencerean evolutionism, and the utilitarianism of Bentham and Mill (Groenewegen, 1990, 28). The mathematical and diagrammatic proofs, for which Marshall is so much acclaimed today, were advisedly relegated by him to footnotes and appendixes (Backhouse 1985, 101–2). Blaug attributes this fact to Marshall's hope to be read by businessmen (1986a, 150), but this explanation does not hold water. Whatever was Marshall's original intention he must have realized that his book became the major source for advanced teaching in economics. Furthermore, Marshall made many efforts to secure the institutionalization of economics as an independent discipline and as a *science* (Kadish 1989; Maloney 1985). Marshall's care not to make his book too mathematical should therefore be attributed not to his wish to appeal to business people but rather to his wish not to turn economics too mathematical.

According to the conventional view, Marshall's approach, on the one hand, and the historicist and institutionalist approaches, on the other, were diametrically opposed. Marshall preferred the deductive method, while historicists and institutionalists opted for inductive, that is, empirical methods. But in fact Marshall was very supportive of historical methods and shared the historicist-institutionalist criticism of the assumed universalism of the deductive method. One of the main faults, for instance, that Marshall found in Ricardo's analysis was the latter's treatment of economic actors, as if all of them were like businessmen in the City of London:

> For the sake of simplicity of argument, Ricardo and his followers often spoke as though they regarded man as a constant quantity, and they never gave themselves enough trouble to study his variations. The people whom they knew most intimately were city men; and they sometimes expressed themselves so carelessly as almost to imply that other Englishmen were very much like those whom they knew in the city. They were aware that the inhabitants of other countries had peculiarities of their own that deserved study; but they seemed to regard such differences as superficial and sure to be removed, as soon as other nations had got to know that better way which Englishmen were ready to teach them (1910, 762).[3]

"But their most vital fault," Marshall further comments on Ricardo and his followers, "was that they did not see how liable to change are the habits and institutions of industry." This fault "led them astray as to the relations between the different industrial classes. It caused them to speak of labour as a commodity without staying to throw themselves into the point of view of the workman; . . . They therefore attributed to the forces of supply and demand a much more mechanical and regular action than is to be found in real life; and they laid down laws with regard to profits and wages that did not really hold even for England in their own time" (ibid., 762–63).[4]

Mark Blaug perceives "an ambivalent attitude" in Marshall's work. "Ostensibly," Blaug notices, "the *Principles* is a study of static micro-economic theory but time after time the reader is told that the conclusions of static analysis are unreliable and that microeconomics fails to come to grips with the vital issues of economic policy." Marshall said that the "Mecca of the economist" is "economic biology," by which, Blaug interprets, "Marshall apparently means the study of the economic system as an organism evolving in historical time" (1985a, 420). Blaug perceives a contradiction between this approach, which "sounds very much like the methodological program of American Institutionalism" and the fact that "Marshall's efforts throughout his life were devoted to teaching, expounding and refining" of comparative static theory (ibid.; see also Backhouse 1985, 102).[5] This ambivalence, though, is merely in the beholder's eye. The Lakatosian historian he is, Blaug cannot but use present-day notions in reconstructing the hard cores of past research programs. From the current perspective of modern neoclassical thinking, Marshall's views indeed seem to be ambivalent. But for Marshall and his contemporaries, the attempt to combine comparative statics with the evolutionary analysis of institutions was very common (Maloney 1985; esp. chap. 5).[6] According to Kadish (1989; 1993b), the explanation of the apparent tension between Marshall's claims about the importance of "economic biology" and the fact that he invested most of his time in writing and revising the marginal analyses of the *Principles* is Marshall's efforts to professionalize economics and present it as a scientific discipline. Marginal analysis was the one tool economists held perfect monopoly over. In contrast, history was a well-established discipline from which Marshall wished to differentiate his own field. This does not mean that he was opposed to historical studies in economics, nor even that he deemed such studies as of secondary importance. As Blaug himself notices elsewhere, John Clapham, a distinguished economic historian (1873–1946) "turned to the study of British economic history as a result of urging by Marshall" (1986a, 47; cf. Kadish 1989, 225). Marshall's support of historical analysis is also evident in the career of another famous economic historian and theorist, Arthur Bowley (1869–1957) (Blaug 1986a, 32). These and many other examples show that Marshall was quite consistent in his support of his-

torical work and considered deductive theory and historical work as
equally essential.[7]

   According to Marshall himself, his outlook was typical of the period.
He attributed this "modern perspective" to changes in biology, and argued that John Stuart Mill was the first economist in whose work the
influence of evolutionary theory had been discernible (1910, 764; cf.
Lowe 1964, 195–200 on Mill). Marshall praised also Cliffe Leslie, Walter
Bagehot, John Cairnes, and Arnold Toynbee, "but above all Stanley Jevons, for developing this modern conception" (Marshall 1910, 765).
Leslie, Bagehot, and Toynbee were three of the leaders of the British historical school. Cairnes (1823–75) was a student of John Stuart Mill, the
last giant of the classical era, and Jevons was one of the leaders of the
"marginalist revolution." Nevertheless, Marshall notices that all of them
adopted the new evolutionary approach. Jevons, who is known today
mainly for his marginal utility theory, was actually known to his contemporaries because of his *applied* works on monetary and other problems (Black 1973, 109). The fact that Marshall treat these economists as
contributors to the same trend shows the deficiency of current historical
reconstructions that perceive them as bitter enemies.

   The "methodological pluralism" of Marshall, Jevons, and others, is
also expressed in John Neville Keynes's *Scope and Method of Political
Economy* (1955; originally pub. 1891), which was then the main methodological book of the English-speaking world.[8] Keynes (1852–1949; John
Maynard's father) was a friend of Marshall, and his book "reflected
Marshall's view that the methodological controversies provoked by the
criticisms of both the German and English historical schools could be
papered over by a moderate exposition of the issues, rejecting the extreme
views of the 'younger' historical economists who demanded a wholesale
reconstruction of economics on an historical foundation but granting
that effective applications of economic theory required an appreciation of
the historical forces that disturbed the pure operation of economic laws"
(Blaug 1986a, 110). The opposition between the deductive English school
and the inductive historical school, J. N. Keynes argued, "is strictly
speaking one of degree only" (1955, 29).

   According to received knowledge, neoclassical economists unequivocally supported *laissez-faire*, which is one of the reasons they are called
neo-classical. This also seems to be a flagrant distortion. John Maynard
Keynes, Marshall's most renowned pupil, notices that "some of the most
important works of Alfred Marshall . . . were directed to the elucidation
of the leading cases in which private interest and social interests are not
harmonious," situations which therefore required government intervention (1924, 27; see also Marshall 1910, 763n). On Jevons, Blaug notices

that he "condemned the maxim of *laissez-faire*, opting for a purely pragmatic approach to government intervention" (1986a, 100). Henry Sidgwick (1838–1900), a pioneer of the Cambridge School who influenced Marshall himself, supported "an utterly utilitarian approach to all acts of governmental intervention, including fiscal measures designed to equalise the distribution of income; a recognition of externalities in production as a source of 'market failure,' . . . and a sympathetic but sceptical attitude to socialism" (ibid., 223–24). John Maynard Keynes actually argues that from the time of John Stuart Mill, "economists no longer have any link with the theological or political philosophies out of which the dogma of Social Harmony was born, and their scientific analysis leads them to no such conclusions" (1924, 25–26).[9] Keynes's testimony is supported by the findings of Jha, who analyzed the contents of *Economic Journal*, the only professional journal at that time, from 1891 to 1915:

> The neoclassical economists were deeply concerned with the various aspects of poverty. . . . Poverty and unemployment were increasingly looked upon as the consequence of economic and non-economic causes over which the labourer had little control. . . . [This view] led economists to support old age pensions and unemployment insurance as desirable forms of state assistance. They also gave their support to the trade union movement, because they believed that a strong trade union movement was a precondition for the establishment of competitive wages and of industrial peace (1973, 201).

To sum up, the leading school in British economics was aware of the complexities of human nature and of the major role that institutions played in shaping human behavior. It saw historical studies as an integral part of economic science and rejected the view that the economy was best left alone. It assigned the state the role of ameliorating the detrimental outcomes of free markets and looked favorably at trade unions as a necessary tool for improving the lot of laborers. A similar way of thinking developed at the same time in American economics, our next topic.

The Economic Rebels and the Establishment of the American Economic Association

If Marshallian economics was very different from the common stereotype of neoclassical economics as extremely pro-*laissez-faire* and deductive, this was much more so in regard to American economics during the so-called "neoclassical era." Ekelund and Hébert explain that "eclecticism had always been the hallmark of American economists," who borrowed from all the European schools and adjusted them to "the uniquely American experience and institutions." For these reasons, "classical and neo-classical theoretical analysis . . . never had the hold upon American economists that it did on English economists" (1983, 402).[10]

While American economics had its unique course of development, it converged with the Marshallian approach toward the end of the century. American economists knew about German, Austrian, and French developments, and many of them, including Richard Ely, John Bates Clark, Simon Patten, Frank Fetter, Arthur T. Hadley, E.R.A. Seligman, F. W. Taussig, and Herbert Davenport studied in Germany. If American economists were attracted to Marshall's work, it was not because they were limited to the English literature due to language barriers. The history of American economics from 1885 is one of the main themes in the presidential address of J. M. Clark (1936). Clark (1884–1963), a professor at Columbia, was one of the most important American economists during the first half of the century (Boulding 1957, 6n; Arrow 1991, 5; Hansen 1953, 11; Stoneman 1979, 2; Blaug 1986a, 53–55) and the son of John Bates Clark, one of the most famous American economists ever and a leading figure in the new American Economic Association. Clark's insight into the history of American economics is therefore very useful. He lists four stages in the recent history of American economics. The first period was the one that followed the establishment of the American Economic Association (AEA) in 1885. The association was established as a reaction of American economists against classical economics, and the founders leaned at first toward the historical method. The marginal neoclassicist period followed, led by Clark's own father, J. B. Clark. However, not many years later, the theory was widely challenged. This third stage began around the turn of the century, but only the practical needs of World War I led to the crystallization of new approaches after the war, the fourth stage in Clark's presentation.

The founders of the American Economic Association, who saw themselves as a "new school," protested the extreme individualistic economics of classical writers and pursued liberal reforms in the fields of labor relations, monopoly regulation, and protective tariffs. In what follows I describe shortly the main figures among the founders of the Association and their ideas in order to render the direction in which the intellectual winds blew.[11]

Richard T. Ely (1854–1943) was among the most conspicuous leaders of the "new school." He "denounced the old school's political economy as deductive and mathematical rather than inductive and historical [and] stressed the need to abandon extreme *laissez-faire* and to humanize economics" (Dorfman 1949, 3:162). Ely was a Christian socialist, who supported factory legislation and regulation of public utilities (ibid.; Blaug 1986a, 72). According to one newspaper, he enjoyed "the confidence of the laboring classes and their recognized leaders" (Dorfman 1949, 3:163) and was accused of upholding socialism in his work. The accusations led to an official investigation by the University of Wisconsin, which accepted Ely's denial (ibid., 3:257). The incident clearly demonstrates, however, where Ely's sympathy rested.

The founders of the Association were generally in favor of labor in questions of labor legislation and union activities. Edmund Janes James (1855–1925) defended labor unions, arguing that the American culture inspired workers "with a desire to share more largely in the material benefits of an advancing civilization, without, however, securing to him a corresponding possibility of doing so under the action of our industrial system" (quoted ibid., 3:161). The only answer to communism and anarchism, he thought, was to better the conditions of workers. Reverend Charles Swan Walker (1846–1933) was more radical, and "even upheld the labor unions' use of boycott" (ibid., 3:174). Henry C. Adams (1851–1921), another leader of the "new school," also defended labor unions, claiming that their importance in balancing the power of concentrated capital is enough to offset their excessive policies. He thought that "the labor movement was a step in the further development of individual rights and harmonized with the basic ideal of Anglo-Saxon institutions, that of equal rights" (ibid., 3:166). Adams perceived his contemporary socialists as "the earnest men of today" and believed the trade unions to be "the great movers of the present" and "the next step toward a nearer realization of Liberty and Brotherhood" (quoted in Furner 1975, 131).[12]

Many "new-schoolers" held an organic conception of society and opposed the individualistic nature of *laissez-faire* beliefs. In 1885, Henry Adams said that "the great problem of the present day is properly to correlate public and private activity so as to preserve harmony and proportion between the various parts of organic society" (Dorfman 1949, 3:173–74). In a monograph published in 1887, Adams argued that "a tyranny which sprang from the unregulated workings of self-interest was just as hard upon the individual . . . as that which sprang from political privileges." "The American view," he continued, "must emphasize the complementary relations of the State and the individual in the development of the social organism" (quoted in ibid., 3:167–68).[13]

Other distinguished leaders of the AEA were Edwin Robert Anderson Seligman (1861–1939) and Simon Nelson Patten (1852–1922). Seligman contributed to the establishment of public finance as "a subject of theoretical as well as practical importance" (ibid., 3:255). He "had been actively interested in . . . a variety of reform movements," but was less radical and more cautious than Ely (ibid., 3:254). Patten was an idiosyncratic critic of mainstream classical economics. He supported tariffs in order to prevent the concentration of farmers on a single crop (ibid., 3:183), and argued that "the traditional laws of economics were not natural laws but social laws, developed by non-progressive people. America required a different set of social laws to achieve fully that progress inherent in its rich material environment" (ibid., 3:183). Patten developed the idea of "economic freedom," according to which all workers had certain rights including the right for comfort, that is, a minimal standard of living, and "a right to relief" for people struck by misfortune (ibid., 3:184–85).[14]

Albert Fetter (1863–1949), who received his education in economics during the period that followed the establishment of the AEA, illuminates more clearly the way of thinking which led to the establishment of the American Economic Association. He says that the founders of the Association protested against what seemed to them to be the irrelevance of the theories of Ricardo and J. S. Mill to the problems of the American economy. During the post–Civil War period political struggles concentrated on new economic issues, including "railroads, public service monopolies, industrial monopolies, organized labor, relations of employers and workmen, the monetary problems . . ., the tariff." "Professional economic opinion," Fetter explains, "gave no help or guidance . . . in all this turmoil of economic transition" (1925, 13; cf. Furner and Supple 1990, 17).

The liberal and heterodox ideas of the rebellious economists were reflected in the way they wanted to define the American Economic Association:

> Ely's prospectus [for the AEA's charter] stated: "We regard the State as an educational and ethical agency whose positive aid is an indispensable condition of human progress." Individual initiative was necessary in industrial life, it said, but "the doctrine of *laissez-faire* is unsafe in politics and unsound in morals." The conclusions of the political economists of the last generation were not to be trusted, it asserted, for political economy was in the first stages of scientific development and its advance was to be achieved not so much by speculation as by an impartial study of economic conditions. The new group was to "seek the aid for the united efforts of church, State, and science, without which the conflict between labor and capital could not be solved" (Dorfman 1949, 3:206).

To make the proposal more attractive to a wider audience, it was toned down before it became the official Charter of the Association. But the original draft clearly demonstrates the founders' rebellious state of mind (see also Furner 1975, 70–75).

J. M. Clark (1936) tells us that a marginalist period was quick to follow the rebellion of the founders of the American Economic Association. This second stage must have occurred very shortly after the first, because the third one took place, according to Clark's Presidential Address, in the early 1900s (cf. Ross 1991, 173), less than twenty years after the establishment of the AEA. It seems strange that so quickly after the insurrection of the founders of the AEA in the 1880s the pendulum swung back to the side of marginalist theory, which, *according to our conception*, is the continuation and refinement of classical teachings. How can we account for this quick transition?

The answer is simple. The contrast between the historicist approach of the German historical school and the deductive nature of marginal analysis is a later reconstruction on the basis of post–World War II perceptions. In the German-speaking world, the contrast was solidified and magnified due to political reasons. Both the German and the Austro-Hungarian Empires were highly centralized, and their universities were controlled by their central governments. When the Second Reich was established, Berlin sought to consolidate its hegemony by appointment of historicist economists, while the Austrian government sponsored the Austrian School and impeded the recruitment and promotion of historicist economists in Austrian universities (Streissler 1990, 158–63). In Britain both the historicists and the deductivists have acknowledged all along the necessity of combining historical research with abstract theory, even though they quarreled over the relative importance of the methods and the appropriate way to combine them. Such reconciliation between historicism and deductive theory was much more common in America, where the influences of many traditions had always been felt (Dorfman 1955, 28). However, in contrast to Marshall, who synthesized marginalism and historical awareness with the classical tradition in the 1880s, the empiricist spirit of the German historical school and the new marginal analysis were allied together *against* the dominant classical school in the United States.

The founders of the AEA perceived marginal analysis as an answer to the problems of classical economics. In his second textbook, *Outline of Economics* (pub. 1893), Richard Ely added an "elaborate presentation of the marginal utility doctrine" and stated that the "constructive work of the Austrian School was fundamental" (Dorfman 1949, 3:257). Henry C. Adams "was among the first to present Jevons' theory of value" (ibid., 3:164), although he later "scrapped the marginal utility economics, at least its expansion into the area of distribution" (ibid., 3:166). But the connection between the radical "new school" and marginal analysis is best exemplified in the work of John Bates Clark, who is considered to be the founder of the American branch of marginalism, and whose contribution to marginalism is often put on par with those of Jevons, Menger, and Walras. Clark was a member of the group which founded the AEA (ibid., 3:206) and, like Ely, thought that unions were important as a counterbalance to monopolistic capitalism (ibid., 3:192–93). Because of these views he also was accused of being a socialist (ibid., 3:195). He "flatly opposed the extreme individualism" and saw society as "an organism subject to the law of ordered change" (ibid., 3:194, 196).

Clark's first book, *The Philosophy of Wealth* (pub. 1886), "showed the influence of his German teachers, being critical of the capitalist system, but also hinted at the marginal utility theory of value of Jevons and Menger" (Blaug 1986a, 51). In 1889 Clark published his major theory of marginal productivity in *The Distribution of Wealth*, for which he is most remembered nowadays. "Clark attributed his own version of marginal utility to the inspiration of his German teacher, Karl Knies" (Dorfman 1955, 28), a leader of the historicist trend. Commenting on Clark's theory from a modern retrospect, Blaug contends that "the name of John Bates Clark stands forever associated with one of the worst fallacies in modern economics: the use of marginal productivity theory to provide an ethical justification for the functional distribution of income, according to which the owners of all factors of production receive exactly what they 'deserve,' namely their marginal products" (1986a, 50). Blaug refers here to the marginal productivity theory. This theory states that the wage is equal to the marginal product; that is, to the money value of the increase in production due to the addition of one more worker. This theory was used by conservatives to argue that wages reflected natural forces and that any intervention, either by collective bargaining or by minimum-wage legislation, would only cause unemployment (Furner 1975, 185–90). Although this conservative position was based on marginal analysis, it was similar in its spirit to the political and philosophical outlook of classical economists to which Clark objected so fiercely.

The apparent gap between *The Philosophy of Wealth* and *The Distribution of Wealth* puzzles modern readers of J. B. Clark (Henry 1982, 166). Jalladeau, for instance, wondered how "the most original critic of the principles of classical political economy becomes paradoxically transformed into a theoretician of the most traditional, hypothetical, and deductive kind" (1975, 210). Conservative economists find in the case of J. B. Clark—"a liberal and optimistic theoretician, who becomes the advocate of the competitive system after having initially much decried it" (ibid., 210)—legitimation and indication that their approach is valid and not ideologically biased. Henry's interpretation is different. He does not dispute the fact of a major shift in Clark's views, but argues "that rather than a fundamental or radical transformation from a socialist (or anti-capitalist) position to a pro-capitalist perspective, Clark underwent a change from support of the small capitalist (what may loosely be called a 'populist') to a position in which he threw his intellectual arsenal behind the large or monopoly capitalist" (1982, 167). Brandis (1985) doubts even this. For him, Clark, the moral philosopher, is the same all along: a scholar whose main concern is the just distribution of wealth. The only change is in the adoption of new economic tools, marginal analysis, that led him to believe in the appropriateness of the market system, *at least under ideal conditions*. The question, however, is whether this adoption of an economic tool should be perceived as a "technical" change only or as a radical change in his outlook.

Clark, no doubt, is a tough nut to crack for historians. But some of the mystery is solved when we understand that marginal analysis was not perceived by Clark to be "traditional, hypothetical, and deductive" as classical economics was. For him, as for Jevons (Black 1973) and Walras (Jaffé 1973), it was a radical departure from classical economics; a departure designed to put economic analysis on a sounder scientific basis. For him, as for Jevons, and even for Menger, marginal analysis was to be combined with historical and statistical analyses. Henry's claim that in his later years Clark employed "rigorous, scientific neoclassicism" might be misleading if we think on the style of marginal analysis *at that period* as identical to the style of mathematical articles in present-day journals. This, of course, is a wrong impression. As was the case with his contemporary Alfred Marshall, Clark supported his marginal analysis by arguments of all sorts and qualified the conclusions of his abstract discussion. Most importantly, he saw his marginal productivity theory as valid only in a static system and emphasized the necessity to study real conditions in order to understand economic realities and govern them (Dorfman 1949, 3:205). Thus, even though wages in the *static* state were equal to marginal productivity, in practice, in the *dynamic* state, the permanent existence of able but unemployed workers weakened the bargaining power of workers and pushed wages below marginal productivity. Unions were therefore necessary to ensure just wages at the same time that monopolistic behavior by unions pushed wages above marginal productivity (Clark 1968, 451–52). Actual policies must be based, therefore, on "close study and careful regulation" (ibid., 451). In any case, the state must be involved in negotiating just wages, because market forces could not be relied on and unionization created monopoly power (ibid., chap. 25). Given this attitude and similar views of J. B. Clark, one can accept Dorfman's criticism of those who have read Clark out of context: "Many statements which [Clark] carefully qualified, such as every man gets what he produces, have been taken by uncritical conservatives as rigid dogma. This made a great nineteenth-century liberal thinker into the symbol of twentieth-century reaction" (Dorfman, 1949, 3:205).

The small detour into J. B. Clark's work was necessary in order to dispel the misconception of his work as being "traditional, hypothetical, and deductive." This misconception has created a false sense of animosity between American marginalists, on one hand, and American economists who were inclined toward historicism, on the other. Although supporters of the Austrian marginal utility theory and the German historical school were in fierce competition with each other in the *German*-speaking world, the *American* economists did not see those approaches as mutually exclusive. Both schools were perceived by "new schoolers" as "scientific" criticisms of the ideologically oriented classical economists. Moreover, the marginalists shared with institutionalists the support of government intervention (Dorfman 1949, 3:251; cf. Ross 1991, 175). This may come as a surprise to those who perceive neoclassical economics—a rather misleading epithet—as the continuation and refinement of classical economics. The political views of most of the American marginalists, like those of Marshall and his influential Cambridge school, were a far cry from the extreme *laissez-faire* of the classical economists.

The profession of economics at the end of the 1880s can be divided into two main camps: the "old school" of conservative classical economists and the "new school" of economists who supported both historical methods *and* marginal analysis, and who, in addition, favored a more active role of the state in the economy. The former camp included arch-conservatives, such as William Graham Sumner (1840–1910) and Simon Newcomb, and more moderate conservatives, such as Charles F. Dunbar (1830–1900), Arthur T. Hadley, J. Laurence Laughlin, and Frank W. Taussig. The conservatives controlled Harvard and Yale, and their absence from the AEA hampered its professional image (Furner 1975, 76–80). Yet the two camps seemed to reach a middle ground in what Dorfman calls "the new synthesis" during the 1890s. The founders of the AEA had always sought to attract more members and, therefore, eliminated "the strictures against *laissez-faire*" from the original charter of the Association (Dorfman 1949, 3:207; Furner 1975, 73–74). At first, this did not help. The economists of the "old school" stayed out, and a *methodenstreit* ensued. But the founders of the American Economic Association still looked for a compromise. "In 1887, eager to attract the young men of the old school, the Council of the Association toned down the constitution." It left out all statements about policies, and kept only the call for "economic research, especially the historical and statistical study of the actual conditions of industrial life." This time they were successful, and "by 1890 most of the leading academic members of the 'old school' . . . were members of the American Economic Association" (Dorfman 1949, 208). A conciliatory atmosphere prevailed: "Economic discussion was less marked by personal animosities; controversy was on a higher level, and generally opposition to any idea was presented dispassionately" (ibid., 3:238; see also Furner and Supple 1990, 9).[15]

The new marginalist approach played a major role in achieving this "rapprochement." As Dorfman says, "the marginal analysis was now definitely in the foreground," and "students arrived at the doctrine from varied directions." The marginal utility doctrine was employed "on different sides of concrete questions," and even though "neither side was convinced," they had the marginalist language in common (Dorfman 1949, 3:243). This environment was a fertile soil for Marshall's *Principles of Economics*, which got indeed many positive reviews (ibid., 3:250). With the new synthesis of classical and marginal economics, American economics moved to a more conservative position. Although "the synthesis which was being made between the classical economists . . . and the historical and marginal utility schools . . . was put together in many different ways . . . the most authoritative combination was conservative" (ibid., 3: 258).

This situation might be conceived as the abandonment of the original revolutionary ideas of the American Economic Association. And yet it also legitimized some of those ideas which became now part of the mainstream. The need in quantitative studies was widely acknowledged, and "even some of the socialist emphasis upon human values could be recognized as a factor in the new equation." In general, economists achieved "an equilibrium among the theories that had seemed so explosive in the eighties" (ibid.). Furthermore, although "orthodox views continued to dominate the scene, . . . orthodoxy was no longer inflexible" (ibid., 3:238). The work of F. W. Taussig (1859–1940), an economist from Harvard, is a good illustration. Taussig was the editor of the *Quarterly Journal of Economics* from 1896 to 1936. In this capacity and as the author of the second most popular textbook, *Principles of Economics* (pub. 1911 and 1939), he "exercised a considerable influence on successive generations of American economists" (Blaug and Sturges 1983, 368). Taussig was among the leaders of the "old school" but at the end of 1886 he was "the first of the 'old school' advocates to join the Association. This was not surprising, for Taussig accepted some of the tenets of the marginal utility school, although skeptical of the fully developed scheme" (Dorfman 1949, 3:265). He also accepted some points of the German historical school (ibid.) and was interested in interdisciplinary studies with psychology (ibid., 3:344). Taussig raised, for example, the possibility that a decline of prices would induce people to sell *more* in the short-run in order to get rid of their inventory before prices fall further (ibid., 4:237). He also claimed that differential costs were a much more pervasive phenomenon than assumed by orthodox theory (ibid., 4:238). Taussig was the first chairman of the new Tariff Commission (1917–19), and during the war he was a member of the Price-Fixing Committee of the

War Industries Board. "These activities reinforced [Taussig's] broad outlook and flexibility in treating traditional theory" (ibid., 4:236).

In terms of policy orientation, Taussig can be described as a "moderate
conservative." He had a "humanitarian drive to achieve a more equitable
distribution of the benefits of material progress," but he also showed an
"extremely cautious bent toward social change" (ibid.). In principle he
admitted the need for government intervention, but in practice he often
objected to concrete measures. For example, he thought that public
works were not efficient and that nothing could be done about "the plight
of the farmers" (ibid., 4:239). Taussig supported, however, other measures, such as compulsory workmen's compensation insurance, public
ownership of dams and power plants, regulation of utilities, insurance of
bank deposits, and monetary policies to prevent financial panics (ibid.,
4:239–42). One should mention also Thomas Nixon Carver (1865–
1961), Taussig's colleague at Harvard and President of the AEA in 1916,
as close to Taussig in the mixture of conservative views with support for
cautious reforms (see Dorfman 1949, 3:354–55; Dorfman 1959, 4:247–
50). Arthur Twining Hadley (1856–1930), an economist at, and later
President of, Yale, was another influential economist at the time, who
advanced some changes in the theory and was flexible in regard to government legislation (ibid., 4:258–64).

There were, of course, other influential figures among neoclassical
economists who opted for opposite views and held more conservative
views than Taussig, Carver, and Hadley. The dominant figures on the
"orthodox" side included many leading economists: James Laurence
Laughlin (1871–1933), Frank A. Fetter (1863–1949), Herbert J. Davenport (1861–1931), Fred Manville Taylor (1855–1932), and Irving
Fisher (1867–1947). Laughlin was the first head professor at the department of Economics at the new University of Chicago and the founder and
first editor of the *Journal of Political Economy*. He "had little sympathy
with the historical school" and conceived economics as a deductive analysis (Dorfman 1949, 3:272). Laughlin was very critical of attempts to in-
tervene in the economy because he considered businesspersons to be "the
greatest force in the intellectual, social, and material development of the
nation" (ibid., 3:273). Fetter, the President of the AEA in 1912, is most
known for his theory of interest (ibid., 3:360–65; Blaug 1986a, 74–76).
He was a Malthusian, a supporter of eugenics, who opposed "democracy
and opportunity" and supported marginal productivity theory with no
qualification (Dorfman 1949, 3:364). Davenport, the President of the
AEA in 1920, "felt that the deficiencies of traditional economics could be
remedied by reformulating and purifying its concepts" (ibid., 3:375). He
opposed labor legislation, and insisted that the efforts of the rich "chiefly
benefited the poor" (ibid., 3:378). Taylor, President of AEA in 1929, be-

lieved in natural laws and natural evolution, arguing that tinkering with "naturally developed" institutions may cause more damage than help (ibid., 3:391).

Irving Fisher's views are unique. Fisher was one of the most famous American economists in the first half of the century, whose contributions to modern economics are still appreciated (Blaug 1986a, 77–81). He was mostly concerned with developing value theory, the theory of interest, and theory of the level of prices (the famous quantity theory). Concerning policy issues, Fisher said that "he himself was an ardent critic of *laissez-faire*" (Dorfman 1949, 3:370), but he seems to have adopted a more *conservative* anti-*laissez-faire* stand. The world, in his view, "was divided into the educated and ignorant." Therefore, "if progress was to be made, 'the former should be allowed to dominate the latter'" (ibid., 3:371). Fisher supported compulsory health insurance and workmen's compensation acts, but objected to regulation of monopolies. He criticized the blind pursuit of individual self-interest which led to cutthroat competition and saw government regulation as justified in such cases, although he doubted the efficacy of the remedy (ibid.).

Although the above five conservatives were famous and influential members of the discipline, the mainstream of the profession was occupied by more liberal economists—from moderate conservatives like Taussig and Carver to staunch liberals like Ely and J. B. Clark. Moreover, the discipline as a whole was much more open methodologically. Historical studies in particular became common for all the theoretical camps.[16] And "value theory, long the central theme of general economic theory . . . occupied less of the attention of the profession" (Dorfman 1959, 5:464). The main reason, according to Dorfman, was that "the dominant neoclassicists . . . felt that value theory was largely a settled issue. In their minds the work of Alfred Marshall in England and J. B. Clark in the United States had produced a satisfactory logical synthesis of the older classical school with the doctrine of utility theory. Innovation and fundamental exploration were therefore simply not necessary. "It was not so much that value theory was considered unimportant but rather, because of its wide acceptance, most scholars felt free to work in other areas" (ibid.; cf. Tugwell 1924a, 392).

The work in those "other areas" (e.g., banking, marketing, labor, international trade), however, was always loosely connected to the core classical or neoclassical theory. The neoclassicists themselves were aware that their theory was not a description of reality, and their study of specific problems was based on history and statistics, very much like the research of "heterodox" economists. The contenders espoused different views in matters of theory and policy. But the medium through which they argued over these issues—verbal discussion on the basis of marginal analysis, descriptive data, historical examples, and common-sense arguments—was the same. This is another example of the difficulty in using the Kuhnian or the Lakatosian frameworks. As an intellectual exercise, we can characterize two distinct "paradigms" (or "research programs") with different assumptions and methodological preferences. And yet, when we examine the works of individual economists, we find that they held various combinations of elements from both "schools." They quarreled over many issues but experienced no "incommensurability gap."

Institutionalism appeared on this background as a response against the tranquil complacency of moderate liberals and conservatives. Unlike the calmness of American economics, the United States witnessed deep cleavages and violent clashes during the same years, and economic issues—labor relations in particular—stood in the center of social and political struggles. Thorstein Veblen (1857–1929), John R. Commons (1862–1945), Robert F. Hoxie (1868–1916), Carleton H. Parker (1878–1918), and Charles H. Cooley (1846–1929), the pioneers of institutionalism, were dissatisfied with the continued reliance of economic theory on deductive analysis and viewed with criticism the moderation of pro-labor positions. Much more than earlier generations, they confided in the power of *empirical* science and thought that governments could use economic science—properly reformed and modified—to improve economic performance, equity, and harmony.

Conclusions: Economists in the Forefront of Social Reform

Conventional histories of economics depict neoclassical economics as deductive, conservative, and focused on marginal analysis. In contrast, we saw in this chapter that both in Britain and the United States, the mainstream of economics accepted and encouraged historical and statistical research and favored economic reforms. Marginalism was widely accepted as one element of theory but was actually practiced by a relatively small group of economists. The fuller picture of economics, however, is much wider and even farther away from the conventional picture. The Walrasian version of marginalism, the Lausanne school, which is the most similar to the post–World War II neoclassical economics, was ignored by most Anglo-Saxon economists. Ménard (1990) says that it is somewhat strange to treat as a school a group which included only two economists (Walras and Pareto), one of whom, Pareto, later renounced his "Walrasian" positions. In addition, Walras was unequivocally against *laissez-faire*. He developed a rigorous analysis of general equilibrium as a tool with which central authority would be able to direct economic activity in the most efficient way. The Austrian school of marginalism was the only one which continued to oppose state regulation, although even there, the earlier proponents of the theory, especially Menger and von Wieser, were much more tolerant toward some level of regulation than both their classical predecessors and their successors in Vienna (Streissler 1973).

The Austrian school was much more successful than the Walrasian one at that time and had many followers in the United States, Sweden (where "the Stockholm school" started to emerge as a center of economic theory), and elsewhere in Europe. In Britain, however, it was not welcomed, and in the German world (including northern and eastern Europe) it had to compete with the historicists who had many followers. During the thirties, Lionel Robbins, with the help of immigrants from the Continent, turned the London school of Economics into a center of Austrian teaching. But this school was put in the shadow of the Cambridge school, which, led by Keynes, did everything it could to undermine the Austrians. The attack on the Austrians was so strong that their most prominent leader, Friedrich von Hayek, had to leave the discipline. It was only in the 1970s, after the decline of Keynesianism, that the Austrian school was "rehabilitated" and Hayek was awarded the Nobel prize in 1974.

In addition to the Austrians, the only other group that opposed the liberal mainstream was composed of those who continued to follow classical economics. This opposition continued to have many followers (Dorfman 1949), another fact that contradicts the models of Kuhn and Lakatos. Yet this opposition was dwarfed by the opposition from the left side of the ideological map. Besides Veblen and other pioneers of institutionalism, the most important criticism came from socialists of various stripes: Marxian, social-democrats, and Fabians. Even many of those who were far from being socialist incorporated Marxian threads in their works. This was especially evident in the growing literature on business cycles, a topic that gained a central position during the first decades of the century. Economists such as Arthur Spiethoff (1873–1957), Albert Aftalion (1874–1956), and Joseph Schumpeter (1883–1950) incorporated institutional elements into their explanations of economic ups and downs in order to account for the failure of markets to reach full-employment equilibrium. Historicist economists joined the attack on the methodological level. In terms of politics, there were both liberal and conservative historicists, but both sides rejected the maxims of *laissez faire*. The historicists had immense influence, and the need to "contextualize" economic behavior and the value of historical research were accepted by most practicing economists.

It is often argued that neoclassical economics was a bourgeois response to the exposition of the faults of classical economics by Marx. This might be indeed the case. But this does not mean that neoclassical economists were as politically conservative as their classical ancestors. Marshall, Ely, Clark, and others have defended capitalism but understood that its defense required rectification of its inherent problems and injustices. We must remember that Britain and America after *The Origin of Species* was very different from Britain of *The Wealth of Nations*. Intellectually, the "Darwinian Revolution" engendered, and was part of, a massive change in the perception of nature, human life, and society. Socially and politically, the accelerating rate of change, the persistence of poverty, and the intensification of labor strife posed a tough challenge for the Smithian belief in natural harmony. At the same time, the growing confidence in the power of science encouraged the belief that enlightened governments, guided by scientific research, would be able to improve and advance the fortune of the human race.

To present the neoclassical economics of today as a natural development of the economics of the neoclassical era, and especially of Marshall, is therefore a severe mistake. Marshallian economics is extremely different from the neo-Walrasian neoclassical economics of the postwar era (Ménard 1990; Yonay 1992). The current view of the neoclassical era as an earlier stage of present-day economics reflects the results of struggles among later-day economists over the meaning of economics, its proper goals and methods, and the past of the discipline. From the currently common perspective in the discipline, modern economics continues Marshallian economics, while institutionalism appears as a strange and exceptional outgrowth, whose demise seems understandable, natural, and desirable. But when one looks at it from the perspective suggested here, it is the rise of institutionalism which suddenly appears as natural and expected. The institutionalist school and the different perceptions thereof are our next topic.

Three

Reconstructing the History of Institutionalism

> Historians, as much as the actors themselves, delight in
> deciding who influenced whom, who had only a marginal
> contribution, and who made the most significant contribu-
> tion. . . . So as not to be confused, we should distinguish the
> recruiting of allies so as to build a fact or a machine collec-
> tively, from the *attribution of responsibility* to those who did
> most of the work.
> (Bruno Latour, *Science in Action*)

INSTITUTIONALISM is one of those "unorthodox" approaches which are
either totally glossed over or treated all too briefly by common textbooks
on the history of economics. Most writers refer to this school as a unique
and exceptional theory, which challenged the mainstream but did not
derail it from its course. The conventional history texts doubt that institutionalism was indeed "a school," in the sense that it had a unified, coherent, and consistent approach to which all the institutionalists subscribed
(Mirowski 1981, 593). The alleged lack of coherence and unity is
brought as a proof that institutionalism has never been a viable alternative to mainstream economics. The authors say that although it might
have had valid critique on orthodox theory, it exhausted its utility by
alerting neoclassical economists to its weaknesses. It is implied that it had
nothing positive to add to the stock of economic knowledge.

The conventional presentation of the history of economics presents
current economics as the culmination of a long process of development
and depicts its past rivals as unworthy alternatives that had no chance to
replace the mainstream due to their own shortcomings. There is nothing
unusual or "unscientific" in this practice of neoclassical economists. As
Kuhn has noticed long ago, triumphant paradigms always revise the history of their fields (1970a).[1] But historians or sociologists, who crave to
understand historical developments, must follow the principle of symmetry; they have to treat equally theories which failed and those that prevailed. To say that a certain approach won because it was "better" is not
an explanation. The more intriguing question is how and why practicing
economists have reached the conclusion that it was better.

This chapter confronts the common views on institutionalism with a different interpretation of institutionalism and its success, achievements, and lasting contributions to economics. As a counterbalance to the conventional view, my presentation might be biased in the opposite direction. My goal, however, is not to "black box" my own description, but rather to reopen the long-closed traditional black box. By presenting a different picture of institutionalism and its role in the history of economics and by juxtaposing this picture alongside the conventional picture, I demonstrate how the history can be interpreted in different ways. The first section gives a general background on the institutionalist movement. In the second section I present some evidence on the success of institutionalism in American economics during the interwar years. The third section discusses the long-standing contributions of institutionalists to modern economics, and the fourth analyzes the question whether there was any "institutional doctrine" that could replace traditional theory. The final section deals with the differences between institutionalism and its contemporary rivals and argues that the differences were not as polarized as they are currently presented. Altogether, the evidence presented here draws a new picture—a picture which is very different from the one we have encountered in most other books on the practice of economics and the fortunes of economists during the first half of this century.

The Rise of Institutionalism (1890–1914)

The term "institutionalism" was first used to describe the work of Thorstein Veblen (1857–1929). Veblen was an eccentric figure and his career was very erratic, not the least because of his boisterous behavior. Nevertheless, Veblen inspired generations of American economists and other scholars due to his sharp diagnosis of American life and poignant criticism of privileged elites. Fundamental to his view of the economy was the separation between the productive elements (the "machine process") and the money-making ones ("the business enterprise"). Workers, engineers, managers, and entrepreneurs were commanded for producing the goods people needed; bankers, big corporation executives, lawyers, brokers, salespersons—all those who did not take a direct role in the production itself—were denounced as parasites. The Veblenian analysis is analogous to Marx's (Harris 1932), but instead of a class struggle between the owners of the means of production and workers, Veblen posited the struggle between the "machine process" and the "business enterprise." He envisioned a society in which the latter would be eliminated but feared that they would actually gain more and more power. Veblen

wrote insightful diagnoses of modern society based on his critical observations of the social practices around him but was not involved in empirical investigations, nor did he think that such research was needed. The
ultra-empiricist image of institutionalism clearly does not befit the great
father of that school.[2]

The second father of institutionalism was John R. Commons (1862–
1945), whose training and career were much more conventional than
Veblen's, and whose criticism was much less combative. Commons was
a student of Richard Ely, who was one of the most famous American
economists at the end of the nineteenth century and a prominent leader
of the group that had established the AEA (see chap. 2). He was mostly
interested in the emergence and evolution of the legal institutions of capitalism and in the development of labor relations between capitalists
and workers. His research method was basically historical studies,
but he took his students to various organizations to watch economic
life in the making and encouraged them to do field work. Unlike the radical views of Veblen, Commons was committed to a reformist program
and was involved in many welfare reforms and labor legislation in Wisconsin. Also in contrast to Veblen, Commons had the social skills and the
desire to organize a "school" around him. He turned the University of
Wisconsin in Madison into a center of institutionalist research, that is,
of rigorous study of the evolution and practicing of various economic
organizations.[3]

The third figure who is often mentioned as the third father of institutionalism is Wesley C. Mitchell (1874–1948). Although he was a student
of Veblen, his work was very different. His vision was the quantification
of economic studies. He believed that quantification would lead to the
discovery of patterns of economic behavior and provide policy makers
with the knowledge necessary to navigate economic life. His main concern was business cycles. His whole work was aimed at taming these
cycles, or at least ironing them out, by deciphering their quantitative in-
terrelations and counterbalancing erratic movements of the market. Although his empirical research was not inspired by Veblen, Mitchell persistently acknowledged Veblen's contribution to his work all his life. His
explanation of the business cycle was indeed based on the Veblenian distinction between money-making and production. In practice, however,
Mitchell is responsible much more than Veblen for the success of institutionalism. Unlike Veblen, the perennial iconoclast, Mitchell was a successful academic entrepreneur. He was involved in establishing the New
School for Social Research and the National Bureau of Economic Research, which he directed for twenty-five years (1920–45). The money
that he managed to solicit from business persons helped him to turn the

Bureau into one of the most prolific centers of economic research. This contribution will be described in more detail later in this chapter.[4]

Under Commons and Mitchell, Columbia and the University of Wisconsin were the two centers of what came to be known as "institutionalism." Because Mitchell, the chief advocate of statistical studies, was identified with Veblen, the term "institutional economics" was assigned to his work as well, and this is why institutionalism was identified during the twenties and thirties with quantitative economics. In 1931, Commons, who actually studied the evolution of economic institutions, began to describe his approach as "institutional" as well. The two centers—Columbia and Madison—were very different in their practices, a fact that loomed large in the criticism against the notion of an "institutional school." But they did share several principles which are widely recognized today as the trademarks of institutionalism: empirical research, suspicion toward deductive theory; emphasis on the changing nature of economic institutions, habits, and norms, special attention to the divergence of market values (prices) from social values, and the belief in the ability of informed concerted action to improve human welfare.

Veblen, Commons, and Mitchell are the "canonized" fathers of institutionalism but they were not alone in their call for the reform of economic science. The other pioneers included Charles H. Cooley (1864–1932), Robert F. Hoxie (1868–1916), and Carleton H. Parker (1881–1958). Cooley, the "fourth founding father of institutional theory" (Dorfman 1963, 41), is known today as one of the parents of American sociology. But he was trained as an economist and taught economics at Michigan. Cooley found the scope of economics too limited and established the department of sociology at Michigan, but he believed that by studying the way people interacted with each other he was actually working on the same problems that economists had been working on for generations.[5] Hoxie, another student of Veblen, specialized in labor economics, and his *Trade Unionism in the United States* (pub. posthumously in 1917) "still stands as one of the few permanent contributions to the theory of labor organization by an American economist" (Dorfman 1949, 3:451; Goodrich 1932a). Parker, who chaired the economics department at the University of Washington, sought to introduce the instincts psychology of McDougall and Thorndike and Freudian psychoanalysis into traditional economics (Goodrich 1932b; Dorfman 1949, 3: 488–89). It is important to emphasize that these three economists—Cooley, Hoxie, and Parker— were highly regarded and very influential at the time. The mainstream historians, who focus on Veblen, Commons, and Mitchell, may create the impression that institutionalism was actually a small group of dissenters, not a "school." By adding to the list at least three other prominent institutionalists, who greatly influenced the discipline, we get a different impression of institutionalism (Yonay 1993). This new image will be further enhanced once we move to the period after the Great War. This is indeed our next topic.

The Sway of Institutionalism during the Interwar Period

The focus on Veblen and Commons in the literature on institutionalism brought about another distortion in the perception of that school. Since both scholars, and especially Veblen, were active mostly before World War I, a widespread impression was created that the institutionalist movement "flourished from the 1890's to the 1920's" (Boulding 1957, 1). Similarly, Backhouse maintains that institutionalism was "equally important" as neoclassical economics "at least until the 1920s" (1985, 221; see also Samuelson 1958, 785n), and Blaug claims that "the institutionalist movement ended for all practical purposes in the 1930s." Even a sympathizing viewer like Mirowski speaks about "an institutionalist school of economic theory in the first three decades of the twentieth century" (1990, 83–84). According to Dorothy Ross, "the turning point came in 1927" (1991, 414) when Mitchell and J. M. Clark supposedly changed their views, a step that "removed the two most eminent and established economists from the leading edge of institutionalist debate" (ibid., 415). Some young institutionalists, she asserts, continued their critique of neoclassical economics but met with a "greater note of impatience" (ibid., 416).

My research shows, however, that institutionalism reached its apogee only during the period between the world wars and declined, rather rapidly, only after the *Second* World War. Two new leaders emerged at that period: John Maurice Clark (1884–1963), who was considered one of the greatest economists of the interwar period (Dorfman 1959, chap. 15; Hansen 1953, 8–11; Stoneman 1979),[6] and Walton Hale Hamilton (1881–1958), who enjoyed a wide reputation as well. At the National Bureau of Economic Research, Mitchell led a host of economists working on national accounting, price indices, and other quantitative projects. The most famous among them were Frederick Mills (1892–1964), Arthur Burns (1904–87), and Simon Kuznets (1901–85). The Commons group of Wisconsin included Selig Perlman, Edwin Witte, Don D. Lescohier, and Arthur J. Altmeyer. All of them were involved in labor legislation and welfare reforms in Wisconsin and on the Federal level. Morris Copeland (1895–1989) pioneered research on the flow of money and worked for many years for the federal government. Gardiner Means's (1896–1988) work (with Adolph Berle) on the separation of ownership and management is a classic which is still widely read among students of industrial organizations. Sumner Slichter (1892–1959) was the authority on labor issues during the period and a constant adviser and arbitrator in labor issues. Harold Moulton, the President of the Brookings Institution for many years, was another influential institutionalist. So were Rexford Tugwell (1891–1979), Leon Keyserling (1908–87), and Edwin Nourse (1883–1974), three of the leading economic advisers in Roosevelt's and Truman's administrations.

It is not easy to measure the influence and power of a past intellectual movement. Obviously we cannot make a survey to see how many economists supported each school, but the above partial list of conspicuous institutionalists indicates that the interwar support of institutionalism was much bigger than the conventional writers allow. Other indications for the place of institutionalists are estimations and interpretations of contemporary economists. While the economists of the time might have failed to see the wider picture and lacked historical perspective, we can learn much from what they said offhand as taken-for-granted facts and even from the very tone of their arguments. Furthermore, what the participants perceived is in some sense the "real trends." If most people believed that one school of thought was declining and another was rising, this is an indication of such a trend regardless of what happened to the actual percentage of supporters among the practitioners in the field.

Thorstein Veblen exposed his view of the field of economics in a paper titled "Economic Theory in the Calculable Future," given at the annual meetings of the American Economic Association in December 1924. Veblen perceived a general tendency in science at large toward "precise objective measurements and computations" instead of "postulates and values which do not lend themselves to that manner of logic and procedure." This spirit, Veblen said, was taking economics with it:

> The economists are somewhat in arrears in this matter . . . yet they show a visible drift in this direction. . . . So that those certified articles of theory at large that have meant so much to the passing generation have been falling into decay. . . . Self-contained systems of economic theory, balanced and compendious, are no longer at the focal center of attention . . . the felt need runs rather along the lines of conjugation between economic science and those fields of knowledge and belief that are cultivated by the material and biological sciences (1925, 50–51).

Veblen, the "father" of this "visible drift," might be biased, but his discussants, J. M. Clark, and Raymond Bye, did not challenge his description. Clark, a fellow institutionalist, agreed that "the forces and tendencies set forth by Veblen do exist," but adds that "other tendencies also exist." The doubt he raised is whether those other tendencies were "mere negligible exceptions to the 'normal' trend" presented by Veblen, or whether they might become a major component of economics *alongside* Veblenian economics (1925, 6). Bye belongs to the rival camp but he also agreed with Veblen that "economists are devoting an increased amount of attention to detailed study of particular institutions and processes, and that this trend is likely to continue in the visible future." Rather than denying this development, he was adopting it as a new component of the established doctrine. The "detailed study of particular institutions and processes did not mean that modern economists broke away from the past and stopped thinking like their predecessors; it was just the influence "of the fact that facilities are now at hand for [empirical] work which formerly were not available" (1925, 59).

A reflection of the change was the relative decline in the publications of large treatises, which pretended to comprehend all the principles of the science. Instead, "detailed monographic and itemized inquiry, description, analysis, and appraisal of particular processes . . . are engaging the best attention of the economists" (Veblen 1925, 50). The current generation of economists, Veblen explained, "go quite confidently into their work of detailed inquiry with little help from general principles" (ibid.; cf. Edie 1927, 434–35). A change was visible also in education. Mitchell says that "if we may judge the future qualifications of economists by the courses which are offered them in our university departments at present, our successors will almost to a man be trained in statistical methods as carefully as they are trained to discriminate among concepts" (in Mills 1928, 41). In this period statistics was considered a part of the institutionalist "research program,"[7] and a proliferation of statistics courses could thus be counted as an institutionalist achievement. William Weld also noticed that "in the schools and colleges there has been an increase in the number of students studying statistics and graphic presentation," and he expressed his belief that "the time is not far distant when most of the colleges and universities will consider statistics to be a necessary part of the undergraduate curriculum" (1924, 427).

Institutionalism, however, was more than the use of quantitative methods, and several institutionalists were dissatisfied with the lack of change in other aspects of economic teaching. For our purpose the most important thing is the *way* they complained about it: they asserted that even though the old principles "find very few defenders now," a survey of economics teaching showed "the remarkable persistence" of these principles due to "the inertia of traditionalism. Teachers have vested interests in those courses in metaphysical economics. They were trained that way" (Tugwell 1924a, 399). The very fact that he could assert such a thing as a well-known fact means, at least, that it was considered a reasonable view among his contemporaries. The formal textbooks used in regular economics courses, however, did change: "Whereas heretofore most courses had been devoted largely to 'principles' . . ., they were now more often divided half to principles and half to problems" (Dorfman 1959, 5:463; a good example is Taussig 1939).

The institutionalists felt that their approach was much more useful in managing the economy and big corporations and were certain that their achievements in this regard would secure the longevity of their research program. They already saw signs of this in the 1920s. George Soule explained, for example, that the recent trend in economics "has been induced partly by a consciousness of the inadequacy of the older theory." But a "much more important" cause, he argued, is "the increased pressure [of business people] for making the science practically useful" (1924, 364). "Many large corporations," Weld told, "have established research departments, in which they have placed trained statisticians to study their own problems." The federal government also contributed to the increasing demand for institutional economists because it did "not accept rule-of-thumb methods" in evaluating properties for Income and Excess Profits taxes (ibid., 426–27).

That institutionalism was on the rise was agreed by rivals of that school. In his defense of a priori economics, Lionel Robbins attacked the "attempt to provide 'concrete' laws of the movement of more complex phenomena, price fluctuations, cost dispersions, business cycles, and the like" (1932, 102). His critique is extremely severe, even nasty. But Robbins admitted that "in the last ten years there has been a great multiplication of this sort of thing under the name of Institutionalism, 'Quantitative Economics,' 'Dynamic Economics,' and what not" (ibid.). He commented on the supporters of this movement that "if they have not secured the upper hand altogether, they have certainly had a wide area of power in America" (ibid., 104). Paul Samuelson, the great champion of the mathematical economics that dethroned institutionalism, dates the 1940s as the time in which "institutionalism withered away as an effective counterforce in economics" (1976, 847). Melvin Reder, in his essay on the history of the Chicago school in economics, also mentions institutionalism as one of the principal contenders in economics until the 1940s (1982, 3).[8]

Probably the best testimony of the high standing of institutionalism was the positions they held in academia and government. In the academic world, Columbia, Harvard, and Chicago were the three main universities during the interwar period, as they are today.[9] Columbia was clearly an institutionalist stronghold, with Mitchell and Clark among its faculty (Arrow 1992, 44); both Tugwell and Keyserling (see below) were graduate students there.[10] The University of Wisconsin, the home of John Commons, which actually ranked third, before Harvard, in the production of Ph.D.s in 1904–28, was the second stronghold of institutionalism.[11]

Harvard, however, was a stronghold of neoclassical economics, with Thomas Carver and Frederick Taussig, two leaders of American neoclassical economics, among its faculty. In 1932 Joseph Schumpeter, a leading European theorist and a bitter enemy of institutionalism, joined the faculty at Harvard (Swedberg 1991).[12] As one recent observer says, one of the "firm opinions" that Harvard economists shared was "that institutionalism was a definite dead end. To a man, the Harvard economists were staunch classicists and neoclassicists, who responded to the institutionalist challenge with condescension" (Camic 1991, 15). Chicago, in contrast, began to emerge as a conservative stronghold only toward the end of the interwar period. Both Frank Knight and Jacob Viner, two of the most famous neoclassical theorists of the interwar era, joined Chicago in 1927 and 1919, respectively, but were still too young to imbue the whole department with their penchant. Paul Douglas (1892–1976), a Professor at Chicago with views similar to the institutionalists' (Silk 1974, 68–69; Reder 1982, 3), related that after he had come back from the Second World War, he "was disconcerted to find that the economic and political conservatives had acquired an almost complete dominance over [his] department." This was *after* the war. Before the war "the department had room for radicals like Lange, liberals like Douglas, middle-of-the-roaders like Viner, as well as the beginnings of a conservative group in Knight, Simons and Mint" (Minsky 1988, 170; Reder 1982, 9). Reder dates the transition of Chicago in 1940–46, when several institutionalists (Paul Douglas, H. A. Millis, and Simeon Leland) left and a few charismatic neoclassical economists, including Milton Friedman, were recruited (ibid., 9–10).

Thus, two of the four leading departments (Columbia and Wisconsin), which accounted together for at least one-fourth, and at times even for one-third, of all new Ph.D.s in economics were clearly under institutionalist domination, strong evidence for the salience of the school. Individual institutionalists also ranked high in the discipline. Mitchell was "one of the two or three most famous American economists of his generation" (Ekelund and Hébert 1983, 418). He served as president of the American Economic Association (1925) and was chosen in 1937 as the President of the American Association for the Advancement of Science, the first social scientist in this capacity since Carroll D. Wright's term in 1903 (Dorfman 1949, 3:473). In 1947 he was the first winner of the prestigious Francis A. Walker Medal, "awarded at intervals of at least five years by the American Economic Association to the most distinguished living American economist" (Dorfman 1959, 5:462). The second winner of the Walker Medal (1952) was John Maurice Clark, another institutionalist who served as president of the American Economic Association (1936). At least six out of twenty presidents of the Association in the period 1925–

44, were institutionalists and many others were sympathizers. Only three can be classified as neoclassical economists.[13]

The institutionalists were also very influential in government. I already mentioned Commons's considerable contribution to the shaping of economic, industrial, and social policies in the United States. His direct impact on social and industrial legislation in Wisconsin became a model for many other states and eventually to much New-Deal legislations, in which his pupils played major roles. Mitchell, Clark, and others also served on many public-policy committees (Dorfman 1959, 5:439n; cf. Barber 1985). Rexford Tugwell was a member of Franklin D. Roosevelt's famous "brain trust" and an Assistant Secretary of Agriculture (Dorfman 1959, 5: 502–3n). When the Council of Economic Advisers was formed in 1946, its first Chairman was Edwin Nourse (Sobel 1980, 21), an institutionalist agricultural economist (Knapp 1979; see also Nourse 1943). While Nourse served as a Chairman, an even stronger adviser behind the scene was Leon Keyserling, who eventually became the Chairman when Nourse resigned.[14] Keyserling was a devout institutionalist and a fierce critic of post–World War II academic economics. In 1953, a Republican administration replaced a Democratic one, but the institutionalists continued to control the Council. The new chairman, Arthur F. Burns, was a close associate of Mitchell, a coauthor of Mitchell's crowning book, *Measuring Business Cycles* (pub. 1946), and Mitchell's successor as the scientific director of the National Bureau for Economic Research. In 1970 he was appointed as the Chairman of the Federal Reserve Board, probably the highest professional position in public service. He held that position for eight years. Another influential institutionalist was John Dunlop, who was very active in mediating labor disputes and served in numerous public positions, including Secretary of Commerce under President Ford.

Evidently, institutionalists continued to exert a great deal of influence after the war in Washington, but in the academic arena they have been gradually pushed to the periphery. Simon Kuznets, Mitchell's student, continued to enjoy a high reputation and to have many adherents. Nevertheless, and despite his Nobel Prize of 1971, he could not stop the decline of institutionalism. Clarence Ayres established an institutionalist school at the University of Texas in Austin (see Phillips 1989), that gained some recognition in the field. At least eight other institutionalists were elected as presidents of the AEA—Simon Kuznets (1955); C. B. Hoover (1954); Morris Copeland (1957); George Stocking (1959); Arthur Burns (1958); Joseph Spengler (1966); Kenneth John Galbraith (1973); and Robert Aaron Gordon (1976). This, however, seems to be more a residue of their past prominence in the field, rather than a testimony of their power in the postwar era.

The younger generation of postwar institutionalists—economists such as Allan Gruchy, Marc Tool, Fagg Foster, Philip Klein, and Wendell Gordon—remained mostly unknown to the economic community at large and to the wider intellectual public. As they were rejected from mainstream journals, they established their own association, the Association for Evolutionary Economics, and their own journal, *Journal for Economic Issues*.[15] Current economists would find, of course, little interest in these works, which are so different from their own, and which they are not trained in digesting and understanding. Yet, for institutionalists, as well as for many other noneconomists, this kind of work seems much more sensible and meaningful. As objective students of science we cannot use the criteria of either group in judging the quality of either approach, and therefore we cannot ignore the existence of an institutional school on the periphery of the discipline. For us it must be part of the domain of economics.

It is impossible to portray the modern intellectual landscape without mentioning the influence of Polanyi, Galbraith, Myrdal, and Hirschman. These scholars have neither been direct students nor indirect followers of any of the prewar institutionalist masters. Yet theoretically and methodologically their works are in line with the work usually identified as institutionalist. Karl Polanyi, whose analysis of the rise of capitalism and excursions into economic anthropology currently enjoy renewed interest among historians, anthropologists, and sociologists (Humphries 1969; Stanfield 1986; Mendel and Salée 1991), was brought to Columbia by its institutionalist economists, who were impressed with his work (Neale 1990). John Kenneth Galbraith, the only postwar institutionalist who reached wide fame and recognition outside economics, has not seen himself as part of the institutionalist genealogy. Institutionalists, however, adopted him and christened him as one of their "forefathers" (Gruchy 1972, chap. 4; Gambs 1975). Gunnar Myrdal, the famous Swedish economist and a Nobel laureate, had started, according to his own testimony, as a neoclassical economist but moved toward institutionalism as he was unsatisfied with the way neoclassical economics developed after World War II (Myrdal 1978). Hirschman's emphasis on the normative system that engulfs the business world and his aversion to abstract models put him much closer to institutionalism than to any other contemporary approach.

Given the centrality of institutionalists at Columbia University and the University of Wisconsin, their predominance in governmental positions for several decades, and their influence over the wider intellectual landscape (especially of Veblen), it seems impossible to consider the institutionalist chapter in the history of American economics as a mere ephemeral episode. This conclusion is supported by numerous testimonies of economists—not only sympathizers—who practiced during that period. It is possible, of course, to argue over the relative power and impact of institutionalists and neoclassicists, but I hope that I have already convinced the readers that there is something wrong with the conventional textbooks on the history of economic thought. Institutionalism did play an important role in the history of economics. Now we should examine the knowledge it produced. Can we accept the common view that institutionalism was mostly a movement of criticism on orthodox economics and that it has not had any constructive contribution to the field? As we will see in the next section, this is another black box that must be opened and substantially modified.

The Institutionalist Contributions to Economics

Conventional historians of economic thought tend to belittle the importance of institutionalism for the evolution of economic knowledge. Those who refer to institutionalism, and who are therefore probably more sympathetic than others, praise institutionalism for some "seminal ideas which become part of the accepted theoretical structure" (Landreth 1976, 363). Other mainstream economists or historians of economic thought do not credit institutionalism even that much. All of them deny that institutionalism offered a new way of looking at, and solving, economic problems. Institutionalists are aware of their image and fight back by focusing on their uniting principles and underscoring their achievements and contributions. The difference in the presentation of the contribution of institutionalism is more in the tone of the presentation and the way the things are said than in content. Boulding even praises institutionalism as "a side stream of dissent," which "may have gouged channels in a direction which the main stream will one day follow—and in part is following" (1957, 3). Nevertheless, Boulding's view on the importance of institutionalism is substantially limited. He says that some other intellectual fields like "the 'new realist' school of legal-economic thinkers [owe] a great deal to Veblen and admit it publicly." But "to the mainstream of academic life he contributed a few scattered disciples, but not much else" (ibid., 7–8). Boulding also praises Mitchell, who "left a vast intellectual progeny in the national income statisticians and the econometricians." But he too, Boulding says, had no impact on *academic* economics. Commons's many achievements in policy making are also noticed by Boulding, but, once again, Boulding claims that these achievements have not infiltrated into academic economics (cf. Ramstaad 1986, 1098n). Boulding's conclusion is therefore mixed. "The direct impact of institutionalism on the main stream of economic thought has been small," but "the indirect influence of institutionalism has been very great" (1957, 11, 12). "The institution-alists may not have given the right answers," he adds, "but they did ask some very right questions" (ibid., 12).

Blaug claims that "the institutionalist movement ended for all practical purposes in the 1930s," but he insists that "this is not to deny that there were lasting influences." Blaug points to the possible responsibility of "the frequent attacks of Veblen and Commons on the narrow focus of traditional economics" for "the recent interest in cybernetics, operation research, management science, organization theory and general systems analysis" (1985a, 710–11). This praise, however, is hedged by the way it is presented. The space allocated to institutionalism—mere three pages—seems to be much less than is justified by a movement of such momentum. These pages are physically detached from the main story on the development of economics; they appear as an isolated appendix as if institution-alism were not an integral part of the history of economic thought.

The contribution of institutionalism to quantitative research is the one element which is widely recognized by conventional observers as well, and therefore I will not dwell much on this here (for details, see Dorfman 1963, 44; Kuznets 1963, 109). Yet the way this contribution is treated by mainstream writers is symptomatic to the mistreatment of institutional-ism. Boulding says that "the pioneering work of the National Bureau on national income statistics in the twenties . . . ushered in a revolution in the economic information system *as profound in some ways as the revolution in astronomy caused by the telescope*. Mitchell, however, made only a small impact on academic economics" (1957, 8; italics added). Similarly, Blaug thinks that "Mitchell's contribution to our understanding of the business cycle and in particular to the *revolution in economic information* that separates 20th- from 19th-century economics is too obvious to call for comment" (1985a, 710; italics added). And yet, like Boulding, Blaug quickly adds that institutionalism "did not fulfill its promise to supply a viable alternative to neoclassical economics" (ibid., 711). These are quite amazing statements. The contribution of Mitchell is compared to the invention of the telescope, one of the most celebrated inventions in the history of science. Similarly, Blaug speaks about a "revolution in eco-nomic information." Nevertheless, it is immediately added that institu-tionalism "made only a small impact on academic economics," or that it had not supplied "a viable alternative to neoclassical economics."

The attitude of Boulding and Blaug exemplifies the merits of the con-structivist approach in the sociology of science. The constructivists un-derline the fact that scholars have very different ideas about the standards science should realize and about the appropriate assessment of how much these standards are met. But even if we could agree upon the standards themselves, we would still face the question of how to compare and judge two competing approaches, when one is conceded as higher on one dimension while the other is considered better on another. The many contributions made by the institutionalists are widely recognized even by mainstream economists and historians, such as Boulding and Blaug. And yet the latter allege that those contributions are less important than those made by neoclassicists. This conclusion reflects the bias of mainstream economics in favor of abstract mathematical theory. Economic theory is considered by most postwar economists to be the main goal of the discipline, and the field where new approaches are tested. Interestingly, the titles of conventional textbooks on the history of economics typically refer to "economic theory" (Blaug 1985a; Landreth 1976; Spiegel 1983; Niehans 1990); "economic analysis" (Schumpeter 1954; Backhouse 1985); "economic thought" (Dasgupta 1985; Galbraith 1987; Oser 1970; Napoleoni 1972); or "economic ideas" (Deane 1978; Routh 1975). There are very few texts on the history of "economics" (Canterbery 1976) or "economic method" (Ekelund and Hébert 1983). In other disciplines we often encounter books titled the "history of physics" or "the history of biology," which describe both the development of theories and ideas *and* the evolution of research methods, experiments, and tools. Economics is quite unique in its extreme focus on pure theory and ideas. Important advances in the collection and analysis of data do not enjoy, therefore, the same exposure in the written histories of the discipline as innovations in theory.[16]

This conclusion is also fundamentally different, as one may expect, from the conclusion reached by institutionalist historians of economic thought. For instance, Allan Gruchy, a postwar institutionalist, disagrees "with those who believe that [institutionalism] is a minor flank attack upon economic orthodoxy which will prove to be ephemeral." Instead, he is certain that "holistic economics," his name for institutionalism, "is the product of a genuine reconstruction which will turn out to be of lasting significance" (1947, viii). Ten years later, Allan Gruchy was a discussant of Boulding's paper mentioned above. In response to Boulding's thesis, Gruchy lists the most famous books of Veblen, Mitchell, Clark, and Means and says that those works successfully "constructed their mosaic of the American capitalist system" (1957, 14). Forest Hill, another discussant at the same session, refuted Boulding's assertion that institutionalists had little influence on academic economics. Veblen, Hill says, influenced the study of industrial organization, labor economics, business cycles, and the theory of the firm (1957, 16). Mitchell's contribution to business cycle analysis, he adds, was recognized in the fact that this contribution "accorded him as the first recipient of . . . the Walker medal." He was clearly, Hill maintained, more than an "economic entomologist" or collector of time series, as Boulding argued (ibid., 17).

The contribution of institutionalists to the collection and analysis of data is not the only one that is belittled and ignored. So is their contribution to policy making. Sometimes it sounds as if the institutionalists are actually *attacked* for dealing with policy instead of theory. In contrast, institutionalist writers stress their involvement in shaping economic policies. For them, this is one of the main criteria according to which scientific approaches are supposed to be judged. Allan Gruchy, for example, says that "what is particularly important about the work of the holistic economists is that it represents one of the most thoroughgoing attempts to close the gap between economic theory and practice" (1947, ix). The main contributor to economic policy was undeniably John R. Commons:

> Commons and his school made an important contribution to economic thinking and policy. Their philosophy found expression in labor legislation, trade-union developments, public utility regulation, agricultural legislation, and trade practices. . . . It was the earlier activities of Commons and his group in Wisconsin who provided the New Dealers with a considerable number of practical instrumentalities and devices, as well as experienced personnel, to direct the new agencies of regulation and administration (Dorfman 1959, 4:398).

Boulding concurs that Commons "was the intellectual origin of the New Deal, of labor legislation, of social security, of a whole movement in this country towards a welfare state. . . . One runs across his students everywhere, both in universities and in government" (1957, 7; see also Samuelson 1976, 846; Ekelund and Hébert 1983, 418; Mirowski 1990, 102).

It became quite habitual to attribute the New Deal to Keynesian ideas. Yet, as everybody knows, the New Deal started *before* Keynes's *General Theory*, a fact Lakatosians cite as evidence that the transition to Keynesianism was less "revolutionary" than commonly argued (Blaug 1975). Leon Keyserling, chairman of the Council of Economic Advisers under Truman and a staunch institutionalist, questions, however, the importance of Keynes's abstract theory. As Sobel explains, "at a time when the Keynesian Revolution was percolating through the economics departments of graduate schools," Keyserling was already involved with framing much of the legislation of the early New Deal. Keyserling emphatically denies that the inspiration for Roosevelt's programs could be found in the works of Keynes. Instead, he traces the roots of the New Deal "to the pragmatic and practical institutionalists, men like Tugwell and himself" (Sobel 1980, 16).

An example of the contrast between Keynesianism and institutionalism is provided by Arthur Burns's response to the signs of depression. Late in 1953 the economy showed signs of recession. Keynesian economists pushed for a full-scale fiscal policy to prevent it. Arthur Burns, the Chairman of the Council of Economic Advisers, took a more careful approach.

While preparing an expansionary fiscal policy, he used a gradual
approach, and followed the indicators closely, week after week. Eventually, the strong measures were not necessary. This was an institutionalist
policy, similar to Keynesianism in its prescriptions, but different in spirit
(Sobel 1980, 56–62; see also Moore 1979, 84). Blaug tells us that in the
late 1940s, Burns "emerged as one of the keenest American critics
of Keynes, not because of any inherent logical defects in Keynes' theories,
but rather because of the haste with which Keynesians rushed towards
policy conclusions on the basis of theories which, Burns felt, had not
yet been decisively tested" (Blaug 1985b, 30). Burns himself said that
Keynesian theory "was no novelty for me. . . . Keynesian fiscal and monetary remedies were commonplace matters. I found myself recommending
Keynesian policies in 1930 and 1931. . . . So did many others. The novelty of Keynes did not lie in the policies he recommended, but rather in
the analytical foundation for his policies" (1985, 19).[17] In contrast to
Keynesians, Burns especially emphasized that it was "essential to look
beneath the surface of the aggregates, such as gross national product,
total employment, and the general price level, in order to discover how
the economy really worked. His continued distrust of models constructed
largely from such aggregates stemmed in part from his view that the aggregates did not adequately reflect what goes on in the economy" (Moore
1979, 82).

Sobel adds that in the 1960s, Burns allied himself "with moderates of
both the Keynesian and monetarist schools. . . . Burns was always ready
to jettison ideological baggage when the occasion demanded" (1980,
176). Burns, Sobel adds, "had no hard-and-fast commitment to either
camp; he usually went where the evidence led him" (ibid., 195). For
Sobel, Burns's pragmatism is evidence of an exceptionally independent
mind. But it reflects not only Burns's character. It reflects also the *gap*
between institutionalism and mathematical neoclassicism. Institutionalists often averred that the economy was too complex to be comprehended
with the help of a few universal and abstract principles. They claimed that
economists had to observe actual economic arrangements and improve
them according to the specific features of the cases. That was what Burns
did both in the Council of Economic Advisors and in the Federal Reserve
Board (Burns 1985, 19).

Given this prominence of institutionalism in economic policy making,
the exclusion of institutionalists from conventional accounts on the history of economics is, again, quite astonishing. And again, one can explain
this overlook by the preoccupation of historians of economics with the
development of economic *theory* rather than policy. Boulding complains
that the influence of Commons is felt "only" "in labor economics, in
social security, in public utility economics, in New-Deal legislation and

administration" rather than in "basic theory" (1957, 8). Any other discipline able to list major achievements such as these to its credit would acclaim those who made these contributions as its heroes. But in economics they are almost forgotten. Commons's "greatest triumphs in the arena of practice were viewed as liabilities in the arena of economic theory in the next generation" (Mirowski 1990, 102). Obviously, policy is not the main economic playing field; theory is.

There is one more important aspect of the institutionalist contribution to economics which has not been noticed so far. Some of the students who were taught and trained by the institutionalists turned out to be leading figures in the postwar neoclassical revival. Among those one can count Kenneth Arrow, Milton Friedman, and Jacob Mincer. It might be attributed to this fact that these economists were less enticed by the mathematization project and more open toward empirical investigations and cooperation with other social sciences even at the expense of mathematical sophistication. Friedman and Mincer, for example, were much more involved in statistical research relative to their colleagues at the Chicago school, and both of them have remained suspicious toward the mathematically sophisticated, but substantively limited, methods of econometricians.[18] Friedman even said once that no one exemplified the " 'scientific spirit' more for him than Mitchell" (in Silk 1974, 54).

In 1959 John Maurice Clark described institutionalism as "one of the great formative influences in the transformation of our economic thought in the past half century" (quoted in Dorfman 1963, 8). One does not have to accept this evaluation as correct, but historians of economics cannot overlook the fact that one of the leading economists of the era, a man who was an avid participant in the scene of academic economics, has expressed such a judgment. Even if his view is exaggerated, it still casts many doubts over the conventional tendency to belittle the importance of institutionalism. It is therefore an encouraging sign that the importance of institutionalism is being reconsidered recently and that practicing economists seek inspiration in old institutionalist theory (Hodgson 1994).

Is There an Institutionalist Doctrine?

The negative evaluation of institutionalism by most historians of economics is mostly due to what the latter consider as weakness in theory. Conventional historians acknowledge the contributions to empirical investigations, to policy making, and to numerous substantive fields, and yet institutionalism is considered unsatisfactory because institutionalists have not offered "a theoretical structure to replace the model they were criticizing" (Landreth 1976, 363; Hausman 1992, 226n). Even their current followers often accept this allegation. The institutionalists, who were aware of this criticism, vehemently rejected this allegation and stressed their belief in the necessity of theory. Nevertheless, their emphasis on empirical research and their criticism of abstract theory exposed them repeatedly to the same allegation.

The accusation in regard to the lack of an institutionalist "theory" is often accompanied by the argument that the institutionalists differed too much from each other. If the theories of individual scholars were not parts of the same whole there would be, of course, no point in speaking about "an institutionalist doctrine." The conventional view asserts, for example, that "what the various [institutionalist] protagonists had in common was antipathy to orthodoxy" (Knight 1952, 45). Institutionalism, Boulding concurs, "is essentially a movement of dissent and has a certain atmosphere of sectarianism" (1957, 1). The idea that institutionalism "is essentially a movement of dissent" was adopted by later writers, who built on this thesis to explain why institutionalism had never been seriously considered as an alternative to orthodox economics. Landreth, for example, argues that because of this "fact," it is impossible to see institutionalism as a school:

> A number of historians of economic theory have found sufficient unity in the thought of certain heterodox economists to classify them into a school known as institutionalism. . . . While there are some common bonds among this group, we cannot find sufficient grounds for such a classification and have therefore grouped these writers by their one unquestionable common element, dissent from orthodox theory (1976, 319).

Backhouse also accepts the view that institutionalism "did not score highly" in terms of "internal consistency and the accuracy with which it summarizes the pertinent parts of its experience" (1985, 240–41). In another example, Ekelund and Hébert say that "not even a self-proclaimed institutionalist pretends to identify a single, cohesive, and consistent body of thought." Institutional economics, they say, "is an umbrella under which many interesting and productive ideas may be hiding" (1983, 424; see also Simon 1979, 499; Blaug 1985a, 710). This last statement is clearly wrong: self-proclaimed institutionalists *have* insisted that "a single, cohesive, and consistent body" of institutionalist thought exists.

Among the post–World War II economists who kept the torch of institutionalism alive, the two main figures were Clarence E. Ayres and Allan G. Gruchy. Both of them put a lot of effort in challenging the atheoretical image of institutionalism. Ayres's denial of the common view is very poignant: "Institutionalism proposes to find [the meaning of economics] in the interplay of institutions and technology, which in turn are its basic analytical principles, just as classical theory has sought the meaning of the economy in the interplay of wants and scarcity, which . . . constitute its basic principles" (1951, 52). Ayres explains that the institutionalists' "zeal for objectivity has led many institutionalists to devote themselves almost exclusively to empirical studies to the neglect of the interpretation of the facts their studies have disclosed." But that does not mean that they have had no theory. Veblen, he adds, "misled a whole generation of students" by saying that he had no theory of value. "But it is our responsibility not to be misled . . . a theory of value is implicit in all of Veblen's work" (ibid.). And he elaborates:

> Veblen saw that tool-using . . . is physically productive, a creative process that underlies all the achievements of mankind; and that the exploits by which some men are always seeking to get the better of others are an impediment to workmanship and creative achievement. This basic ethical principle—the instrumental theory of value . . .—runs through all of Veblen's work, and is one of the foundation principles of institutionalism (Ayres 1951, 53).[19]

Unlike Ayres, Gruchy does not seek to rehabilitate Veblen. Instead he claims that the antitheoretical image of institutionalism might have been different had it been "based more on the work of Commons, Mitchell, Clark, and other post-Veblenians than on Veblen's work" (Liebhafsky 1980, 23).[20] One of the major themes of Gruchy's lifetime work "was that of correcting the stereotyped caricature of institutionalism . . . that still permeates the minds of contemporary orthodox economists who have conveniently utilized the stereotype to avoid dealing with the problems with which heterodox economists consistently confront them" (ibid.). Gruchy's view of the essentials of the institutionalist approach is different from Ayres's. According to his summary, "the institutionalist theory of capitalism runs in terms of the continued march towards industrialization, the spread of collective action, the growing inability of the free market system to remove automatically discrepancies between the nation's income and product flows, the development of imbalances between prices and costs and between savings and investment, and the expansion of government action to reduce these discrepancies and imbalances" (1957, 14). While Ayres concentrates on the interaction between technology and society, Gruchy, focuses on the inability of a market economy to produce socially desirable outcomes, and hence, the need for an active government. Their differences notwithstanding, the interpretations of both Ayres and Gruchy are rooted in Veblen's theory, and especially in the idea that the pecuniary logic is different from the logic of production.

From the constructivist point of view, the answer to the question whether institutionalists had a theory depends on how one defines theory, and there is no one conception of what theory is that is agreed by all philosophers and scientists. Current neoclassical economists internalized a rather unique view of theory, which is very different from the notion of theory held by institutionalists. The former view theory as simple models, which abstract from reality and demonstrate the effects of given variables on some other variables, using formal and rigorous deductive analysis. The institutionalists preferred depth and width of theory, even at the expense of elegance and rigor. Their theories, which have been similar to those pervasive in most other social sciences, are supposed to account for fundamental historical processes.

The meaning of theory was thus part of the conflict between institutionalists and neoclassical economists, an issue we will discuss in chapter 4. For now, the point that we should remember is that we cannot accept the judgment of writers who were trained within the dominant neoclassical paradigm as an objective evaluation. When they accuse institutionalists of having no theory, what they mean is that institutionalists had no theory *of the neoclassical type*; this is the only type of theory they recognize. Institutionalists lacked, of course, such a theory. This, however, does not mean that they lacked theory in some other sense of the word.

The same logic applies to the accusation that institutionalists lacked internal unity to be considered a viable alternative. There is no doubt that the institutionalists were not a homogeneous group. Many institutionalists accepted the market economy as a basis for social action to bring about better results. Others denied any role for the market. Consequently, they differed in their attitude toward neoclassical price theory, which is based on market economy. These differences were reflected in the way the past was interpreted. While most institutionalists accepted the contributions of the great economists from Smith to Marshall as important, others rejected the works of all or some of those economists. Other differences were revealed in their methodological approaches. Veblen was not very interested in empirical research; Commons was mostly a historian; and Mitchell indefatigably fought for quantitative economics.

The question, however, is the significance of these differences. Do they mean, as the critics of institutionalism claim, that it is impossible to speak about "an institutionalist doctrine"? According to the constructivist approach there are no absolute answers for questions of this sort. The answers are a matter of interpretation. Labels such as "classical" or "neoclassical" economics indicate certain general ideas that were part of the work of many individuals. But these labels by no means indicate that the economists involved had identical principles and beliefs. "Simple labels," Arrow says, "are never adequate" (1992, 45). This is true also in regard to the label "institutionalism." The people referred to as "institutionalists" seem to share certain tenets despite the gaps among them on methodology, policy, and theory.

When rival approaches clash, it is often the case that each one tries to challenge the other by drawing attention to internal contradictions within the beliefs of the contender or among its advocates. In such cases we would witness a trial of strength in which the criticized party tries to show its unity and coherence. And this is, indeed, what the institutionalist writers have done. Clarence Ayres, for instance, admits that "no critical consensus has evolved" among the heterodox economists, but at least the institutionalists "acknowledge Veblen as a common source of inspiration" (1938, iii–iv). Ayres also claims that the most basic institutionalist principle is that "the relative scarcity or relative plentifulness of all resources [are determined by] the state of the industrial arts. . . . That is the paramount fact of the modern economic system" (1957, 26). He argues that "the recognition of that fact is the most constructive achievement of institutionalists generally. Formless and inchoate as the writings of institutionalists have been, that emphasis runs *through them all*" (ibid., italics added).

Speaking about the generation of institutionalists that followed Veblen, Allan Gruchy explains that they "did not slavishly follow the lines drawn in earlier years by Thorstein Veblen" but "brought new emphasis to the work of revamping economic thought." The younger generation, Gruchy adds, "were prone to be somewhat less speculative and more concerned with immediate economic and social issues than was Veblen. They were more willing to envision economic reform within the limits of the existing private-enterprise system." Yet Gruchy insists that these differences do not mean "that these younger revisionists of the postwar period had developed a basic approach to economic studies which was different from Veblen's approach. On the contrary, their work was in its essentials within the Veblenian tradition" (1947, 2). He therefore concludes that the works of the "outstanding members of the holistic [i.e., institutionalist] school . . . fall into the mold of a common intellectual pattern" (ibid., 541; see also Hodgson 1994, 68–69).

Mark Blaug, a neoclassical historian, praises Gruchy's book as "a *tour de force* of interpretation" but is not convinced of its main thesis (1985a, 712). In his opinion, the interpretation "unfortunately collapses the moment it is probed." Blaug, who has never been part of the institutionalist movement, cannot see any sense in Gruchy's argument concerning the "main message" of institutionalism. Looking at the works of various members of the movement through his own perspective of what counts, he sees no commonalities. In contrast, John Adams, a contemporary institutionalist, conceives Gruchy's "perception of an underlying unity in the writings of the major American institutionalists" as one of Gruchy's "giant ideas" (1980b, 3). Who is right, Blaug or Gruchy and Adams? Apparently, the institutionalists shared many beliefs but disagreed on many other things. What part is more significant? This, the constructivist approach is never too tired of repeating, depends on one's perspective and cognitive or material interests. It is useless to assume that there is any measure of consensus against which one could compare the unity of institutionalism and determine whether they were unified enough to be considered "a school." What we can do is to follow the debate over unity itself and find out how the belief that institutionalism was not unified turned into a black box.

The "Old-Fashioned" Neoclassical School and Institutionalism

The discussion on the unity of institutionalism brings up another important aspect of the interpretation of that movement. The critics of institutionalism, we saw, agreed that institutionalism was "essentially a movement of dissent"; what the institutionalists had in common "was antipathy to orthodoxy" (see previous section). The previous section has documented the attempts of institutionalists to demonstrate their positive achievements. This presentation may create the impression that they were indeed united by their objection to orthodox theory. But did all the institutionalists share "antipathy to orthodoxy"? Today institutionalism is almost universally perceived as the antithesis of "mainstream" orthodox theory, but we have to be careful in basing our historical interpretations on current constructions. In chapter 2 we saw that the Marshallian type of neoclassical economics was very different from the current version of neoclassicism. Marshallian economics and the American "new synthesis" of the 1890s acknowledged the role of institutions, repudiated simplistic hedonistic psychology, accepted the necessity of historical and statistical studies, and favored greater involvement of the government in the economy. So what were the institutionalists so upset about? Why did Veblen attack orthodox theory? Can we really speak of a struggle between two clearly distinguishable networks of economists, two distinct schools or paradigms?

The conventional approach to the history of economics is built on clear definitions of schools and theoretical approaches, and therefore the relations between any two movements can be characterized either as completely contradictory or as compatible. The constructivist approach, in contrast, treats intellectual schools as labels fluidly assigned to various groups either by themselves or by others. The map of the discipline that eventually appears depends on the negotiation among different definitions of the situation. When an agreement has been achieved, it has a power of its own; by being assumed by participants, it is constantly rein-forced, and thus, it can become more "real" than it has originally been. But it is still a fluid map; new participants, new practices, and new ideas can always change its contours.

When we study the social life of economics during the twenties and thirties we can easily sense a competition among several groups. At the time, the camps were not clearly defined. The term "institutionalism" itself has just entered the lexicon, and discussions were conducted on its meaning. Originally it was coined as a label to describe the work of Thorstein Veblen only. Sociologically, one could discern two concrete "schools," that is, dense networks of economists who were related to each other; one around Commons in Madison, and the other around Mitchell and the NBER. There was also a wide trend of using statistics, which included many other researchers with a variety of theoretical positions beside Mitchell's group. The neoclassical camp was even less clearly defined. When economists spoke about "orthodox" economics what they usually meant was the British political economy from Smith to Marshall, but it was not certain what it meant in the 1920s. As we saw in the previous chapter, many neoclassical economists (i.e., economists who are recognized as "neoclassical") supported moderate state intervention and empirical research. Others looked less favorably toward such practices. Irving Fisher, Frank Knight, and Frank Taussig—to mention only three of the leading neoclassical authorities—differed a great deal in their beliefs about economic policies and the way economists should go about their disciplines.[21]

Nevertheless, I find the labels "institutionalists" and "neoclassical" useful in analyzing the economic discourse of the interwar period. In the next chapters we will learn more on the views of institutionalists and the differences between them and the neoclassical economists. But in order to give the reader some notion on the differences and to justify the crude division of the discipline into two camps, I summarize here the main differences between them. The institutionalists emphasized, of course, empirical research much more than the neoclassicists. Many of them accepted the neoclassical analysis of hypothetical conditions as valuable for a limited range of interests, but they were much more likely than Marshall to stress the limits of this practice due to irrational components of human behavior, the rigidities of institutions, and the evolutionary development of the economy. They, therefore, pushed toward quantitative and historical studies and hoped that exact quantitative data would allow them to find laws of economic development and regulate the economy safely.[22]

The neoclassicists were less sanguine concerning the ability of empirical work to give clear-cut solutions to economic problems. They were aware of irrational behavior and of the role of institutions in channeling human action but believed that deductive analysis based on the assumption of rationality was the most profitable course for economics nonetheless. They never mistook their analysis for a description of reality. They viewed the orthodox value theory only as a starting point and fully agreed that empirical research was essential for accounting for specific phenomena and for policy making. Because of their more restrained expectations of economic research, the neoclassicists were more cautious in their policy recommendations. They had the same goals as institutionalists but favored more restrained intervention because of their doubts concerning the ability of economists to ensure the realization of these goals.

Whether these are large or small differences is a matter of taste and perspective and the decision how to present them depend on strategic and tactic calculations. If the protagonists expressed harsh criticisms of each other during the interwar years, this might be attributed to the fact that in the twenties these two approaches were the main contenders, and in that context their differences might have appeared large. Yet it would be wrong to assume that the relations between the two parties were entirely antagonistic. Several prominent institutionalists—most notably, Veblen, Tugwell, and Ayres—wished to discard neoclassical theory in its entirety. But others—especially Commons, J. M. Clark, Copeland, and even Mitchell—conceived themselves as part of the mainstream of economics. Commenting on his own work, John Commons claimed that there was nothing new in his analysis; the only change was in rearranging old ideas and concepts in somewhat new fashion: "Everything therein can be found in the work of outstanding economists for two hundred years. . . . The things that have changed are the interpretations, the emphasis, the weights assigned to different ones of the thousands of factors which make up the world-wide economic process" (1990, 8). Mitchell also acknowledged the value of classical theory and conceived institutionalism as an enterprise of making the old theory more applicable (e.g., 1924, 15, 18; in Working 1927, 20). The institutionalists, Arthur Burns reminisces, "were not content with the Marshallian synthesis. They didn't abandon it. They found a use for it, but they also found it incomplete and inadequate for dealing with the problems of the times" (1985, 17; see also Yonay 1991, 164–66; R. A. Gordon 1963, 125).[23]

The social relations between the advocates of the camps were as diverse as the positions of both sides. Mark Perlman, an economist with background in both parties whose father, Selig Perlman, was a well-known institutionalist colleague of Commons at Wisconsin, describes in an interview how the students at Wisconsin were exposed to the ideas and theories of both institutionalists and neoclassical economics. When I talked on the two schools with Jacob Mincer, a neoclassical economist at

Columbia who is associated with the Chicago school, he was referring to "what you call institutionalism" or "what you call neoclassical economics." Obviously, he knew what I was referring to by these labels but felt uncomfortable with them, probably because, like Perlman, he did not conceive the two camps as completely inimical.

The best proof that the two groups were not polarized as one may think today is, perhaps, the existence of many economists whose positions were somewhere between institutionalism and neoclassical economics. This group included some of the most distinguished economists of the interwar period: Allyn Young, Thomas S. Adams, Alvin Johnson, Henry Seager, and Paul Douglas. I will deal with the first three of these economists, because their ideas illustrate the fuzziness and vagueness of what appear often as clear-cut borders between institutionalism and orthodoxy in conventional textbooks. Allyn Young (1876–1929), one of the most prominent American economists during the interwar period, is sometimes referred to as a neoclassicist because his "enduring contribution was in the development of value analysis and money" (Dorfman 1959, 4:222). But, as Dorfman adds, "his interest went far beyond these areas" (ibid.).[24] Young explicitly protested against the "fruitless quarrels of the methodological sects, against their intolerance, and against their pretensions to exclusive possession of the only right points of view and the only effective methods of research" (Young 1927, 10). Economic research is retarded, Young lamented, "because of our intolerance of methods and points of view other than our own" (ibid., 6). For Young, orthodox theory and institutionalism were complementary: "the *contractual* approach," the Marshallian one, "views social arrangements as deliberate contrivances resting upon voluntary agreements—instruments which men use in attaining their purposes." "In the *institutional* view," he explained, "these same arrangements appear as social habits, the products of history, not really shaped by the rational prevision of men . . . man himself . . . is the product of life in society" (1927, 6).

Young had more confidence in orthodox theory than the institutionalists. The theory, he declared in the 1929 edition of *Britannica*, was "an instrument of proved effectiveness for predicting some of the results of economic changes with a fair degree of certainty" (Dorfman 1959, 5:465). But he was very careful in applying its results. The marginal productivity theory, for example, was somewhat misleading in his opinion. Taken by itself, he wrote, it "had no particular significance except as a 'corrective to the even more misleading notion' that rewards were not in any manner dependent upon productivity" (Dorfman 1959, 5:465). At the same time Young was very interested in economic history and devoted a great deal of effort to the study of the Industrial Revolution. His belief that "the economic system grows and evolves like a living organism by means of successive adjustments and adaptations" (quoted in Dorfman 1959, 4:224) was virtually identical to the institutionalist position. The reason I did not classify Young as an institutionalist is his much more modest expectations concerning the ability of economic science to solve social and economic problems. He expressed his "fear that we are in danger of expecting from systematic research more than systematic research can possibly give us." Young does not agree with those "who think that through research . . . the social sciences might be as completely revolutionized . . . as the physical sciences were. . . . As a result, we are asked to believe, society would be in command of its own destiny" (Young 1927, 23–24). This is an explicit warning against the institutionalist confidence in the power of empirical research, which Young could not share due to his own belief that there were no permanent and exact laws that governed human behavior (ibid., 8). Yet, more like the institutionalists than the Marshallians, Young believed that "uniformity and regularity" could emerge out of the "arbitrary or capricious happening" if we applied the scientific creed of "patient and methodical inquiries which we call research" (ibid., 1). He also agreed with institutionalists that "the increase in the number of able men who are bringing the spirit of scientific inquiry into the study of economic problems gives us ground for hoping that we shall learn how to deal with those problems more effectively and more wisely" (ibid., 25). Young also stressed the importance of the assiduous collection of new data and the "need to supplement our statistical inquiries which have to do with aggregates and averages, by historical studies in which the individual and concrete aspects of economic activities shall be emphasized" (ibid., 19, 21).[25]

Thomas Sewell Adams (1873–1933), a Professor at Wisconsin and later at Yale, was involved in the legislation of income taxes and consulted both federal and state authorities in matters related to taxation (Dorfman 1959, 4:215). Adams taught "economic theory based primarily on Alfred Marshall's *Principles*" (ibid.) but he "evidenced little interest in the more theoretical and abstract aspects of public finance. For him, such matters as the analysis of tax shifting and incidence were overshadowed by the practical problems of making fiscal policy work" (ibid., 4:221). Adams also urged the Bureau of Labor Statistics to hire graduate students in economics to field work, so that they "could become acquainted with actual labor and industrial conditions" (ibid., 4:217). On the other hand, Adams shared with Young and the Marshallians the doubts in the power of science: "Political economy which is mere science," he wrote, "is not enough partly because it is an impossibility, partly because there is something more excellent" (Adams 1928, 3–4). An economic branch which dealt with taxes could "never be merely or principally a science." In this and in many other branches of economics "in which the 'underlying uniformities which the economics seek,' are vitally dependent upon the conscious and concerted action of social groups" (Adams 1928).

Alvin S. Johnson, a student of J. B. Clark, and for some time his personal secretary, was a professor at Cornell and the President of the AEA in 1937. Johnson's main interest was the orthodox price theory, but he treated the theory as a starting point, not as a description of reality. Although "he has been held in high regard by circles representing the dominant viewpoint of formal economic theory, . . . his active mind, especially in matters of practical proposals, has often enough cut across that tradition" (Dorfman 1949, 3:420). Johnson "expressed dissatisfaction with the limitations of 'orthodox' economics," which left out of discussion many problems that could not be put in terms of supply and demand (ibid., 3:423). His view on the nature of economics (1922) is very similar to the way institutionalists conceived of the discipline.

Conclusions: A Prospering, Mighty, and Fertile School

The conventional narrative of the history-of-economic-thought literature depicts institutionalism as a nebulous label attached to the works of a very few early twentieth-century economists who criticized orthodox theory. Those economists were very different from each other and they were united only by their strong dislike of the economic tradition that preceded them. They might have had some influence over economic policy-makers and they encouraged quantitative research. But since they had no alternative theory, their utility was exhausted as soon as orthodox economists heeded their criticism and mended the established theory accordingly. That is why they failed to attract many followers and to survive long enough to have a permanent impact on the discipline. Understandably, they disappeared from the economic arena in the 1920s.

In this chapter I offered an alternative narrative, one told mostly by institutionalist writers. According to this narrative, institutionalism continued a radical trend in American economics, one which was already quite powerful in the 1880s. It included dozens of economists and reached its zenith only during the interwar period. It was very critical of the established doctrine, but it did not seek to throw it out completely. The institutionalists suggested an alternative view of the economy and offered new ways to study it. Their teaching was very persuasive and attracted the attention of policy-makers and economists. Even many neoclassical economists shared the institutionalists' desire to make economics more empirical and recognized the need in increasing the role of the state in the economy. The decline of institutionalists started only after

World War II, but their sway in Washington lingered for a decade or two thereafter. To sum up, the institutionalist chapter is an important link in the history of economics without which we cannot understand its past evolution and many of its modern aspects. Its enduring mark in economics is evident in the welfare legislation in the United States and the measurement techniques and economic forecast procedures common in our days.

Which of these two narratives is closer to the historical reality? According to Latourian principles, when two conflicting claims clash, each party has to recruit allies to convince potential juries that its claim is valid. In our case, the orthodox approach has managed to erect a powerful network of allies and its view has become hegemonic. For the last decades its view has been widely accepted as the whole truth and used as a black box in the discourse of historians, sociologists, and political scientists, while the institutionalist narrative has been almost extinct. I believe that this closure was achieved too early, and my main goal was, therefore, to convince the readers that it should be reopened. My pro-institutionalist narrative might have been overstated, but the evidence presented in this chapter shows that the accepted narrative is grossly misleading. A discussion of this evidence, both by critics and supporters, can further refine our picture of modern economics. Meantime, those who want to learn more on the institutionalist views and the nature of their disagreement with neoclassicists are invited to read the next chapters, in which various aspects of the debate are analyzed.

Four

The Struggle over the Meaning
of Science

What is Science? We cannot define the word with the precision and concision with which we define *Circle*, or *Equation*,
any more than we can so define *Money, Government, Stone,
Life*. The idea . . . is too vastly complex and diversified. It
embodies the epitome of man's intellectual development . . . a
particular branch of science, such as Physical Chemistry or
Mediterranean Archeology, is no mere word . . . but a real
object, being the very concrete life of a social group constituted by real facts of inter-relation.
  (Charles S. Peirce, *Collected Papers*, vol. 7
    [quoted in Mirowski 1990])

"Scientific," like "democracy" and "American," is becoming
a shibbolethic password which the naive think they have only
to pronounce with sufficient glibness to be welcomed among
the respectable and recognized elect.
  (A. B. Wolfe, *"Functional Economics"*)

Good Science, like God, patriotism, and the flag, are rhetorical devices designed to be impossible to argue against—devices often used in the absence of a good case on the merits.
  (J. S. James, *"The Drug-Trials Debacle and
    What to Do About It"*)

THE TRADITIONAL VIEWS of science assume the existence of one fixed set
of rules, the Scientific Method, that unifies all sciences, distinguishes between production of scientific and nonscientific knowledge, and ensures
the validity of the former. Dispassionate observation, controlled and
replicable experiments, logical calculations, and unassailable mathematical proofs make scientific knowledge objective, universal, and independent of individual and social interests. Of course, different scientific fields
adjust the concrete components of the Scientific Method to their own
special requirements and circumstances, but such adjustments themselves
are determined according to the logic of the Scientific Method. They do

not reflect the variety of science, but rather the variety of the realities studied by science.

Historical and anthropological studies have found, however, that science does not work according to this mythical Scientific Method. First of all, it has been found that criteria of validity and quality in science vary substantially from one field to another (Knorr-Cetina 1991). Second, the research has exposed how the methods followed by various scientific fields are determined in negotiation and conflict among practitioners with distinct attitudes (Latour and Woolgar 1979; Latour 1987). Even experimentation, the quintessentially scientific method, was accepted as a valid method only after long struggle with those who warned that experiments opened the door to serious mistakes due to the limits of our senses (Shapin and Schaffer 1985). Descartes perceived Newton's reference to "force in distance" as unscientific; Pasteur kept double books because the experiments he conducted failed to prove his argument; and Einstein refused to surrender to the empirical findings of quantum mechanics because they contradicted his most basic views of the universe. The constructivist view therefore emphasizes the variability of scientific cultures and their heterogeneity.

Disciplines are also influenced by the criteria of other disciplines, especially of highly prestigious ones. Approaches and methodologies have to be black boxed like facts or theories, and such stability is achieved by connecting them to stable networks of celebratedly successful disciplines. When a new field is established, or an old approach challenged, the practitioners try to tie their views to stable and powerful existing networks. In any period there is one science which is considered by members of the larger society to be the leading exemplar of science and serves as a model for "good science" in remote disciplines. Mechanics was the most prestigious field following the success of Newton. Darwin's theory may have bestowed this supremacy to biology (Marshall 1910, 764). Chemistry also reached a period of glory following its success in "creating" new materials late in the nineteenth century, and, finally, Einstein's relativity theory and the invention of atomic energy may have uplifted physics back to the most preeminent position.[1]

In many fields we find that a conflict has been ignited by a new approach, which speaks in the name of progress and "science," and which seeks to substitute quantitative, exact and *allegedly* objective methods for more qualitative, less exact, and less reproducible ones. Snow (1964) spoke about "two cultures," scientists versus humanists, but we might better view this as a difference between two styles of academic inquiry, one of which is more common in the natural sciences and the other in the human sciences. Harwood, for instance, found such a division in his study of the "hereditarians" versus the "environmentalists," in relation to racial IQ differences: "Whereas Jensen's supporters' position is characteristically rational, quantitative, abstract, atomistic, and static, his critics' position is inclined to be intuitive, qualitative, concrete, holistic, and dynamic" (1979, 236).

Due to the diversity of science and its multifaceted nature, each party in a scientific struggle can draw upon a copious repertoire of philosophical arguments which have been made during millennia of ontological and epistemological discourse. It is important to emphasize that it is *not* argued here that metaphysical views are the cause of paradigmatic disagreements. This might be the case, but it is equally plausible that philosophical views are only the rationalization for preexisting different substantive views (MacKenzie and Barnes 1979, 198). The long philosophical discourse includes a variety of opinions and views, and scientific disputants might be viewed as "shoppers," who turn to this discourse for suitable philosophical justifications, which would help them to turn their plain views into black boxes.

The struggle between neoclassical and institutional economists is one example of the struggles over the "right method" in science. The core of the institutionalist attack on neoclassical economics is in the realm of methodology (Blaug 1985a, 708). Their stress on inductive methods and their claim that quantitative studies are a prerequisite for the establishment of general laws contrasted the deductive nature that characterized neoclassical economics, although the latter also recognized the need for empirical research. It is therefore not a surprise that methodological arguments concerning the nature of science and the criteria of good science occupied the center stage of the debate. Institutionalists argued that their empirical approach was more compatible with the methods of modern experimental science. Some neoclassicists (but not all!) defended qualitative methods and presented their practice as an "art." Other neoclassicists reminded their colleagues of the achievements of theoretical reasoning and accused the institutionalists of amassing countless facts without suggesting any theory to explain them. As in other disciplines, both institutionalists and neoclassicists used many examples from physics and biology. There was hardly any methodological essay that did not make a reference to one of the more prestigious natural sciences. Neoclassicists brought the laws of mechanics as a model, and as a justification, for their pursuit of simplified laws of economic behavior. Institutionalists, on the other hand, drew attention to the laborious and assiduous collection of data on movements of planets, which preceded and, in their opinions, allowed the discovery of the laws of mechanics.[2] They also used evolutionary theory as a model for economic science. Economic systems, they argued, were not mechanical systems. They were, rather, evolving organisms that constantly changed.

In this chapter I describe this struggle and the nature of arguments brought by both camps. The focus is on the "allies" that each party brought and on the ways these allies were being tied to the goals of the parties. The structure of this chapter is in the form of a dialogue. I start from the core of the institutionalist criticism, and then I review the counterarguments of the neoclassicists, the rebuttals of institutionalists, the neoclassical rejoinders, and so forth. This is *not* a chronological description of an actual debate. When the analyzed materials were written, the various arguments had already been part of the discourse, and the participating discussants anticipated the arguments which would be brought against their claims and preempted them. Yet it is possible to reconstruct a logical order of arguments, which is also the most convenient way to comprehend the debate. The chapter is divided into two parts. In the first part I follow the exchange of arguments which started from the accusations made by institutionalists that neoclassical economics was not scientific because it was not based on empirical research. The second part deals with a counterattack of the neoclassicists, in which they accused the institutionalists of having no theory to make sense of the data they had been collecting. We will see that the institutionalists and the neoclassicists actually professed very similar methodological beliefs. Therefore, the third section explains the essence of the disagreements which kept institutionalists and neoclassicists apart even when they declared their allegiance to the same principles.

The Institutionalist Attack

Institutionalists: Science Is Inductive

If one has to choose one element of institutionalism as the core of the approach, the emphasis on empirical research is a good choice. Probably the main allegation of institutionalists against orthodox economics was the lack of a serious attempt to describe what really happened "out there" in the economy. And the most respected ally that the institutionalists recruited was *Science* itself. They made the argument that proper science, *as it was practiced in all other disciplines*, was based on the laborious collection of facts, the search for recurring patterns, attempts to generalize the data, and, finally, the construction of theories to make sense of the amassed facts and generalizations. The established neoclassical doctrine, the institutionalists argued, was uniquely outmoded in its reliance upon deductive methods:

Tradition has established as the proper method of theory, deductions from hypothetical and drastically simplified premises rather than inductions from observations, the study of case material, or the use of statistics; and has caused its students to feel no necessity for checking doctrines by reference to the facts—a process regarded as quite essential in all other sciences. Furthermore, it has rendered theorists content with extremely general and highly abstract explanations of economic phenomena (Slichter 1924, 304).

Albert B. Wolfe's essay began with professing "The Demand for a Scientific Economics," already implying that the existing approach was not scientific. He argued that neoclassical theory was "static and taxonomic, *a priori* and deductive, unrealistic, scholastically over-refined, and based on antiquated and unscientific psychology" (1924, 445). Classical and neoclassical economics, he further asserted, "do not give us a *realistic* theory, that is, a theory which explains economic life as it actually is and based on an *adequate* inductive method" (ibid., 467). Wolfe made the further accusation that neoclassical generalizations were derived not from actualities but "rather [from] *metaphysical* postulates and hypotheses." Valid theory, he maintained, should be "dynamic, evolutionary and relative, concerned broadly and objectively with processes rather than with the precise implications of conceptual definitions, scientifically inductive rather than formalistically logical in method, and realistic" (ibid., 445–46; italics in original).

This view was a central recurring theme in many of the methodological writings. George Soule argued that by not following this fundamental method of science, namely, inductive research, economists perpetuated "the primitive state of economic science" (1924, 360). He added that neoclassical economists "have fallen in love" with the neatness of the theoretical system they had developed and refused to abandon it in favor of scientific methods. The result, in Soule's opinion, was that economic doctrine had become more like metaphysics than a description of reality (ibid., 360–61). Lionel Edie explained the fact that "economists are so much in disagreement nowadays" by the fact that "economics is at last undergoing a real transition under the impact of the spirit and method of modern science" (1927, 408). John Candler Cobb (1926) presented the theory that each scientific discipline was going through "a natural evolutionary development from qualitative toward quantitative methods." Economic theory had just outgrown the qualitative stage, and it was now following its older sisters—the oldest sister, astronomy, chemistry, and the youngest, medicine. Quantification allowed economists to "formulate the theories and principles of economics into concrete problems, and to attack them one by one, by intensive inductive method" (1926, 426–27).

Neoclassicists: Physics Is Also Theoretical

The recruitment of science by institutionalists could be answered by two tactics. Neoclassicists could point at those aspects of the prestigious sciences that were more similar to the deductive methods of neoclassical economics. Or, alternatively, they could say that economics was not a (natural) science, and that the methods of natural science were therefore irrelevant. Traditional views of science (including the Mertonian, Kuhnian, and Lakatosian) tend to assume that academic schools must adhere to consistent views. Constructivists, in contrast, find that schools often employ contradictory arguments. Such was the case with the neoclassical response: some neoclassicists opted for the first alternative, pointing especially to the achievements of theoretical physics. Others, or the same neoclassicists in other occasions, insisted that economics was not (just) a science; it was an art as well (Lowe 1964, 199). I will begin with the first line and discuss the second later.

Frank Knight, the central neoclassical theorist, said that "there is a close analogy between *theoretical* economics and *theoretical* physics." In both fields, he added, application of the principles required adaptation to particular conditions, "but the application of principles is impossible without principles to apply." Laboratory physics could not have achieved its astonishing progress "without the aid of a relatively separate development of mathematical theory." Similarly, applied economics could not progress without the development of pure theory (1924, 259; emphases added). Raymond Bye admitted that chemists and physicists used detailed observations in their studies but added that they were still interested "in the ultimate constitution of matter," which was basically a theoretical question. Bye mentioned also Einstein's theory of relativity "which was an achievement of purely abstract theory," and yet was celebrated as one of the greatest feats in the history of science. In astronomy, he added, "such theoretical questions as the origin of our solar system and the organization of the stellar universe" were practiced "side by side with such definite [empirical] researches as the measurement of stellar parallax and the observation of solar eclipses" (1925, 60–61; see also Bye 1924, 285). Furthermore, in the absence of the possibility of laboratory experimentation," economics was justified, according to Bye, in being *even more deductive* in its nature than physics (1924, 285). In his view, "the carefully sifted results arrived at by generations of keen thinkers checking each other's results" were as strong safeguards as experimental results in assuring the validity of economic theory. Thus, Bye flanked the institutionalist argument: yes, economics was a science, and indeed, science should be based on empirical research (alongside deductive reasoning). But in economics the experimental part was problematic. It was therefore legitimate, and even desirable, to bolster the deductive part to make up for the relative lack of experimental evidence.

Institutionalists: The World Is Too Complex to Be Studied Deductively

Now it was the turn of the institutionalists to strike back, and they did it by recruiting the complexity and the fluidity of economic systems as allies. The institutionalists perceived the social world as a very intricate system, which contained many interrelated elements, all of which were in constant change. If the world had been simpler, the argument went, we might have been able to study it deductively by the power of pure reasoning on the basis of a few simple and indisputable postulates. But "the difficulty of analyzing economic institutions by abstract thought or detached reflection has led to an attempt to apply new [inductive] methods of scientific inquiry" (Edie 1927, 408–9; see also Hale 1924, 225). Deductive reasoning was, indeed, part of any science, but in a human science like economics, the inductive part should be *greater*, not smaller, than in the natural sciences. F. C. Mills said, for instance, that theory did "not accord strictly with the facts in any scientific field." But in certain of the physical sciences, the gap was "reduced to a minimum" due to "absolute sameness" of the units of analysis (e.g., all atoms of hydrogen are the same) and the certainty of measurement. In a field like economics, "in which a multiplicity of causes operate and in which there is a high degree of variation in the data, a much larger body of inductive evidence is needed" (1924, 55).

Neoclassicists: "Theory Is the Economist's Vacuum Tube"

The neoclassicist response to the challenge of complexity was that the neoclassical theory, in spite, or maybe because, of its simplicity, was the best strategy to grasp the nature of economic systems. Jacob Viner, for instance, admitted that "many forces combine to produce an economic phenomenon," and these forces "change so rapidly and as yet so unpredictably in their intensity and their relative importance." Since the world was so complicated and changed so quickly, he reasoned, we must abandon any aspiration of attempting to replicate its exact mechanism. What we could do, Viner thought, was to analyze the "usual operation" of the "dominant forces." As imperfect as it might be, this was the best we could do (in Mills 1928, 32).[3]

The neoclassicists summoned natural science again to persuade us that such a strategy was valid and desirable in science: "The phenomena of the world are complexly built up of many interacting forces. Scientific analysis requires that they be broken up into their elements in order that they may be more easily understood" (Bye 1924, 288). Bye's example, again, was from the study of gravity by observing objects in vacuum tubes. By using these artificial conditions, physicists discovered laws of falling bodies that made it possible to understand the real world. Economic theory "is the economist's substitute for the experimental conditions of the physicist's laboratory. It is his vacuum tube" (1924, 288). Frank Knight employed a similar analogy in defending the use of the assumption of rationality by neoclassical economics. He did not deny the power of irrational motives in human behavior, but he saw them as "*aberrations* from the fundamental tendency and hence in subordination to it" (italics in original). These aberrations, he continued, "are of the nature of friction, divergence of materials from conditions taken as standard, and the like, in the workings of the laws of mechanics in actual machines" (1924, 259). Friction, gravity, and vacuum tubes thus became warriors on the side of neoclassical economics in its methodological trial of strength.[4]

Institutionalists: Economics Differs from (Natural) Sciences

As convincing as the metaphors of vacuum tubes and friction were, the institutionalists showed no less resourcefulness. The differences between natural and social sciences were marshaled again *en force* to debilitate the allies that neoclassical economics brought from physics. George Soule's essay can be conceived as a direct response to Bye's essay. The "economic man," Soule averred, was "not a counterpart of the apple in a vacuum" (1924, 361). The method of the natural science "was at first conceived proper for the human sciences." But social sciences were crucially different from the natural sciences in the sense that physical units were identical to each other while social units were not: "In order that Newton's deductions might have validity," Soule explained, "it was necessary to assume that one body of given mass in a given relationship to a system of bodies would behave like any other body of like mass in the same relationship to a like system, that such dominant identity of behavior extended throughout the physical universe, and that it would not be changed in the passage of time" (ibid.). This was not the case with economics, where universal qualities "make up a far smaller part of the phenomena of human behavior than they do of the behavior of falling apples." "The atmosphere of circumstance," he added "is so much more important to man-behavior than it is to apple-behavior" (ibid., 361–62; cf. Mäki 1994).

Rexford Tugwell's argument emphasized the fact that unlike apples, human beings could change the circumstances of their existence. He blamed the classical economists for assuming "that there were immutable laws continuously governing social development" (1924a, 391). As examples he mentioned the Malthusian law, the iron law of wages, and the law of diminishing returns, and argued that the economists who formulated these laws forgot that "no enlightened society will tolerate the free working out of such forces." "We already have," he added, "a vast organized politico-social machinery for seeing that [these laws] do not work out in the way that is described by the economists as though it were inevitable and benevolent" (ibid., 392). In this way Tugwell recruited human volition which made the strategies of natural science unfit for economics.

Tugwell's discussion of the law of diminishing returns illustrated his objection to the practice of neoclassical theorists of formulating general laws of economic behavior. That law says that when we add more of one factor of production, while other factors are constant, we would get less *additional* product. Applied to the whole economy, in which land is constant, the law would predict that the growth of the population, that is, of labor power, will not lead to an equivalent growth of production (Blaug 1985a, chap. 3, 426–27). In reality, Tugwell asserted, the growth of product has exceeded the growth of population. Yet, economists did not abandon the law, and argued, instead, "that the law of diminishing returns has only been temporarily circumvented by invention, discovery and substitution and that the law is always there just the same" (1924, 392). In form, this is similar to what physicists would say about the argument that airplanes refuted the law of gravity. But Tugwell argued that the difference was in usefulness: "The law of gravitation has in fact been useful in innumerable experiments that have established some truth or uniformity. But you can never point out that the law of diminishing returns has been useful in the same sense. Nor can you successfully contend that the laws of marginal value have ever helped to establish any further useful generalizations (ibid., 393).[5]

Neoclassicists: Economics Is Not a Natural Science

Strangely enough, the same shield that the institutionalists raised to deflect Bye's and Knight's clever uses of physical metaphors, was used also by neoclassicists to deflect the general inductive attack of institutionalism. I refer to the argument that economics and other social "sciences" were not really sciences, or that they were essentially a different kind of science, thus calling for different kinds of methods. Knight was one of the few chiefs of neoclassical economics who refused to model economics after physics even though he himself used physical metaphors to defend orthodox theory. "In the realm of physical nature," Knight argued, "the exact methods of science have carried understanding and control enormously farther than common sense could go. But this was because the data are relatively stable, reducible to classes of manageable number, and especially classes with recognizable and measurable indices." None of these features, he stressed, "seem to hold good of human data" (1924, 267). Unlike data in natural science, which were "relatively stable [and] reducible to classes of manageable number," data on human beings were in constant change, and the multitude of variables rendered it impossible to reduce it "to classes of manageable number." Knight also maintained that "the problem of understanding and controlling human behavior is radically different in character from that of explaining the material world and using it. Physical objects are not at the same time trying to understand and use the investigator!" (ibid.). Knight fervently challenged the aspirations of many institutionalists and more than a few *neoclassicists* to be like physics. He argued that economists had to "recognize that man's relations with his fellow man are on a totally different footing from his relations with the objects of physical nature and to give up . . . the naive project of carrying over a technique which has been successful in the one set of problems and using it to solve another set of categorically different kind (ibid.).

Viner also rejected the desire for economics to be like physics. It was true, he admitted, that "in the physical sciences progress has consisted in the discovery of quantitative differences underlying what first appeared to be solely differences in kind." But "the varied character of [the economic] subject matter and the wide range of diverse problems with which it deals makes of economics an ill-ordered and sprawling discipline." From this feature of economics Viner concluded that "methodological analogies from physics should not be applied to economics as a whole without the most serious qualifications and reservations" (in Mills 1928, 31).

The fact that neoclassicists used two allies which seem to negate each other—the similarity of economic laws to laws in physics, and the fact that social science differed from natural science—is a good example of the complexities of scientific discourses. From a constructivist perspective, however, it is not hard to explain this phenomenon. This is similar to an adroit lawyer who builds the defense of her client by preparing alternative, often mutually contradictory, lines of defense. Similarly, the neoclassicists argued that economics should not be like natural science, and it should not be judged according to the criteria of natural science. But even if one decided it should follow natural sciences, orthodox theory would still be exonerated, because it did posses the quality of *theoretical* natural science.

I conclude here the first round of arguments. The institutionalists who wanted to counter the last argument had either to repeat the initial arguments or to mobilize other kinds of allies. If the general philosophical arguments were not convincing enough, a resort to arguments about the nature of reality or relevance to policy making might perform the job. This will be our subject in the following chapters, but before this we have to follow the neoclassical counterattack on the methodological and philosophical battleground.

The Neoclassicist Counterattack

Neoclassicists: The Place of Theory in Empirical Research

One of the tactics that neoclassicists employed to deflect the frontal attack of institutionalists on deductive methods was to point at the importance of deductive reasoning in physics. But this was more than just a defensive move. It served also as the fulcrum of the neoclassical counterattack on institutionalism. The main accusation made against the latter was that institutionalists cared only about collecting data. Empirical data, the neoclassicists claimed again and again, have "to be digested, interpreted, generalized upon, and comprehended into a system of principles. . . . A mere mass of separate, uncoordinated facts about industry would be chaos, not science. There is a unity and plan to economic life" (Bye 1925, 59–60).

The connection between theory and empirical research was, thus, a central topic in the ongoing trial of strength. One voice that joined the attack on the institutionalist trend belonged to John D. Black, who supported the call to a much larger emphasis on empirical research, but who nevertheless believed that theory was also lacking and should be improved. Black testified on his own field, agricultural economics, in which there were "tons of data collected on all sorts of subjects." "The great need," he told his audience was "not more data to analyze quantitatively, but a better grasp in qualitative terms of the elements of the problems" (in Mills 1928, 44). At the same roundtable discussion Jacob Viner expressed similar criticism. Theory was vital. The quantitative studies that the institutionalists proposed were bound to fail, because

> Without some capacity to fit isolated phenomena into some general system, there can be no sense of proportion, no guide as to the significance and the proper interpretation of the empirically-discovered relationships between small groups of detailed phenomena, no working dominance over the wilder-

ness of single instances which the economic world must seem to be to the economist who does not believe in general theory, no effective machinery for the creation of new hypotheses which even the most empirically-minded of statisticians would find essential as a stimulus to really creative quantitative work (ibid., 35).

Institutionalists: We Do Not Deny the Importance of Theory

The institutionalists knew that the accusation of the neoclassicists might hurt their efforts and therefore vehemently denied that they took theory less seriously. The main line of the defense of the institutionalists was evident in Mitchell's presidential address from December 1924. This address started with the statement that "we all practice both qualitative and quantitative analyses." There was no point in trying to prove that "one type should predominate over the other," because it was obvious that "qualitative analysis . . . cannot be dispensed with, if for no other reason, because quantitative work itself involves distinctions of kinds, and distinctions of kinds start with distinctions of quality" (1925, 1).

The importance of this issue for the participants was seen in Mitchell's frequent reiteration of his position: "No one has denied the usefulness of quantitative analysis on one side, or of qualitative analysis upon the other. At most there are differences of emphasis," Mitchell replied to his critics in the roundtable discussion of methods where Black and Viner attacked the quantitative advocates (Mills 1928, 40). He elaborated more in another roundtable discussion, summarized by its Chair, Holbrook Working: "It is a blunder, [Mitchell] held, to identify quantitative method with induction and the process by which orthodox economic theory was developed with deduction. In all thinking it is necessary to pass from the confused data yielded by observation to comprehensive ideas, and back to particular facts" (Working 1927, 20). Mitchell's awareness of the accusation against institutionalism was evident in his lectures on *Types of Economic Theory*. In the lecture on Commons, Mitchell observed that since Veblen's first publications, many essays on institutional economics "end with the complaint that institutionalists have done little except criticizing economics of the standard sort and have not gotten round the task of putting anything in its place" (1969, 2:701). Mitchell perceived Commons's *Institutional Economics* (pub. 1934) as the remedy of this problem. That book "covers a wide range of economic problems and certainly deserves consideration as a valiant attempt to provide the constructive contribution which had been demanded of institutionalism" (ibid.).[6]

Many other institutionalists emphasized the importance of theory. John M. Clark, having asserted the limits of the deductive method, added that induction alone was also not sufficient because it did not provide us with an explanation. The core of science, he thus concluded, was the combination of the deductive and the inductive methods (1924, 74; see also p. 78; Veblen 1948, 217). Rexford Tugwell also supported a combination of the deductive and the experimentalist approaches (1924a, 399–400), arguing that "as a matter of fact deduction lies at the very heart of induction. The best theorist is the man who knows best the methods . . . of induction" (ibid., 399). Tugwell took us back to natural science by mentioning that Newton, Darwin, and Pasteur were among the few who excelled in both kinds of work, inductive and deductive. On the other hand, he also referred to Laplace, Lamarck, Franklin, and Priestley who "were not great inductive workers," but contributed a lot to the history of science nonetheless" (ibid., 401). The mobilization of these deductive scholars by Tugwell, the staunch advocate of empirical research, indicated his wish to underline his commitment to theoretical practice.

Lionel Edie, another enthusiastic supporter of detailed empirical studies, also emphasized that "the revival of pure theory is the hope of quantitative method" (1927, 410). Speaking about the young generation of institutionalists, he said that their main task was to dissolve "the heterogeneous facts into new hypotheses pertinent to the problems confronting us." But "thus far," he acknowledged, "they have shouldered a little of the responsibility" (1927, 410–11). As a consequence, "the mass of special studies tends to result in a kind of intellectual anarchy" (ibid., 434). Edie, however, believed that the lack of theory was a reaction to the past preoccupation with theory, not an inherent feature of institutionalism. Like Mitchell, he thought that the problem was already being addressed by the studies of Commons and Hamilton on the historical development of property rights and labor relations. "Such efforts are all too rare," he admitted (ibid., 411), but he had no doubt that the problem would be addressed by institutionalists in years to come. Similar points were made by many other institutionalists (e.g., Cobb 1926, 426–27; Mills 1924, 54), a testimony to the importance institutionalists attached to the refutation of the accusation that their approach lacked theory.

The Evaluation and Perception of Theory

If the institutionalists were so scrupulous in treating theory with respect, why were they so harshly censured by the neoclassical economists? One answer might be that this criticism was just part of the "demonization" of

the enemy. Parties in academic feuds, as in other struggles, often exagger-
ate the opponents' views in order to render those views less credible. But
this is not the whole explanation. Although the neoclassicists and institutionalists agreed that inductive and deductive methods were complementary, they did dispute the nature of theory and its role. A clue to the
difference can be found in a controversy which flared during a roundtable
discussion on "The Present Status and Future Prospects of Quantitative
Economics" during the Annual Meeting of the American Economic Association in December 1927 (Mills 1928). The roots of that controversy,
however, were in Mitchell's visionary presidential address three years
earlier.

In that presidential address, Mitchell emphasized the importance of
theory. But at the same time he emphasized that theory could help *only* if
and when it was relevant to empirical studies, unlike the old orthodox
theory. Mitchell asked, "When a [current] theorist puts any one of his
problems to a statistician, does the answer he gets ever quite meet his
questions? And when a statistician attempts to test an economic theory,
is his test ever conclusive?" (1925, 3). The answer, he said, was negative
because orthodox theory was built in such a way that empirical data were
irrelevant. To use Popperian terms, Mitchell argued that the old theory
was unfalsifiable. What, then, was the use in quantitative work, Mitchell
asked. His answer was that if we had the Jevonsian (i.e., neoclassical)
theory in mind, then there was no use indeed in quantitative research.
Jevons and Marshall, he maintained, did not formalize problems that
could be answered by empirical research. That was their fundamental
flaw. Theory was vital but only one that could interact with empirical
findings: "What we must expect is a recasting of the old problems into
new forms amenable to statistical attack. In the course of this reformulation of its problems, *economic theory will change not merely its complex-
ion, but also its content* . . . there is little likelihood that the old explanations will be refuted by these investigators, but much likelihood that they
will be disregarded" (ibid.; italics added).

Mitchell's presidential address drew a lot of angry reactions by neoclassicists, who interpreted it as a call to discard the old doctrine in its
entirety. Led by Jacob Viner, they capitalized on this statement to delegitimize institutionalism:

> We have been told that the economist of the early future will not be interested
> in the questions for which the older economists sought answers, but will con-
> cern himself with new problems and only such problems as can be investigated
> by the new quantitative techniques. We have also been told that for some time
> into the future the new economists . . . will be content to make detailed investi-
> gations narrowly confined in their range and to build up mass of information

as to the empirically-discovered relationships with narrow ranges of concrete phenomena (Viner in Mills 1928, 34).

Viner warned that these promises sounded like those made by German historicists a few decades before, promises that had led, in his view, nowhere (for more on the references to the German historical school, see chap. 8).

Both camps clearly supported a methodology which combined deductive reasoning and inductive collection of data, but as Mitchell said, "there are differences of emphasis" (in Mills 1928, 40). It is easy to concede that theorists try to conceive the world as they know it; hence, they are "empiricist." And similarly, observing the world requires some kind of theoretical scheme to make sense of the data. And yet, institutionalists and neoclassicists conceived the relations between empirical work and theory differently. First, the neoclassicists and institutionalists diverged in their attitudes toward the fundamental principles of orthodox theory. Mitchell and most institutionalists did not believe that *contemporary* theory would be much help in constructing generalizations. Hence they sought to build a new theory from scratch. The neoclassicists, on the other hand, saw the contemporary theory as the starting point and criticized the radical institutionalists for their willingness to discard that theory. Viner was probably typical in doubting the ability to build a completely new theory on the basis of recently collected data. In his opinion, economists must start from a general theory, of which neoclassical theory was the only specimen, and modify it according to empirical results.

Related to this was the belief of neoclassicists that the orthodox theory was still useful even in its current level of development. In a clear opposition to Mitchell, Viner said that the problems posed by classical and neoclassical economists were still relevant. Many economists, he told us for instance, "sought for light on the post-war problems in the English literature of the first two decades of the Nineteenth Century" (in Mill 1928, 35). Raymond Bye admitted that some modifications in the old doctrine were essential but he did not "anticipate that the resulting principles will be so vastly different from our present generalizations as some critics would have us believe" (1925, 59). Bye, like the institutionalists, professed a combined inductive-deductive methodology but differed from them in believing that orthodox theory could stand the test of empirical investigations: "More painstaking study of particular processes and institutions, more inductive and experimental work, is likely to develop. Doubtless this will lead to considerable refinement and revision of our general theory. But there will continue to be an active interest in that theory, and abandonment of it is neither to be expected nor desired" (ibid., 61). This was, of course, very different from the assessment of institutionalists who were very skeptical of the potential of orthodox theory to help solve the immediate problems of the economy. I will return to this subject in chapter 7 when I analyze the trial of strength over relevance.

Realism and Broadness vs. Rigor and Elegance

So far we saw that the institutionalists did not believe that orthodox theory could be helpful in illuminating modern economic life, whereas their neoclassical opponents believed the theory was still fecund and seminal. This gap derives from a divergent perception of the role of theory. A. B. Wolfe, an institutionalist, was interested, for instance, in depth and width at the expense of elegance and neatness. Economics, he thought, should try to explain behavior and to include psychological motivations in its scope. Such a research program, he said, "will doubtless for a long time to come lack the assurance and the esthetic symmetry and definiteness of the older . . . systems." But this price was worthwhile, because the new research program "will not be the pleasing indoor sport" that the old theory had been (1924, 466).

Wolfe was aware that since "the natural sciences have developed constantly in prestige," many economists, especially younger ones, would import the "standards of scientific objectivity and accuracy developed in the natural sciences" (ibid., 448). But in his opinion, this was a mistake: "A true scientific method for economics must take recognizance of the peculiarities of the data with which economics has to deal. It cannot be built up on analogy [with natural science]" (ibid., 463). In economics, psychological factors were the motivating power and their inclusion inevitably made theory less precise. In his opinion, the inclusion of important factors is more important than neatness and accuracy: "An economics which admits to consideration some type or types of motive, and yet excludes other of great, if not possibly equal, importance in their influence on the intensity and direction of economic activity, *cannot be scientific* (ibid., 464; emphasis mine).

John Maurice Clark was also concerned with the trade-off of scope and accuracy and unhesitatingly preferred the former:

> What if economics as a theory of efficiency opens up problems requiring evidence not amenable to academic canons of accurate and absolute demonstration? What does scientific procedure demand? Scientific tactics says: "Limit the study to evidence about which absolute and accurate statements can be made." But scientific strategy says: "It is unscientific to exclude any evidence relevant to the problem in hand." *This comprehensiveness is scientific*, even if it involves some sacrifice of other qualities for which science likes to strive.

The core of scientific method lies, not in induction, nor in deduction, but in taking account of all relevant facts and excluding none (1924, 74–75; italics in original).

Clark was opposed also to the search of a theory which was universally true. "Human behavior in economic life was so many sided," he said, that any attempt to come with formulas which would be "one hundred per cent accurate" must be "in the form 'whatever is, is'; preferably camouflaged into a semblance of meaning" (ibid., 77–78). Such a formula did not help us to interpret behavior. What we need, he maintained, was to "simplify in order to interpret; . . . a never-ending search for generalizations that are significantly true, and for that very reason are often neither one hundred per cent accurate, nor universally accurate" (ibid., 78).

Clark's search for "generalizations that are significantly true" was probably the best way to describe the concept of science that institutionalists held. Scientific theories in the human sciences should not be in the form of universal laws but should rather explain historical developments and changes of economic institutions and motivations (cf. Wilber and Harrison 1978; Ramstaad 1986). That was the concept of theory that Mitchell had when he argued that Henry L. Moore's quantitative work was not only more relevant practically, but also more significant *theoretically* (1925). Henry Moore (1869–1958) was one of the pioneers of the use of statistics in economics and one of the first to use regression analyses to study the elasticity of demand for various crops. Moore, Mitchell said, did not solve the problem that Alfred Marshall posed, because he could not control external variables (as required by the *ceteris paribus* clause of the comparative statics of neoclassical theory), nor measure the influences of infinitesimal changes in prices (as required by marginal analysis). But Moore's work made it possible to evaluate the *actual* price elasticity of demand for particular commodities. Because of this, Mitchell claimed, Moore's work was more relevant not only practically, but also more significant *for theory building*. It could be connected to a variety of social, psychological, and economic factors and thus advance our theory of real human economic behavior. On the other hand, Jevons's calculus of pleasures and pains, or Marshall's assumptions of a motivation to consume and a distaste for work and waiting may or may not be valid. Either way, it was not relevant, Mitchell reasoned, because these concepts were not measurable and, hence, useless both practically and theoretically.

Morris Copeland (1931) was very perceptive in noticing the differences in the meaning of theory. "Hypotheses concerning industrial government or the organization of our railroad system," Copeland argued, "*are economic theories* as truly as hypotheses concerning variations in price, production and distribution" (1958, 52; italics added). Copeland perceived institutionalism as realizing "newer phases of economic theory." These phases, Copeland said, "aim to take account of certain features of society that the Industrial Revolution has made prominent: disparity in bargaining power, sales efforts, a variety of restraints on competition, overhead costs, changes and ambiguities in our legal system."

The views of Wolfe, Clark, Mitchell, and Copeland illustrate the institutionalist response to the accusation that institutionalism had no alternative theory to replace orthodox theory. Institutionalism, they believed, did offer a new kind of theory. It was a theory of institutional change and industrial organization, of changes in tastes and technologies, of labor relations, and of psychological motivations and social norms. It was very different, in its form and content, from neoclassical theory, but they insisted it was not a bit less "a theory." They acknowledged that their theoretical approach was still incipient but were sure it would thrive and replace the older theory.

Conclusions: Contesting Perceptions of an Economic Science

In the beginning of the chapter, I brought the argument of institutionalists that science is primarily the collection of data, an inductive pursuit of the realities of the world. Neoclassicists responded by saying that science was also theoretical reasoning from facts to their logical conclusions. Next, neoclassicists accused institutionalists of having no theory, which was as vital a part of science as data collection. The institutionalists denied this allegation fiercely and claimed they had a *new* type of theory. The summary of the struggle institutionalists and neoclassicists conducted shows that the dispute whether the institutionalists had a theory or not stemmed from the differences in viewing the nature of proper theory. Thus our historical journey enables us to answer the question whether institutionalists had a theory or not (chap. 3).

Those who have followed the analysis and the constructivist argument to this point would probably anticipate the answer: It depends! It depends on who is answering. Institutionalists and neoclassicists had *different* notions of what theory was. Speaking about the "paradigmatic" gaps among various schools, Henry Briefs calls our attention to the fact that "since each of the approaches points and seeks a distinct kind of invariance or lawfulness, the doctrinal results of 'other' approaches may seem to result in no laws at all [as institutionalism is seen by neoclassicists—Y. Y.] . . ., or in abstract and rigorous relations lacking relevance to the concrete reality of the time and space [as neoclassical theory is conceived by institutionalists—Y. Y.]" (Briefs 1960, 7). The institutionalist theory's "refrain that there were no 'natural' grounds for economic institutions was read [by postwar neoclassical economists] as implying that institutionalism left no systematic economic theory" (Mirowski 1990, 102). To put it in other words, institutionalists did have an "institutionalist kind" of theory, but they lacked the "neoclassical type" of theory (Wilber and Harrison 1978; cf. Hausman 1994, 195).

Historians and sociologists cannot, and should not, aspire to decide whether the institutionalist theory is a proper theory or whether the current neoclassical theory is good or bad. All they can do is to say what past or present practitioners have thought of either theory and suggest explanations for the fortunes of various doctrines. Of course, methodologists and philosophers, and practicing economists as well, are concerned with the evaluation of theories and methods in economics. But the question of whose concept of theory is better is part of the ongoing struggle over the way the discipline should go. There is no absolute criteria that can be employed in order to find the "true" answer to that question. It is a dispute that can be resolved (not necessarily peacefully and to the pleasure of everybody) only by methodological and philosophical trials of strength of the type described in this chapter.

The same struggle over the meaning of theory continued after the Second World War. Ayres (1951, 52), for example, averred that "to insist . . . that only curve-plotting is economic theory is to forget the theoretical presumptions from which alone the significance of curve-plotting derives." Ayres (1957, 26) criticized the conventional price theory:

> It simply is not true that scarce resources are allocated among alternative uses by the market. The real determinant of whatever allocation occurs in any society is the organizational structure of that society—in short, its institutions. At most, the market only gives effect to prevailing institutions. By focusing attention on the market mechanism, economists have ignored the real allocational mechanism. Hence the hiatus between economics and other social studies, all of which are concerned with various aspects of the institutional structure of society.

This means that a full economic theory must include the conceptualization of the organizational structure. If this cannot be achieved by using rigorous deductive reasoning, that is too bad; but according to J. M. Clark's criteria, the comprehensiveness of theory is more important than rigor.

For institutionalists, attempts to comprehend the special structure of the American economy, in contrast to other capitalist societies, or trials to conceptualize recent changes in capitalism, in governmental policies, in the structure of corporations, and so forth are the daily bread-and-butter of economic theory. This is in contrast to orthodox theory, which preferred rigorous analysis of abstract relationships, which were mathematically solid and, in principle, universally applicable. Chandler Morse, a postwar institutionalist, rejected, therefore, "the frequent misconception that the institutionalists denigrated theory." The institutionalists, he said, "did disapprove of *some kinds of theory*, but their aim was a positive one, to push theory into closer contact with life and reality" (1958, vi; italics added).

I should add a few words for the noneconomist readers of this book. For such readers, the institutionalists' view of theory may seem so trivial that they might fail to understand the whole dispute. It is therefore important to understand that economists have a completely different notion of theory than other social scientists. For many economists, the theories which are common in sociology, psychology, and political science, be they Marxist, Weberian, Freudian, behaviorist, pluralist, or whatever, are "loosely formulated hypotheses" based on "intuitive evidence" which "conceal moral judgment." This is a paraphrase of Reisman's evaluation of Galbraith's approach (1981, 84), but such idioms are commonly expressed by economists when they encounter theories which deviate from the mathematically couched models common in economics. Only the latter is considered by them as scientifically solid because it relies on unassailable mathematics and is devoid of any ideological content. Thus Paul Samuelson, the prophet and pioneer of modern mathematical neoclassicism, could claim with no hesitation that Galbraith, a modern institutionalist, "has no principles. There are few testable, researchable propositions in his writings that could serve for the purpose of Ph.D. theses or articles in learned journals. How can a jury prove his attitudes and insight right or wrong?" (1976, 849). Galbraith, Samuelson continued, "does provide a ware that is in great demand: a critique in viewpoint against the prevailing orthodox in economics." But according to his standard, there was no theory in Galbraith's work.

Many of the present-day theoretical disputes share the same feature: they also involve deep philosophical and epistemological controversies (Pheby 1988; Mäki 1994). Many advocates of modern neoclassical theory defend their approach by claiming that there are no alternative theories. Hausman perceptively interprets that such defenses—advanced, *inter alia*, by Friedman (1953), Koopmans (1957), and Grether and Plott (1979)

> implicitly demand that any alternative to accepted theory must preserve a peculiarly "economic" realm to be spanned by a single unified theory. They are not merely defending simplicity, unity, and broad scope as methodological desiderata. . . . Instead one finds a constraint in operation here against considering a narrow-scope hypothesis, regardless of its empirical vindication (1992, 236).

This preference for simplicity and unity is not a requirement of science as such but *one view* of science. A similar gap separates, for instance, the view of "the current ['Walrasian'] orthodoxy concerning the use of economic models" and the approach of Milton Friedman, who "works from inside what he describes as a 'framework' . . ., something much looser than a specific model" (Backhouse 1993a, 126). Apparently, Friedman is ready to adopt a view of science which is much closer to the institutionalists' conception of theory than to the common perception in economics (ibid., 128).[7]

Since science treasures both simplicity and empirical vindication, when two approaches offer different "baskets" of these goods the choice is the result of subjective tastes and not of a universal methodology. The fact that almost all economists—at least in the U.S.—share similar tastes is not a proof that their preferences are scientifically superior. It is rather a testimony to their power to banish economists with other preferences from the discipline (Gieryn 1995).

As Gieryn claims, the practice of debating what is "science" is typical for scientific discourses, but its outcomes can be different in various schools. In other disciplines, in other countries, and in a few minor universities in the U.S., practices which have been repudiated by mainstream economists as nonscientific are still considered as the backbone of science. The wish of modern economists to follow the procedures of "hard science" in order to banish disagreements and controversies "has been a vain hope." It simply shifted economic disputes to "the rubric of 'the philosophy of science'" (Mirowski 1990, 76). This is inevitable because there are not any given, eternal, and incontestable procedures of "hard science."

Mirowski himself is, therefore, wrong in attributing the decline of institutionalism to an inner contradiction in its teaching. Mirowski asks how could institutionalists

> praise scientific discourse as the only relevant truth criteria, and simultaneous [*sic*] eschew scientific practice as it was understood in mid-twentieth-century America? Where was the mathematical formalism and axiomization, the systematic hypothesis-testing according to the canons of classical statistical inference, the mathematical models, and the style of studied anonymity of the physics report? (1990, 105)

The answer is simple. In 1945 it was not sure yet what "science" meant for Americans in general, and for economists in particular. There was still a contest between pragmatists and logical positivists, between institutionalists and mathematical economists. It seems that the advocates of "mathematical formalism and axiomization" and of mathematical models prevailed.[8] But that was the result of ongoing negotiation between 1945 and, roughly, 1960, a result which could be attributed to many factors from the immigration of many logical positivists to the U.S. during and after World War II to the eruption of the Cold War. The result, however, was not the same everywhere. In sociology and psychology, the predominant views were closer in spirit to institutionalism than to the mathematical models of (certain kinds of) physics and economics. Nor is the outcome fixed and stable. Current economists, like the economists of the interwar years, like physicists, chemists, biologists, and sociologists, continue to make arguments about what is "a science" and what is the meaning of science in economics. This methodological discourse is an essential part of the debate about the validity and relevance of economic theories (Weintraub 1989). It cannot be ruled out of economics as many practicing economists wish,[9] nor can it end with conclusive and unequivocal answers according to a given Scientific Method (McCloskey 1985; Weintraub 1989).

Methodological controversies are common in all sciences. The case described by Dean (1979) sounds typical of many fields in the human sciences. But Dean dealt with taxonomic schools in botany, and his account demonstrates that this type of trial of strength is not unique to the human sciences. In the case of taxonomy, the traditional school originated from the work of Linnaeus in the eighteenth century, and is based on observed morphology of plants. In the 1920s, this approach was challenged by researchers who were influenced by recent advances in genetics. They sought to base their taxonomy on genetics, by making experiments on hybridization. The proponents of the new approach claimed that the old approach had "its value, and hence its excuse, in the biological exploration of new and distant countries." Yet, they argued that "permanent taxonomic results must await the application of statistical and experimental methods in the field." Building on the prestige of experiments in physics, they boasted that their experimental methods would "turn taxonomy from a field overgrown with personal opinions to one in which scientific proof is supreme" (quoted in Dean 1979, 213). The defenders of tradition were ready to admit the virtues of the new approach as an *addition* to existing practices, but emphasized that in order "to be of maximum use to science," biological classification had to "come to terms with art" (quoted in ibid., 220).

Another example is the way experiments are conceived in medical research. Alvan Feinstein from the Yale School of Medicine distinguishes between "fastidious" and "pragmatic" perspectives (1983). Advocates of the first approach "prefer a 'clean' arrangement, using homogeneous groups, reducing or eliminating ambiguity, and avoiding the specter of biased results" (1983, 545). Their opponents, the pragmatists, think that medical experiments should be aimed at resolving clinical problems and should therefore "incorporate the heterogeneity, occasional or frequent ambiguity, and other 'messy' aspects of ordinary clinical practice" (1983, 545). The struggle between these two approaches has been going for a long time (Marks 1987), and, as Steven Epstein (1995) shows, the balance between the two views in AIDS research has changed in favor of the pragmatist conception due to the pressure exerted by AIDS activists. Quoting a report of the National Academy of Sciences, Epstein argues that the "basic scientific conceptions of what it means to 'prove,' to 'verify,' or to 'reproduce' findings in biomedicine . . . have been challenged and reshaped by AIDS activists."[10]

These are just two examples of a ubiquitous characteristic of scientific conflicts. The long history of science is replete with such struggles. Economists are dubious of methodological disputations in economics and claim that "economic methodology is sterile, that progress never occurs, and that debates go on and on without the participants ever reaching a consensus" (Hands 1993, 143). "This lack of consensus," Hands explains, "is often cited as a reason for not participating in methodological discourse" (ibid.). He therefore attempts to convince his readers that economic methodologists did reach agreement over many issues. My answer is different: the very continuation of disputation and controversy is a sign of a vibrant and lively science. As these debates go on, some agreements are reached ("black boxes") but other disputes are likely to erupt. Economists should ask how to make this discourse better rather than seek how to proscribe it altogether.

Five

Bringing People and Institutions Back In: The Struggle over the Scope of Economics

> Different persons, according to their choice of profession,
> find the money-motive playing a large or a small part in their
> lives, and historians can tell us about other phases of social
> organization in which this motive has played a much smaller
> part than it is now. Most religions and most philosophies dep-
> recate, to say the least of it, a way of life mainly influenced by
> considerations of personal money profits. On the other hand,
> most men to-day reject ascetic notions and do not doubt the
> real advantages of wealth. Moreover, it seems obvious to
> them that one cannot do without the money-motive, and that,
> apart from certain admitted abuses, it does its job well.
>   (John Maynard Keynes, *The End of Laissez-Faire*)
>
> The economists approached the task of discussing such
> problems as how can nations best organize themselves to
> increase their wealth, [and] how wealth is distributed. . . . Yet
> the explanations that they gave were unavoidably colored
> by their spontaneous working ideas of what human nature
> is and how it operates. This is characteristic of economics
> today as in the past.
>   (Wesley Mitchell, *Types of Economic Theory*)

WHEN ECONOMISTS consider the meaning of science, they often draw on
the leading and most prestigious domains: physics, chemistry, and biology. But the question of what science is quickly gives its place to the more
concrete question of how to apply the meaning of science for the unique
subject matter of economics. The answer to this question depends to a
large extent on the way human beings are perceived (cf. Lawson 1994).
That is why human nature and social organizations were marshaled into
the struggle between institutionalists and neoclassical economics and
used to defend the positions of both parties. Institutionalists argued that
the simplifications of pure economic theory, unlike the laws of natural
science, were not helpful in understanding economic phenomena, because
people and social organizations were influenced by a much larger number

of factors, and, also, because of the ability of people to learn and adapt their behavior. Similarly, some neoclassicists claimed that exactly due to these reasons, social scientists must not aspire to imitate natural science. Human behavior was not as regular as the behavior of heavenly bodies or as the movement of blood in our veins. Searching for laws of such behavior on the basis of empirical research would not lead us to any meaningful results. The best we could do, they thought, was to understand the "economic"—that is, the rational—aspect of human life.

This chapter deals with those aspects of the contest between institutionalists and neoclassicists, which focused on the nature of human beings and social institutions. The first part of the chapter describes the attack of institutionalists on the assumptions of hedonism and rationality, which, they argued, underlay orthodox theory. The second part is concerned with the defense of neoclassical economists. Unlike the trial of strength over methodology, the neoclassicists chose not to play on the court of human nature. Their defense of neoclassical theory was, mostly, to plead guilty and admit that classical and early neoclassical thinking was steeped with misconceived notions of human nature. They maintained, however, that neoclassical theory did not depend on those erroneous psychological conceptions, and, therefore, its conclusions were not implicated by them. In fact, they tried to reshape the boundaries of the economic discourse by arguing that psychological motivations were irrelevant for economic analysis. The third part focuses on the attempt of institutionalists to provide economics with an alternative conception of human beings, a conception which was centered on the influence of collectivities on the structure of personality.

Exorcising the Economic Man: The Institutionalist Critique

A. B. Wolfe, an institutionalist who fostered bright hopes in regard to the cooperation between economics and psychology, contended that orthodox economists were the victims "of psychology, adequate to explain a certain limited type of motive, but inadequate to the needs of [the new] generation of theorists" (1924, 468). This accusation refers to the hedonistic psychology held by the British utilitarian philosophers during the eighteenth and nineteenth centuries. In economics this psychology was incarnated in the conception of the "economic man." The hedonistic economic man (women were invariably ignored!) was supposed to behave "mechanically" in such a way as to maximize his pleasure and minimize his pain: Wolfe attacked this view very harshly and was followed by many other institutionalists (e.g., Mitchell 1924, 14–17; Mills 1924, 42–43; Tugwell 1924a, 388–94).

The institutionalist arguments can be divided into three main claims. First, they recruited the nonmaterial and nonselfish interests of people. The existence of such interests, they said, refuted the basic assumptions of neoclassical economics and nullified its conclusions. Second, irrational behavior was brought in together with a new concept of human beings as social creatures. Again, this idea was employed in order to convince the readers that the conclusions drawn from neoclassical analysis were invalid. A third major ally was the idea that labor was not only a pain which must be endured, but also a source of satisfaction, an argument that had many implications for orthodox economic analysis.

Institutionalists claimed that human beings had interests which were not material, and which were thereby neglected by neoclassical economists. Wolfe vehemently rejected classical economics "which would attempt rigidly to exclude from the economist's consideration every motive which is not clearly and directly 'economic,' that is to say, pecuniarily hedonistic" (1924, 464). He believed that such an approach was so absurd that one did not need "extended argument" to convince unbiased economists that it "cannot be scientific." Institutionalist economics redressed this deficiency in economic theory. A new generation of theorists, Wolfe said, began "to see the human organism as a whole and to see that 'economic' motives are neither all hedonistically acquisitive nor capable of being dissected out and treated in entire independence of the rest of the psychic processes of the individual and the community (1924, 467; see also Tugwell 1924a, 408). Paul Douglas, who shared many of the institutionalist attitudes,[1] actually attempted to classify all the "non-commercial incentives." Each item on the list can be viewed as a soldier in the allied institutionalist army in the battle over the nature of human beings. The list goes as follows:

1. The desire to benefit humanity.
2. The fascination, or joy, of work itself.
3. The desire to project one's own personality in the work at hand.
4. The desire to be esteemed by one's fellows in the same field of activity.
5. The desire for the esteem and approval of the general public.
6. The craving for notoriety.
7. The desire for power over men and over things (Douglas 1924, 188).

These motivations were common knowledge for most intellectuals in those days, and by arguing that neoclassical economics denied them, institutionalists put a question mark over the soundness of neoclassical economics as a whole.

The trial of strength over human motivation involves, however, more than the psyches of people in the place and time in which the trial occurs.

It involves "Human Nature" itself. The question is not just what determines the behavior of people in the immediate society, but how people *in general* behave. This trial of strength cannot, therefore, be settled only on the basis of psychological studies of people in our society. Contenders have to convince us that their views are valid in regard to simple and ancient societies as much as to our own modern and complex society. An empirical research might have found that in the acquisitive society of modern America the "pecuniarily hedonistic" motivation was indeed so strong as to make other motivations practically insignificant for understanding economic phenomena. Institutionalists emphasized, however, that one could not mistake current structures of motivations for "Human Nature" in general. The acquisitive quality of American society was a product of specific conditions, not a reflection of universal human traits. Douglas therefore stressed that whatever we might discover in contemporary society, Human Nature was very much different from the economic man:

> The evidence seems irrefutable that alongside the economic motive, which is undoubtedly real and powerful, there are in most of us, these non-commercial incentives as well, which are, at present, utilized only to a small fraction of their capacity. It is one of the problems of our social life to offer these desires an opportunity to function for the common good and to stimulate them in that direction. The false conception of the exclusively economic man has blinded us to these other characteristics of mankind and has helped to make our age one where the emphasis is laid upon acquisition (1924, 188).

The idea that people were materialistic because of the cultural environment could be accepted only if another basic assumption of orthodox economists, namely, rationality, was undermined. The rationality of the "economic man" means that actors behave in such a way as to maximize the realization of their desires; to maximize their utility in the economic language. Institutionalists rejected this view and brought a great deal of evidence to convince their colleagues that irrational urges were powerful determinants of human behavior. Here again, all the institutionalists had to do was to draw attention to common examples of behavior that contradicted evident interests of the actors themselves. The issue here is not the sacrifice of one's own economic goals in the pursuit of other people's welfare or in order to achieve nonpecuniary desire. What irrationality means here is that people achieve suboptimal outcomes either due to mistakes, lack of patience, short-sightedness, the pursuit of immediate satisfaction, or as a result of uncontrollable psychological urges.

The institutionalists attacked the idea of the economic man as a human calculator. "Even business men," Sumner Slichter said, "are far from

being the carefully calculating, unemotional, intellectual machines which
the [neoclassical] theory of free enterprise assumes them to be. Often they
are too busy, too careless, or too lazy to investigate thoroughly the alternatives presented to them" (1924, 320). Wage earners and consumers are
even more "inclined to be careless and indifferent to their interests in
business dealings. Most of them are amateurs when it comes to buying
and selling. They have not been trained to suppress their whims and fan-
cies, their optimism and their credulity, and to be matter of fact, skeptical
and not too easily convinced by clever talk" (ibid., 321).

Alongside the evidence of irrationality, in the strict economic sense,
institutionalists recruited the view of human beings held by pragmatists
and symbolic interactionists to strengthen the validity of their argument.
The pragmatists and symbolic interactionists emphasized the susceptibil-
ity of men and women to many influences from the surrounding community. The rationality of the "economic man" means that one behaves according to one's *real* desires; not the "false" desires society inculcates in
us. The assumption is that human needs and desires are universal and
constant and cannot be manipulated by others (Stigler and Becker 1977;
see discussion in DiMaggio 1994, 29). The institutionalists, following
pragmatists and symbolic interactionists, refused to accept this assumption and thought that human beings' basic needs and wants were determined by social forces.

Pragmatism went even farther and rejected the very distinction between "society" and "individuals." Such terms assume that there are
independent individuals, on which society exerts influence. But for pragmatists there are no individuals independent of society. What people
think, the language they think in, their emotions and desires, and even the
way they perceive themselves—all these are shaped and constituted
by society (e.g., Dewey 1963 [1938]; Mead 1962 [1934]). Institutionalists built upon this view to attack the individualistic approach of neoclassical economics. Edie (1927, 406) quoted Thorndike—a famous psychologist at that time—with approval: "Perhaps nine-tenths of what
commonly passes as distinctly human nature is . . . put there by institutions, or grows there by the interaction of the world of natural forces and
the capacity to learn."

Mitchell stressed the fact that specific economic circumstances give
man "practice in dealing with certain problems, familiarity with certain
conventional ideas, sympathy with certain standards. These circumstances help to develop his power of intelligent analysis in certain directions, and to limit them in others." "What a genius can accomplish,"
Mitchell added, "depends on whether the circumstances of the time afford him the stimulus and the opportunity for developing the line of activ-

ity in which he is gifted" (1967, 1:5–6; cf. Dewey 1963). The behavior of individuals, another institutionalist wrote, was, "standardized by existing institutions, and that what commonly appears to be intrinsic in human nature, and therefore axiomatic and unchangeable, is after all merely a characteristic of institutions" (Edie 1927, 408).

The institutionalists' effort to replace the individualistic vision with a social one, like many other battles, had two aspects: defensive and offensive. While the contenders looked for evidence to support their own positions, they did not neglect the search after "incriminating evidence" against their opponents. An example is Edie's claim that the belief of orthodox economists in individualism was itself a cultural product. He recruited "more recent social thinkers" to convince the readers that individualism was just an appearance which concealed the lack of personal freedom:

> For long, philosophers assumed that individualism meant perfect freedom to set independently of all restraints. However, more recent social thinkers look upon individualism as a form of domination wherein the subjects are commonly ignorant of the taboos, customs, and precepts which dictate their conduct. The so-called freedom of *laissez-faire* has too often been in reality merely a slavish obedience to traditional standards of choice and outworn institutional arrangements (1927, 436).

The third element in the attempt to break the neoclassical network involved the conventional assumption that work was pain (in the Benthamite terminology) that people wished to minimize. Orthodox theory assumed that labor was irksome, that is, that people by nature did not like to work and worked as little as they could. Institutionalists, following Saint-Simon, Fourier, and many others, challenged this view. Work, they reasoned, occupied a large part of our life. It was therefore "irrational" to ignore it in calculating human welfare. Paul Douglas, for instance, said that "no allowance is made [in orthodox theory] for the possibility that some of the desires . . . may be satisfied either in whole or in part by the process of the work itself" (1924, 154). Mitchell explained that for past economists the maxim that "man was condemned to eat his bread in the sweat of his brow . . . was a hard fact which the economist had to accept." Human welfare could be maximized only by "enhancing the output of goods . . . not in making the process of production pleasant" (1924, 31–32). Mitchell rejected this view and asserted that economists should care not only for outputs, but for the quality of work as well. John Maurice Clark also mobilized modern ethics, which "emphasizes rather the well-rounded development and use of human faculties." In his view, the basic needs "have successively worked themselves past the point of diminishing return." New incentives for work must therefore focus "on other things than wage scales" (1924, 89; see also Edie 1927, 431). Neoclassical analysis has been based on total separation of consumption and production. The satisfaction begotten by work could be introduced into neoclassical theory, but that required a major revision of the theory and has never been realized.[2] The institutionalists thought that such revisions were essential and critical.

Rearranging the Boundaries of Economics: The Neoclassical Defense

Whereas we found many participants who defended the deductive approach, virtually no economist in the materials I examined came out to defend the assumptions of hedonism and rationality. Extreme enunciations of individualism, hedonism, and rationalism could be found in the ideological and political discourse of the interwar era. But the absence of similar declarations from the professional discourse in economics undoubtedly indicates that in that arena hedonism had lost its grip. That does not mean, though, that neoclassical economists abandoned the theories that hedonism had been associated with earlier.

Raymond Bye's position reflects the way neoclassical economists looked at the issue in the 1920s. He first cited the criticism that orthodox theory was "based on a concept of rational, hedonistic consumers whom modern psychology shows to be non-existent." Buyers, he admitted, were not "economic men" who "carefully [weighed] each dollar's purchase against possible alternative purchases; they spend irrationally, foolishly, swayed by various emotions, advertising, social customs, fads, imitation, and what not" (1924, 276). His defense of neoclassical theory was simply to deny any connection between *contemporary* neoclassical theory and the views that the institutionalists imputed to them: "Few, if any, economists of repute now hold the marginal utility theory in its original form," he argued (ibid.). "The marginal utility theory in its original form" is a reference to Jevons's patently hedonistic formulations. But Bye maintained that Jevons's contribution could stand alone without its hedonistic underpinnings:

> Whether human beings are rational or irrational . . . they make their purchases in accordance with the law of demand. . . . The marginal utility theory erred in assuming that it constituted a complete explanation, and that utilities were evaluated by purchasers in a rational way. Many economists have now discarded these assumptions. . . . The demand for commodities no longer appears as a rational manifestation of economic men guided by utility, but a mere

working out of certain characteristics of human choices which explain their observed tendency to follow the law of demand in a market. . . . It is now possible to set forth the theory of demand without any taint of hedonism (ibid., 277–78).

The "law of demand" simply states that people would buy less of a commodity if its price rises. This is a simple observation that could be explained by modern psychological variables without assuming that people make complex calculations before any economic decision.[3] The spirit behind Bye's quote is quite obvious. Hedonism and rationality had been long-standing allies of orthodox economists. Now that they went out of fashion, the supporters of orthodox theory tried to dissociate themselves from them. "The rationalistic assumption of human conduct," Bye said, "was never necessary to economic theory; it was simply dragged in because hedonism was the dominant philosophy." Therefore, he concluded, we could correct their psychological explanations to accord with modern psychological views and thus maintain their theoretical generalizations about demand (ibid., 278).

Bye's defense was in accord with the Marshallian teaching. Jevons thought that it was possible, in principle, to ascertain the exact utility a consumer had from a certain good, so that it would be possible to say that she enjoyed a cup of tea 2.35 times more than a cup of coffee. The marginal analysis of consumption postulated that the satisfaction people got from any additional unit of the same good was decreasing as they had more of that good, and this was supposed to be demonstrated empirically. The problem that marginalist economists faced was that nobody at that time managed to measure utility, a fact that served as a powerful weapon in the hands of their enemies. Marshall, therefore, tried to retain the theory by cutting its bonds to hedonistic and rationalistic psychology. His solution, recounted by Bye, was to assume decreasing utility on the basis of observations and common sense without assuming that human beings were rational and hedonistic in all their endeavors. This strategy excluded psychology from economics: "In fact, a complete theory of human choices is not essential to the theory of value. Why men buy what they do is an interesting query, an answer to which is well worth seeking. . . . But for most purposes of economic theory the choices can be taken for granted, and their explanations left to the psychologist" (Bye 1924, 278).

Adam Smith, Maltus, J. S. Mill, Marx, and scores of other early economic thinkers dealt with human needs and desires in length. The early marginalists, and especially Jevons, emphasized psychological motivations even more than their classical predecessors. The attempt to banish such motivations was therefore an abrupt turnabout in the development of economic theory. The fact that neoclassical economists were ready to adopt such a drastic change indicates that human nature was a very powerful ally in the institutionalist alliance. It constituted a real threat for the old doctrine and the only way out was by changing the rules of the game and cutting off the psychological wing.

The exclusion of psychological issues from economics is an example of a strategy which can be seen occasionally in struggles between competing networks. The strategy is to define the scope of a field according to what the network does best. Psychological motivations were legitimate subjects in economics from Adam Smith to Jevons. But as the advocates of the theory had run into difficulties in dealing with them satisfactorily, they tried to rule out the whole issue. This strategy, which has actually been followed by post–World War II economists up to the present,[4] was, of course, fiercely resisted by institutionalists. Referring to formulations similar to those of Bye, John M. Clark derided this trend:

> Some forms of the doctrine of marginal utility are even more clearly tautological. Our old friend, the "economic man," is becoming very self-conscious and bafflingly non-committal. Instead of introducing himself to his readers with his old-time freedom, he says: "I may behave one way and I may behave another. . . . You must take my choices as you find them; I choose as I choose and that is all you really need to know." The poor thing has been told that his [hedonistic] psychology is all wrong, and he is gamely trying to get on without any [psychology] and still perform as many as possible of his accustomed tasks. He has become a symbol (1924, 77).[5]

One of the main themes in A. B. Wolfe's essay was exactly the importance of psychology in economic science. His essay "The Demand for a Scientific Economics" included a section on "Psychological Data in Scientific Economics" (1924, 461–69). The main goal in that section was to fight the inclination of some economists to eschew psychological data because it was " 'subjective,' indeterminable, and unamenable to direct observation." "The function of the economist, according to this view," Wolfe explained, was "to describe the external, superficial organization and operation of the price system. Study of its motivation is ruled out" (ibid., 461–62). Wolfe argued against such a position that "an adequate psychological knowledge is a *sine qua non* of a realistic, a true, and a functional economics" (ibid., 468). It is worthwhile to quote his reasoning at length:

> No one regards economic organization as a purposeless mechanism. Describe it without reference to its functions and you have something as barren as Spencer's sociology. One cannot any more describe and understand the functional process of an economic society without considering the motives which

actuate them than one could explain the operation of a steam engine without mentioning the steam. . . . Human motives . . . come in as links in the casual sequence determining human behavior, economic behavior included. A non-psychological economics must therefore be regarded as either a superficial fragment, or as positively non-scientific. It is Hamlet with Hamlet left out (ibid., 462, 466; see also Mitchell 1924, 23).

Wolfe offered an alternative vision of the scope of economics. Economists, he believed, should study everything that had bearing on the economy, including suggestion, imitation, emulation, habit, customs, class standards, class prejudice, moral, political, and aesthetic sentiments, rivalry, desire for recognition, gregariousness, balked dispositions, suppressions, repressions, and sublimations. This is only a partial list of psychological motivations that "must come in for recognition and evaluation whenever observation shows them to have significant influence" on production, market prices, distribution of income, and consumption (1924, 465).

There were several topics that the institutionalists hoped to advance by incorporating psychological factors, and the most obvious one was the question of how preferences were determined. Neoclassical economists left this question aside for other disciplines to explain. The institutionalists brought this as a glaring neglect of neoclassical economics to perform its responsibility of explaining economic behavior: "Instead of taking wants for granted . . . according to . . . traditional economics, present-day students [i.e., the institutionalists—Y. Y.] feel it necessary to take them as primary problems of inquiry and analysis" (Edie 1927, 430–31). Another topic was the study of business cycles. J. C. Cobb argued, for example, that Mitchell's book from 1927 on business cycles "clearly shows the importance of psychological factors . . . and conclusively proves the need for the development of quantitatively stated psychological data" (1928, 66). By marshaling tastes and behavioral determinants of business cycles, institutionalists implied that even if we wanted to explain narrow economic matters, we must employ psychological knowledge quite massively.[6]

Definitions of scope of scientific field cannot be "proven" or "confirmed." Controversies over scope, like controversies over definitions, can be waged only by reference to the usefulness of alternative definitions. Neoclassicists sided with the exclusion of psychological factors, among other reasons, because they did not believe in the possibility of studying such factors "scientifically." Psychological issues, they said, were " 'subjective,' indeterminable, and unamenable to direct observation" (Wolfe 1924, 461). This takes us back to the argument over the meaning of science, on which we focused in the previous chapter. Wolfe (1924, 462), in response to the exclusion of psychology, first charged that the scope suggested by Bye was "barren." Wolfe also presented a very rosy picture of the prospects of the proposed scope to engender achievements which were useful, either for specific recognized problems in the field or for other social groups whose support and resources were valuable. In chapter 7 we will see how institutionalists recruited usefulness to promote their definition of the scope of economics.

Social Institutions as Allies

In this section I deal with another primary component of the institutionalist network, which is closely connected to human beings. This component is the social organization that human creatures construct. If economics was a science of human behavior, and human behavior depended on social organization, it followed that social organization was a vital variable in explaining economic behavior. The same conclusion could be reached from the acknowledgment that many noneconomic motives affected economic behavior. If people were influenced by religious sentiments, political affiliation, and cultural urges, then religious, political, and cultural institutions must be included in the stories economists told. That is why social institutions were also brought by institutionalists into their struggle against neoclassical economics. And, of course, this is why they are called "institutionalists."

Originally, the term "institutionalist" was restricted to the work of Thorstein Veblen. Other names suggested by the leaders of the movement conveyed the same idea: "collective economics" (Commons); "social economics" (J. M. Clark); "administrative economics" (Means); or "holistic economics," as suggested by Gruchy to include all the variants of institutionalism (1947, 5). All these titles indicate an attempt of institutionalists to tie the broader society and its institutions to their alliance in order to support the claim that institutional economics was a broader and a more useful approach than what the competitors had offered.

The institutionalists promoted a collectivist approach to social life to replace the individualistic tendency of neoclassical economics. According to the latter, "a bargain between two persons concerns primarily those two persons" (J. M. Clark 1924, 91–92). Clark suggested instead that "the most important effects of private bargain consist in the part they play in the qualitative evolution of the personal characteristics and social relations of the human race at large." Such a premise, if accepted, would wipe out all the conclusions of neoclassical theory. The whole structure of orthodox theory has been built on the assumption that "every person is an island." The welfare of one individual does not depend on the welfare of another. Hence, exchange between two individuals is their own business. But Clark asserted exactly the opposite: what two individuals made between them *did* influence the whole society. Clark gave two examples: the business cycle and labor relations. These were two "community problems," and they could not be left to individuals.

Morris Copeland employed an analogy of society with a living organism. He hesitated "to personify the group" but claimed that such an analogy was helpful because there were several points of resemblance between groups and organisms. First, "individuals like the cells of the organism are dependent on each other." Second, "the group has certain characteristics . . . in a large measure independently of the constituent individuals involved." And finally, "certain sub-groups . . . [can] be construed as having special functions" (1924, 129–30).[7] Such a conception of society is totally opposed to the neoclassical view. If individuals were dependent on each other, then they would not care only for their own personal welfare, as the neoclassical analysis assumed.

Lionel Edie said that the collectivist notion "may at first glance seem harmless and unimportant" for the conventional analysis of neoclassical analysis. But when this notion was "applied vigorously in all phases of economic thought, there is reason to believe that it points the way to a profound reconstruction all along the line" (1927, 408). Edie emphasized two implications. First, it meant that social change could be achieved only by changing institutions: "Each individual has to learn the entire modern cultural pattern from birth," and therefore, "the only chance of modifying the behavior of his own or future generations is to modify external institutions" (ibid., 407). As Albert B. Wolfe explained, "the individual is helpless, by himself," so that "the creation of opportunity is essentially a cooperative social process and function" (1924, 481). Second, Edie called attention to the "resistance of institutions to internal change" as illuminated by recent ethnographic studies. Such resistance included "standards of industrial behavior" that tended "to persist long after they have outlived their usefulness" (1927, 407). The "resistance of institutions to internal change" was recruited to show the inadequacy of the neoclassical approach, which implied that economic agents instantaneously adjusted to new conditions in the market. This was a derivative from the assumption of rationality implicit in neoclassical analysis even when neoclassicists distanced themselves from that assumption. Edie therefore suggested that we needed "careful historical analysis of our chief economic institutions . . . [in order to] explain, first, how economic processes have developed out of the past; second, how they function in the present; and third, how they may be modified and controlled in the future" (ibid., 414).

The offensive against the neoclassical approach was carried more aggressively by Sumner Slichter. Slichter complained that economic theorists "consciously endeavor to prevent social institutions and usages from intruding themselves into the formulation of economic doctrines" (1924, 304). "Machinery, science applied to industry, corporations, trade unions, cooperative organizations, trade . . . associations, the credit system, [and] commercial and investment bankers" were treated, he said, as they had been treated in "the theories of Adam Smith" (ibid.), although all these factors had changed substantially since Adam Smith. The implication was obvious: the orthodox doctrine was severely inappropriate, because it ignored the most basic elements of the economic system. Without dealing with institutions such as unions, trade associations, banks, and so forth, one could not understand economic phenomena. J. M. Clark exemplified this by pointing out that in the modern economy "the dominant actors in economic life are corporations and unions." The role of individual entrepreneurs declined, and the function of the entrepreneur had "become split up into a large group of functions, shared by different persons and even by different corporate entities" (1924, 93). Under such circumstances, "the ability of corporate organizations to stimulate loyalty, or to make loyal behavior the best policy, or both, is the vital necessity of private enterprise" (ibid.). Although it was possible, as in present-day theory, to assume that the firm behaved like an individual, it was also clear that the relations among the various components of complex organizations complicated the behavior of such organizations and caused deviations from what was expected to maximize profits. This line of argumentation carries us to the next chapter, where I discuss the recruitment of "the economy" itself into the ongoing struggle between the two approaches.

Conclusions: Changing Concepts of Human Nature

Hedonism and rationality became part of the black box titled "Human Nature" in the structure of the classical paradigm during the first three-quarters of the nineteenth century, and it was not removed from that structure with the transition to neoclassical economics during the last decades of the century. But "Human Nature" was a black box which contenders could easily challenge, because even lay people had firsthand experience of it. Scientists may claim to have "better," "scientific" tools to study human nature, and therefore they assert that their knowledge is more valid than commonsense knowledge. But those who disagree with the dominant views *inside* the scientific community can always mobilize common knowledge against the scientific expertise. It follows that the content of the black box labeled "Human Nature" was very sensitive to general cultural views of what human nature is. It was a subject that scientists could not monopolize, and therefore it was one channel through which values and ideologies could easily intrude into the realm of social science.

The institutionalists capitalized on this vulnerability in the orthodox structure of black boxes. Based on what common people knew from daily life, institutionalists recruited three chief allies against the economic man. First, they reminded their readers that people wished to achieve much wider goals than their own material success. Often, they told us, people cared more for the welfare of their family members or of the whole community than for their own selfish interests. This was a point with which most readers—including practicing economists, new graduate students, and the public at large—agreed based on their own experience. It was therefore easy to cast doubt on any theory that seemed to run against this accepted knowledge.

Second, irrational behavior was brought in together with a new concept of human beings as social creatures. Again, this idea was employed in order to convince the readers that the conclusions drawn from neoclassical analysis were not valid. People did not maximize given universal goals, nor did they seek idiosyncratic interests of their own. Rather, they pursued socially learned goals. Economists could neither take human desires as given nor could they leave the study of those desires to others; they must include these desires in their explanations. The third ally was the idea that labor was not only a pain to be endured, but also a source of satisfaction, an argument that could have revolutionized economic theory if it had been accepted.

The advocates of neoclassical theory chose not to challenge these claims. This decision indicates that the allies recruited by the institutionalists, that is, the institutionalist conception of human beings and their interaction, were well established within the larger intellectual community of that period. The neoclassicists either agreed with those conceptions or realized it would not benefit them to challenge them. Whatever the motivation—intellectual or political—their acceptance further reinforced the new view of people and society and turned it into a black box. Rather than attacking this new black box, they denied its supposedly pernicious implications. Orthodox theory, they said, did not depend on antiquated hedonistic psychology, although it was historically associated with such an approach. In fact, it did not rely upon *any* psychological approach. It merely laid out universal laws of behavior which are useful for the analysis of behavior everywhere and at any time. This strategy prompted a struggle over the scope of economics: should economists deal with the determination of psychological components that bore upon economic behavior, or should they leave it to other students of human behavior? Institutionalists thought that economic analyses must deal with *all* determinants of behavior if they wished to understand *economic* behavior. Neoclassicists maintained that division of labor would be more efficient in the production of knowledge. Obviously, this is a choice that cannot be resolved by following universal and objective rules. It is dependent on the *goals* of science, not on "facts" and logic.

Six

The Free Market on Trial: The Struggle over the Gap between Reality and Theory

Every individual is continually exerting himself to find out the most advantageous employment for whatever capital he can command. It is his own advantage, indeed, and not that of the society, which he has in view. But the study of his own advantage naturally, or rather necessarily, leads him to prefer that employment which is most advantageous to the society.
  (Adam Smith, *An Inquiry into the Nature*
    and Causes of The Wealth of Nations)

The business man's place in the economy of nature is to "make money," not to produce goods. The production of goods is a mechanical process, incidental to the making of money; whereas the making of money is a pecuniary operation, carried on by bargain and sale, not by mechanical appliances and powers. . . . the less use a business man can make of the mechanical appliances and powers under his charge, and the smaller a product he can contrive to turn out for a given return in terms of price, the better it suits his purpose. The highest achievement in business is the nearest approach to getting something for nothing.
  (Thorstein Veblen, *The Vested Interest and*
    the Common Man)

WHEN TWO CAMPS compete in science, each party tries to show the inadequacy of the black boxes of its rival in order to undermine the whole network of allies assembled by that rival. This, however, is not an easy task. In the complex and abstract domain of science, the meaning and significance of each black box can be comprehended only in the context of the whole enterprise. Uncommitted practitioners or uninitiated novices whose souls the contenders wish to conquer cannot be convinced in the validity of the black boxes before they choose one party and undergo its training course. Yet practitioners may appeal to common sense and argue that certain arguments of the other party are obviously invalid. This type of reasoning is especially relevant in economics, a science whose materials

are part of our everyday life. Institutionalists exploited this fact and attacked orthodox economics as an approach whose inadequacy and in-
compatibility with the known facts were notoriously obvious. The conditions of the economy in real life, they maintained, were so far from the
assumptions of neoclassical theory, that a theory based on those assumptions was not useful *even as an approximation* to reality.

The neoclassical analysis started with the model of perfect competition. By perfect competition economists meant first of all the lack of concerted action in the form of monopolies, oligopolies, trusts, labor unions,
and governmental regulation. It was assumed that there were countless
sellers and buyers in each market, and because they all competed against
each other, no single buyer or seller had the power to establish the prices
they wanted to pay or get. No firm, for example, could charge a price
higher than production costs, because if it did, it would be in the interest
of other firms to offer a slightly lower price and "steal" the other's firm's
clients (e.g., Samuelson and Nordhaus 1989, 41–43, 541). Only when
firms united together (or are too few to begin with) and had no competition could they dictate any price they deemed desirable or at least "have
some measure of control over the price of the good" (ibid., 567). The
same was true about workers who could control wages only if they were
organized (ibid., 701–2). The model of perfect competition also assumed
that economic actors had *perfect knowledge* about the goods offered in
the market, their qualities, their exact properties, and their prices. There
was also a hidden assumption that all goods and services were *marketable*, and that each supplier got a full payment for the service or good she
provided (ibid., 44). There were no free lunches, unless the service or
good was so abundant as to satisfy all wants, nor could someone cause
injuries to others without compensating for it (ibid., 771–73).

By recruiting the irrationality of human beings, the institutionalists already challenged the utility and validity of neoclassical analysis. If individuals were susceptible to "irrational" urges and pressures, than the
availability of perfect knowledge would not suffice to ensure maximum
welfare. But it was possible to tighten the siege on the orthodox doctrine
by showing that even *if* people were rational, the neoclassical model
would not work due to *structural* features of the economy. And indeed,
such a claim constituted an important element in the institutionalist critique on neoclassical doctrine.

Another aspect of neoclassical theory was the proposition that the best
results for the economy as a whole could be achieved by perfect competition. This was based on the assumption that rational individuals, either as
firm-owners or as consumers, were best qualified to find the best combinations both in production and consumption. The competition in the
marketplace promised that they would be able to discriminate between

factors of production, workers, and products and find the "best buy," thus promoting efficiency in the economy. This view was elaborated and refined in the "new welfare economics" of the 1940s and 1950s, but the roots of this view were in the work of Adam Smith, who argued that when an individual "intends only his own gain . . . is in this . . . led by an invisible hand to promote an end which was no part of his intention" (Smith 1961, 166).[1]

The conclusion that "common welfare coincided with the private interests of each individual under conditions of free competition" (Copeland 1924, 107) was derived logically, and hence, unassailably, from certain simple assumptions. The institutionalist attack was aimed, therefore, at these assumptions, rather than at the conclusion itself. The institutionalists' attacks on the assumptions of rationality and hedonism and on the individualistic nature of orthodox theory were already described in the previous chapter. This chapter deals with the institutionalist attacks aimed at the gap between the structure of the economy and the way this structure is postulated by neoclassical theory. Neoclassicists, though, did not pretend that the real economy was perfectly competitive. Deviations in the forms of monopolies, government regulations, externalities, and imperfect knowledge were well known to everybody. The neoclassicists argued, however, that abstract models were just approximations to real-life conditions. There were factors which were not included in the theory, and which accounted for the observable deviations of the real world from the predictions made by theoretical reasoning. Yet they insisted that the model of the economy suggested by neoclassical theory was good enough to help us make sense of economic phenomena, because it included the most essential insights into the workings of the economy.

To refute this last argument, it was not enough to present just a few real-life cases which contradicted the theory. Statements like "all swans are white"—to take a famous example—or "all industries are competitive," can be convincingly challenged by one black swan, or one uncompetitive industry. It is inherently more difficult, however, to challenge a statement in the form of "*most* industries are competitive *enough* to be *usefully* analyzed by a model of perfect competition"—the type of assertion made by interwar neoclassicists (cf. McCloskey 1994b, 136). In order to defend their own approach, and to cast doubts on the neoclassical structure, institutionalists had, therefore, to persuade their colleagues that the deviations from perfect competition were *too numerous* and *too systematic,* thus making the neoclassical model of small or no use *even as an approximation.* Some of the institutionalists believed that the perfect competition model had been useful in the past, when the economy had been simpler. Others did not accept even this. But they all agreed that "the rapid technical and institutional development of the last century and a half renders it impossible any longer to accept the eighteenth-century analysis of the efficacy of free enterprise" (Slichter 1924, 308). The attempt of institutionalists to reopen the black box of "approximately competitive markets" is the subject of this chapter.

The gist of the institutionalist critique is provided in Morris Copeland's essay. Copeland saw some truth in the classical approach, which emphasized the efficiency achieved, in principle, by a market economy. But he also saw much truth in the socialist view, which has "more frequently looked on the darker side of life and found waste of natural resources, chronic idleness of people and of industrial apparatus; nonliving wages, insecurity of workers, wasteful use of their services and inhuman treatment; diversion of human effort into the production of armaments, luxuries, adulterated products and advertising; ample incomes to nonworkers; and autocratic control by a capitalist minority whose title is hereditary" (1924, 107; cf. Taylor 1928). Each of these items—waste, idleness, nonliving wages, and so forth—was mobilized by the institutionalists to unsettle and destroy the orthodox network.

The first section of this chapter focuses on evidence showing that market values were not a good measure of the social values of goods and services, thus shooting at the core of the theory of value on which the whole neoclassical edifice is built. The second part deals with economic agents' systematic lack of relevant knowledge, another pillar of the same edifice. The following section concentrates on the waste caused by competition itself, a reversal of the most important political implication of neoclassicism. The fourth section is concerned with power disparity in the economy and its consequences. The issue is not the injustice of the system but the loss of productive capacity due to inherent labor unrest and lack of cooperation. The fifth and last part of the chapter considers some differences among institutionalists and the nature of the neoclassical response to the attack at this front. Neoclassicists actually said very little about these subjects, and this fact will be discussed in this concluding part as well.

Making Money and Making Goods: Nonmonetary Evaluation of Welfare

The institutionalists offered an alternative framework for the model of free-market and perfect competition. They made a fundamental distinction between the practice of extracting pecuniary profits, on the one hand, and the production of goods and services, on the other. This distinction was one of the main themes of Thorstein Veblen's approach, in which we can find polar distinctions between "pecuniary employment" and "industrial employment," or between "business enterprise" and "the machine process," or "vendibility" and "serviceability" (Blaug 1986a, 256). The first concepts in these couples refer to the profit motive, and the second to the actual process of real production. Such a distinction is not feasible in the neoclassical framework. Under the basic assumptions of the latter, only "serviceable" things can be sold. Every productive factor must be *fairly* remunerated for its services. Given free competition, any factor which is unpaid can move, or be moved, to places where the remuneration is higher. For a similar reason, it is impossible to have unfair profits. Factors of production cannot be rewarded *more* than their economic value, because any producer who pays them more would end up with higher costs, and, hence, uncompetitive prices. Income can only be earned fairly, and only for productive services.

Morris Albert Copeland's essay "Communities of Economic Interest and the Price System" was concerned specifically with the divergence between prices and values. Such divergence was caused by the fact that the price system did not reflect real gains and costs:

> If our property and other civil-economic rights were such that each person or organization, in entering or refraining from any transaction, had to bear all costs and could reap all the gains of so doing, we should probably be safe in assuming the coincidence of individual interests and the common welfare. . . . Under such circumstances consumers' demand might shape business policy rather than conversely, and technological efficiency might be the chief task of business management. But it is obvious that things are far otherwise today (1924, 114–15).

Because of this situation, "making money does not *necessarily* mean making goods nor making goods *always* mean making money" (ibid., 114; Taylor 1928). The general welfare, Copeland declared, was not ensured any more by the practice of individuals who cared only for their own self-interests. Paraphrasing Smith, Copeland said: "Each, seeking his own general gain, helps to bring about a result which was no part of his intention. But that result is not always the common good of the self-seeking parties; it may be a common misfortune" (Copeland 1924, 114). Lionel Edie underlined the fact that "what each can get for himself depended less on his efficiency in producing goods for the use of others than on his efficiency in encroaching upon the gains of others by driving shrewd price bargains" (1927, 425).[2] The fact that people could gain by speculation, manipulation, or sheer fraud was in itself a strong argument in behalf of the institutionalist thesis. The neoclassical approach downplayed these practices because under the assumptions of perfect knowledge and rationality, people could not be gullible. But the question was still open whether such deviations were frequent enough to make the model unavailing. Institutionalists therefore brought examples from the real world—recruited allies, in the Latourian language—to prove their point.

The first ally was the existence of advertising and salesmanship. The very existence of these practices is somewhat anomalous in the neoclassical framework. Advertising makes sense as a way of disseminating information, but it is clear from the way it is done that the target of the advertisers is not only to inform consumers about their options but also to shape their preferences. Slichter, for example, argued that "modern business . . . spends such huge sums and employs so many experts in persuading men to attach far more weight than they otherwise would" to various luxurious commodities (1924, 312). An "impressive array of specialists—advertising copy writers, press agents, artists, psychologists, salesmen, window dressers, and others," make it "their life work to shape men's desires in the interest not of mankind but of business" (ibid., 310). The energies of these specialists are thus being used for unproductive purposes, while consumers are being duped to waste their income on useless products. Moreover, enterprises intentionally create pain, as is the case with fashion, which is purchased "less to gain pleasure than to avoid the discomfort of being out of fashion" (ibid., 312). Lionel Edie concluded on the basis of these arguments that "the rational element in our choice-making loses its supremacy," because of the "very elaborate technique for dominating the mind of the buyer by appeal to his irrational nature" (Edie 1927, 431, 433).

The existence of each of the occupations related to salesmanship and advertising, our everyday experience of buying things we do not need, and the huge amounts spent by people on things that appear to have little use were brought into the trial of strength to give more credibility to the idea that more than a few business practices caused harm to society. The fact that institutionalists wanted to underline here was not only the irrationality of consumers but also the *shrewd rationality* of business entrepreneurs, who employed science and specialists "to take advantage of every failure on [the consumers'] part to guard their interests." "Prospective buyers are minutely studied and classified. Every desire, hope, fear, whim, prejudice, or impulse which might possibly lead people to buy is sought out" (Slichter 1924, 321–22; cf. Mitchell 1924, 30; Copeland 1924, 113; A. B. Wolfe 1924, 467). Advertising and salesmanship were not a minor phenomenon in the modern economy but a central feature thereof that must be considered in the evaluation of its functioning.[3]

Pollution and other environmental hazards were another ally of institutionalism. Here the argument was simple: if enterprises were not required to pay for pollution, *rational* businesspersons would find it "profitable to pollute the air or the streams, [and] to locate their plants regardless of the effect upon the value of adjoining property" (Slichter 1924, 314). This was also the case with the safety of workers: rational employers would rather compromise the health of their employees than their profits. These examples showed that the market mechanism did not guarantee social welfare. "Industrial accidents, industrial disease, pollution of the air by smoke or of the streams by discharge of waste in them are among the costs which are easily preventable but which it usually pays industrial establishments to let fall on others rather than to eliminate" (ibid., 345; see also Mitchell 1924, 21–22; Copeland 1924, 110).[4] Overutilization of natural resources was another fact that institutionalists tied to their offensive to prove the inefficiency of the free market. In the case of natural resources, Slichter claimed that free competition provided "no incentive to discriminate against enterprises which disregard the general welfare" by overutilization of these resources (1924, 309). The market mechanism encouraged rational entrepreneurs to think about their short-term individual interests and blinded even rational people as far as long-run interests were regarded (see also Copeland 1924, 114).[5]

Another fact which was brought to support the general thesis that markets discouraged efficiency was the practice of firing workers during recessions. In his path-breaking *Studies in the Economics of Overhead Costs* (pub. 1923), John Maurice Clark argued that from the social welfare point of view, it was better to employ all workers during depressions, while for each firm it was profitable to dismiss them. Overhead (or indirect) costs are fixed costs which firms have to pay regardless of how much they produce. When a firm invests in capital in the form of machinery or buildings, it has to pay for these machines even if it does not utilize them. Labor is similar in the sense that one has to incur costs in order to reproduce it, that is, to keep it alive. But unlike machines, employers can discharge workers during recessions and let them reproduce themselves at no cost to the employers (Edie 1927, 425; Slichter 1924, 314; Copeland 1924, 107, 134). Beyond the evident unfairness of this practice, it involved a huge waste for society at large. Resources are idle because it does not pay for private owners to use them, but it is obvious that by using these resources, the society as a whole could be better off (cf. Copeland 1924, 111).

Advertising, salesmanship, pollution, lack of occupational safety, overutilization of natural resources, and depressions, were the more frequent examples given by institutionalists to deviations from general welfare due to the profit motive of private interests. The modern economic language specifies the term "externalities" to all those cases in which someone creates a nuisance for which she is not required to pay (negative externalities; external diseconomies), or in which someone is not paid for her services (positive externalities; external economies) (Nicholson 1990, chap. 21). The modern neoclassical solution is to allow for state regulation to overcome this apparent market failure, either by establishing explicit guidelines and standards of pollution, by the use of taxes, or by simulating the market by selling a limited number of pollution permits (ibid., 617–29). In any case, externalities are perceived as exceptional cases in which the market fails to perform its regulatory duties. It is a concept whose very existence reinforces the image of the market as the most efficient mechanism of allocation and distribution.

For the institutionalists, the concept of externalities—if they had been familiar with this jargon—was much wider. Advertising also "pollutes" the minds of citizens by creating wants where they have not existed before. Firing a worker also creates a damage which the firm does not have to pay for (e.g., discomfort for the worker, extra burden on welfare agencies, increasing crime, riots). Similarly, overutilization of natural resources decreases the welfare of future generations without any compensation for this injury by present-day producers and consumers. In sum, the institutionalists perceived externalities as *the main characteristic of modern economies*, a feature that impeded the ability of the invisible hand to foster optimal welfare. A *visible* hand of rational planning was needed to secure the best economic results.[6]

Lack of Knowledge and Its Implications

The divergence of private interests from public interests was enough, in Slichter's mind, "to indicate quite conclusively that, *even were men fully informed of their own interests and entirely rational in their choices*, the value of competition as a protective agency would be extremely limited" (1924, 314; italics in original). But the institutionalists marshaled other allies in an attempt to make their network stronger. Their next target was the assumption of perfect knowledge, which lay in the heart of the perfect-competition framework. The goal was again to show that the divergence from neoclassical assumptions was neither local nor trivial. Economic actors, they said, lacked *basic* knowledge on *crucial* issues. Furthermore, given the complexity of required information and time constraints, it was unlikely that they would ever have useful knowledge on many issues.[7]

The attempt to bolster the chronic lack of knowledge as a black box occupied a significant part of Slichter's essay (1924), and I follow his arguments. Slichter began with business enterprises, who among all economic actors were best qualified to gather the information that was relevant to their activities. And indeed, he argued, they could "afford to investigate goods, prices, the existing and prospective conditions of it of buyers." Yet there was "much information of vital importance . . . which even they [were] unable to gather." Slichter gave the example of "determining the competency of applicants for employment." Since employers often could not discern the more qualified workers, "the incentive which [wage earners] have to develop skill is very substantially diminished" (1924, 314–15). This was a systematic deviation that might keep the economy far away from the desired optimum.[8]

Business enterprises were the most likely to have valid knowledge on their practices. "When we turn to wage earners and consumers," he continued, "we find a far more serious absence of requisite market information" (ibid., 315). Slichter first examined the ability of workers to choose rationally the best work for them, based on wages, work conditions, and accident and disease rates. Concerning wages, he said that "while there are statistics on wages, it is compiled only at the industry level, and the findings are not given in a way that common workers can understand it" (ibid.). "Information concerning the physical and nervous strain of the work in different occupations, and in different plants is almost totally lacking." Workmen's compensation acts "resulted in the collection of voluminous statistics on industrial accidents," but these statistics "relate in large degree to *industries* rather than to specific occupations or jobs, and . . . the existing data do not show the relative hazards in individual plants." Moreover, the available data was not brought to the attention of workers and have not been "reduced to a simplified, understandable form so that workers can easily compare the risks of different employments" (ibid., 316–17). On the risk of industrial disease, he added, there was almost no information whatsoever.

We should note here the way that Slichter lined up his allies. First, there were no statistics. Second, if there were, then they were not in a form that workers could understand; and if they could understand them, then they were too general to inform them about the specific conditions necessary for rational decisions about their specific jobs. Furthermore, this was true not only for wages, but also for accident rates. With regard to frequencies of industrial diseases, work-related strain, and unemployment, the information was even scarcer. Without this vital information, workers could not maximize their utility in the way that neoclassical theory assumed, and again, this applied to the *whole* labor force. *The divergence from perfect competition was pervasive.*

Slichter then added the third element of this front: consumers also lacked vital information about the products they bought: "The consumer . . . has so many things to purchase and so little time in which to buy them, that [collecting information] is impracticable. Often the appraisal of quality requires technical training and knowledge and, not infrequently, the making of tests which, of course, are usually out of the question (ibid., 318–19). Consumers did learn from experience, Slichter admitted, but this was a "slow and costly way of discovering which goods are superior" (ibid., 320). The consumer, he further observed, did not maximize his utility: "If he is reasonably well satisfied with a certain brand, he is likely to continue to use it rather than to experiment with others"—a precursory expression of the satisficing notion that Herbert Simon introduced into economics many years later.

Slichter's allies—the difficulty of finding out the skills of new workers, the lack of sufficient knowledge on the jobs we are offered, our inability to consider all brands and test their quality—were known facts from personal experience, and their recruitment contributed to the effort to taint the assumption of perfect knowledge as too unrealistic to be useful. But there is one more aspect of the absence of information that is less visible. This is "the extraordinary uncertainty in the demand for goods which exists despite the great need for them, the unprecedentedly great ability to buy them, and the extensive efforts made by business to stimulate purchasing" (Slichter, 1924, 328). Macroeconomic ups and downs, the business cycles, leave business enterprises uncertain concerning the demand for their goods and services. Free competitive enterprise "is peculiarly unfitted to function well in the face of uncertain demand, and at the slightest uncertainty it restricts production." Hence, "chronic underproduction *is an inherent characteristic of free enterprise*" (ibid., 330, italics added).

Competition as a Source of Waste

Thus far the institutionalist attack challenged two key black boxes of neoclassical analysis: they maintained that market prices did not reflect real values, and they claimed that economic actors did not have the information necessary to make rational decisions. In this section we will see how they assaulted another sacrosanct principle of the orthodox doctrine. Competition, they argued, led to waste of resources. This was, of course, a sharp contrast to orthodox teaching, which had always perceived competition as an unqualified blessing and offered a return to a regime of competition as a solution for most economic problems.

In his essay, Slichter listed several reasons why markets were not efficient. First, "in the field of marketing, competition usually results in an enhancement rather than a reduction of expenses" (1924, 342). "The expenditures of each are likely to nullify those of the others so that the result is about the same distribution of business but higher selling costs to all" (ibid., 343).[9] Another problem was the irresponsible risks taken by firms under stiff competition. This was, according to Slichter, the root of the crisis in banking, a crisis which was solved only by abandoning the principle of free enterprise and the creation of "special machinery to impose on the banks the credit policy which the public interest demands" (ibid., 309).[10] A third problem caused by too much competition was "the wastes resulting from unstandardized raw materials, equipment, or products" (ibid., 346). Producers have an interest to keep a clientele by making machines, which are incompatible with similar machines made by competitors. This is rational from the individual firm's point of view, but it lowers the welfare of consumers and imposes unnecessary expenses when consumers have to change from one environment to another or to combine both. The difficulties many of us have in moving from an IBM/ PC to a Macintosh environment, or vice versa, is a good example of this inefficiency.

Another problem was that "competition forces producers to scrap old-style equipment prematurely" (ibid., 346). In order to retain competitive prices, producers have to use the most efficient methods, which means that they have to buy the most sophisticated machinery. But if the machinery was getting more advanced all the time, they were driven to buy new machines before they had had time to cover the costs of the old ones. This was one example of a more general problem of "firms with high indirect costs [which] can drive out firms with lower total costs" (ibid., 341). Indirect (overhead) costs are fixed costs that do not depend on the quantities produced, such as machines, management expenses, advertising, offices, and public relations. A firm with high indirect costs and low direct costs (which do vary with quantities produced) can sell in lower prices than a firm with a reverse cost structure. According to neoclassical analysis, the price of a good (P) must equal the marginal cost of producing it. Marginal cost (MC) is the cost of producing one more unit, and it is assumed to rise as more of that good is produced.[11] If P is higher than MC, it will pay to produce one more unit, because the firm can sell it for more than it costs to produce it. If P is below MC, the firm will cut production as the cost of producing the last unit is higher than what the firm can charge for it. Slichter accepts this logic, and deduces the possibility of a firm with a low MC to drive out a firm with higher MC but lower *total* costs due to lower fixed (indirect) costs. This leaves alive the firm with the higher overall costs, an apparent inefficiency.

The point in which Slichter departed from the conventional neoclassical analysis was in considering the possibility that two firms in the same industry would have different cost structures. The neoclassical analysis assumed that cost structures were the same across the same industry, an assumption, or a black box, that institutionalists challenged.[12] Hale, for instance, raised the possibility that "the price of finished products may be much higher than the cost *to some producers*," while "the price is no greater than the cost of producing at the margin" (1924, 201; italics in original). This brought systematic and permanent "above-normal" profits for some producers, a possibility which contradicted neoclassical teaching. This analysis was similar to neoclassical analysis in its abstractness and deductive reasoning but violated a fundamental premise of neoclassical theory in order to make the analysis more realistic. As in the previous cases, neoclassical theorists were aware that cost structures of firms were not identical in reality, but they were inclined to assume that they were similar enough to be treated as identical without missing any essential feature of the economy.

Morris Copeland raised another problem caused by competition: the case of increasing returns (decreasing costs[13]). Increasing returns is a situation in which the multiplication of all the factors of production by the same constant yields more than a proportional increase of the output. Copeland argued that in such a case, "free competition *must be* cutthroat competition" (1924, 110n). According to the neoclassical analysis, firms try to sell more until MC and P are equal. Under the assumption of constant or decreasing returns, when production rises, MC rises as well, and therefore equilibrium must be reached. But in the case of decreasing costs, as the firm produces more, its MC *declines*. There is an incentive for each firm to cut its prices and steal clients from competitors. This may lead either to cutthroat competition, which may destroy all competitors, or to the breakdown of free competition as firms merge together to prevent ruinous competition or are taken over by a single firm.

Given the drawbacks of competition that institutionalists identified, it is probably not surprising that they have not joined the lamentation about the rise of big corporations and the emergence of monopolistic competition. Yet later writers have argued that the main faults that institutionalism found in capitalism was the fact that the modern economy was governed by a few big corporations with monopolistic power. It is believed that this feature of the modern economy was one of their most powerful arguments against neoclassical theory. Our study of interwar institutionalism fails to confirm this belief. The decline of free competition was mentioned by several institutionalists but did not play a major role in any of the institutionalist essays I examined.[14] Although I did not find it to be a major theme in the institutionalist critique, the neoclassical model was criticized harshly by *some* critics because of its incongruity with a real world of bigger and bigger corporations (cf. Bye 1924, 276). It is therefore an intriguing enigma how such a powerful attack on the old doctrine was almost totally sidestepped by the institutionalist literature.

The solution of this puzzle is implicit in what I have said so far. The arguments institutionalists arrayed show that competition was not perceived by them as a marvelous arrangement in the first place. Hence, they felt no need to grieve its decline. If they wanted to establish that competition was harmful, they could not censure its decline as a major problem in their onslaught on the neoclassical approach.

Imperfect, or monopolistic, competition was one of the central topics in neoclassical thought during the late 20s and early 30s. Piero Sraffa (1898–1983) and Joan Robinson (1903–83) at Cambridge, Edward Chamberlin (1899–1967) at Harvard, and others have developed neat and rigorous models of imperfect competition that turned into fundamental black boxes of modern neoclassical economics (Shackle 1967, chaps. 5–6; Samuelson 1971; Ekelund and Hébert 1983, chap. 20). For neoclassicists, this work was essential in order to find the way to restore perfect-competition outcomes. For institutionalists, monopolies and monopolistic competition were established facts, and the question was how to regulate them and get the best out of this new reality. The institutionalist program for maximizing social welfare involved, therefore, more coordination and a larger dose of central planning, not as a substitute for markets but as mechanisms for improving market functioning:

> Many expenditures can be controlled only by the cooperative action of large number of establishments. This, however, requires some sort of super-plant organization able to impose its will upon individual firms. . . . Some sort of super-plant organization is needed to avoid the great waste in the exploitation of oil and natural gas. . . . Advertising and selling expenditures cannot be kept down by the independent action of competitors . . . stabilization of both styles and prices is beyond the power of individual business establishments acting independently (Slichter 1924, 345–46; cf. Cyert 1988, chap. 6).

The solution was coordination, not competition. "Super-plant organization," which was considered sacrilegious by the orthodox doctrine, was suggested as salvation by institutionalists. Mitchell was even more explicit in arguing that the exploitation of modern technology necessitated a cooperation on the highest level. Instead of many small businesses working alone against each other, "production ought to be organized on a continental scale. Every industry ought to be carefully adjusted to every one of the industries with which it interlocks" (1924, 30). Mitchell knew that such a practice would involve a problem of monopoly power, that could be used against unprotected consumers. He was also aware of the inefficiencies involved in monitoring giant production. Yet he believed that proper regulation and careful planning could reduce such negative effects to a minimum, thus making the advantages of large scale beneficial for the society as a whole (ibid., 30–31).

The Missing Dimension: Power Disparity and
   Labor Relations

The institutionalists marshaled externalities, lack of knowledge, and wasteful competition against neoclassical theory and the associated policy of *laissez-faire*. These allies could have been enough to discredit the whole neoclassical structure of black boxes, but the war effort of the institutionalists was augmented by an attack from another front. Power, the institutionalists claimed, was unequally divided between economic sectors, and those who had more power could tilt the economic system in their favor. The neoclassical approach assumed that private enterprise was harmonious, thus ignoring the basic conflict of interests that underlay capitalist economies. The institutionalists, in contrast, perceived this conflict as another reason why capitalist systems did not work as efficiently as orthodox theory anticipated.[15]

Again, the institutionalists drew examples from economic life around them. The first example that they brought to substantiate the above argument was the way industrialists used "skilled employment experts" in order to discover and hold those workers "who are willing to endure long hours, extremely heavy work, or extraordinarily great risks for little or no extra compensation." As a result, "competition for labor comes to be based less purely on wages and working conditions and more upon skill in obtaining and holding the most docile, most easily satisfied, and least discriminating workers" (Slichter 1924, 322).

Another factor in the lack of balance between workers and business was the greater ability of employers "to wait or to take advantage of alternative opportunities" (ibid., 323). This vast power disparity made the neoclassical theory of wages entirely useless, claimed Slichter. The theory argued that the wage of a worker was equal to her marginal productivity, that is, to the additional net revenues the firm gets from employing that one more worker. If the wage is less than this, it is profitable to employ more workers. Assuming perfect competition in the labor market, the firm would have to offer the workers higher wages. With more workers, marginal productivity is *assumed* to decline until equilibrium is achieved. The parity of marginal productivity and wages is a fundamental neoclassical black box, on which many models have been built (Blaug 1985a, chap. 11; Samuelson and Nordhaus 1989, chaps. 27, 30). For example, a common neoclassical explanation of unemployment is the existence of a minimum-wage statute and collective contracts with unions that fix the wage rate *above* marginal productivity. That makes it uneconomic to hire more workers, because the value of what they would add to production is less than their aggregate income as sanctioned by law (Stigler 1946).

The institutionalists who challenged this black box sought after allies to show that in real life it was not reasonable to expect wages to equal marginal productivity. This was not easy to prove because marginal productivity could not be directly measured. The trial of strength in that point, therefore, had to be waged by recruiting indirect evidence. Slichter recruited the lag of wages behind the increase in productivity of workers. Total productivity of an industry (or the whole economy) is easier to estimate than marginal productivity, and by claiming that average wages lagged behind total production, Slichter put a question mark over the marginal productivity theory. Another argument was the practice of business persons to "put up with a more or less serious shortage of workers rather than pay more than they consider labor to be worth," which depended more on "what they have been used to paying" than on calculations of productivity (Slichter 1924, 325). Employers "do not hasten to raise wages with marginal productivity because of the great uncertainty of modern business. Although they may at the moment be able to pay more," they are constantly afraid of an economic downturn around the corner (ibid.).[16]

Thus, norms of businesspersons and uncertainty were both brought in as structural factors which kept wages below marginal productivity. In addition, Slichter brought in the immobility of workers. Neoclassical theory assumed competition, which, in the case of the labor market, meant that employers could choose the workers who asked for the lowest wages, and employees could choose the best-paying employers. Slichter, however, argued that in fact, employees were not really free, because they learned "from experience the difficulties of finding a satisfactory place, and this renders them loathe to leave a reasonably good place" (ibid., 327). This barrier was strengthened by the fact that seniority on the job gave workers "a certain standing in the eyes of the management . . . [and] a feeling of some security against lay-off." Lionel Edie supported the assault on marginal productivity theory with studies by Alvin Hansen, Paul Douglas, and Arthur Bowley—three recognized authorities in the field of labor economics—which showed "the inconsistent relationship between physical productivity and financial reward" (1927, 423). Slichter also offered an alternative black box: "wage earners have learned that, regardless of what employers can *afford* to give them, wages, hours, and working conditions are, as a rule, no better than managements, in view of the economic strength of the men, find it expedient or necessary to grant." Bargaining power is therefore "esteemed and respected by labor, and hard work, technical proficiency, and cooperation tend to fall into disrepute" (Slichter 1924, 339–40).

By bringing the disparity of power between employers and consumers and between the former and employees, institutionalists wished to establish something more than the unfairness of the system. Their chief goal was to call neoclassical theory into question. The ability of business enterprises to extract higher profits at the expense of both consumers and labor served this goal. If consumers were outsmarted by producers, and labor had no room to maneuver, then no matter how similar other elements of the economy were to the ideal perfect-competition model, a free market regime would not maximize social welfare as claimed by orthodox theory; state intervention was needed.

But that was not all. Slichter raised yet another argument. The polarity of labor and capital, this labor specialist claimed, deprived managements of "the benefit of suggestions and criticisms from those who are in the best position to observe points of waste and to suggest changes, namely the workmen and the minor officials" (1924, 332). "Managements are responsible to capitalists," he explained, "and administrative policies are designed to advance the interests of the capitalists. . . . The officials can scarcely encourage workers to criticize policies designed to benefit investors, often at the expense of the wage earners." Furthermore, managers did not want workers to "develop an attitude of self-assertion and independence which would render them unwilling to submit with docility to the management of industry," and therefore they did not encourage workers to submit suggestions for improvements. Workers, in turn, were afraid that such suggestions would cost them their jobs because of the changes they entail (ibid., 333, 340; Edie 1927, 425). The neoclassical framework left no place for such important considerations as the nature of labor relations and the motivation of workers. Its model implied that workers were homogeneous; their production could not change due to better treatment, and this approach, Slichter averred, was a serious theoretical flaw.

The last point made by Slichter ties his argument about labor to his earlier arguments and to his claim that competition was not the best regime. One of the reasons "for the acute differences between capital and labor" under existing arrangements, he explained, "is the fact that wages and conditions of work are . . . settled in each plant separately. This gives each enterprise a powerful incentive to obtain an advantage by paying less or offering less favorable terms than its rivals" (1924, 350). This is another reason to favor super-plant coordination. Such coordination would make it easier to compensate workers more fairly, and thus, increase social welfare.

Conclusions: Economic Realities and Economic Models

Slichter summarizes all the deviations from perfect competition conditions. His summary was so emphatic and declarative, that it is worthwhile to present it at length:

Incomplete and fragmentary as our survey has been, it has indicated that the faults of free enterprise are by no means simply incidental and exceptional. . . . We have found that the most fundamental requirement of free enterprise—an interest on the part of individual buyers and sellers in discriminating against those who disregard the common welfare—is lacking, not in a few scattered instances, but in many. We have seen, furthermore, that even when individuals do have an interest in discriminating, they frequently lack the information, the time, the willingness, the intelligence, or the bargaining power to do so. We have observed that free capitalistic enterprise habitually underproduces, that, owing to the uncertainty of markets, it *must* underproduce if business enterprises are to remain solvent; that it fails lamentably to get managements to concentrate upon the improvement of technique and the elimination of waste and forces them into a fight for markets so fierce and of such vital importance that a large share of the best executive ability must be devoted to the struggle; that it not only fails to obtain the cooperation of labor in production, but also causes wage earners consciously to withhold their aid and often to fight against technical improvements. . . . Finally, we have seen that the existing industrial organization is largely responsible for a deep-seated and extremely bitter conflict between capital and labor, of such magnitude and intensity in some countries that it shakes the foundations of the social order itself (Slichter 1924, 351; italics in original).

The themes in this summary reappear in the writing of other institutionalists. Yet the institutionalists did not negate that the orthodox model has some value. John Maurice Clark, for example, said that "as a tool of analysis, [neoclassical theory] is invaluable; but as the sole source of truth, it is woefully inadequate" (1924, 101). His position was also reflected in his evaluation of Adam Smith, who "grasped the element of mutual aid running through exchange, [and] saw its organizing possibilities." Smith's contribution was "the validity of price as an economic organizing force" (ibid., 83). Yet Clark insisted that value theory of neoclassical economics captured *only one aspect* of economic life. He therefore agreed with the "new generations" of economists, the institutionalists, who discovered that real-world arrangements "fail to produce the expected efficiency and instead cause waste and social loss rather than pure mutual gain in the process of free exchange (ibid., 84). Neoclassical theory did hold some important truth, but it failed to account for many facets of economic life. It was useful as a starting point, but the analysis had to go beyond it (see also Clark 1936, 4–5).

Clark was not alone among institutionalists in attempting to exploit the merits of orthodox theory without subscribing to its basic conclusions. Commons himself stated that "institutional economics cannot separate itself from the marvelous discoveries and insight of the classical economists" (1931, 648). Copeland also asserted that "the broad, general truth of the classical explanation . . . appeals and persists because of its comparative simplicity as well as its approximate truth." But, like Clark, Copeland immediately added that "it is only an approximation." Furthermore, the approximation was "so rough and crude that it fails to account for any of the imperfections of coordination" (1924, 107). Later he explained that "we cannot get very far by assuming [as orthodox theory does] a static society, with *free* competition and constant or increasing costs for each enterprise, for by so doing we rule out nearly all the factors to which imperfection in the functioning of exchange coordination are due" (ibid., 119).[17] Orthodox theory admitted the existence of imperfections, but it could not treat these imperfections "except as deviations from the theoretical norm." Thus, "Business depression have been construed as *abnormal* times, trusts as *unnatural* monopolies, non-living wages as true only for the *short-run*, and many *social* evils have been blamed on individuals and the inaccuracies of their felicific calculations" (ibid., 107–8; italics in original). Copeland asserted that these properties of the economy should be treated theoretically, because they were systematic features of the economic complex. The institutionalists, in sum, wanted to modify some boxes of the neoclassical edifice and kick out several others. But they mostly wanted to add new walls to the existing building of orthodox theory.

In chapter 3 we discussed the question whether the institutionalists had an alternative theory. We saw in this chapter more evidence that they did. They agreed that economics should be a science of welfare and that the market could not be relied upon to determine the real value of goods and services, although it did serve as a starting point for an overall evaluation. They also agreed that orthodox theory did not provide the tools for analyzing general welfare. The common goal of Clark, Copeland, Douglas, Tugwell, Slichter, Hale, and Wolfe (all in Tugwell 1924b) was geared toward the identification of a general scheme of social welfare and methods to achieve it. Strangely enough, the neoclassical essays on institutionalism that I encountered in the methodological writings of the twenties ignored this most essential contribution of institutionalism. Raymond Bye's essay (1924) is the only one in the analyzed corpus which tackled a few of the institutionalist claims, and even he seems to miss the crux of the institutionalist critique. In his 1924 essay in *The Trend of Economics*, Bye grasped well most of the criticisms against neoclassical theory on the methodological level (see chap. 4) or in regard to the nature of human behavior (see chap. 5). But in regard to the suitability of orthodox theory for capturing the structure of the modern economy, the only critique that he mentioned was that "monopoly control of supply, the stratification of society into non-competing groups, lack of mobility of capital, and similar conditions result in a marked discrepancy between value and disutility costs" (1924, 276; see also 1925, 59). The problems of cutthroat competition, systematic lack of knowledge, structural and dysfunctional disparities of power, and many other problems raised by institutionalists were not mentioned at all. The focus was on the decline of competition, an issue that was the least important in the institutionalist attack on neoclassical theory.

Bye's defense of neoclassical theory further shows that he either was unaware of the institutionalist attack or that he preferred to ignore it. His main argument was that modern neoclassical theory (of the 1920s) got rid of the outmoded psychological concept of disutility. He referred to the work of Herbert Davenport, Carl Gustav Cassel, and Thomas Carver, three prominent neoclassical theorists around the turn of the century. Those economists, he argued, got rid of the psychological interpretation of prices and based it, instead, on supply and demand analysis (1924, 278–79). Bye took pride in this modern version of marginal analysis and perceived it as an appropriate answer to the severe criticism that had been leveled toward orthodox theory (ibid., 280). *But this modern theory was exactly the theory that the institutionalists disputed.* The institutionalists agreed that in principle, in a market system, "the available resources [are] being devoted only to the production of those commodities for which the highest prices are offered," as claimed by Bye. But due to advertising, salesmanship, lack of information (and inability to reach necessary information), and many other reasons mentioned in this chapter, the highest prices were not necessarily offered for the things people needed most. Nor did these prices reflect all the used resources or the impact on the environment. The health of the workers, and other factors, were also not sufficiently reckoned with.

Bye's defense of the concept of marginal productivity was a case in point. We saw above that Slichter had a grounded objection to the theory based on what he considered to be common practices of employers and employees. Bye, however, responded to a much simpler and less sophisticated criticism. He argued that "when it is said that labor is paid according to its marginal productivity, what is meant is not that labor gets what it produces. . ., but that it is paid *according to its value to the employers* who are bidding for it in a competitive market" (ibid., 281; italics in original). This is a proper answer to a common misunderstanding that confuses *total* product and *marginal* product.[18] The main point of the institutionalists was different. They focused on the fact that the *value to employers* diverged substantially from the *value to society*. On this topic Bye was silent. Nor did he say anything on the arguments concerning, for example, the immobility of workers due to their age, their lack of security, and the inability of consumers to judge the quality of products.

One cannot assume that Bye's attitude was representative of the neoclassical position. We saw earlier that Frank Knight was another defender of neoclassical theory whose views were quite different from those of Bye.

They also differed in their political positions. Bye accepted the possibility that governmental intervention was needed. He maintained, however, that any attempt to control the economy should be done according to "the laws of economics," that is, according to neoclassical theory. A good example was trade policy. In contrast to the common *laissez-faire* ideology which totally proscribed tariffs, Bye said that tariffs which were introduced according to economic theory, as suggested by Friedrich List and Henry Carey, were not out of the question (1924, 297). This was pretty much the attitude of Marshall and his students. Knight, in contrast, was known as a stubborn opponent of any governmental intervention, which was the reason he is known as one of the forebears of the Chicago school. Knight, however, based his opposition to government not on economic theory but rather on broader social and political concerns: "That men are not completely rational in managing their affairs is true, but hardly implies that a government, which must be run by men, will be both wise and benevolent in managing those of everybody" (1957, 21). He was aware—probably unlike some of his progeny at Chicago—that a free-market economy was not perfect, but thought that it was preferable because "it has the supreme merit of enabling people to co-operate without specific agreement on values" (ibid.). As Silk explains, "Knight was deeply pessimistic about the human race and its pretensions of altruism; he thought the dominant trait of mankind was greed, and he thought it essential to build an economic system which recognized that fact" (1974, 51). That is why he "held that the state, even when it sought to do good, was far more likely to do evil" (ibid.). Free enterprise was better, in his view, not because it was more efficient, but rather because it allowed individuals to explicitly pursue their interests without the repressive powers of the state (Dorfman 1959, 5: 479).

Knight's view represented the minority within the economic profession between the world wars. It deviated not only from the radical attitudes of institutionalists, but from the reformist zeal of Marshallians in Britain and the founders of the AEA as well (see chap. 2). For our interest in this chapter, however, the main point is that Knight, like Bye, did not confront directly the arguments made by institutionalists concerning the compatibility between economic theory and the modern economy. His stands were derived from ethical and social considerations and not from the perception of private enterprise as efficient (see also the essays in Knight 1946). It was only after the Second World War that the mathematical economists addressed the points made by institutionalists and analyzed situations of imperfect knowledge, unequal power, externalities, and so forth.

All along this chapter I referred in footnotes to many of the modern treatments of problems that the institutionalist literature brought up.

Some people may consider those treatments as sufficient and claim that institutionalism completed its service by pointing our attention to the flaws of the primitive neoclassical theory (chap. 3). That is the explanation often given by mainstreamers for the demise of institutionalism. On the other hand, others would argue that much of the institutionalist critique is still valid. The mathematical theorists modified the models in order to answer *some* of the problems raised by the critics of neoclassical theory but have not addressed *the main arguments*: the profusion of externalities, the systematic lack of knowledge and inability to collect data, and the inherently antagonistic relations between various sectors of the capitalist economy. One does not have to accept this evaluation in order to appreciate the contribution of institutionalists to modern economics. The fact that some of the most recent models in economic theory deal with problems which were brought up by the institutionalist thinkers is in itself a testimony that their contribution is larger than what even the most generous conventional textbooks concede. It is also a hint that modern economists may still find some inspiration in the long-forgotten writings of institutionalist economists, either for the extension of neoclassical models or for a new revolution in economic thought.

Seven

The Struggle over Social Relevance and the Place of Values

> Since no paradigm ever solves all the problems it defines and since no two paradigms leave all the same problems unsolved, paradigm debates always involve the question: Which problems is it more significant to have solved? . . . The question of values can be answered only in terms of criteria that lie outside of normal science altogether.
> (Thomas S. Kuhn, *The Structure of Scientific Revolutions*)

> The specialist in general theory . . . must drop the superstition, which too long has impaired the usefulness of his work, that the explanation of how value is determined is the central task of economic theory beside which all others are of little consequence. . . . The problem of value determination . . . can possess only subordinate significance in comparison with the question of how industry can be made to operate more closely in conformity with the general well-being.
> (Sumner Slichter, *"The Organization and Control of Economic Activity"*)

> It is a sign of the maturity of a discipline that its main problems are not drawn from immediate, changing events. A genuine and persistent separation of scientific study from the real world leads to sterility, but an immediate and sensitive response to current events stultifies the deepening and the widening of analytical principles and techniques. The leading theoretical chemists are not working on detergents or headache remedies and the leading economic theorists need not be concerned with urban renewal or oil embargoes.
> (George Stigler, *Essays in the History of Economics*)

SCIENTIFIC VALIDITY measured in terms of logical analysis and compatibility with reality is not the only criterion for choosing among scientific approaches. When there are two competing approaches, which are both valid, or when scientists cannot agree which approach is valid, they can resort to a criterion of an entirely different character. This criterion is the usefulness of the competing approaches and their relevance to practical needs.[1] The way we have defined black boxes, they include more than conventions of how to do research (i.e., methods), accepted facts, and agreed upon explanations (i.e., theories). They include also shared goals of scientific research. Scientists spend time and energy trying to convince each other and the world at large of the importance of their individual and collective pursuits. Defending a research program by reference to its practical utility often leads to arguments concerning the "do-ability" and applicability of research programs. Each party makes promises concerning the prospective ability of its paradigm to solve various problems. The time span of these promises is often quite long and the promises are understandably very speculative. Hence, opponents frequently challenge the promises, and disputes over prospects of research programs to solve practical problems ensue.

I will begin this chapter by discussing the accusations made by institutionalists concerning the inability of neoclassical theory to address important practical problems. Orthodox economics, they said, was irrelevant, if not outright damaging for policy making, because of the unrealistic nature of its assumptions and its undue concentration on abstract value theory. The institutionalists argued that by following their own inductive research program, economic science would be able to provide solutions to many pressing economic problems. These promises are the subject of the second section. The third section reviews the neoclassical response which had two aspects: casting doubts on the utopian promises of institutionalists and making promises about the prospects of the neoclassical research program itself. Neoclassical theory, its proponents claimed, was neither finished nor stagnant; it was a project that had proved itself in the past and would yield many fruits in the future. The last section deals with the role of values in economic science. This issue is related to the trial of strength over relevance because the neoclassicists argued that the best way to help solve practical problems was to focus on pure theory in an unbiased way by excluding any discussion of values. Institutionalists claimed that such an omission would lead to a barren science and asserted that values could be handled scientifically and without subverting scientific norms.

Institutionalists: Overpriced Value Theory

One of the main claims of institutionalists was that practical needs necessitated much more emphasis on empirical research. People might debate in the abstract the virtues of a deductive approach relative to an inductive one, the institutionalists agreed. But urgent economic problems required research that paid careful attention to the realities of human nature, social institutions, and the economy. Rexford Tugwell, for instance, argued that orthodox economists "managed to create the structure of classical theory [only] by doing a good deal of violence to what were then hidden actualities." This, he argued, was one of the reasons that "their economic theory cannot help us to understand the problems of human economic behavior any more" (1924a, 390). He claimed that the laws of neoclassical theory "are not useful in the sense that natural laws are useful" because they were not based on a study of the real economy. Instead of attempting to find laws which described the reality, economic laws "became, in the hands of the classical school, ends in themselves . . . they were merely logical exercises" (ibid., 393).

Similarly, Wesley Mitchell characterized pre–World War I economics as dry, dull, and impractical. He complained that economics had become "an academic discipline, cultivated by professors and neglected by men of action, modest in its pretensions to practical usefulness, more conspicuous for consistency and erudition than for insight" (1924, 19). And George Soule complained that "the plain fact is that whereas most people trust the word of the natural scientists as a matter of course, neither the ordinary leader of public life nor the ordinary private citizen has . . . thought of accepting economics as a body of contemporary and exact knowledge from which guidance may be derived in action" (1924, 359). Soule blamed the "primitive state" of the discipline which was due to the lack of empirical work. Institutionalism therefore appeared as the solution that might turn economics into a practical science referred to by leaders and informed citizens (ibid., 360).

A common complaint of the critics of orthodox theory was that it had concentrated its efforts on one problem, value theory.[2] Valuable though it might have been (and not all of them agreed that it was valuable), they argued that it was wrong to ignore all the other issues. The institutionalists, Joseph Dorfman says, "conceded that a good deal of value theory was valid . . . , but they contended that it was too limited and narrow and that its importance to economic science had been overstressed" (1959, 5:465–56). A. B. Wolfe caustically remarked that the marginalists had used analytical geometry and calculus "to pile up a formidable mass of 'value theory' which left objective reality to one side, [and] helped to solve no actual economic problem" (1924, 468). Sumner Slichter claimed that instead of studying the economic system, economic theory had "exhibited a remarkable tendency to concentrate attention upon a single problem, regarding it as the central one in economics, and feeling no necessity for extending its inquiries beyond the limits thus set" (1924, 306).

The "infatuation" of neoclassical theory with value theory is exemplified in their use of Robinson Crusoe. The story about Robinson Crusoe's desert island is a rhetorical device, which is often used in teaching economics (cf. Madison 1990, 40–41). The idea is that Robinson Crusoe, as the sole resident of the island, can decide how to divide his time between, let's say, picking bananas and coconuts. Given his skills in picking fruits ("the technology") and his tastes, one can find out how Crusoe would allocate his resources (i.e., his time) in an optimal way. It would also be possible to determine the relative values of bananas and coconuts, that is, how many bananas each coconut is worth. This is the basic question that value theory has dealt with, although it has proceeded, of course, to worlds in which there are several factors of production, more than one person, and more products. Yet the theory still deals with very simple worlds relative to our real one. Institutionalists were very critical of the fictional world of Mr. Crusoe. As William E. Weld told us, "in fact, this island has been neglected in recent years by the students of economics. The present-day economist is profoundly interested in human welfare, and the doctrine of 'truth for its own sake' in such an engrossing world of actualities does not have the chance to make itself felt" (1924, 425).

According to the institutionalists, the main concern of economists should be "the problem of the organization and control of economic activity" (Slichter 1924, 353). Economists should stop being preoccupied with the determination of prices and focus on the question of how to direct industry in a way which will maximize the happiness of the community (ibid.). Slichter gave a long list of new realities which emerged since Adam Smith's time but were ignored by theory, such as corporations, trade unions, cooperative organizations, trade and employers' associations, and commercial and investment banks (cf. Taylor 1928, 270). Slichter then elaborated on the kinds of questions which were not discussed by neoclassical economics despite their importance. Among other things he mentioned the influence of market organization and institutions upon prices, the effects of buying and selling policies on actual behavior, the impact of the credit system on savings, the impact of science on the longevity of capital, and the way labor productivity depended on wages (Slichter 1924, 304–5; cf. Edie 1927, 427–28). Orthodox theory was not useful for managing modern industries, Slichter implied, because it had ignored all these topics.

I end this section with Tugwell's description of the reaction of many contemporary students to the neat and sophisticated orthodox theory. His sarcastic description informs us about the atmosphere in economics during the twenties, although we cannot know precisely how many economists felt that way:

> So it was that classical theory . . . stood triumphantly symmetrical, an absolute! And so it is still too much taught. By a series of assumptions and with the use of certain chosen illustrations it can be worked up to climactically. . . . And

when the thing is complete—there you are! Value! But someway or other the student goes away from the demonstration unsatisfied, frustrated, angry, feeling rather as though a logical trick had been played upon him (1924a, 393).

Institutionalists: Promises and Alleged Successes

The institutionalists not only complained about the preoccupation of neoclassicists with value theory, they also called attention to many practical problems, which waited to be addressed. They passionately argued that economists had to concern themselves with these issues, and expressed their certitude concerning the power of their own empirical approach to solve many important economic problems. Often they claimed that promising results had already been achieved. The way those arguments are tied together is nicely seen in the references to the experience of the First World War. Wesley Mitchell emphasized the economic problems that the war brought and the problems of economic adjustment in its wake. He mentioned several of the main questions of the day—should the U.S. collect its loans to the Allies, how to reduce the domestic debt, and so forth, and concluded: "The list of problems bred by the war need not be completed; it is long enough to suggest how varied and how searching are the demands that will be made upon the constructive capacity of economists" (1924, 20–21).

Mitchell was sure that these pressing needs would nail down the commitment of economists to the institutionalist path. The war seemed to prove, at least for Mitchell and his fellow institutionalists, that the improvement of economic performance required adaptation of policy to diversified specific circumstances. This practice seemed to be facilitated by the institutionalist kind of empirical research, rather than by the abstract neoclassical theory, which appeared to be too general to offer concrete solutions. Mitchell thus added that the war experience disqualified the arid preoccupation with value theory, and though this had not had much influence on theory *yet*, "the next few years should harvest heavy crops from the sowing of the war. . . . The war [is] just beginning to make its influence felt in the slow-moving social sciences" (ibid., 20).

Mitchell also emphasized the positive experience with government planning during the war. He underscored the policies of central planning and underlined the collection of data by government agencies that made these policies effective: "Thousands of men who participated in the work of the War Boards learned to think in terms of the nation's needs, to collect quantitative data . . . and to effect a strange blending of government and private initiative" (ibid., 20). The success of empirical work and governmental intervention thus proved the merits of institutionalism, or at least that was what the institutionalists hoped. As George Soule said, the experience of the war had changed the perspective of economists, and many of the best of them "left their grazing on the arid hillsides of traditional theory and began to crop the juicy lowlands of fact" (1924, 364–65; see also Clark 1936; Dorfman 1949, 3:493). Based on the war experience, Mitchell hoped that many other problems, which were not related to the war, might be solved by economists who studied the actual functioning of economic institutions and by government intervention in steering the economy based on empirical findings provided by economists. Included in the goals that Mitchell expected economists to achieve were control of business cycles, conservation of natural resources, and elimination of waste in industry (1924, 21–22; cf. Soule 1924, 365).

The ability to prevent waste was stressed by numerous institutionalists. Mitchell, for instance, assigned to economists the role of finding out whether the organization of industry "on a continental scale" could increase production because of better coordination, or would be unproductive, because it "necessarily involves bureaucratic control [which would] lead to a new type of inefficiency." Mitchell also claimed that "we need careful quantitative analyses of efficiency under various conditions" (1924, 30–31). He believed that the economic science of the institutionalist type would be able to give definite answers to that question. Similarly, Mitchell asserted that economists could find whether advertising was beneficial to the economy as a whole, and "the bearings of inequality of income upon savings, personal efficiency of workers, industrial depressions and the like" (ibid., 30). All these are complex issues, but Mitchell treated them as solvable with the help of the empirical tools that institutionalism promoted. He was even more sanguine with respect to the prospects of psychological research and the contribution of such research to economic studies (ibid., 23).

Mitchell exhibited an extremely optimistic belief in the potential of institutional economics and argued that "where scientific work is possible there is slight excuse for hesitation" (1924, 30). He worked laboriously to realize the goal of scientific guidance for economic policy, and one of his achievements was the establishment of the National Bureau for Economic Research (NBER, est. 1920), which has remained one of the major research institutions in economics.[3] The task of the NBER, as Mitchell saw it, "would be nothing less than to gather statistics and commission monographs that would enable a national leader . . . to fabricate an all-embracing program" (Sobel 1980, 43).

Mitchell's student, Rexford Tugwell, expressed a similarly optimistic belief in the ability of science to solve quickly and conclusively formidable and vague questions. For example, he asked, "How far can human beings adjust themselves to industrial conditions?" We know that they have some capability of adjustment, he said, "but just how far? That we do not know. And we can formulate no worthwhile program until we find out. . . . And inductive measurement can be of the very greatest service here" (1924a, 407). Similarly, he "seduced" readers to support institutionalism by expressing his belief in the ability to find out *inductively* how deep economic motives are. Are they deeper, for example, than sexual motives? He believed that science, in the fashion of institutionalism, could answer this question, and that an answer to this question was a prerequisite for the formulation of any policy (ibid.).[4]

There are countless other examples of institutionalists who depicted a utopian picture of the achievements that could be reached by the adoption of their research program. I will give only one more outspoken example from Lionel Edie's essay. He assured readers that by adopting empirical methods, economists would accomplish the same level of success as other sciences. They would be able to control the economy, he promised, and their control will be "analogous to the *bacteriologist* who masters the microbe and controls disease, or to that of the *physicist* who discovers new knowledge of the atom and gives new control over energy, or to that of the *electrician* who discovers how to regulate radio activity (1927, 436; underlines added). This is a good illustration of the aspirations institutionalists fomented and publicized in order to convince the community of economists in the merit of their research program. It should be emphasized, though, that this was not necessarily a tricky manipulation to attract supporters. The institutionalists probably believed in these promises themselves, and in any case, their sincerity is not at issue here.[5] The main point is that such "utopian" visions were offered by the contenders. As we will see, this practice was not limited to institutionalists; neoclassical economists also made promises, as do all scientists who have a "cause" to promote.

Given the extremely optimistic nature of their promises, the institutionalists knew that they had to work hard to convince their fellow economists. They therefore tried to demonstrate the feasibility of their vision by claiming that their research program had already been applied successfully. Speaking about quantitative research, John Cobb said that "how far this [quantitative] tendency will go in economics and what it will accomplish is idle speculation." But he insisted that "it is beginning to work and has indicated the probability of important results" (1926, 427). George Soule was less modest. Referring to recent developments in collecting quantitative data and to the experiments in economic policy, he bragged that "the result was a growth almost miraculous" (1924, 364–65). Lionel Edie, who examined "several hundred monographic economic studies," found that "the most salient common characteristic is the discovery of new knowledge about economic behavior."[6] He maintained that even though each of these studies yielded "microscopic" increments of knowledge, "nevertheless, in their totality these increments give increasing knowledge of, and therefore increasing control over, human nature in relation to economic institutions" (1927, 435–36).

This closes up the case of institutionalists: Starting with the failure of the neoclassical doctrine to pursue contemporary economic problems, they presented their research program as having the required conceptual gadgets and methods to handle those problems. Furthermore, they promised to solve the problems and pointed to some preliminary achievements in order to enhance the credibility of these promises. Now we turn to the other side and see how neoclassical economists coped with this seemingly unstoppable attack.

The Neoclassical Attack: Doubting the Institutionalist Strategy

The neoclassicists used the same tactics as the institutionalists in order to defend their approach and cast doubt upon their opponents. They tried to prove that the promises of the institutionalists were doomed to fail and drew a utopian picture of the future which their own research program could allegedly bring about. An example of the first move was Jacob Viner's deprecation of the institutionalist contribution: "The new quantitative work [of institutionalists] has suggested refinements and corrections, but its contribution has so far been modest in its proportions" (in Mills 1928, 35). While he admitted that quantitative methods could help solve several problems, Viner predicted "that for many years at least there would be much within the traditional range of economic inquiry which will wholly resist quantitative inquiry, and that it will also be many years before economists discover how to apply quantitative analysis to a wide range of problems which seem by their inherent nature to be ill adapted for such analysis" (ibid., 32).[7] It was unnecessary to prove that the quantitative method promoted by institutionalism was in principle flawed. It was enough to argue that the fruits of this method were bound to ripen only in the far future in order to establish the necessity of neoclassical theory for the time being. Viner thus turned the institutionalist argument of practicality on its head: it is the institutionalists who fruitlessly played with dreams for the future. Meanwhile, neoclassical theory gave immediate solutions to current problems.

Moreover, there were inherent properties of the economy, which limited the potential of quantitative research. Viner explained that "economic phenomena are always the product of a host of factors." Hence, it provided "a fertile field for the application of probability theory," that is, to quantitative research. Yet there were "comparatively few factors," which carried dominant weight, and which changed "so rapidly and as yet so unpredictably in their intensity and their relative importance." Because of this, the deductive reasoning of neoclassicism which concentrated on these few factors would "often render more service than the most subtle elaboration of probability theory" (ibid., 32).

The dean of the opposition to institutionalism in the post–World War I period was Frank Knight. In a letter dated May 18, 1923, Knight wrote to Mitchell that he was "the farthest in the world from having anything against the study of economic institutions. But . . . I am very skeptical about the development of any science in that field" (in Mitchell 1969, 2:735). It is this skepticism in the prospects of *success* of the institutionalist research program, and *not* different conceptions of human nature and society, that led Knight to criticize institutionalism. Knight's skepticism was the common thread in his resistance to the institutionalist research program, in a score of later articles. He knew that good economic advice must be based on actual experience and knowledge of history. But he did not believe in the possibility of reaching meaningful conclusions by a scientific study of the institutional aspects. Economic science could only help illuminate the rational aspect. It should focus on this feasible and important task, rather than waste its energies on *futile* attempts to find laws of human behavior (see chaps. 4 and 5).

This was similar to the objection of Marshall and other empirically conscious neoclassicists to statistical "tests" of the theory. Philip Mirowski (1989b) maintains that the view of "old-fashioned" neoclassicists on the role of statistics was very different from the institutionalist position. The institutionalists wanted to use statistics to improve theory and were ready to make sweeping changes based on statistical results or any other kind of empirical knowledge. The "old-fashioned" neoclassicists, on the other hand, conceived statistics as important for the practical application of theory but did not believe that the theory itself could be improved according to empirical data. Mirowski cites a letter from Marshall to Henry Moore. The latter tried to build empirical demand curves, and was praised by Mitchell in his presidential address as advancing Marshall's abstract theory and making it more useful both for policy making and theory construction (see chap. 4). In his letter, Marshall stressed that he "deliberately decided not to follow" Moore's research. His experience "of the last forty years has confirmed me in the belief that your method is not likely to have practical fruit," he wrote to Moore (Mirowski 1989b, 222n). Marshall gave two main reasons. First, most economic variables depended on too many factors to separate the impact of each. Second, many factors could not be measured and quantified. These arguments take us back to those made by the neoclassicists in chapter 4.

In spite of their objections, the neoclassicists supported statistical research and even conducted it themselves. Mirowski emphasizes the fact that "many of the leading lights of marginalism were also instrumental in the development of probability theory and statistics: Jevons, Edgeworth, Bowley, Keynes, Slutsky, and Wald, only to name the most illustrious" (1989b, 222). How can we reconcile their objections to the institutionalist research program with their own engagement in statistical research? The answer lies in the place allocated to statistics in their overall plan. In contrast to the institutionalists, the neoclassicists did not feel compelled to link neoclassical price theory to "explicit empirical evidence or to pollute their value theory with stochastic concepts" (ibid., 223). An example is Arthur Bowley's work. Bowley thought that the role of the statistician "was to assist economic theory, not to challenge it," an attitude "to be contrasted with that of Henry Moore and Wesley Mitchell working in the United States at exactly the same time" (Blaug 1986a, 34). The plans of institutionalists to overhaul economic theory based on statistical studies was met with ridicule and "extremely disparaging comments" by leading neoclassicists such as Walras and Marshall, who "used their influence to discourage interest in those directions" (Mirowski 1989b, 221–22).

In order to understand the approach of "old-fashioned" neoclassicists, we have to understand the distinction they made between "theoretical economics" on one hand, and some other kind of economics which dealt with aspects of the economic system which were closer to real life. It is quite clear that Marshall, Knight, and other neoclassicists understood that orthodox theory was valid in capturing only one facet of economic life; a universal and perhaps the most important aspect, but nonetheless only one (see chap. 4). Therefore they had no problem in accepting the idea that it was necessary to supplement orthodox theory with "applied" or "historical" studies:

> Such a mass of interrelated data seems to call for a combination of three methods of treatment which must logically be sharply differentiated. The first is economic theory in the recognized sense, a study, largely deductive in character, of the more general aspects of economic cause and effect, those tendencies of a price system which are independent of the specific wants, technology and resources. The second division, or applied economics, should attempt a statistical and inductive study of the actual data at the particular place and time, and of the manner in which general laws are modified by special and accidental circumstances of all sorts. . . . The third division of economics is the philosophy of history in the economic field, or what some of its votaries have chosen to call "historical" and others "institutional" economics, studying "the cumulative changes of institutions" (Knight, 1924, 264).

By "applied economics" Knight referred to the quantitative research of Mitchell at Columbia and the NBER, and "institutional economics" was his characterization of Commons's research program at Wisconsin. The role of applied economics was to conduct "a statistical and inductive study of the actual data at the particular place and time, and of the manner in which general laws are modified by special and accidental circumstances of all sorts." Knight emphasized that "this branch of the science is subject to very narrow limitations" because the data being gathered "lack the stability, classifiability and measurability requisite to scientific treatment" (Knight 1924, 264). More important, Knight believed that applied economics could succeed only when it relied upon theory as a benchmark. He compared applied economics to applied physics and said that in both fields "the application of principles is impossible without principles to apply. It is no argument against the practical value of pure theory that taken alone it does not yield definite rules for guidance" (1924, 259). Similarly, Knight limited the function of historical and institutional studies and doubted their ability to yield "scientific" results in the strict meaning of the concept. Historical and institutional economics, he argued, was "a field for the exercise of informed judgment rather than for reasoning according to the canons of science" (ibid., 264).

Raymond Bye (1924, 273–75), who argued that the theory of value and distribution should continue to stand at the center of the field, raised another justification for empirical research: the need in descriptive information *in* fields which *lack theory*, such as consumption and uncertainty. He added, however, that it was "difficult to conceive of an 'institutional economics' which can ever take the place of current economic science." "A mere description of the organization and technique of institutions," he explained, would "furnish much information of value to the business man and statesman, and help to build up an applied economics as distinguished from the broader general or 'pure' science," but naturally, it was the "pure science" which was more important even for practical matters.

The institutionalists did not accept the separation between "pure theory" and "applied economics." In chapter 4 we saw their methodological arguments. Here I seek to emphasize their appeal to practical reason. Thus, Spengler maintained at a roundtable meeting during the AEA annual conference that a practically good theory "must give due weight to the role of institutions and must allow for more flexibility in economic behavior than is assumed in the classical analysis" (in Homan 1931, 136). A similar contention is made by Sumner Slichter. In contrast to Knight, Slichter insisted that "the problem of industrial organization and control is . . . a fit subject for theoretical speculation, and there are advantages in having it investigated by theorists as well as by specialists in other fields." In order to reach useful solutions, practical problems needed "to be studied not merely as a problem of marketing, banking, railroads, agriculture, or municipal utilities, but as a general problem of economics." Whereas Knight doubted the ability to reach general conclusions about the evolution of economic institutions, Slichter believed that "the comparative method should be used and an effort made to arrive at general laws and principles, to build up . . . a general theory of economic organization and control" (Slichter 1924, 353).

For institutionalists, any theory which kept the institutional variables out was a theory of "empty boxes," to use John H. Clapham's term. Clapham was an English economic historian who wrote a famous article, "Of Empty Economic Boxes," which was published in the *Economic Journal* in 1922 and stirred up a vigorous debate. Clapham attacked Marshallian theory, according to which "increasing-cost and decreasing cost industries . . . ought to be taxed and subsidised [respectively] so as to maximise economic welfare." Clapham agreed but wondered "how are we to tell which industries conform to the one category rather than the other?" (Blaug 1986a, 48). In a similar fashion, institutionalists believed that many concepts of orthodox theory which were inherently incapable of operationalization were merely "empty boxes," because they could not be used for either policy construction or for the advancement of theory.

The Neoclassical Defense: Theory Is the Key to Powerful Policies

Not only can we not rely upon the cheerful assurances of institutionalists, the neoclassical economists said, we also have no reason to do so. Even if the critique of institutionalists was valid in certain points, this was not a reason to abandon orthodox theory, which was being constantly improved. The neoclassical doctrine, its advocates asserted, was not stagnant. They willingly admitted that there was "still room for further development in the pure theory or mechanics of economic relations" (Frank Knight in Working 1927, 19), but claimed that the theory was "in process of evolution" (Bye 1924, 272). "As our knowledge of allied sciences grows," Bye explained, "[and] as the tools of observation and measurement available to the economist become more perfected, our generalizations are becoming more accurate and useful" (ibid.).

In order to prove that their promises were not rubber checks the neoclassicists pointed at their recent achievements. Bye, for instance, said that "meanwhile, the theory of value and distribution itself is undergoing an evolution which gives it greater precision and validity" (1924, 275). There was already much good literature in the field of applied economics," Bye added, and a "great deal more that is better is sure to be produced in the next few decades" (ibid., 291). Bye refers mainly to "recent developments of the theory of distribution, as exemplified in the marginal productivity theory." He explained why these developments "may be regarded as a distinct advance." For example, "The one-sided supply analysis of classical economics has been blended with the equally one-sided productivity analysis into a well-rounded whole." This is Marshall's famous contribution. Another innovation is the replacement of "the cruder term specific productivity" with "the more scientifically precise and unobjectionable phrase marginal productivity." The iron law of wages, which stated that workers were doomed to receive subsistence wage (the wage-fund theory) "has given way to a theory which admits the influence of standards of living and various hereditary and environmental factors in determining the wages of the different labor-strata." And a new theory of interest included psychological and productivity factors. Concerning the theory of profits, "great advance has been made over the classical theory, which regarded profits as almost synonymous with interest . . . . Emphasis is now placed on the strategic position of the entrepreneur, who, as the risk-taker and director of industrial processes, acts as the shock absorber of the industrial system (ibid., 283).

Bye's essay was written in 1924, only thirty-four years after Alfred Marshall established marginal utility theory as a black box in economics. Since then, English economists (Pigou, Wicksteed, and Marshall himself), Swedish (Wicksell, Cassel), Austrian (Böhm-Bawerk, Wieser, von Mises, Schumpeter), American (Carver, Taussig, Davenport, Fisher), and others developed neoclassical applications in many fields. The debates between the Austrians, the Walrasians, and the Marshallians led to theoretical elaborations, and Bye avowed that this "evolution is bound to continue."

Bye also made a concrete promise "which would go far to meet the objection that the present theory is abstract and unreal." He asserted that future theory would focus much more "upon specific rents, profits, wages and interest rates instead of confining it so largely . . . to the more general determination of those incomes" (ibid., 284). This promise was an answer to the accusation that by speaking about "the wage rate," or "the interest rate," neoclassical theory ignored systematic differences between various kinds of workers, or between various interest rates. But Bye thought that this was not an inherent problem of neoclassical theory: it could be handled satisfactorily within its framework.[8] Bye argued also that "we must pay more attention to the frictions and obstacles of a dynamic world, which interfere with the conditions of free competition and perfect mobility assumed by the older theory" (1925, 59). Another avenue for advancing neoclassical theory was raised by Frank Knight, who believed that the passage of time was the most important element missing in neoclassical economics, that should, and could, be introduced into it (in Working 1927, 19).

The defenders went farther than promising that future developments in theory would solve the problems critics had found in neoclassical theory. They also claimed that the way to solve existing weaknesses in the theory and make it more useful was by making the theory *even more rigorous* and comprehensive. The problem, they said, was not the abstract nature of neoclassical theory, as the institutionalists claimed. On the contrary, the problem was the fact that the theory *was not abstract enough*. More rigorous, deductive, and abstract reasoning was necessary to make the theory powerful and useful. For instance, Jacob Viner raised the possibility that the old neoclassical economics was not "excessively general in its pursuit of wide generalizations," and this was why some economists were "accepting the criticism of the Lausanne school that it deals simultaneously with the variations in too few factors to give an adequate bird's-eye picture of the general system of interrelationships as a whole (in Mills 1928, 36).

Lausanne is where Leon Walras, and later Vilfredo Pareto, taught. Walras's version of neoclassical analysis was much more rigorous and abstract than the version of Jevons and Marshall, which had dominated neoclassical thinking since the end of the nineteenth century. The few supporters of the Lausanne school advocated the analysis of all markets simultaneously (general equilibrium), while Marshall and his students maintained that various markets could be analyzed only one by one (partial equilibrium), and claimed that such an analysis was good enough for all practical matters. Viner disagreed; in his opinion a return to the teachings of Walras and his school would advance neoclassical thinking since current problems were caused by the insufficient development of mainstream theory. Thus, while the institutionalists inferred from the flaws of Marshallian neoclassical economics that economics should be more empirical, Viner believed that the solution was to make the theory more mathematically rigorous. This could be achieved only by making it less empirical and more abstract.[9]

Referring to Clapham's accusation of empty boxes, Frank Taussig, a leader of neoclassical economics, agreed "that too many of our concepts and propositions are in *vacuo* and that we are but ill informed about the way in which the facts of economic life fit into them." Yet he felt that "the rapid accumulation of statistical data and their analysis by the best statistical methods were 'putting more and more into our empty boxes'" (Dorfman 1959, 4:238). It is important to note that they will fill the boxes of the existing doctrine, not build new ones; empirical studies are important for applications, not as a basis for a new theory.

The institutionalists attempted to cast doubt on the promises of neoclassicists to renew and advance orthodox theory, similar to the attempt of neoclassicists to cast doubt on the institutionalist promises. One way to achieve this goal subtly was by blurring the distinction between classical and neoclassical economics. Wesley Mitchell, for instance, said that the neoclassicists thought that marginal analysis was "radically different from Ricardo's type of theory . . . [but] Jevons, Menger, Walras,

[John Bates] Clark and their disciples did not really produce a new species of economic theory; what they had found turned out to be merely a new variety of the Ricardian species" (1924, 15). Tugwell, in a similar fashion, argued that "the early classicists marked out the way which was to be pursued by the English mathematical school, the Austrian psychological school and finally to be rounded into its perfect form by Alfred Marshall and certain Americans" (1924a, 392). Bye spoke enthusiastically on "recent developments"; he believed that the recent works in neoclassical economics were "more scientifically precise and unobjectionable," and asserted that "the theory has also been bettered in many details." Mitchell and Tugwell "cooled him down." The innovations Bye talked about might seem like great changes, but actually—the institutionalists claimed—they "did not really produce a new species of economic theory." They merely created "a new variety of the Ricardian species." These changes were certainly not enough, they implied, for adjusting the theory to the new needs of modern society and to its scientific capabilities.

The similarity of the neoclassical economics to its classical predecessors is still an open question in the historiography of economics. Some present-day economists accept the claim made by Mitchell and Tugwell; others do not. What is of interest here is the way the controversy over the relevance of the competing research program spilled over to a dispute over the interpretation of past works and their relations to contemporary works. This subject will occupy us in the next chapter, but first we have to examine another "spill over": the struggle over the place of values in the science of economics.

The Scientific Study of Value: Should Economics Be an Ethical Science?

The disputes over the goals of economics, its scope, and its methods led to a very fierce debate about the connection of economic science to values. Is economics only a "positive" science which has the sole task of describing reality, or is it also a "normative" science which is endowed with the role of assessing and judging economic institutions? The struggle over this question is closely interrelated to the debate which research program was more useful, which is the reason we discuss it here.

The pioneers of economics, or of political economy as it was known until the end of the nineteenth century, were interested in broad questions of social policy, politics, morality, and religion. For them, the treatment of economic problems naturally involved matters of values and social goals. It is only during the neoclassical era that "there has been a tendency for neoclassical economic theory to become more purely descriptive, analyzing the phenomena of economic life in a colorless, impersonal way, relegating the consideration of questions of public policy, or the goodness or badness of existing institutions, to the background, or omitting them altogether" (Bye 1924, 289). The substitution of the term "political economy" by the term "economics" reflected this trend toward "positive economics" and away from "normative economics" (Black 1983).[10] Yet many economists disputed this tendency. While "some regard this tendency as a mark of progress," Bye explained, "others decry it as a sign of decadence" (Bye 1924, 289).

Within the United States, the first battle over this issue was conducted during the 1880s and involved the founders of the AEA on one side, and the supporters of classical orthodoxy on the other side. Ely, the vociferous and polemic leader of the "new school" who laid the foundations of the AEA (see chap. 2), claimed that economists should prescribe "rules and regulations for such a production, distribution, and consumption of wealth as to render the citizens good and happy" (quoted in Ross 1991, 114). For Ely, "economics was concerned not with economic arrangements as they existed in the present, . . . but with what ought to be in the future" (Ross 1991, 114). He was supported by Henry C. Adams and by Richmond Mayo-Smith, who claimed that economics must direct state action and "say what will be the consequences of such action, and whether it will be for good or evil" (quoted in Ross 1991, 114). The older school, on the other hand, argued in favor of a complete separation between the "science" of economics and the "art" of its application in the political sphere (Lowe 1964, 199). As in Britain, Dorothy Ross says, they wanted to use the authority of science to undermine socialist ideology and support the existing economic order. Frank W. Taussig, a leader of that school, "even suggested that the sphere of state economic action be given over entirely to sociology or political science" (Ross 1991, 114).

The struggle of neoclassicists and institutionalists was connected to this emerging debate. The institutionalists continued the tradition of the AEA founders and felt that the trend toward positive economics "robs economics of its vitality and significance, making it a dry exercise in dialectics instead of an interesting and important contribution to human improvement. They would make economics a science of welfare, rather than a science of wealth" (Bye 1924, 289). For the institutionalists, this issue was one of their central rallying cries, and virtually all of them ardently opposed the separation of "positive" and "normative." In what follows I describe first the opinion of modern neoclassicists, who employed the separation of economics and values to strengthen their claim for scientific status. I then move to the institutionalists, who attacked the new neoclassical approach as barren and argued that a fruitful approach must couple a description of "what is" to normative discussions of "what ought to be."

Bye defended the separation of positive from normative questions. Pure science, he maintained, should present the world as it is. Then applied science can apply the objective knowledge to specific questions and in relation to views of how the world ought to be. He admitted that "the ultimate reason and justification for the great mass of scientific investigation . . . is undoubtedly its usefulness in promoting the welfare of mankind. . . . Economic science must show us ways of increasing the prosperity of the race if it is to justify its existence." The question, however, was "by what means we can best go about it" (1924, 289). He believed that "the surest procedure is to make a clear separation of pure from applied science. . . . Purely descriptive knowledge, impartially arrived at by disinterested observation, is a necessary preliminary to the solution of any problem" (1924, 290). Hence, he perceived the growing separation of economics and ethics as "an encouraging sign." It stripped "economic laws of their ethical bias" and made it possible to understand the "nature of things as they are." This put us "in a better position to locate defects and find means for their removal," and therefore reformers must first acquire "a thorough knowledge of pure economics if they are to achieve useful results" (ibid., 290–91).[11]

One of the claims of those neoclassicists who supported the separation of economics and values was that economists should not decide for other people what was a good service, and what was not. This belief was expressed sharply by Herbert Davenport: "What is the economist, that he should go behind the market fact and set up a social philosophy of ultimate appraisals?" (quoted in Wolfe 1924, 469). Neoclassicists therefore preferred to take a "neutral" position and to discuss how to get as much as possible of what people wanted, without pretending to judge the values of the things being sought after. This, they claimed, was the province of other fields.[12]

Institutionalists strongly objected to this reasoning. Their view was clearly stated in A. B. Wolfe's essay in *The Trend of Economics*. Wolfe argued that economics dealt with wealth *not for its own sake*, but rather because wealth represented the opportunity to gain some satisfaction. Efficiency could be assessed only by referring to this satisfaction. But if this satisfaction was the ultimate goal, then "the efficiency of our economic organization is to be measured not alone by the technical efficiency of its productive processes, but by the extent to which it succeeds in distributing products and services where they will do the most good" (1924, 476–77). J. M. Clark (1924, 73) also concentrated on the concept of "efficiency." He stated that this concept inevitably involved evaluation, and the question is whether the theory of economic efficiency could stop "short of the whole problem of ideals of good conduct and welfare; in short, of morals and ethics?" If there were such a universal and objective standard of efficiency, it would then be possible to have an economic science, which is independent of subjective values. Clark, however, did not believe that such a standard existed. He reviewed the attempts to define efficiency, first by some material standard, and later by the concept of utility, "so that economic efficiency has become, at bottom, a psychological conception" (1924, 73). He then concluded that any separation of economics from ethics *cannot be done without introducing a bias. The economic standard of judgment will become a standard which, from the broader social point of view, is limited or warped, either by excluding certain values (for instance, those on which the market sets no value which their creator can collect) or by accepting certain partial or imperfect judgments of value (for instance, the judgment of a laborer as to the fatigues and other sacrifices of production)"* (ibid., 73–74; italics in original). Efficiency must be evaluated on the basis of ultimate goals, and the goals of society "are supposed to have something ethical about them," Clark emphatically added.

The problem that Clark and Wolfe raised is a reflection of the problem of externalities (see chap. 6). If someone makes something which has some value for society, but which is not rewarded by the market ("positive externality"), then it is not enough to study the market in order to understand all aspects of social welfare. Negative externalities pose, of course, a similar problem: if someone inflicts damages and is not required to bear the costs, it is still the job of economists to consider those hurtful effects in their study of welfare. Goods and services which do not improve welfare, that is, do not make people happier, such as fashion and "conspicuous consumption," should not be reckoned in the calculation of social welfare, even though they are profitable for individual firms. As Morris Copeland claimed, if all persons "had to bear all the costs and could reap all the gains" of their activities, "we should probably be safe in assuming the coincidence of individual interests [as reflected by market prices] and the common welfare" (1924, 115). But this was not the case, and given the existence of externalities, "the necessity for economists to take some stand on the issue has become of increasing importance" (ibid.).

The notion that economists should deal with all aspects of human welfare, and not only with market transactions, was clearly related to the view of institutionalists on human nature. Both the recognition of nonmaterial interests and the repudiation of hedonistic conceptions led to the conclusion that a theory of welfare could not limit itself only to marketable goods and services. Taking "consumption as the end of all things corresponds to hedonistic ethics," Clark argued (1924, 89), and this meant that economists could not limit themselves to the study of markets and prices. They had to consider all spheres of human life and employ a realistic conception of human nature in order to know what added to human welfare. This idea was very important for institutionalists, and they built a large array of arguments to establish it as a central black box of economic science. I identified six such reasons given by institutionalists.

First, John Maurice Clark argued that a change of the legal order may change the "wealth" of a society by giving more or less exclusive rights to owners of some property. Paradoxically, "an invention, once made public, is not 'productive,' and the inventor is not a productive factor" because everybody can make use of the invention without paying for it. But if the inventor could keep patent rights and sell the invention, then it would become "wealth" (1924, 88). This argument exposed the illogical nature of the neoclassical definition of wealth, which is based on market valuations. If we want to measure the welfare of society, Clark and many other institutionalists asserted, we cannot rely upon market values, which change according to arbitrary legal statutes. And if we cannot use market values, we must rely upon our own judgment.[13]

A second argument in favor of the institutionalist approach was the long list of problems which persisted in spite of material richness or even because of them. Morris Copeland mentioned, among other things, "waste of natural resources," "chronic idleness of people and of industrial apparatus," "non-living wages, insecurity of workers," and "production of armaments, luxuries, adulterated products" (1924, 107). All these examples came to one thing: suffering is prolonged in spite of the enormous advances in production. Something must be wrong if orthodox theory asserted that modern societies were much better-off than they had been a few decades earlier, while most of the population, the workers, were getting very low wages and lived in a constant fear of being laid off. Davenport might have had a point in arguing that economists should not make decisions for citizens about the importance of goods and services. But to deny that a society was better-off when income was transferred from the rich to a poor family on the verge of starvation appeared illogical to Copeland and to his fellow institutionalists.[14]

Third, several institutional economists thought that even if a separation of economics from ethics "could be done, it would be nothing less than disastrous for a young science that hopes to become more and more important and useful and for a world which needs to have the work of the economists directed toward the betterment of its material situation" (Tugwell 1924a, 420). Here we return to the domain of relevance. A. B. Wolfe (1924, 469) warned that the view that economists should not consider at all "whether [economic] service was beneficial or harmful," might turn economics into a useless discipline. He cited Charles Horton Cooley, the economist from the University of Michigan who helped institutionalize American sociology. Cooley maintained that conventional value economics had become "almost wholly a short-range study of mechanism, remarkable for elaborateness within a confined area, but not at all remarkable for breadth or for any light it throws on the wider economic and social significance of the mechanism which it treats" (quoted in Wolfe 1924, 469–70).

Fourth, the institutionalists denied that there was any contradiction between understanding the economy as it was and discussing its virtues and vices. These were two related practices, which should be pursued separately according to Bye. Yet in order to implement the "positive" aspect well, the economist "should be highly conversant with existing social purposes, constructively critical of them, intimately aware of the present effects of social forces in detail, actively concerned with possible alternative ways and means of achieving . . . goals" (Homan 1928, 352). This view entailed the separation of the "positive" from the "normative" *but invested economists with the responsibility for both* (Copeland 1924, 121). The evaluation of economic institutions and policies was essential, Slichter argued, and this task involved appraisal. But it was a task "which the economist can scarcely escape, for, if he does not study how the economic system works, who will?" (1924, 307). Philosophers did not know the "positive" aspect and could not make well-informed judgments about what was good for the society *economically*. "The economist is best equipped to investigate the common economic interest" (Copeland 1924, 123), and it should, therefore, be her role to evaluate the overall social results of economic policies.

Fifth, whether we liked it or not, *it was impossible to divorce economics from ethical norms*. A. B. Wolfe maintained that all the older schools, including classical economics and neoclassical marginalism, were based on ethical criteria (1924, 474–76). Even the work of business economists—his term for a new trend in neoclassical economics—reflected their value-preferences by revealing "a sort of irritable contemptuousness for any economics which does not accept profit and physical output as criteria of economy and 'prosperity'" (ibid., 476). The "logical gymnastics [that] the pure science economists are put to in their attempt to evade ethical norms and valuations," Wolfe scoffed, confirmed that "non-ethical economics" was impossible (ibid.). Some institutionalists went even farther and argued that the allegedly non-normative analysis of neoclassical theory was *more* ideologically biased, because it was based on hidden value judgments, whereas institutionalists discussed values openly.[15] George Soule, for instance, claimed that "the imaginary system of economic universals [of orthodox theory] . . . brought about a feeling that attempts to control economic phenomena through the exercise of human will or ingenuity were fruitless and hence probably immoral" (1924, 363). If, according to the theory, nothing could be done to redress a regrettable situation, the neoclassicist would be inclined to justify the situation as inevitable, regardless of how much she despised that situation. Soule argued that such a conclusion cloaked a very concrete ideology.[16]

Wage policy is a good example. Bye accepted the normative view that wages were too low but argued that the goal of raising wages could be achieved only if the laws of economics were heeded. The goal could be achieved only by raising marginal productivity or by limiting the supply of labor, not through collective bargaining: "A better knowledge of economic theory would have prevented many a trade union abuse and pointed out the path to real wage increases" (1924, 297). The institutionalists rejected the idea of economic laws, and Slichter explicitly argued that wages were determined not according to marginal productivity, but rather according to the power of workers (see chap. 6). Laws that explained why collective bargaining could not work were therefore not based on science; they were a rather apologetic justification of the existing order.

The sixth argument in favor of normative economics was that welfare could be studied scientifically even though it involved values. Copeland argued that economists could study empirically what things were valued by the society (Copeland, 1924, 123). A. B. Wolfe asserted that while economics was "necessarily a science of means and ends. . . . ethics is also fundamentally a science . . . of means and ends." Wolfe maintained that economists could not "escape the task of taking into consideration the relative value of the conflicting ends themselves." But "taking into consideration" did not mean that economists had to decide what values should actually be considered as more important. They had to register what the public thought and take note of conflicts of ultimate goals when they found them (1924, 477).[17]

"Positive" economists, who did not want to make any value judgment, were forced to resort to material wealth as measured by market prices as the only criterion for welfare susceptible to scientific analysis. They did not say that material wealth was the only thing that counted. But they insisted that this was the only thing that economists could speak about *as economists* (cf. chap. 5). Institutionalists responded to this by arguing that (1) market prices depended on arbitrary legal statutes; (2) the satisfaction derived from material wealth depended on its use and its distribution; (3) the neoclassical approach ignored important aspects of welfare; (4) economists could deal with factual and normative issues separately, and they were the only ones who could evaluate properly economic welfare; (5) neoclassical economics itself was biased by the nature of its premises; and (6) social goals, which might serve as criteria for evaluating social welfare, could be determined scientifically by studying human beings and finding what they were actually satisfied by.

It should be remembered, however, that in this issue, the institutionalists were supported by a large faction of neoclassicists. Frank Knight, one of the most prominent neoclassicists during that period, concurred, for instance, that the coupled treatment of goals and means by economists was unavoidable and, more than this, desired:

> [It] is in fact necessary and proper for the question of objectives to occupy a large if not the main part of social discussion. For social science cannot, like the natural sciences, be restricted to the problem of means for achieving objectives taken for granted. Not the winning of power, but its use is, and must be, the leading question (1928, 247).

Knight thought that the attempt to separate values and facts stemmed from a feeling of "pronounced irritation" on the part of a large proportion of social scientists due to the uncertainty concerning the appropriate method of social science. This feeling caused a considerable number of younger men to "seek escape in the methods of the natural sciences," and the positive-normative dichotomy was part of this attempt. Knight considered this attempt hopeless. He argued instead "that the situation from which escape is sought is not so bad as it seems" (ibid.). Social science was different from natural science and one should not aspire to the same level of certainty and immediate applicability as in the natural sciences. Economics should consist of a discourse on human problems, and that is why the separation of values from science was completely misguided.

Conclusions: The Coupling of Validity and Relevance

This chapter demonstrated that alleged relevance to practical needs played an important role in the trial of strength between institutionalists and neoclassicists. Both parties presented their visions of the contributions their approaches would make to the solution of urgent economic problems and cast doubt on the promises of their rivals. Institutionalists argued that their empirical research program was much more suitable than the obsolete neoclassical approach for proper understanding and handling of current economic problems. Neoclassicists, on the other hand, claimed that institutionalists would drown in the complexities of the countless social factors they wished to study. They maintained that their own neoclassical approach would be much more useful because it tackled *only* the most central aspects of economic behavior. They admitted that by abstracting from reality, they ignored pertinent facets of economic behavior. But they insisted that this was the most fruitful strategy to comprehend the economy and govern it.

Promises for the future cannot be proved. In contrast to substantive theoretical or methodological reasonings that can be subjected to rigorous logical examination, promises deal, by definition, with the unknown, and are therefore inherently speculative. Thus, even those positivists who believe that decisions in science should be made solely on the basis of solid "facts" and sound logical reasoning must admit that when two competing strategies are offered, the choice often involves beliefs in the unproved potentialities of these strategies. This conclusion is supported by a common practice of scientists. It is common in science to say that it is not "fair" to judge a new theory, research method, or technique in its early stages, and practitioners from all fields justifiably demand to subject their methods and ideas to the "test of time." In other words, they ask us to ignore visible contradictions and problems on the ground that proper answers and solutions may emerge during the development of their innovations. Kuhn took account of this aspect and noticed that new paradigms are often less powerful in their outset than the established paradigms they wish to replace (1970a, 154). In choosing scientific strategies, we thus face again "a situation in which there can be no proof," which therefore calls upon the use of "techniques of persuasion" (ibid., 152). Such practices mean that decisions are reached on the basis of arational, aesthetic, and metaphysical views (ibid., 155–59), a conclusion that jibes with ours in chapter 4.

Can we make a rational decision on the basis of an examination of the past records of the competing research programs? The answer is no, and the reasons are similar to those we explicated in earlier chapters. First, the reliance upon past records is not a simple "automatic" practice but rather a process of assessment: is a certain "achievement" really an achievement, and can it really be attributed to the school which claims it as its own? Was the War Industries Board of World War I, for instance, really successful? Was its success due to the "institutionalist" approach of its economists? No universal, uncontested answers exist for such questions. The same is true with regard to failures. Institutionalists claimed that "orthodox theory" failed to offer solutions to the urgent problems of the post–World War I period. But did it really fail? Who should answer such a question? Many people indeed complained about the economic situation, which, for all practical matters, means that there was a "crisis." But would the outcomes have been better had institutionalists controlled economic policy making? Or would the situation have been worsened? There is no absolute and indisputable way to answer such questions apart from substantive beliefs about the economy. Answers also depend on theoretical frameworks and methodological approaches. The only way to reach a conclusion is to conduct trials of strength in which contenders would raise conflicting arguments and debate competing views. "Successes," a popular adage says, "have many parents; failures are orphans." This is true in science as it is valid elsewhere, and institutionalists and neoclassicists exemplified this "principle" by claiming the successes for themselves and blaming their rivals for the failures.

There is, however, a second, not less severe problem in using the past as the basis for judging the ability of competing schools to provide suitable answers to the pressing needs of today. Whatever the successes and failures of the past, they do not prove the ability to tackle *current* problems. We should not necessarily support those approaches that had many achievements in the past—even if nobody challenges these successes—because this would be a prescription for stagnation. Nor can we infer from an indisputable failure in the past that a research program is hopelessly impotent in solving the challenges of the future. The neoclassicists did capitalize on past successes, but this only confirmed the institutionalists' contention that orthodox theory was an obsolete approach, inadequate for the *new* problems of mature industrial economies. Neoclassicists, however, admitted that their approach needed revisions to be able to handle new problems and insisted such revisions were already under way.

Past successes (and failures) do not prove the ability (or inability) to solve current problems. Yet such a record, like examples from other disciplines and philosophical arguments, have an impact on the evaluation of the contending research programs by uncommitted practitioners who have to make their choices. This is why the advocates referred to the achievements their respective schools had allegedly realized. The institutionalists "explained" that their research program was still young, but they pointed to several studies that, according to them, already increased our knowledge of economic realities and our ability to treat economic problems. Neoclassicists understood that references to long-past achievements would not convince the contemporary audience in the suitability of their approach and therefore stressed the recent developments in their theoretical treatment of present problems.

While the past may provide some indications of practical capabilities, a conviction in the potential of a research program to solve urgent present problems ultimately relies on a belief in the validity of its interpretation of the world and the adequacy of its research methods. Neoclassical economists believed that their theory took into consideration the most essential elements of the economy and trusted the practical conclusions they derived from it. In their opinion, the orthodox theory of value was most valuable in the construction of economic policy. Institutionalists, on the other hand, believed that by breaking "the closed circle of the old economic universals," they were able to generate "at once a more useful practice and a more vital theory" (Soule 1924, 365).

Here we come full circle: the practical value was supposed to help us decide which approach was more valid, at least pragmatically; but the belief in the practicality of a scientific approach ultimately depended on its assumed validity. Hence, claims of usefulness should not be viewed as an independent criterion for good science. It should be conceived rather as one "front" of the overall debate among contending approaches. As scientific advocates debate "facts" and theories, so do they argue over usefulness, and the arguments are inextricably woven together. A theory is claimed to be valid because it "solves problems," but the belief that a theory really solves problems ultimately relies upon its assumed validity.

Many historians of economic thought tend to explain the rise and fall of scientific schools by stating that winning approaches were "more practical," or "more relevant" for the problems of their times, while the losing schools are frequently presented as "irrelevant" to the solution of pressing problems.[18] Based on our ongoing analysis, we have to reject such explanations. It would not suffice to say that institutionalism expanded in the 1920s because it offered practical solutions to the problems of the day, as it would be too simple to explain its decline in the 1950s by some hypothetical loss of its potential practicality. The question is not which theory was "really" more useful—a question that we, as outside observers, do not have the tools to answer—but which theory was more successful in convincing practicing economists that it was more useful.

In our case, we can say that institutionalism rose after World War I because there was a sense—not a proof by any means—that it offered better solutions to contemporary problems. The war threw the world economy out of balance, and the huge debts of governments, internally and to other governments, further exacerbated the situation. A sense of chaos in the economy always encourages doubts about the adequacy of economic science, and thus helps the opposition to shake established doctrines (Wiley 1983, 46). In addition, the surprising success of managed economies during the war raised another question mark concerning the traditional teachings of orthodox economics. But neither the postwar difficulties nor the success of the war economy provided decisive proof that institutionalism had better solutions. The winning nations in World War I, we know, failed to heed the advice of mainstream economists (Keynes 1988 [1919]). The latter could therefore shift the blame for the difficulties on politicians, as they certainly did, and not without justification. Similarly, the success of the managed economy during the *war* did not show that such a system would be more efficient during *peace*time, as Keynes perceptively warned (1924, 35). The success of institutionalism was therefore not a direct and logically unavoidable consequence of the changing atmosphere. It rose because its advocates were able to seize upon the atmosphere and convince many of their colleagues that the established doctrine indeed "failed," and that their alternative approach, among the many alternative approaches, had the best chances to "fix" the economy.

The same principle applies to the explanation of the fall of institutionalism after the Second World War. Nowadays, neoclassical economists often claim that institutionalism failed because it had no substantive program to replace the orthodox policies it criticized (see chap. 3). Since mainstream economics is dominated today by the Keynesian-neoclassical synthesis, this "explanation" has been accepted by many economists and noneconomists. We, however, should be aware that such contentions are self-serving and cannot be accepted at face value. The few surviving followers of institutionalism, for example, claim that their school had concrete programs, which were applied during Roosevelt's New Deal and Truman's Fair Deal. They even assert that the success of the economy in the 1950s and 1960s was due to institutionalist policies (see chap. 3). For modern economists, this would probably sound as a ridiculous claim. But the outside observer should not privilege the "common knowledge." She must investigate why and how most economists came to believe that institutionalists had no concrete program. This is the question historians should deal with, instead of constructing a Whig history which simply explains that one theory lost because it was replaced by a better one.

There are many examples for similar trials of strength over relevance in other disciplines. In the case of taxonomy the traditional taxonomists argued that whatever the merits of the experimental approach *in principle*, it just did not do as an answer to practical needs because it is "the work of a lifetime," and "one can hardly expect taxonomists . . . to wait so long (Faegri 1937 as quoted in Dean 1979, 220), a claim which is amazingly similar to arguments made by both neoclassicists and institutionalists. The advocates of "pure science," Richard Whitley says, often defend themselves by claiming future applicability for their "scientific" work (1984, 55). The experimental taxonomists, the "pure scientists" in this context, admitted that the old taxonomy "has its value" for certain immediate needs. But "permanent taxonomic results," they argued, "must await the application of statistical and experimental methods" (Dean 1979, 213). They believed, in other words, that in the future, after elaborations and refinements of the new method, the latter would be *even more useful* than the old methods which appear more productive in the short-run. Such a claim was made by both the institutionalists and the neoclassicists. The former had just begun developing statistical tools and claimed that the results were soon to come; the latter set themselves on the mission of rigorous reformulation of orthodox theory which, they believed, would make the theory applicable to daily economic life.

Another example is provided in the study of MacKenzie and Barnes on biometry and Mendelism. Biometrists pointed to the predictive power of their statistical analyses, and thus held the same position as institutionalists. Mendelists argued, in contrast, that their approach explicated the *mechanism* of evolution, and thus had the *potential* of improving predictive possibilities to a previously unimaginable level (MacKenzie and Barnes 1979, 194–95), an argument which in many respects resembles the contentions of the neoclassicists such as Knight and Viner. In general, questions of "do-ability" are raised in the attempts of competitors to present their rivals' goals as "utopian," "undoable," "unfeasible," and so forth (Fujimura 1987). The rivals meet such doubts by demanding patience and by brushing failures aside as temporary difficulties (Law 1973).

Trials of strength over relevance continue in present-day economics as well. Mathematical economics, which has dominated postwar economics, has often been accused of excessive formalism. This accusation is voiced every now and then by distinguished economists, by supporters of heterodox schools, by scientists from other fields, and by business and government officials. Claims similar to those made by institutionalists sixty and seventy years ago are often used by these recent critics. And as their interwar predecessors, the advocates of mainstream, mathematical, neoclassical economics continue to defend their approach, to point to alleged achievements, and to promise more impressive successes in the future. Similar trials of strength take place inside the mainstream as well as among competing alternatives. Neo-Keynesians claim that their approach does not only capture "reality" better than the theories of their rivals; they also aver that it offers better tools to solve the economic problems of our period (Hahn and Solow 1995). Their rivals also think that their policy prescriptions, extreme or attenuated *laissez-faire*, is the best solution to the same economic difficulties. Alternative approaches, such as Neo-Marxism, institutionalism, post Keynesianism, neo-Austrian economics, Schumpeterian economics, and others maintain that they have better solutions than mainstream economics. But each one of them also asserts that its answer is more useful than any of the other alternatives. And as was the case in the 1920s and 1930s, so does the present struggle involve questions of scientific validity, perceptions of reality, and competing interpretations of theories and facts.

Eight

Evolution or Revolution? The Struggle over the History of the Discipline

> There can be small revolutions as well as large ones, and some revolutions affect only the members of a professional subspeciality, and that for such groups even the discovery of a new and unexpected phenomena may be revolutionary.
>
> The Depreciation of historical fact is deeply, and probably functionally, ingrained in the ideology of the scientific profession, the same profession that places the highest of all values upon factual details of other sorts. . . . The sciences, like other professional enterprises, do need their heroes and do preserve their names. Fortunately, instead of forgetting these heroes, scientists have been able to forget or revise their works.
>
> (Thomas S. Kuhn, *The Structure of Scientific Revolutions*)

THIS CHAPTER deals with the way in which contenders in a scientific conflict relate their contentions to past works in their field. There are three dimensions to the connection between the past and ongoing scientific struggles. First, scientists have to decide whether to present their ideas as continuing the past or as a break-away from it. Second, the contenders construct the history of the field in such a way as to make their contributions look like natural developments from the past. They may emphasize the work of selected practitioners in the past and downplay the role of others, or they may present earlier approaches in such a way as to make their own approach appear to be the next logical stage of development. They can also, on a third dimension, interpret past work according to the story they tell, in such a way as to justify their own work (Gerrard 1993, 60). One way or another, the past is a focal point in conflicts among paradigms (Brown 1993).

The first question a new group of scientists must ask is how to connect its program to the works previously carried out in the field. Should they claim that they continue a magnificent tradition? Or should they proclaim to break away from a mistaken line of inquiry which leads nowhere? In science, "progress" is a primary value, but given the uncertainty of scientific results, the authority of past scientists, whose contributions to the advancement of the field are highly recognized and respected, also has its own legitimizing power. The choice is not between innovation, on the one hand, and loyalty to the past, on the other. It is obvious that merely sticking to past achievements would not lead present scientists to the recognition that they seek as *original* scientists. The real choice is how to *frame* one's novel results. In other words, the question that scientists face is not whether to innovate or not, but rather how to *package* their innovations (Pinch 1990, 658; cf. Perrin 1987; Mendelsohn 1974).

The choice how to present a new contribution is *not* determined by the degree of similarity of its content to old teachings. Even a party which advances opinions which *seem* to be patently in contrast to the views of the "Founding Fathers" of a certain field does not have to give up the attempt to recruit those Founding Fathers. They can recruit the *spirit* of "sacred writings" or they can advance new interpretations of the "sacred writings" that are compatible with their novel ideas. Arguments may be made that would the Founding Fathers be alive today, know what we know today, and be acquainted with modern methods, they would have adjusted their views to be like those of the recruiting party. In fact there is no objective way of knowing the "degree of similarity" between a current program and an older tradition apart from the arguments made by interested contenders. What we later hear about similarities and differences reflects the outcome of the struggle, and, hence, cannot be presented as the independent causes of how new approaches are perceived. As Nature cannot explain the outcomes of scientific controversies (Latour 1987), so it is impossible to use the writings of the Founding Fathers to explain the outcomes of scholarly controversies over the interpretation of those writings. The actual decisions of scientists depend on concrete contemporary circumstances in the fields they work in and on general values of the surrounding environments. A sense of "crisis" may push economists to speak more in terms of "breaking away," even if they offer only minor changes. During more tranquil times they would be more likely to present their work as "continuing the past," even if they want to change the face of the field entirely.[1]

Defying the laws of nature, the best strategy for any group of scientists would be to try to have their cake and eat it too. They would try to present their work as very innovative but at the same time find "evidence" in the writings of the Founding Fathers that these radically new ideas are also in line with the spirit of the Fathers. But since it would not be easy to persuade an audience that both of these claims are true, scientists often have to choose which aspect to stress: continuity or change. We should also be aware that the members of a single paradigm do not necessarily share the same view of the past. Their opinions in this issue are not only a matter of cognitive similarity, but also a political decision and a matter of personal "tastes." Even if practitioners share the same theoretical positions, they may adopt different strategies to advance these ideas as a result of their different assessments of the balance of power in the field or due to different personal temperaments.

The first section of this chapter deals with the neoclassical strategy of presenting the institutionalists as extreme revolutionaries, who ignored the great achievements of Adam Smith, Ricardo, John Stuart Mill, Jevons, Marshall, and the other masters of economics. The institutionalists pleaded "not guilty" and concentrated their efforts on establishing the connections between their approach and those great economists traditionally revered by the discipline. Their efforts in this regard are described in the second section of this chapter. Not all institutionalists, however, pledged allegiance to the classical and neoclassical tradition, and many of them added the authority of nonconformist economists to their efforts to stabilize the institutionalist network. These aspects are covered in the third section of this chapter. The last section summarizes and discusses the way in which the past was used by interwar practitioners.

A "Revolutionary" Stigma: The Neoclassical Attack on Institutionalism

Raymond T. Bye led an attack on institutionalism, in which he claimed that institutionalist economics is going to discard all the marvelous achievements of the past. Bye began his essay by distinguishing three possible reactions to any change: conservative, revolutionist, and evolutionist. The conservative "clings tenaciously to the past, resisting all progress"; the revolutionist "sees only the defects . . . and, too eager for future possibilities, . . . he would throw away all the old"; and, finally, the evolutionist "knows that the world moves onward, but he regards this process as one of orderly growth. Therefore for him progress means no rough breakage with the past" (1924, 271). Referring concretely to the institutionalists, Bye argued that those "severe critics, . . . impatient at the abstractions and strained logic of neoclassicism . . . would throw away much or all of classical teachings, hoping to substitute for it a new economics, resting on sounder premises and using a better methodology" (ibid.). The institutionalists, he implied, were extreme radicals, who in spite of their good intentions might cause great harm to the discipline by abandoning the teachings of their predecessors.

Such accusations were typical. Neoclassicists, for example, exploited Wesley Mitchell's declaration in his 1924 presidential address that "there is . . . much likelihood that [old explanations] will be disregarded" due to quantitative investigations (Mitchell 1925, 3). John Black claimed that this statement "has done considerable harm." Although Mitchell denied that his statement disparaged theory, Black contended that "young men who know little of economic theory have taken it to mean that [theory] is nothing for them to worry about, . . ., that all they need to do is get busy with some data and develop some principles of their own" (in Mills 1928, 44). Jacob Viner's attack in that same roundtable meeting (ibid.) was much harsher. Viner took issue with Mitchell's assertion that the new economists would "be content to make detailed investigations narrowly confined in their range and to build up a mass of information" (ibid., 34). He explained that Mitchell's predictions were "almost precisely identical . . . to the prophecies of the German historical school some sixty years ago." It was this resemblance, he added, that concerned him so much. The German school was successful in revolutionizing the learning of economics in Germany, and the result was, according to Viner, a sheer failure. "German economics," he said, "is now obviously struggling to repair the resultant damage, and . . . to regain the exalted position which it occupied before the historical school won its costly and temporary victory" (ibid., 24).[2]

The way that the German historical school was introduced into the historical narrative is a typical case of how parties in scientific disputes attempt to implicate their rivals by associating them with negatively valued names from the past. By equating institutionalism with the German school, Viner drew on the attitudes prevalent in the field. He did not analyze the German historical school's position and its implications but assumed that the school had been a disaster for the advancement of economic knowledge. Like Viner, Frank Knight did not bother to say what is wrong with the German school or to analyze the similarities between that school and institutionalism. He casually mentioned "the father of the new Historismus in American economics, Dr. Thorstein Veblen" (1924, 249), thus creating an impression that institutionalism was nothing but a new version of the German school, and hence, equally misguided and dangerous.[3]

Institutionalist writers were aware that "an avowal of historical method nowadays is likely to be construed as a repetition of the defects of that method as used by some students [i.e., the German historicists— Y. Y.] in the past" (Edie 1927, 414). They could have counterattacked either by challenging the negative valuation of the German historical school—thus opening a closed black box that defined the German historical school as a failure—or by dissociating themselves from that school. They chose the second option and admitted that "in the hands of some of the adherents of the German historical school, history tended to become either an encyclopedic description of raw facts or an attempt to formulate certain universal laws of development" (ibid.). Mitchell also denounced the German approach for moving from the extreme of too abstract a theory to the equally erroneous extreme of discarding the whole structure of abstract theory (Mitchell 1924, 18).

Yet the institutionalists also emphasized the positive aspects of the German school: "It is indeed a narrow view," Edie said about the criticism against German historicism, "which encompasses only the defects of their work, and ignores their contribution to inductive method, to economic realism, and to evolutionary interpretation of economic institutions (1927, 414; cf. Gay 1930; Young 1927). This is another example of the "forensic" tactics of pursuing two contradictory lines of defense simultaneously: we are not like the German historicists, the institutionalists seem to say, but even if you—the impartial jury—find us to be similar to the Germans, please notice that the latter have made several important contributions to economics.

The neoclassicist, who presented themselves as the guardians of the past, faced a different dilemma. Since the notion of progress is central to the scientific ideology, pledging allegiance to the long-dead masters of the discipline may expose the pledgers to the accusation that they were doctrinaire believers, who promoted a religion rather than a science.[4] Thus, they had to be sophisticated enough in mobilizing the past in such a way as not to contradict their simultaneous claim for innovation. Bye's solution was to speak about *evolution* as the golden path between revolution and conservatism. "Older theories are being modified and corrected; but progress is being made . . . by building from what has gone before" (1924, 272). "It is not to be expected," he said on another occasion, "that economics will forever fit into the mold that was cast for it by such men as Adam Smith, David Ricardo, and John Stuart Mill. There would be no progress in our science if we did not modify, refine, and supplement their crude generalizations" (1925, 59).

In the previous chapter we saw that the neoclassicists displayed the recent developments in their theory and promised to make many more innovations. To maintain this impression of innovativeness, Bye, Viner, and others condemned fellow neoclassicists, who wanted to preserve the doctrine unchanged, at least as harshly as they condemned the institutionalist opponents of neoclassical theory. For example, Bye denounced those "exponents of neo-classical economics" who "have become enamored of its dialectics and logical symmetry, and continue to dispose it to their disciples in much of its original form" (1924, 271). This devastating attack is as taxing and unrelenting as any of the attacks waged by the most extreme institutionalists. But Bye did not conduct this attack in order to debunk the neoclassical approach in principle. On the contrary, he did it to escape the criticism aimed at the old theory by distancing himself and orthodox theory itself from its doctrinaire backers.

Institutionalists as the Guardians of Tradition

In the textbooks on the history of economic thought institutionalism is presented without exception as an antithetical approach to neoclassical economics. We noticed ourselves in earlier chapters the strong objection that institutionalists raised to the old doctrine. We may think, therefore, that in this case, the institutionalist protagonists had no other choice but to wage a direct attack on the established doctrine and to openly deny any ties to Smith, Ricardo, Marshall, and the rest of the economic pantheon. It seems as if there was no way that they could claim to be the followers of those economists. Bye and Viner, it can therefore be argued, have not "stigmatized" institutionalists as revolutionary; they simply presented the "simple truth" about them. Would not the institutionalists themselves disavow any tie to the past?

Nevertheless, they did not. Many of the institutionalists conceived themselves as the *legitimate successors* of the traditional economists and refused to denounce their predecessors: "Saying that 'Adam Smith is out of date' or 'Mill's work is obsolete,' is temptingly easy and only too common" (Cobb 1928, 64). Instead of disowning earlier generations, the institutionalists brazenly claimed that they continued along avenues envisioned by the discipline pioneers themselves: "Fully a generation ago, vision of the trends of economic science which are now materializing [i.e., institutionalism—Y. Y.] was in the minds of leading economists" (Edie 1927, 438). The institutionalist strategy was to emphasize those elements in the work of past economists that resembled their own program. As we saw in chapter 3, this was not a bogus scheme; there were real similarities between the work of institutionalists and those who had preceded them. But for our analysis here, one should not care how similar they "really" were. What the reader should mind is the tactics used by the institutionalists to convey the impression of similarity. That we tend to assume today that the institutionalists totally broke away from the generations before them is a testimony to the success of Viner, Bye, and others to turn their view into a part of the dominant network and the failure of institutionalist to black box their perception of history. But as historians we must free ourselves from conventions and examine how the institutionalists themselves presented their relations to previous teachings.

The institutionalists maintained that the "attempt to apply new methods of scientific inquiry" were not new "but are simply a matter of greater emphasis upon methods which have long been recognized" (Edie 1927, 408–9). William Weld, for example, included Marshall and Pareto among those who "have been desirous of reaching . . . inductive principles" (1924, 432). Wesley Mitchell even presented the emerging quantitative approach as a mature stage of traditional economics. "The method of Ricardo and the method of the modern quantitative worker," he told an audience at the AEA Annual Meetings, "are identical" (in Working 1927, 20). A figure that many institutionalists referred to was Alfred Marshall, the epitome of neoclassical economics. Notwithstanding his role in enshrining neoclassical economics, the institutionalists emphasized that Alfred Marshal had been inclined toward empirical research and had felt the need for greater emphasis on such research. In his 1925 presidential address, Mitchell quoted Marshall as saying that his own qualitative work should be supplemented by statistical work, which had not yet been possible due to lack of data (1925, 1). Frederick C. Mills reminded us that "Alfred Marshall long since called economic laws 'statements of economic tendencies,'" which meant that he abandoned the view that economic laws truly described the behavior of real people (1924, 49; see also Edie 1927, 438; Cobb 1928, 67).

Other protagonists of orthodox theory were also mentioned. Lionel Edie recruited William S. Jevons. In a lecture given in 1876, Jevons anticipated a vigorous growth of "concrete" historical and mathematical economics alongside the old "abstract" science. Edie quoted from Jevons's famous book: "Economics might be gradually erected into an exact science, if only commercial statistics were far more complete and accurate than they are at present." Jevons was further quoted as arguing that "the deductive science of Economics must be verified and rendered useful by the purely empirical science of statistics. Theory must be invested with the reality and life of fact" (quoted in Edie 1927, 439; on Jevons see also Mills 1924, 44 and 49n). Francis A. Walker, one of the most respected American economists of the nineteenth century (1840–97), was similarly quoted as promoting in 1889 the new scientific spirit, by which he meant the "more careful observation of phenomena," and the use of statistics (Edie 1927, 439). "Similar sentiments," Edie continued, "were expressed by Patten, Dunbar, Cairnes, Ely, [John Neville] Keynes, Giffen, and many others" (ibid., 440). These economists were all part of the pantheon of economics, and by stressing their support of empirical studies, institutionalists sought to mesh them into their own network.

The opponents of institutionalism could argue that, the above statements notwithstanding, those great economists of the past did not pursue statistical work themselves. It seems that this method was not considered important enough by those economists. Scholars often support many ideas in general but realize only those ideas that they deem most vital. This argument threatened the institutionalist recruitment of the distinguished past economists. They needed therefore to explain the fact that the economists they mentioned had not employed quantitative methods themselves. One explanation was given by George Soule, who pointed at the lack of sufficient data and statistical tools in the nineteenth century, an explanation supported by Marshall and Jevons in the above quotations. Soule explained that "the premature flowering of economic theory" was a "necessary fault in the pioneers," because the quantitative way was not open for them. But this inclination "was exaggerated by their followers, and in some cases was even exalted into a conscious method" in contrast to the spirit of the pioneers (1924, 360–61). If the Founding Fathers were alive today, Soule implied, they would have supported the institutionalist party in its struggle with contemporary neoclassical economists.

Another way to construct the new agenda as continuing the practice of past economists was to say that the old way of doing economics was suitable for studying the simple economy of the past. Classical and neoclassical theory, the argument went, gave a valid account of the economy in the nineteenth century. Nevertheless, the world changed so much that the old theory lost its explanatory power. William Weld, for example, suggested that the *ceteris paribus* clause, on which the deductive reasoning of comparative statics was based, was useful to analyze the simple economy of the nineteenth century. In such an economy it was possible to find two situations which differ in one thing only, "others things being equal." But in the modern world, Weld explained, "the so-called 'other things' are less likely to be equal" (1924, 426). Similarly, Sumner Slichter gave a whole list of new realities which had emerged since Adam Smith's time, but had been ignored by orthodox theory (1924, 304). Whether economic theory was deductive and abstract because quantitative tools and data were not available, as Soule and Mitchell maintained, or because the simpler economy of the nineteenth century could have been properly comprehended by such a simplified theory, as Slichter and Weld contended—the bottom line is the same: classical theory might have been the best possible one in the nineteenth century but was inadequate for modern times (Taylor 1928). The new institutionalist approach, its advocates claimed, retained the spirit of the classical theorists and adjusted the basic principles of those scholars to modern economies and to the possibilities of modern science.

It seems, on the face of it, more difficult to argue that the institutionalists held the same view of human behavior that the heroes of the past have held. Classical writers, so we have learned, introduced the concept of "homo economicus" into economic thinking. Hedonism and rationality, the two most essential features of that "economic man," were two of the main accusations that institutionalists made against orthodox theory. The institutionalists could not exonerate the classical economists in this issue without undermining their arguments concerning human nature and society (chap. 5). What they did was to argue over the meanings that the classical forebears had assigned to the conception of the "economic man" and to say that it was not part of their "hard core." An example is provided by John Maurice Clark, who pointed to the similarity between his own approach to human nature and the classical view of Adam Smith (1924, 97). Clark found evidence that the classicists did not support the idea of rationality; they only thought that individuals could choose better than governments.[5]

Paul Douglas devoted much space to repudiate the conception of "economic man" in his essay in *The Trend of Economics* (1924). Yet Douglas contended that the institutionalist view was not so much divorced from the thinking of classical and neoclassical economists. For instance, Nassau Senior (1790–1864), a prominent classical economist who explicitly elaborated the behavioral assumptions behind the economic-man conception, did not assume "that men desired wealth for its own sake." "On the contrary, Douglas continued, "he forestalled such criticism . . . by admitting that men's 'wants are as various as the differences in individual characters.'" Douglas reminded us that Senior's *An Outline of the Science of Political Economy* (1836) had mentioned the wish to get power, distinction, leisure, bodily and mental amusement, and to benefit friends and the public. Senior promoted the concept of the economic man on the ground that money "seems to be the only object for which the desire is universal" (ibid., 153). The same logic drove J. N. Keynes to support the "economic man." He agreed that "there may be other incentives to effort" than material ones. But he asserted that "in order to introduce the simplicity that is requisite in a scientifically exact treatment . . ., it is legitimate and even indispensable to begin" by assuming that the desire for wealth "operates without check" (ibid., 154).

Douglas commented that "little objection can perhaps legitimately be offered to such a method, if those who employed it were aware of the limited character of their conclusions." "Error creeps in," He alluded to his contemporary orthodoxy, "when the economist forgets that the result is only 'a first approximation toward the truth,' and that other ignored forces may invalidate it" (ibid., 155). The approach of Senior and J. N. Keynes was unobjectionable in itself, Douglas maintained, but it was abused later by neoclassicists who failed to understand its gist, and "have either denied or minimized the existence of [nonmonetary] motives, or have brushed them aside with the statement that, for the sake of 'simplicity,' any consideration of them may be excluded" (ibid., 155). The currently dominant neoclassical view thus appears as a debased incarnation of the Founding Fathers' view of human nature. Institutionalism, in contrast, is presented as advancing the conceptions of classical writers into modern times. It was neither a revolutionary step, nor a radical rejection of the past but simply a revision of old concepts according to new knowledge and modern ideas.[6]

The institutionalists also looked for support in the more recent works of distinguished neoclassicists themselves, economists who expressed ideas similar to theirs. Douglas (1924, 155), for instance, added that his contemporary Frank Taussig (1859–1940) was "a noteworthy exception" to the fault of neoclassical economists who "have either denied or minimized the existence of [nonmonetary] motives" (ibid., 155). Taussig was a leading figure in American neoclassical economics around the turn of the century, and the editor of the prestigious *Quarterly Journal of Economics* (1896–1936). His recruitment carried therefore a significant weight. Mitchell, in another example, favorably commented on Marshall who was "more realistic than [John Stuart] Mill in that he does not use 'an artificial definition of a man' but insists that he deals with real men" (1969, 2:218). Mitchell also referred to Henry Sidgwick, "who succeeded John Stuart Mill as leader of the English utilitarians." Sidgwick "averred that he ate his dinner because he was hungry, not because he anticipated pleasure" (1924, 15), a poignant hint against hedonism. Similarly, John Bates Clark was quoted as saying that "the ultimate foundations of political economy . . . include a modern view of human nature and of intensified social activity" (Edie 1927, 438–39).

The institutionalists' view of human nature was closely related to their emphasis on the role of social institutions in human life, and institutionalists looked for hints to similar recognition in the works of the Founding Fathers. Mitchell argued, for instance, that "the orthodox economists [were not] wholly hostile to [the institutionalist] kind of work." He specifically referred to John Stuart Mill, who "emphasized the influence of institutions upon distribution, and placed his hopes for the future upon institutional change" (1924, 18). Mitchell, however, criticized Mill because "such excursions into institutionalist economics were not considered to be really a part of economic theory—they were 'application of social philosophy' in the language of Mill's sub-title" (ibid.). Thus, on the one hand, Mitchell found cognitive affinity between institutionalist thought and the writing of a prominent classical economist. On the other hand, he criticized that scholar for "differentiating economic theory from the study of economic institutions" (ibid.). This allowed Mitchell to create the impression that the institutionalists took the classical view forward and improved it, while contemporary neoclassicists, who ignored institutions even more than Mill, were actually regressing.

We reach now what appears to be the deepest gap between institutionalism and classical economics: the support of active government by the former and the endorsement of *laissez-faire* by the latter. We all know about Adam Smith and his notion of the "invisible hand," about David Ricardo, the stock broker whose ideas served the interests of the rising capitalist class, and about Thomas Malthus, who denied the ability of reforms to change the harsh conditions of the working class. It appears therefore unthinkable that there was anything in common between the classical economists and the institutionalists, who favored an active government and believed in the ability of well-informed reformers to improve common welfare manifold. Nevertheless, the institutionalists did try to break the alignment of *laissez-faire* policies with the mythical Founding Fathers of the discipline and forwarded evidence to show that the institutionalist interventionist views were prefigured by some of the distinguished economists of the past. Wesley Mitchell, to take one example, claimed that orthodox theorists were not fans of private property and free competition for their own sake. They supported these institutions because they saw them as necessary means to achieve economic growth. But they would have had no problems in adjusting the means, if the conditions were different:

> The classical attitude toward economics from Adam Smith to Marshall is an effort to gain understanding of actual economic behavior . . . for practical purpose—to improve economic organization. From Adam Smith who pleaded for economic freedom to Marshall who wanted to abolish poverty, the classical economists were at bottom reformers. They were critics of economic organization. To think of them as champions of capitalism is to reveal ignorance of their writings;—though I suppose all of them thought that private property . . . was necessary to stimulate labor and waiting as human nature now stands (1969, 2:219).

Abbott Usher's presidential address (1934) is a good example of the way old theories are reinterpreted in the light of new knowledge and interests.[7] Usher devoted his whole presidential address to dispel the misconception, in his opinion, of associating classical economics with the extreme position of *laissez-faire*. He admitted that "classical and neoclassical economic theory is commonly associated with a form of liberalism that was more largely directed toward the repeal of old laws and regulations than to the constructive development of institutions to meet new social problems" (1934, 1). This was the case, he explained, because the classical economists lived amidst a society which was replete with obsolete economic regulations that had hindered the expansion of industry and commerce. They believed that by abolishing governmental intervention, society would be able to produce more wealth.[8] But Usher argued that new concepts and knowledge were gained since the original classical economists had died. Given this new knowledge, the same classical principles, he implied, would actually lead to calls for active government (cf. Taylor 1928, 270; Young 1928).

One of the new concepts with which the classical writers were unfamiliar, and would have led them to reconsider their positions, was the idea of evolution, of constant change. Because of this concept that had been very central since the middle of the nineteenth century, "we cannot assume that our institutions are approximately mature and adequate." We have to be keenly aware of "the imperfections of adjustment" and adopt "positive, conscious action" to overcome these imperfections. Furthermore, "any given society will always find its institutional mechanism inadequate and imperfect, because changing conditions create new needs and problems for which self-regulating mechanisms cannot instantly be created. Regulation is thus essential even in a society that tends to be self-regulating" (Usher 1934, 4–5). Usher vehemently professed that even the classical writers would have believed "that social evolution is a constructive process which involves active participation of both individuals and state," had they known the principles of evolution and its role in the history of nature and human beings. Moreover, they would have recognized that "there is no guiding hand other than the collective wisdom of each generation. By reason of persistent imperfect and maladjustment, the remedial activities of the state must be extensive and . . . vigorous" (ibid., 5).

John Maurice Clark praised classical economics as a big step relative to previous doctrines, but by the same token he implied that it had to be modified to fit modern circumstances. "As against the chief doctrines they had, at the time, to combat," Clark explained, "these classical assumptions were true." The alternative to classical economics was "the interests and sophisms of class exploitation." And since "these interests and sophisms retain a dangerous degree of vitality," the principles of classical economics "retain essential truth" (1924, 82). Nevertheless, these very principles were inferior to modern conceptions, because they "ignore many democratic and human values which are now striving for practical recognition" (ibid.). Institutionalism, in Clark's opinion, built on the classical tradition. It retained the valid aspects of it and added an analysis of those properties of the economy which were missing in the original classical analysis.

Clark's view was reflected in his appraisal of Adam Smith. Smith, Clark explained, "was born into a world whose official economics was utterly distrustful of free exchange." Smith, Clark told us, "grasped the element of mutual aid running through exchange, saw its organizing possibilities and contrasted these with the crippling effects of contemporary sorts of interference" (ibid., 83; cf. Young 1927, 4). This was a giant step forward, but we must continue and comprehend other aspects, like the externalities which the institutionalists called attention to again and again. The problem, Clark thought, was that later economists enshrined the letter of Adam Smith's work rather than absorbing its spirit. Hence, the limitations of classical theory "are chiefly the work of later writers than Adam Smith, who seldom allowed his thinking to be cramped by its own machinery" (1924, 84). In this fashion, Adam Smith was vindicated, while orthodox theory as contemporarily practiced was indicted.

Recruitment of Unorthodox Authorities

So far we have seen that the neoclassicists tried to present institutionalism as revolutionary, while institutionalists presented it as evolving from the leading theories of the past. This, however, is not an exact picture. Two qualifications have to be made. First, not all institutionalists saw themselves as following the path of Adam Smith, David Ricardo, John Stuart Mill, and Alfred Marshall. Second, the institutionalists also drew on the work of past critics and rivals of orthodox economics. This section deals with these tactics.

While most institutionalists expressed their appreciation for the contributions of the great masters of English political economy, some of them did not accept this respectful view. Best known among those who fiercely attacked orthodox theory was, of course, Thorstein Veblen. Veblen's antiestablishment view needs little discussion as it is well known and frequently documented (Gruchy 1947, 35–50; Landreth 1976, 320–25; Mitchell 1969, 2:626; the essays in Blaug 1992a). Although there is no doubt that Veblen was one of the main sources of inspiration for all institutionalists, many of the latter, including his own pupils, were much more sympathetic toward orthodox theory. In the materials I analyzed, Rexford Tugwell is the only one who lashed out at the entire tradition of the English political economy. Referring to the belief of Adam Smith in the harmony of interests, Tugwell called it a "mystic paradox" and said that were it "not so tenacious, it would not deserve serious consideration" (1924a, 408). Adam Smith is not the only victim of Tugwell's critique. In explaining what seems to him to be the deterioration of economic thought, he claimed that one of the main causes was the academization of economics. Economics suffered because the teaching of a science—the inculcation of an existing doctrine—contradicted the practice of science, the production of new original ideas (1924a, 410). Tugwell's sweeping critique certainly carried the aura of revolutionary rhetoric. He expected revolutionary changes that would be carried not by academic scholars but by special research institutions and economic practitioners in government and business. Similar views against orthodoxy were expressed by Clarence Ayres, Veblen's student and the most prominent leader of institutionalism during the postwar years. Slichter also attacked Ricardo and mainstream economists after him, but unlike Tugwell and Ayres, he spared Smith, who, in his opinion, responded appropriately to the economic problems of *his* time.

Veblen and Tugwell constituted the minority among institutionalist thinkers. Mitchell, Commons, Clark, Copeland, and many others treated the works of past economists much more respectfully and saw themselves as the followers of those famous pioneers of the discipline. These more moderate institutionalists, though, did not limit their references to the past to mainstream teachings. They established their continuity with classical and neoclassical writers wherever they could, but used the works of past critics of orthodox theory as well. Citation of unorthodox sources may be less helpful in establishing the credibility of institutionalism among conservative colleagues, but it may help them to secure and tighten their black boxes. The fact that institutionalist ideas had been suggested before by economists in different places and at different times added to the impression that those ideas contained some grain of truth. It was easier to disparage a group of current economists than to disregard a continuous tradition, even when this tradition departed from the main current.

Thus, Mitchell referred to the criticism on Ricardo's economics by Richard Jones, "who knew enough of economic history and of contemporary conditions outside of England to appreciate that Ricardo's whole system applied to an institutional situation recent in its development and limited in its scope" (1924, 17). Mitchell also mentioned Sismondi, who "investigated the development and cultural consequences of the industrial revolution in England," and John Rae, who "showed how different institutions affect invention and accumulation of capital" (ibid., 17–18). Richard Jones (1790–1855), John Rae (1796–1872), and Jean Charles Leonard Simonde de Sismondi (1773–1842) were indeed three famous critics of the classical system whose works were recognized as important despite their "heretical" views. Mitchell drew support from socialist thinkers as well. He mentioned Robert Owen, William Thompson, Saint Simon, and Charles Fourier, who "sought to devise a new set of institutions which would insure a juster distribution of labor and income" (ibid., 18). In this case, the socialists' support in the importance of institutions appeared side by side with John Stuart Mill's opinion, the views of some respected economists from the classical era, and the work of the German historical school. Thus, even if the socialists were not "credible sources," their support added to the overall weight of the argument. There must be something good in the institutionalist claim, Mitchell implied, if economists as different from each other as Fourier, John Stuart Mill, Sismondi, and Roscher shared its main principles (ibid., 18). Mitchell was not even afraid of recruiting Karl Marx, who "knew how to use contemporary documents as an effective supplement of economic theory if not as its basis" (ibid.), and argued that the objection to Marx's political views should not blind economists to the virtues of his methods. These virtues were praised by Morris Copeland as well. Copeland wished to synthesize the Marxist approach with the orthodox view and admitted that, of the two, "in some respects the Marxian view is the more realistic"(1924, 107).

Conclusions: How to Be Both Traditional and Innovative

Institutionalists drew on both orthodox and unorthodox economists. As is the case with any significant change, the new empirical stress and other institutionalist innovations could be perceived either as an evolution of the past or as a revolutionary departure from it. Evolution, after all, brings about many "revolutionary" developments, and the labeling of a change as evolutionary or revolutionary is a matter of judgment and taste, as well as the result of social negotiation. Most institutionalists endeavored to show that their ideas were in line with the principles of the Founding Fathers of the discipline. This did not prevent them from airing very sharp criticisms on many aspects of older works, but they emphasized those statements of the accepted doctrine that were most similar to theirs and interpreted the intentions of deceased economists in such a way as to fit their own goals.

Wesley Mitchell is a good example of a scientist who chose to present his work as continuing the tradition, rather than as a breakaway. Mitchell would be the last one to deny the "revolutionary" significance of those quantitative methods that he so passionately advocated and promoted. As we saw, he went as far as to argue that the new methods would change the whole focus of economic research, a statement that got him in trouble among his fellow economists. But nevertheless, he still presented his approach as a mature stage of old doctrines. In a roundtable in the AEA Annual Meeting of 1927, Mitchell insisted that there was no place for struggle between the orthodoxy and the new approach (in Working 1927). A year later, when Mitchell was harshly criticized for abandoning the old theory, he answered that the representatives of traditional economics overstated the claims made by institutionalists and "passed over in silence" what institutionalists said in favor of the established doctrine. "I know no competent economist," he said in response to criticism by Viner and others, "who would subscribe to the one-sided views which have been imputed to persons unnamed [probably himself—Y. Y.]" (in Mills 1928, 39–40).

The institutionalists used any source that they could: they were not sheepish in citing socialist, Marxist, and other unorthodox economists. In general, the institutionalists tried to build the strongest defense they could for their ideas, using past works where and when those works were instrumental in endorsing their case. The neoclassicists were equally "opportunistic." They did not have to bother to show their loyalty to the Founding Fathers, because that was not disputed by their opponents. While institutionalists were accused of being too revolutionary, the neoclassicists were accused of being too traditionalist. As a consequence, their strategy was the reverse of the institutionalists' strategy, emphasizing the differences between their ideas and older theories. But the neoclassicists also tried to present past economists as closer to modern ideas of good science, so that their own resemblance to those economists would be less damaging. For instance, they agreed with the methodological arguments of the critics but denied the fact that such a criticism was a breakaway from the past. "It is not that the men of the past were not interested in precise knowledge of industrial phenomena," Bye explained, "but that they did not know how to get it. They were obliged to reason speculatively and qualitatively, because they lacked the tools for empirical and quantitative work" (1925, 59). Frank W. Taussig also asserted that "no one has ever denied" the value of quantitative work for economics, and no one "completely neglected it." The recent emphasis on such work was merely "due to the enormous growth of the available quantitative material, and the development . . . of expert methods" (in Mills 1928, 41). A similar opinion was given at the same roundtable session by Jacob Hollander, another reputable veteran neoclassicist who served as the President of the AEA in 1921 (ibid., 30).[9]

We can see this line of defense as an attempt of the neoclassical "loyalists" to jump on the empirical bandwagon by presenting the past as empirically oriented. But as we said about the institutionalist representations, we should not treat the neoclassical ones as a conscious and deliberate distortion of history. Empirical elements could be found in classical thoughts as acknowledged by both institutionalists and neoclassicists, each group for its own reason. The neoclassical defense of earlier teachers was very similar to the arguments of the empiricist institutionalists, and especially to the arguments of Soule (1924) and Mitchell (1925), who explained the rise of quantitative economics by the recent availability of data and the development of statistical techniques. The difference between the neoclassicists and the institutionalists was subtle. The defenders of the established theory argued that the tradition had always been based not only on deductive fantasies, but on observation as well.

By defending past practices, they defended their own practices of the same nature. The institutionalists implied that the classicists recognized the importance of empirical studies in principle and made some pioneering research. But orthodox theories, they added, had not been based on *systematic* research. The neoclassicists brought forth the argument to contain the inductivist trend and to preserve the existing precedence of deductive reasoning by claiming that the current approach was not so lopsided as argued by the institutionalists. The latter made the argument in order to show that the core of the changes sought by them was in line with the original ideas of earlier economists but had not yet been realized.

The neoclassicists blamed institutionalists for abandoning the teachings of the past. But at the same time, when those old teachings contradicted the beliefs of modern neoclassical economists, the latter were not timid in denouncing those same teachings. Bye, the staunch defender of orthodox theory, admitted that both the classical economists and the institutionalists conceived "normative economics" as an integral part of the economic vocation. Nevertheless, in this case he denounced the classical position and held that modern economists should learn from their mistake: "The economics of the classicists, with its apologies for the present system, its defense of laissez-faire, its sweeping assertions about the impossibility of raising wages, and so on, was pseudo-science . . . because it made the mistake that some misguided reformers would now like to see repeated" (1924, 290). This is a good demonstration that practicing scientists are not so much interested in preserving the past as they are interested in finding support for their own ideas in the past. Since the institutionalists criticized many properties of past theories, Bye marshaled the revered names of the past against institutionalism. But when the ideas of those same great economists were closer to the position of institutionalists, he had no qualms about criticizing them harshly.

This "opportunistic" strategy of both institutionalists and neoclassicists may leave the impression that the economists of that period were immoral and dishonest. This was clearly not the case. First of all, the statements that the disputants cited from older writings were not forged. Second, their interpretations of past works were not only instruments to deceive others. They also reflected the way that they understood those works themselves. If the two parties had different interpretations of Adam Smith, for example, it was because each party read Smith through the perspective of its own approach. As in the case of "Nature," there is no singular outside objective interpretation that can be brought as the "real" meaning of a scholar's ideas. Economists may recruit things that Marshall, for example, wrote in various publications, draw on certain testimonies of Marshall's pupils and friends, bring evidence from private letters, and so on. Eventually they may even convince others that their interpretation is correct, thus making it into a black box. But like the black boxes of "natural facts," the validity of all such interpretations is provisional. It can hold until someone offers another interpretation and is able to mobilize enough allies from Marshall's writings and other sources to convince others that her interpretation was better.[10]

Even if we could reach an agreement about the views of one scholar, we would be left with the much more complicated task of reaching an agreement about the meaning and significance of an intellectual trend. The tradition of English political economy from Smith to Cairnes commonly known as "the classical era" is a collaborative project, encompassing 150 years and hundreds of scholars. It is difficult enough to reach agreement on the interpretation of only one prolific writer. It is virtually hopeless to try to reach agreement on the meaning of "classical economics," which encompasses the works of Smith, Ricardo, Malthus, Senior, James and John Stuart Mill, Cairnes, and many others. And, of course, it is very unlikely that all these economists had exactly the same views. This does not mean that every interpretation of "classical economics" is equally legitimate. Barbara Herrnstein Smith, an avowed relativist, forcibly argued (1988) that the claim that we could never know what was the "true" meaning of a literary work did not mean that any interpretation thereof was acceptable and that all interpretations were equally good. It seems ridiculous to say that the classical and neoclassical traditions were not deductive and abstract. When we compare them to other research programs, we can easily see that they were more deductive and abstract than most. The institutionalists did not deny it either, and therefore this fact was black-boxed. Both camps also agreed that there were inductive elements in the practice of classical and neoclassical economists. Similarly, there was no argument that classical economists supported *laissez-faire*. The question is *why* did they use mostly deductive methods? Was it because they did not have an alternative at the time? Or was it because they thought it was the best method for economics in general and forever? *Why* did they support *laissez-faire*? Did they support it for its own sake? Or did they support it because it was better than the common inhibitions on free trade at the beginning of the Industrial Revolution? Both interpretations appear to be compatible with the written evidence, and therefore both the institutionalists and the neoclassicists could find evidence in the classical writings to support their claims that the classicists were like them.

A similar note can be made in regard to the connection between the German historical school and institutionalism. Many modern writers claim that institutionalists were indeed influenced by the German school, and show the similarities between the two. Jack Myler's dissertation on *German Historicism and American Economics* documents the connections in detail. He lists five similarities: emphasis on inductive research, focus on processes of change, a collectivist approach as opposed to individualism, moral relativism, and support of governmental intervention (1956, 349). In some cases the connection is quite obvious on a personal level, as in the case of American economists—such as Richard T. Ely, John R. Commons's mentor—who was a student of Knies, a prominent figure in the German school. However, the fact that we can show many similarities between the German historical school and institutionalism, and even direct channels of influence, does not mean that institutionalism was an American offshoot of German historicism. The institutionalists' attempt to dissociate themselves from the German school was not simply a bluff. Veblen, the other "father" of institutionalism, along with Commons, was very critical of the German school, as were Mitchell, Tugwell, and others.[11] "From the beginning, the Americans followed the German historical school *in a discriminating fashion*" (Dorfman 1955, 28; emphasis added). As Myler said, the German historical school might have provided "the intellectual seedbed for the institutional approach" (1956, 348), but the "seedbed" could have fostered different kinds of plants. We should also remember that historicism was not "the sole source of institutional doctrine" (ibid., 349). There is no doubt that the American institutionalists were proficient in the English tradition, and even though they challenged it, they absorbed many of its concepts and attitudes. Commons's first major book, for example, attempted to combine marginalist notions concerning value and distribution with historicist ideas and reformist concerns" (Rutherford 1990, xv). Moreover, American economics has its own unorthodox tradition, with figures such as Henry Carey (1793–1879) and Henry George (1839–97). Not all deviations from the orthodox doctrine, therefore, had their origin in German influence.

The same conclusion holds for the controversy over the meaning of classical economics or the true intentions of Adam Smith, Ricardo, or Marshall. We do not have to say that both the institutionalist and the neoclassical readings of earlier works were equally convincing, but the decision whose interpretation was better could not be decided by us—the bystander observers on that struggle—since our familiarity with those classical works is much more limited than the expertise of both parties of that controversy.[12] All we, historians and sociologists, can do is to document the arguments made by both sides concerning the history of economics and investigate the role such arguments played in the wider conflict between institutionalist and neoclassical economists.

A similar process takes place today whenever the interwar period itself is discussed. Interpretation of that period bears upon current struggles, and, therefore, the historical analyst is unavoidably involved in the ongoing competitions among present-day schools and approaches. The cur-

rently prevalent perception of institutionalism as a breakaway from earlier traditions is the result of the sweeping victory of mathematical economics in the postwar period. It simply left no institutionalists to write
the history of their approach from their own perspective. And those accounts from the institutionalist point of view that were published were
pushed aside and ignored.[13] That is why I found it necessary in chapter 3
to present a picture of institutionalism which is different from the one
that can be found in most textbooks on the history of economic thought.
According to the view of this writer, that presentation is not supposed to
be perceived as the ultimate truth. It was offered as a countervailing
weight to the conventional presentation in an attempt to open a black box
that has been closed too rapidly and coercively.

Those who accept the common image of institutionalism as radical and
revolutionary may object and argue that their view is supported by the
explicitly virulent attacks on the established doctrine by Veblen, Ayres,
and Tugwell. Indeed, those attacks might have helped the neoclassical
camp to successfully brand the institutionalists as "radical" and "revolutionaries," a stigmatization that Veblen, Ayres, and Tugwell would have
probably accepted willingly. Furthermore, this image of institutionalism
is supported by a large group of postwar institutionalists, whose avowed
extremism supports the radical image of past institutionalism (Mirowski
1990). But the success of later economists to define institutionalism as
revolutionary cannot be explained solely by the views of that small group
despite its prestige and influence within institutionalist circles. Commons,
Mitchell, and John Maurice Clark were not less influential, and more
institutionalists preferred their attitudes toward orthodox theory. Many
contemporary followers of institutionalism have also advanced this moderate view and conceived their approach as supplementary to mainstream
economics. They have challenged the conventional narrative told by neoclassical mainstreamers and by their more radical peers and emphasized
those past institutionalists who were not interested in abolishing traditional theory. Allan Gruchy, for example, says that "the institutionalists
do not repudiate or dispense with pure or basic economic theory. What
they have done over the years is to take the basic theory of Marshall,
Keynes, and others and place it in the larger setting of a theory of the
evolving economic system" (1957, 14; see also Adams 1980b, 6). John
Adams also agrees that modern institutionalists are "more willing to bor-
row some of the language and concepts of orthodoxy and have toned
down the overheated criticism of Veblen" (1980b, 11).

To prevent any mistake, it is not argued here that the moderate image
is truer than the radical one. To repeat our general principle, there is,
of course, a factual basis for perceiving institutionalism as radical. But
there is *also* a basis to perceive it as a continuation of past trends. Accord-

ing to the constructivist approach in the sociology of science, our task as historians and sociologists of economics is not to decide which basis is bigger. This determination would be the result of conflict and negotiation among economists; not the cause of the conventions eventually agreed upon. Moreover, we may attribute the current radicalism of institutionalists to the successful stigmatization of earlier institutionalists as radical. The success of the neoclassical rivals to push institutionalism out of the discipline core left the moderate institutionalists without ties to powerful sources and facilitated the efforts of radical institutionalists to take over the institutionalist movement. Thus, it is possible that the extremist image of institutionalism has *produced* a reality of present-day extremity rather than *reflected* it. As historians we should be very careful not to use this image as evidence concerning the nature of institutionalism in the past.

The principles that enable us to depict the same research program either as revolutionary or as conservative holds for other research programs as well. It is possible, for instance, to portray modern, mathematical, neoclassical theory as revolutionary as it deviated from the Marshallian approach in many key issues (see chap. 9). The fact that its similarities with the Marshallian tradition are stressed reflects the choices of mathematical economists and their success in repressing other economists who purported to have followed Marshall and claimed to be his true followers *and* economists from their own camp who thought of themselves as radical innovators.

There are many examples of controversies about the past of this nature in other disciplines as well. MacKenzie and Barnes (1979, 192–97) provide us an example from biology. Biometrists and Mendelists disputed each other's claims to the Darwinian and Galtonian heritage. In sociology the interpretations of Marx and Weber have been fiercely debated. In psychology many scientists recruited Freud to advance their own agendas. Such interpretive controversies are not limited to the academic world. Religious sects often debate the interpretation of "holy scripts" and claim to constitute the true heirs of "the holy tradition." Artistic and literary circles also seek to follow past masters and argue over the essence of those masters' works. And political leaders, who profess that they realize the vision of great national heroes, must establish the similarity between their contesting programs and the ideas of those heroic figures. The past is always a major battleground of present-day wars.

Nine _____

Epilogue: The Fall of Institutionalism and the Rise of Modern Economics

The theory of general economic equilibrium . . . is an "intellectual experiment"—a particular method chosen for describing how a market economy works under various simplifying and unreal postulates. These postulates were not intended by its creators to be more than intermediary steps in the process of analysis—they were simplifications which were intended to be removed later when the theory was brought into closer approximation to real life. But it was an inherent consequence of the *a priori* approach of this school that its followers should be preoccupied with the properties of the notion of "equilibrium"—which meant that progress took the form, not of removing the scaffolding but of constantly *adding* to it. Making the theory more rigorous made the whole construction even more abstract (and hence more distant from its ultimate goal) since it involved the discovery (or recognition) of additional assumptions implied in the results.

(Nicholas Kaldor, *"Recollections of an Economist"*)

BEFORE World War II, institutionalism was well established in major universities and the government, and its influence on New Deal legislation was substantial. Nevertheless, by the late 1950s it was already considered outdated. The explanation of this rapid decline requires another study, but based on my research I can offer some preliminary thoughts on this sudden change of fate. I hope that these thoughts, as sketchy as they are, would complete the story about institutionalism and demonstrate the ability of the actor-network analysis to account for both its rise and decline.

My argument in this chapter is, in a nutshell, that institutionalism did *not* lose the war described in the previous chapters. It was defeated, along with its longtime rival "old-fashioned" neoclassical economics, by a new approach, which first appeared as a major force in the 1930s and skyrocketed soon after the Second World War. This new winner was mathematical economics. Despite frequent assertions, this approach did *not* evolve out of an existing approach.[1] It drew some inspiration and help from earlier exponents of mathematical economics, but it was mostly the creation of individuals who worked alone and swam against the dominant currents of the period. The power of mathematical economics was augmented by the development of econometrics as a new approach to quantitative research that differed from the way institutionalists practiced such research.[2] The relations between mathematical economics and econometrics was not tranquil, and the tension between their basic beliefs and methods produced bitter methodological disputes. Yet under the sponsorship of the Cowles Commission, the contrasts were ignored, and a new overarching philosophy was created that presented the mathematical and econometric enterprises as complementary.

If anyone could claim to be the "natural" heir of the old Marshallian neoclassicism it was Keynes and his associates and disciples at Cambridge, who maintained the methodological strategies of Marshall and his general outlook of economics.[3] Keynes opposed both the mathematization of economic theory and the attempt to verify it by econometric tools. Yet postwar economists co-opted Keynesianism into the rising mathematical-econometric alliance, thus creating the winning neoclassical-Keynesian synthesis.[4] This synthesis has dominated economics at least since the 1960s. The Keynesian component has been under attack since the early 1970s from various "conservative" approaches (monetarism, rational expectations theory, real business cycle theory), but it is still one of the main parties, and it is accepted by many that the whole macroeconomic discourse is Keynesian even today (Friedman and Samuelson in Blaug 1990b). The next three sections deal, respectively, with the three components of the winning coalition: mathematical economics, econometrics, and Keynesianism.

The Rise of Mathematical Economics

During the 1930s a group of American graduate students in the United States started to develop mathematical economics. The emergence of this group was an extraordinary phenomenon. Those young economists were not disciples of older mathematical economists, although they got some help and encouragement from the very few economists who had been interested in mathematical economics, including Irving Fisher and Harold Hotelling. They pursued their mathematical interests, deviant from the dominant trends, and sometimes had to overcome resistance from their own teachers. Nevertheless, they persisted in their endeavors and their numbers increased constantly until they became the mainstream of economics sometime during the 1950s. Among these pioneers were Paul

Samuelson, Kenneth Arrow, Milton Friedman, George Stigler, Robert Dorfman, Armen Alchian, Joe Bain, and Abram Bergson.[5]

The emergence of this group in the United States coincided with the consolidation of a similar group in the London School of Economics. In Britain the leaders of this movement included John Hicks and Lionel Robbins. Both were *not* trained at Cambridge, the core of British economics, where the efforts to develop mathematical theory were not welcomed. Due to the unexpected death of Allyn Young in 1929, who had been appointed only three years earlier as the head of the economics department at the LSE, Robbins was appointed to that position, and it was he who established the LSE as a center of the new movement. Robbins's appointment put the LSE on a new track. The original course of the LSE, under the influence of Sidney Webb, led toward empirical and historical studies. This attitude was very similar to the spirit that motivated the institutionalist movement (Kadish 1993a). The fortuitous event of Young's death, as well as the way Hicks stumbled upon Paretian theory (Klamer 1989), show that in Britain, as in the United States, mathematical economics was *not* an evolution of an existing school. Indeed, Jevons, Walras, and Pareto "had already introduced mathematics into economics. But after 1930, this activity *underwent a rebirth*" (Samuelson 1970, 844; italics added).

The new mathematical research program had two main elements. First, it included a transformation of Marshallian economics into a mathematical form as a basis for further rigorous derivations. While institutionalists and many neoclassicists in the interwar period felt that price theory had been completed (see chaps. 6–8), the years after World War II witnessed a flood of articles, each focusing on a certain element of the theory, couching it in a newly born jargon, and deriving rigorous conclusions out of it. The analyses have assumed that consumers maximized their utility and firms their profits. The mathematical economists did not necessarily believe that these assumptions about maximization were true. But they nonetheless defined the discipline as a science of rational allocation of resources and left it to other social sciences to study real economic behavior.[6]

The basic technique has been one of maximization and minimization under constraints. Calculus, especially Lagrangian methods, became the basic instrument in the economic theorist's tool kit. Various conditions were analyzed: perfect competition, monopolies, duopolies and oligopolies, schemes of taxation and subsidies, technologies of increasing, constant, and decreasing returns, various production functions, and so forth. The pages of the main American journals (*AER*, *JPE*, *QJE*) during the 1950s are full of such papers.[7] Concepts like externalities, public goods, elasticities, income and substitution effects, complementary and substituting goods, indifference curves, isoquants, and many others were defined in an exact fashion, and the mathematical economists studied the implications of hypothetical coefficients and combinations of factors.[8]

The second major aspect of the mathematical revolution was general equilibrium theory that originated in Walras's work. Marshall treated each market separately. He knew, of course, that prices and quantities of other goods influenced the market of any single commodity, but he thought that these influences were too complex, and therefore he treated them as exogenous in the analysis of a single industry (Marshall 1920, book V, esp. chap. 6 and notes xiv–xxi of the Mathematical Appendix; A. K. Dasgupta 1985, 100; Bladen 1974, 382–85). Walras, in contrast, believed that it was possible to analyze the connections between all markets, and the pioneers of the mathematical revolution followed his lead (Stigler in Breit and Spencer 1986, 103–4; Ménard 1990).[9]

The economists who analyzed general equilibrium started with the simplest assumptions of perfect competition, no government intervention, and perfect knowledge of all economic actors. They asked whether there was a solution to the system of equations which described the preferences of all consumers and the production functions of all commodities. The idea was not to find the actual preferences and the real production functions. This was obviously an impossible task, although Léon Walras and his early disciples might have entertained such an idea (Ménard 1990, 119). Instead the mathematical economists wanted to know if a system of equations that described a whole economy was solvable *in principle*. After conditions of existence were identified by Arrow, Dubreu, and McKenzie, these investigators and other theoreticians investigated whether and when there was only one solution, and whether the solutions were stable or not. These questions have occupied many of the best mathematical minds in economics for a very long period. They still constitute one of the main branches of economic theory today.[10]

The Mathematical Economics-Econometrics Alliance

A big push toward mathematical economics was given by the establishment of the Econometric Society and the publication of *Econometrica* as a new journal dedicated to mathematical articles. Today the term "econometrics" is reserved for statistical studies, but at that time it meant the use of mathematics, including both abstract, deductive mathematical modeling *and* the use of empirical data and statistical procedures for testing theories. The Econometric Society and *Econometrica* provided forums for presentation and publication, and increased the unity of the mathematical devotees. More important, both the Society and the journal were supported by the Cowles Commission, a private and affluent fund dedicated for economic research. The Commission also organized summer conferences that were very instrumental in establishing a unified international group, devoted to the development of economics as an exact science.[11]

The Econometric Society achieved a rearrangement of the forces in economics by turning quantitative research from an ally of institutionalism into an ally of mathematical pure theory. Institutionalists envisioned statistics as a tool for devising new theories, leaving behind concepts that could not be operationalized, and adding new psychological and institutional variables. In contrast, the conception that was developed by econometricians at the Cowles Commission perceived econometrics as an instrument for adjudicating between rival models which originated in the old neoclassical theory (e.g., L. Klein 1985, chaps. 10–11). The Cowles Commission itself had embarked first on a course of quantitative research in the institutionalist fashion. But as the connections between the Commission and the Econometric Society got stronger in the early 1940s, economists from the Society were appointed to the Commission and changed its course (Malinvaud 1991, 50–51).

The "great battle" between the old institutionalist conception of statistical research and econometrics was fought in the late 1940s when Tjalling Koopmans wrote an extremely critical review of Wesley Mitchell's and Arthur Burns's *Measuring Business Cycles* (pub. 1946). The Review, titled "Measurement Without Theory," was actually an attack on the approach used by institutionalists in quantitative research (usually referred to as the NBER method after the National Bureau for Economic Research where Mitchell established a large research group that worked under his aegis). Rutledge Vining responded in 1949 and defended the method of Mitchell and Burns. The exchange between Koopmans and Vining, which also included Koopman's "Reply" and Vining's "Rejoinder" in the same year, revealed the fundamental gap between the institutionalists' views and the approach of the Cowles Commission.[12] When the exchange took place, the so-called "NBER method" was still considered legitimate. But in a short period the approach of Koopmans and his colleagues (Frisch and Tinbergen in Europe, Klein, Marschak, Tobin, and others in the United States), became the only legitimate method in the field of economics.

A similar crucial exchange took place between Lester, Machlup, and Stigler and involved the merits of marginal theory itself. Lester, an institutionally oriented labor economist, cited empirical evidence against the basics of the neoclassical approach (1946). His article motivated Fritz Machlup to write an article in defense of marginal analysis (1946). In the same year George Stigler wrote an article which relied upon marginal analysis to condemn minimum-wage legislation (Stigler 1946). The next year Lester replied to Machlup and attacked Stigler (Lester 1947), and the exchange continued with Machlup's (1947) and Stigler's (1947) responses.[13]

Like the exchange between Vining and Koopmans, this exchange indicated a watershed in the history of institutionalism. At that point it was still considered a legitimate and serious contender in the discipline, but thereafter it rapidly lost its power. The optimism of institutionalists just after the war (e.g., Gruchy 1947, 1) changed into a sense of failure and despair. At the Annual Meeting of the AEA in December 1956, Kenneth Boulding (1957, 1) did not hesitate to argue that "there is not today anything which would be called either an institutionalist 'movement' in economics nor even an institutionalist group." He admitted that "there are a few economists today who would call themselves institutionalists," but these, he claimed, "tend to be isolated individuals" (ibid., 1). In 1958, the institutionalists established a separate organization (Gambs 1980), a step that signaled the demise of institutionalism as a significant power within mainstream economics.

The alliance of pure mathematical economic theory and econometrics was not achieved without problems. The London School of Economics, which became the center of mathematical economics in England, was under the strong influence of the Austrian School. The latter supported a subjectivist approach and objected *in principle* to macroeconomic studies. It perceived the role of economics as developing logical implications of fundamental postulates which were known by introspection. In the United States this approach was supported by Frank Knight and immigrants from Europe who subscribed to the Austrian School, such as Fritz Machlup.[14] Lionel Robbins's *An Essay on the Nature and Significance of Economic Science* (1932) is the most famous methodological work of that approach.

Six years after Robbins's book, Terence Hutchison published *The Significance and Basic Postulates of Economics* (1938) in which he advocated the opposite empirical approach. Hutchison was influenced by Popper's notion of science, which regarded as science only those theories which were refutable. A priori knowledge was ruled out as unscientific.[15] The debate between Robbins's *a priori* approach and Hutchison's empiricism was conducted in the 1940s and 1950s in a series of articles and responses in the professional journals (Hutchison 1941, 1956; Knight 1940, 1941; Machlup 1955; 1956).

The dispute has never been resolved, but it was successfully swept under the rug under the influence of Milton Friedman's *Essays in Positive Economics* (1953). Friedman maintained that the reality of assumptions was irrelevant, and that the only criterion to judge theories was their success in prediction. In this way he hoped to avoid the accusation that pure economic theory was not scientific, in the Popperian sense, because it was inherently irrefutable, or worse, repeatedly refuted by daily observations. Friedman thus gave an empirical Popperian dress to a methodology which was basically the one supported by Robbins.[16] McCloskey has noted that in practice economists do not follow Friedman's methodology (1985, 16–19), in the sense that they do not abandon fundamental assumptions even when their predictions fail. Yet this methodology is still professed by most practicing economists (McCloskey 1985, 9; O'Brien 1974, 17; cf. discussion by Hausman 1989).[17]

Keynes, Keynesianism, and the Transformation of Economics

Surprisingly enough, this discussion of interwar economics has not even touched upon the "Keynesian Revolution" yet. This is not a mistake. The "Keynesian Revolution" has been considered the most celebrated event in the field of economics in this century, but from a methodological point of view it was less revolutionary than the innovations of the mathematical economists and the econometricians. Keynes was a student of Marshall and his basic view on the nature of economic science was always Marshallian. Speaking about Marshall's students, including Pigou, Robertson, and Keynes, Schumpeter argued that they were

> formed by [Marshall's] teaching and started from his teaching, however far they may have traveled beyond it. After 1930, Keynes himself and most of what may be termed the third generation did indeed renounce allegiance. But so far as purely scientific analysis is concerned, this means less than it seems to mean. And though some of them grew to dislike Marshall, not only his modes of thought but also his personal aura, his stamp is still upon them all (1954, 833; See also Briefs 1960, 35n; Jensen 1983).

Keynes's main work was in the field of monetary theory and business cycles, the two topics that comprised macroeconomic research before World War II. Macroeconomic theory of national product had not been much changed by the marginalist revolution of the 1870s. That revolution focused on micro-theory of consumer behavior and firms, leaving the classical theory unchanged. Say's Law, according to which supply created its own demand (making prolonged involuntary unemployment impossible), was formulated early in the nineteenth century, and remained in the textbooks until Keynes's *General Theory* (Hansen 1953, 6). Marxists, institutionalists, and other critics have long doubted the classical doctrine, and the Marshallian economists themselves became increasingly skeptical about its validity. Keynes's work was part of a growing literature on macroeconomic issues (cf. Clarke 1988). It was aimed at revising classical macroeconomics, *not Marshallian microeconomics* (Oser 1970, 390; Galbraith 1987, 235–36; Routh 1975; Deane 1978).[18]

The institutionalists accepted the Keynesian Revolution as their own victory. They supported, of course, the conclusion that government intervention was needed and thought that Keynes moved toward recognition in the importance of institutional research. In 1947, John Maurice Clark claimed that *General Theory* was a step in the right direction, but it was still restrained by Keynes's wish not to alienate traditional economists (Clark 1947; see also Gruchy 1947, 71n). Keynes opposed both mathematical economics and econometrics. *General Theory* contains only rudimentary mathematics and in very small doses. This was not due to lack of mathematical knowledge on Keynes's part. Keynes underwent good training in mathematics and statistics, and in 1922 he even published a book on the theory of probability. But like Marshall he consciously avoided the use of sophisticated mathematics and statistics in his work and expressed his dissatisfaction with mathematical efforts of others. In his essay on Jevons, Keynes lamented "how disappointing are the fruits . . . of the bright idea of reducing economics to a mathematical application of the hedonistic calculus of Bentham" (quoted in Black 1973, 111). This statement would probably fit Keynes's opinion with regard to the sequel of Jevons's enterprise by modern mathematical economists had he lived long enough to witness those efforts.

On Keynes's objection to econometrics we can learn much from an amusing, but instructive, story which Jan Tinbergen, a pioneer of modern econometrics, relates. Tinbergen and a few collaborators found statistical evidence to support one of the crucial assumptions of Keynes in *The Economic Consequences of the Peace* (pub. 1919). Tinbergen told Keynes about it, "expecting that he would consider this to be a strengthening of his position." Instead, Keynes responded by saying, "How nice for you to have found the correct figure!" (Tinbergen 1988, 78). Tinbergen explains that Keynes intuited the right answer, and this is a gift of a genius. This explanation misses the main point. Keynes was not an intuitionist, and the above anecdote does not prove Keynes's indifference to empirical research. On the contrary, Keynes was very knowledgeable in economic matters based on personal experience and broad reading of business news and analyses. His objection to econometrics stemmed from a conviction that econometric tools could not reveal new economic knowledge, as he wrote in his pointed review of Tinbergen's attempt to test business-cycle theories with statistical tools (Keynes 1939; see more comprehensive analysis in Patinkin 1976). Interestingly, Keynes voiced clear and strong objection to the use of price indices and national income figures (1964 [1936], chap. 4; Carabelli 1992). His objection is stated in the beginning of *General Theory*, and it is an explicit reversal of his view in his 1930 *Treatise on Money*. Therefore it is difficult to see this position as just a heedless statement. Yet post–World War II economic discourse has completely ignored *this* part of *General Theory*.[19]

The mathematical economists mathematized Keynes's theory, and the econometricians turned Keynesianism into their centerpiece (Brirfs 1960, 35n). There is contradictory evidence concerning Keynes's reaction to the common mathematical version of the *IS-LM* curves, first developed by John Hicks in his 1937 review of *General Theory* and pervasive in most postwar textbooks.[20] Keynes sent an approving letter to Hicks, but some interpreters believe that the approval was merely out of politeness. In any case, Hicks's presentation was the basis of many more mathematical elaborations in the postwar era after Keynes's death in 1946 (S. Weintraub 1977a).[21]

Econometrics started in the area of microeconomics. H. L. Moore and his student, Henry Schultz, and the pioneers of economic statistics in Europe were interested in deriving empirical demand curves both as a test to the theory and for practical reasons. Only in the late 1930s did econometricians begin to build statistical models of the whole economy (Arrow 1991, 4–5).[22] For them, Keynesianism was like a heavenly blessing. It focused the attention of the discipline on macroeconomic questions and provided them with problems that seemed most suitable for statistical work. With the increasing availability of national data, the econometricians found a rich meadow to graze in, and econometric models became the second pillar of modern economics (Lawrence Klein in Breit and Spencer 1986, 24).

Keynes was a shrewd academic entrepreneur who wished to have an impact on academic economics as well as on economic policy. It is therefore difficult to distinguish between his fundamental beliefs and the compromises he made to convince his intended audiences. J. M. Clark might have gone too far in depicting Keynes as a "closet institutionalist." Keynes seemed to have an avid interest in theoretical work, but he also "saluted Commons as 'an eminent American economist'" (Mitchell 1969, 2:731; Keynes 1963 [1925], 334–36).[23] I do not wish to express any categorical view about Keynes's real intentions. The interpretive literature on Keynes is vast. But it is quite clear that the Keynesianism which developed after Keynes's death in 1946 was not what he himself envisioned.[24]

The mathematical and econometric conversion of Keynesianism created an unbeatable coalition of mathematical modeling, econometrics, and Keynesianism, which dominated economics in the 1950s and 1960s.[25] Even monetarism, which has been perceived as the rival of Keynesianism, is actually one of the variants of the dominant coalition.

Milton Friedman, the monetarist, and Paul Samuelson, the Keynesian, share the acceptance of mathematical economics, to which both have made numerous contributions, and of econometrics as the methodological armory for deciding between their models. The differences between them are about the coefficients of certain equations, not about the methodology or the general approach.[26]

The Old and the New Economics

The "New Economics" of the post–World War II era is thus composed of three principal elements: mathematical modeling in microeconomics, "Keynesian" discourse in macroeconomics, and econometrics as the empirical arm of the previous two theoretical pursuits. Institutionalism has been pushed aside, but it was not the only loser. "Old-fashioned" neoclassical economics, its main foe for many years, lost as well. Even though mathematical economists and econometricians have proclaimed Marshall and Keynes as their heroes, the way they approached economic problems was very different from that of Marshall and Keynes.[27] The new coalition did not refrain from striking even at the holiest of "old-fashioned" neoclassical economics: Alfred Marshall. Samuelson, for instance, complained that "the ambiguities of Alfred Marshall paralysed the best brains in the Anglo-Saxon branch of our profession for three decades" (quoted in Groenewegen 1990, 24). He belittles the work done before mathematical economics, saying that "the sleeping beauty of political economy was waiting for the enlivening kiss of new methods, new paradigms, new hired hands, and new problems" (in Breit and Spencer 1986, 60).[28] Even more disparaging of Marshall is Lionel Robbins's stricture. Robbins praises Marshall's *Principles of Economics* as one of the best treatises, but at the same time he rebukes Marshall:

> We have all felt . . . *a sense almost of shame at the incredible banalities* of much of the so-called theory of production—*the tedious discussions* of the various forms of peasant proprietorship, factory organization, industrial psychology, technical education, etc., which are apt to occur in even the best treatises on general theory. . . . One has only to compare the masterly sweep of Book V of Marshall's *Principles*, which deals with problems which are strictly economic in our sense, with the *spineless platitude* about manures and the "fine natures among domestic servants" of much of Book IV to realise *the insidious effect* of a procedure which opens the door to the intrusions of amateur technology into discussions which should be purely economic (1932, 65; emphases added).

Marshall, Keynes, Taussig, Knight, and other "old-fashioned" neoclassicists considered historical, psychological, and sociological knowledge as absolutely necessary for proper economic policy making. Their constant gaze was set upon policy issues. They believed that economic theory gave important hints for how to conduct the economy, but they were fully aware that good policy needed much more than proficiency in abstract theory. This approach to the field has eventually been lost. Gradually Walras replaced Marshall as the icon of neoclassical economics. On the cover of the third edition of his famous textbook (1955), Samuelson drew the "Family Tree of Economics," which includes only the most famous economists: Adam Smith, David Ricardo, John Stuart Mill, Marx, Marshall, and Keynes. In the fourth edition (1958) Walras is entered in the same circle with Marshall. This addition symbolizes the transformation from "old-fashioned" to mathematical neoclassical economics.[29]

The "old-fashioned" neoclassicists also fought for their lives, although the distinction between the old and the new was not very clear for the participants themselves. Speaking about econometrics and Keynesianism, Lawrence Klein writes that "for 10 or 20 years opposition was fierce" (in Breit and Spencer 1986, 22). We can see this conflict, for example, in the critique by George Stigler (1943) and I.M.D. Little (1950) of the "new welfare" economics. Both were dissatisfied with the separation of economics and ethics and with the narrowing of the field only to those statements that could be mathematically proven.[30] Stigler's criticism was part of a discussion in a session on the new mathematical welfare economics at the annual meetings of the AEA at which the merits of the new "rigorous" approach were hotly debated.

"Skirmishes" like this erupted several times in that period. In the field of international trade, for example, Jacob Viner rejected Haberler's *Theory of International Trade* (pub. 1936). Haberler's book was "the first book which successfully reformulated the old classical theory of comparative costs in the modern language of general equilibrium theory" (Blaug 1985b, 75). According to Blaug, Viner's rejection in his *Studies in the Theory of International Trade* (pub. 1937) was mostly a quarrel about the respective merits of 'partial' [i.e., Marshallian] versus 'general' equilibrium analysis" (ibid.; see Viner in Mills 1928, 36). For similar reasons, Milton Friedman rejected the arguments of Lange in his *Price, Flexibility and Employment* (Weintraub 1991b, 1).[31] But objections of this sort could not prevent the mathematical machine from rolling forward.

Gerard Debreu (1991, 1), one of the most prominent mathematical economists, provides in his presidential address to the American Economic Association several statistics to illustrate the change of economics since World War II. He found that in 1940, "less than 3 percent of the refereed pages . . . [of *AER*] include rudimentary mathematical expressions." In 1990, "nearly 40 percent . . . display mathematics of a more elaborate type."[32] Debreu provides more evidence to demonstrate the

mathematization of economics. For example, many of the best economists, as defined by several different criteria, are mathematical economists, and more than a few faculty members in the best economics departments got their Ph.D.s in mathematics. And today, he adds, "graduate
training in mathematics is necessary" (Debreu 1991, 2).

The mathematization of economics magnified the traits of economic
theory which institutionalists had so fiercely criticized, and which "old-
fashioned" neoclassicists had started to rectify. Economists today know
less than at any time before about economic history and the history of
their discipline (Klamer and Colander 1990; Yonay 1992). Different institutional arrangements and norms are totally overlooked.[33] Many economists, though not all, believe piously in the rationality of human behavior to a degree that none of the great economists from Adam Smith to
Keynes ever believed. The acquaintance of economists with other social
sciences has decreased manifold. And the support of economists in *laissez-faire*, both in terms of the proportion of the advocates and the fervor
of their belief, has become more powerful than at any time since the early
days of classical economics. The institutionalist critique that drew the
attention of earlier neoclassicists has vanished almost entirely, and modern neoclassicists do not pause even for a moment to reflect on it.

This picture of a dramatic turnabout contrasts with the way conventional historians of economics tell the story of modern economics. Nor
does it correspond to either the Kuhnian or the Lakatosian theories of
changes in science. But it does not contradict the constructivist approaches in science studies. Indeed, it is a surprising shift given the balance of power and the allocation of resources during the prewar years.
But since human agents—scientists and others—can act on the world, the
drastic transformation is not inconceivable. Yet, to explain how it actually happened, we must follow the history very closely. This project must
await further research.[34]

Ten

Conclusions: The Evolution of Economic Analysis

Pure science and impure economics both require of the scientist that he should live most of his thinking life along some spoke remote from the true hub of society which he is a member; and from the true hub of the now in which he is. This produces the characteristic and expectable two-facedness of the modern scientist: scientific morality and social immorality. . . . The scientific mind, in being totally scientific, is being unscientific. We are in a phase of history where the scientific pole is dominant; but where there is pole, there is counterpole. The scientist atomizes, someone must synthesize; the scientist withdraws, someone must draw together. The scientist particularizes, someone must universalize. The scientist dehumanizes, someone must humanize. The scientist turns his back on the as yet, and perhaps eternally unverifiable; and someone must face it.
(John Fowles, *Aristos,* 9:35–36)

Science is a public good, which must be preserved at all costs, since it is a source of variety. It causes new states of the world to proliferate. And this diversity depends on the diversity of interests and projects that are included in those collectives that reconfigure nature and society. Without it, without this source of diversity, the market—with its natural propensity to transform science into a commodity—would be ever more doomed to convergence and irreversibility. In the end it would negate itself. Like Carnot's cycle, the economic machine can only function with a source of heat and a source of cold!
(Michel Callon, *"Is Science a Public Good?"*)

THE CONVENTIONAL VIEW on the history of economics perceives a straight development from Adam Smith and classical economics, to Alfred Marshall and neoclassical economics, and then to the Keynesianism of the 1930s. The developments of the postwar period are depicted as the logical conclusion of this long development. Mathematical economists have merely "translated" Marshall into rigorous mathematical models that have enabled them to correct mistakes and to deduce more rigorously the implications of specific conditions and assumptions. Similarly, rigorous econometrician models of the whole economy allowed macro-economists to put the Keynesian and rival theories in exact form and test their adequacy statistically. The study of the interwar struggle between institutionalists and neoclassical economics challenges this grossly oversimplified and misleading picture. It demonstrates that the nature of economic science in our period is not a logical conclusion of prewar processes. On the contrary, interwar economics was edging away from the abstract and deductive pole, putting a higher premium on the empirical study of the institutional aspects of economics. This trend was evident in the approach of Alfred Marshall and his students, including Keynes, and in the popularity of many views that sturdily attacked orthodox economics head-on.

Institutionalism was one of those critical approaches that gained a great deal of influence during that period in the United States. Unlike the current tendency to belittle that school, institutionalism undoubtedly constituted one of the major intellectual forces in interwar American economics. Institutionalists held key positions in academic settings and controlled two of the four leading economics departments in the United States (Columbia and Wisconsin). Wesley Mitchell established the National Bureau for Economic Research, and was among the founders of the New School for Social Research. John Commons founded a new journal (*Land Economics*), trained a large group of economists who investigated various aspects of economic policy, and helped to initiate social welfare plans, first in Wisconsin, and later as part of the New Deal. These achievements were recognized by contemporary economists, who bestowed respect and rewards on their institutionalist colleagues. Mitchell and J. M. Clark gained the highest award of the American Economic Association, the Walker Medal, and served, along with several other institutionalists, as presidents of the Association.

Even if institutionalism was a poor alternative to orthodox economics—as is often argued today—our story indicates that it was a significant episode in the history of American economics. Whatever one thinks about the merits of institutionalism, it is obvious that during the 1920s and 1930s, the economic profession was preoccupied with the institutionalist critique, and major concessions were made by orthodox economists as a result. The later return of economists to even more extreme abstractions might indicate the inherent barrenness of institutionalism, as neoclassical economists say today. Or it may reflect the defeat of institutionalists in the struggle over resources, as the constructivist approach implies. But in any case, a historical account of the development of economics cannot ignore this episode.

The success of institutionalism in those years and the centrality of the debates analyzed in chapters 4 through 8 indicate that the mathematization of economics after World War II constituted a major change in the practices and beliefs within the profession. Of course, there are more than a few continuities between postwar economics and the Marshallian tradition, and therefore the label "revolutionary" to characterize postwar economics is as problematic here as elsewhere. It was extremely revolutionary in some aspects; it was quite traditional in others. In any case, mathematical economics emerged only after a bitter conflict with both institutionalists and traditional neoclassicists. There was no logical necessity that it would gain such a domination, as previous developments were not determined by pure and universal logic and indisputable facts. The triumph of mathematical economics, like the successes and failures of previous schools, is the outcome of struggles between two or more schools and the negotiation among them. This aspect, which is totally missing from Kuhnian and Lakatosian approaches, is essential for our understanding of the dynamics of science. Historians should study the process that resulted in these developments, not to justify them *ex post facto* as the inevitable growth of knowledge.

Many historians of economics imply that a good theory would prevail over worse and weaker theories. The quality of a theory is assumed to be the most important determinant of its destiny; in order to explain its success or failure we must evaluate its quality, and this evaluation is presumed to be an objective property of the theory. Thus the history of economics collapses into philosophy of economics, as anyone can notice by casual reading of the history of economics literature. Neil de Marchi has made the same observation by noticing recently the affinity between the standard logic of modern neoclassical tools and the Lakatosian rationalist construction of the history of science (1991). The logic often implied by present-day economists is that if one can construe a model of rational action that fits ostensibly irrational human behavior, this model should be preferred over explanations in terms of psychological drives, habits, or social customs (Klamer 1990; Mehta 1993). The Lakatosian rationalist reconstruction (as interpreted by De Marchi and other economists) also looks at the development of science in retrospect and justifies the choices of scientists as rational (Brown 1993). If economists have made good choices, no more explanations are needed. Like economists who build models, they prefer neat models over more realistic but clumsier theoretical principles (cf. Hirsch et al. 1987).

For those who accept the validity and usefulness of the pervasive practice of economic model-building, this approach might appear as a strong argument in favor of Lakatos. But there are many others for whom hypothetical rational reconstructions, either of economic or scientific choices, are not persuasive at all. They would argue that it is possible to come up with an *a posteriori* rationalization of any action, making such an explanation uninteresting and useless. They would look for the explanation of human action by understanding the motives of the actors (e.g., Lavoie 1990a), by detailed study of historical evolution of economic institutions (e.g., Veblen 1948; cf. Nelson 1994), or by observing real economic behavior (DiMaggio 1994).[1] It might be evident to the reader that the author of this book is inclined toward the second group of scholars, but this is not the point here. What is important is that the evaluation of the historiography of a scientific discipline is inextricably tied to the evaluation of current practices prevalent in that discipline.

If the goodness of institutionalism, Marshallian economics, Keynesianism, mathematical economics, and econometrics is not the appropriate explanation for their respective fate, where should we look for an explanation? As suggested in the first chapter, the explanation can emerge only from a rigorous study of the wide and complex network of people, ideas, cash flows, practices, and artifacts that were involved in the production of economic knowledge. Since this network—or more accurately, the plethora of partially overlapping networks that have produced economic knowledge in various locales—is immense and dynamic, it is obviously beyond the scope of this volume to explain the rise of institutionalism during the interwar years and its postwar demise. Our main goal was to shed some light on one part of the network, namely, the part dealing with the philosophical and methodological foundations of economic knowledge, its goals, and its prospects, and all this in the American context only. As limited as this project has been, I hope it was enough to cast some new light on the recent history of economic thought and reopen a few black boxes that were closed prematurely. In the rest of this chapter I want, nonetheless, to examine three much broader questions in light of what we have learned so far. The first section discusses how to explain changes in economic knowledge, the second deals with the question of whether economic science has progressed, and the last section tries to give some clues of how to examine whether economics is a good science or not.

The Translation of Mute Objects: How to Explain Economic Knowledge?

Although any pretense to offer an explanation at this stage would be patently premature, we can raise serious doubts concerning some of the explanations offered from other theoretical perspectives and gain, at least, an idea of what a constructivist explanation would look like. It is possible to summarize the deficiency of all the explanations that have been offered so far by noticing a feature they all share. All these explanations assume that there are fixed and stable entities that may serve as the "causes" of the outcomes of scientific competition among economic schools. The scientific discipline, economics in our case, is posited as the "dependent variable," and the debate revolves around the significance of various "independent variables," such as political pressures, ideological commitments, religious beliefs, philosophical doctrines, economic booms and recessions, concrete economic and social problems, major scientific achievements, the views of prominent scholars, logic, and facts. This common approach assumes that each one of these variables can either enhance the chances of a party during a scientific struggle or reduce them. Scholars from various schools of thought and different theoretical perspectives have argued over the relative importance of each of these factors, but all of them have presupposed that the connection between the "cause" and the "outcome" is stable and fixed.

Within the Lakatosian framework, the ability of the theory to yield novel empirical findings or novel theoretical explanations is the key, and it is assumed that this novelty is an intrinsic feature of the theory. The reasons this project has failed are discussed and analyzed by many papers in De Marchi and Blaug (1991), although the editors try to save the Lakatosian perspective as much as possible. Basically the problem is that the progressiveness of a research program, which is supposed to be the main causal variable, is treated as an objective variable. But the innovativeness of a new theory is not naturally given, of course. Human agents have to convince their colleagues that their innovations are really novel, that they are valid, and, not less important, significant for human life. The institutionalists and the neoclassicists tried to do exactly that. Both were able to muster enough support until World War II but failed to do so after the war.

The Kuhnian approach suffers from the same problem. Within the Kuhnian framework, anomalies, that is, contradictions between the theo ries and the empirical evidence, are the causes of change in science. The accumulation of anomalies and the growing recognition of their existence create a "crisis" and eventually lead to a "scientific revolution." The "anomalousness" is assumed to be given. They can be ignored or brushed aside, but the objective historian can unequivocally determine that an "anomaly" has existed. Although Kuhn himself was aware that a fact can be considered an "anomaly" just from within a paradigm, economists who have used his model have often used their judgment to determine the existence of "anomalies." Anomalies, and hence crises, were not considered to be products of human construction but as given facts, as the causes of changes in economic theory. Thus, the rise of institutionalism might be attributed to contradictions between orthodox theory and the success of the managed economy of World War I. Keynesianism has been often attributed to the "anomaly" of the Great Depression, and the rise of new classical economics is currently attributed by many practitioners to the "anomaly" of stagflation in the mid 1970s.

According to our approach, however, the "anomality" of these events is a human construct (Star and Gerson 1987). Moreover, even when the existence of an anomaly is acknowledged, its importance and significance might be debated, and therefore its impact depends on the decisions and actions of various contenders. Harvey (1980) and Star (1989) provide examples of how the responses to "anomalies" were influenced by the social context in which they were "revealed" and defined (see also Callon 1980b). Kuhn himself has never explained when scientists feel uncomfortable enough to give up their hopes to find a solution within the existing paradigm (but see his comment in 1970a, 79). Sensing this difficulty in evaluating the growth of economics, George Stigler claimed that "Kuhn's assertion that a crisis is necessary for the emergence of a new paradigm is virtually a tautology" (quoted in Bronfenbrenner 1971, 140–41). Stigler, in this sense, is a precursor of the constructivist view. In Latourian terms, a crisis occurs when the dominant network loses many allies (or a few powerful ones).[2] This is not necessarily confined to the discovery of "anomalies." The dominance of a certain paradigm might be undermined for many reasons: the initiative of a politically skillful scientist from the opposition, a new discovery, an influence from another discipline, or a new philosophical or cultural ideal. Such developments influence the availability of potential allies and their weights and thus impact the balance of power in the discipline. "Anomalies," that is, the perception that some accepted facts are unaccounted for by the dominant theory, are but one factor that can cause people to abandon the dominant paradigm, but they are not the only reason.

For an illustration let us look at the Great Depression, one of the best examples of a contradiction between theoretical teaching and empirical reality. Many historians of economics have brought up the Depression as the major determinant that undermined the dominance of neoclassical theory and allowed Keynesianism to rise and be established as the new mainstream. But this is an *a posteriori* reconstruction. At the time of the Depression it was not known how it would impact the struggle among various schools, and the advocates tried to align it with their views of the economy. Keynesians used, of course, the Great Depression to advance their theory, and institutionalists perceived it as another proof for the necessity of general planning. But neoclassicists had an explanation that accorded their outlook as well. For them the crisis was the outcome of increasing intervention of governments and the failure to prevent monopolies (see the papers in D. V. Brown et al. 1934, and esp. Schumpeter

1934).[3] Furthermore, neoclassical economists argued that the Depression exposed the failure of institutionalists, who held a great deal of power in the United States during the 1930s and failed to anticipate and cure it (Robbins 1932, 104). If such a claim looks disingenuous today, it is because we have been trained to think about the Great Depression in a specific way. We thus cannot say that neoclassical economics declined because of the Great Depression. The proper way to put it is to say that neoclassical economics declined inter alia because there were some economists who successfully *used* the Great Depression in such a fashion as to implicate neoclassical theory.

Kuhnian explanations also fail to explain how a new paradigm is chosen in the wake of a "crisis." Kuhn refused to say that new paradigms win because they were "better." It is just their perceived *potential*, especially in solving conspicuous problems, that convinces many scientists to espouse them. Laudan properly points to the fact that Kuhn's model lacks a satisfactory explanation of the way a new paradigm gains hegemony: "The things [Kuhn] has to say are, when taken together, inconsistent, and, when taken separately, are unconvincing" (1982, 264; cf. Mulkay 1975, 513–16). In the terms of the ANA we would expect that the supporters of both the new and the old approaches will point to the problems that their respective approaches can best solve. It is reasonable, of course, that the approach which gives a convincing solution to those problems which are considered more important, will be the one that will have more chances to win. But we do not have to assume, as Kuhn does, that there are certain problems which are recognized by *all* members as equally troubling. What is important is socially constructed. The role of the scientific revolutionaries is, as in politics, to convince enough members that they have better solutions to the problems that disturb those members.[4]

The Lakatosian and Kuhnian types of explanation seek the cause of change in the interaction of scientific knowledge with reality. They are called "internalist" explanations, because they remain *inside* the world of knowledge. Many scholars who have not been satisfied with these explanations have offered instead explanations that seek the causes of economic knowledge in the social surroundings of the discipline. An example of this *externalist* view is Dorothy Ross's analysis of economics in the end of the previous century. Ross rejects the explanation of the marginalist success by its professional, scientific nature: "Neither professionalization nor science," she says, "are univocal terms; rather they are shaped by cognitive, aesthetic, and value judgments imbedded in history" (1991, 177). Quite perceptively she notices that science meant something else in Germany and France than in the U.S. and Britain, and therefore marginalism met more resistance in the former countries.

So far her reasoning is similar to the constructivist logic (see chap. 4), but having rejected the "internalist" factors, Ross turns to the "external" one, culture, and her constructivism turns into positivism: "Marginalism won its success in England and America not just because it embodied a sophisticated economic theory but because it met the *standards of sophistication operative in those cultures*" (1991, 177; italics added). The wider culture is treated as an external force, "a cause," that has influenced the internal world of economics. What we saw in this book is different. We saw that even in the same society the "standards of sophistication operative in [that] culture" were not given and uncontested. Rather, they were the subject of dispute within the American scientific culture in general, and economists were avid participants in this dispute. There might have been general principles agreed upon by all, or most, American scientists that differed from those accepted by German scientists. But the interpretation of those principles and their meaning for economics were open for debate. Both parties in our story tried, of course, to mobilize them on their behalf and to convince the others that those principles entailed the vision of science they espoused. The end result was as much a product of their efforts, skills, and choices as it was a product of the original ideas themselves.

Our approach is thus equally critical toward internalist and externalist explanations. Explaining economic knowledge by personal feuds or ideological and political forces is as problematic as the Whig history of internalists. Whereas the latter assumes that Nature is the ultimate umpire in science, the externalists assume that Society performs that role. It is assumed that each external force supports one scientific party or another; it cannot be mobilized by both (cf. Latour 1987, 142–44). There is a variety of external explanations that have been offered by various scholars, and all of them share this predicament. Ross's culturalist account is in many respects the broadest and most sophisticated, but others have been raised by a score of historians, sociologists, and economists and, hence, merit a brief mention.

One of the most popular accounts of the rise of modern economics attaches the destiny of economic theories to political ideologies. Thus it is offered that marginalism appeared in the last quarter of the nineteenth century as a response to the Marxist challenge, and its success—it is often argued—stemmed from its service for the dominant class. Following Mark Blaug, Ross argues that "the social and political relevance of marginalism was its great attraction" during the end of the last century (1991, 178).[5] "Marginalism," she says about J. B. Clark's work, "must have been attractive because its higher level of abstraction seemed to escape the ideological contention of the Gilded Age and allow the legitimation of capitalism on the basis of science rather than moralism" (1991,

179). According to Ross, marginalism won because it appeared objective and scientific. This explanation, however, does not hold water because at that time it was not established yet what objectivism and political neutralism implied in economic research. During the ideologically charged days of the 1930s, many people resorted indeed to science in a search after "objective" answers for the grave economic and social problems. Lionel Robbins, the supporter of mathematical neoclassicism, offered them deductive apriorism as an answer. The deductive method was based on logic, and, according to Robbins (1932), left no room for personal preferences. Terence Hutchison, on the other hand, offered logical-positivism as the proper strategy against the infiltration of ideological biases. The deductive method, he reasoned, was based on philosophical assumptions which might disguise ideological preferences (Hutchison 1938, 137–43; cf. Tugwell 1924a, 414). Thus, both parties recruited the same ally, "ideological neutrality," in defending themselves and indicting the opponents (cf. Coats 1983b, 7; Proctor 1991).

After World War II the mathematical economists won. This triumph, like that of the marginalists in the 1870s, has again been attributed by many scholars to the ideological neutrality of the mathematical method. The mathematical *appearance* might, indeed, have helped the pioneer mathematical economists spread their theories, including those that entailed government intervention. Yet, this appearance is exactly what we must explain. From our constructivist perspective, it is wrong to say that mathematical economics won because it offered a more objective way to conduct economic research. It won because, first, objectivism was accepted as a required feature of science, and, second, because mathematical economists succeeded in presenting themselves as objective. Critics of mathematical economics argue, in contrast, that the aura of objectivity is just an illusion (e.g., Mirowski 1981, 597); under the apparently impartial appearance of mathematics many ideological premises and implications reside.

Ross's explanation attributes the success of marginalism to the abstractness of neoclassical theory, not to its specific content. Its support of capitalist society was achieved indirectly by cloaking economic disparities and injustices in an esoteric, scientific jargon. Other scholars have identified a more direct association between dominant economic theories and the dominant capitalist ideology and have argued that neoclassical economics (in the 1870s) and mathematical neoclassical economics (in the postwar years) won because their contents supported directly the interests of dominant interests. For example, it is claimed that John Bates Clark's version of marginalism justified the existing distribution of income (e.g., Blaug 1986a, 50–52). Or, as another example, the standard demand and supply analysis led to the conclusion that minimum wage legislation was ineffective, a conclusion favored by employers.

This line of reasoning errs twice. First, it assumes a simple connection between political interests and economic theories; each theory, it is assumed, has a clear and unambiguous political implication. Second, it assumes that "interests" are objectively given and known to all; they are not a matter of social construction. It is easy to show that the first assumption does not fit the evidence as many theories have been employed to support completely different ideologies. J. B. Clark's theory, for example, has been offered liberal, as well as conservative, interpretations. Clark offered a theory that seemed to justify the distribution of income, but argued that this theory was applicable only under static conditions, not in the dynamic world. Clark and many of his prominent colleagues rejected, undoubtedly, the Marxian analysis but promoted many radical reforms, activity for which they were bitterly attacked by powerful business persons and their representatives in academic administrations (chap. 2).

The institutionalists of the interwar era also believed in the necessity to reform American capitalism in order to save it from communism and fascism that loomed over interwar Europe. This may have contributed to their success in the 1920s and 1930s, but such an account leaves us with no explanation of their eventual decline. Most postwar institutionalists, indeed, adopted more radical views, but this might have been the *outcome* of their marginalization rather than its *cause*. At the same time Arthur Burns, one of the most prominent institutionalists and Mitchell's close friend and collaborator, adopted conservative policies and served under Eisenhower and Nixon as Chairman of the Council of Economic Advisers and Chairman of the Federal Reserve Board.

We can see a similar diversity within the neoclassical camp. The most prominent American neoclassicists during the interwar period, Knight and Viner, were more conservative than their British counterparts, Marshall, and his pupils, who thought that the modern state had to be more involved in the management of the economy. Their conservative approach notwithstanding, they lost their academic standing during the conservative years of the late 1940s and the 1950s. The mathematical economists and econometricians who took over the field after the war (e.g., Samuelson, Arrow, Tobin, L. Klein) were much more liberal than the "old-fashioned" neoclassicists. They had to overcome fierce political resistance in their struggle to make their knowledge useful in managing the national economy. Their academic victory was the *key* of their political power, not the outcome of such power they had commanded earlier (Yonay 1992). Joseph Stigler and Milton Friedman were also pioneers of the mathematical revolution, which has not prevented them from reaching very conservative conclusions.

The conclusion is that economic theories can be interpreted in diametrically conflicting ways to support different political interests and ideologies. Hence, political interests cannot serve as explanations for the victory of one economic approach over others. But there is even a more profound reason why we cannot use political interests as the causal variable. This reason is that the interests themselves are not given. They are constructed by human agents in social negotiation, and economic theory plays a significant role in this process. Keynesian ideas, which dominated American economics in the 1950s and 1960s, met a deep sense of apprehension from the business community. The Keynesians had to work hard to convince businesspersons that the latter's interests were actually served by Keynesian policies (R. M. Collins 1981). Nowadays it is often argued that Keynesianism won because it furthered the interests of capitalism, but at the time of its ascent capitalists had opposed it vehemently. There might be an "objective" compatibility between Keynesianism and the "real" interests of capitalists but how could this compatibility promote Keynesianism if real living capitalists actively opposed it?[6]

Another kind of external explanation that can be often found in the literature on the history of economic knowledge assigns changes in theory to the economic situation and to specific economic problems that society faces at the time (e.g., Leijonhufvud 1976, 75; Ward 1972, 23). In time of inflation, for instance, it is only logical—the advocates of this kind of explanation say—that theories that purport to solve this problem, or that actually solve it, would become more powerful. During a prolonged recession, on the other hand, one can expect theories that explain unemployment to be more dominant. Thus, the adherents of this view would see the transition which took place during the 1970s from a Keynesian framework to a monetarist/real expectations framework as natural development given the prominence of inflation in those years.

On the face of it, this explanation sounds very reasonable. Economic knowledge is practical knowledge, and its development is motivated by real needs of society. What could be more natural than expecting it to respond directly to changes in the exigencies of the time? The constructivist logic, however, quickly exposes the inadequacy of this apparently persuasive explanation. According to this type of explanation, the solution for the most urgent economic problem is the most powerful ally whose mobilization is decisive in struggles among competing economic schools. But as is the case with all allies, the question which side this ally endorses is *not* a given fact. It depends, again, on the actions of human actors, economists, who must persuade their colleagues that their approach offers the best chances to solve the crucial problem. If only one school offered a solution that nobody challenged, then it would make sense to assume that this school would be preferred. But in most cases, all competing schools would claim to have a solution for the stressing needs of the economy, as we saw in chapter 7 in regard to the problems of the American economy after World War I.

Even after an economic problem has being solved, the advocates of various theoretical approaches argue over the question of who should be credited with the success, or whether it was indeed a success. We already mentioned two such cases. The first case is the *constructed* success of the War Industries Board (WIB) during World War I. This success was generally attributed to the institutionalist spirit, but Keynes, for example, warned that its achievements might have been due to the unique collective spirit of the war. Recent economists are not even sure that it was such a great success. The association between the postwar prosperity and Keynesianism, which is widely accepted as an explanation for the hegemony of Keynesianism during the 50s and 60s (e.g., Silk 1974, 246–47), was challenged very early by the institutionalists who assigned it to the prudent direction of Arthur Burns as the Chairman of the Council of Economic Advisers under Eisenhower and other institutionalists in various government positions (chap. 3). Similarly, the argument that the inflation was harnessed due to the monetarist policies of central banks is also a claim made by a certain party and not an incontestable fact.

Furthermore, even the question what is a "problem" is not an external factor that impacts economics from the outside. Sociologists of social problems know that the definition of a situation as a "social problem" is the outcome of social negotiation (Spector and Kitsuse 1987). To define a situation as a "social problem" some work of definition is needed. First, it has to be shown that the situation is "bad"; that the outcomes are undesirable. But this is not enough. The situation would not be defined as a "social problem" unless it is accepted that there is a "solution"; that the outcomes could be bettered. Thus, airplane accidents are not considered a "social problem" if they are not assumed to result from correctable conditions, such as pervasively negligent maintenance or insufficient government control. If they are perceived as a "natural" concomitant of flying, they are "bad" but not a "problem." Air accidents can become a "social problem," however, if someone manages to convince the public that the accident rate could be lowered. It is the same with the economy. Low rates of growth are not considered a "problem" if people do not think that growth is feasible. And indeed, the lack of growth in preindustrial societies was not considered a problem.

Obviously, economists are not passive participants in the construction of "economic problems" but are very active in the identification of certain situations as "problems," because one must refer to economic knowledge in order to argue that the economy could be better. Unemployment, for instance, became a "social problem" when Keynes and others convinced powerful social actors that it could be eliminated. Perhaps it ceased to constitute a "social problem" more recently as many contemporary economists persuaded powerful groups that nothing could be done to lower it.

Another type of externalist explanation seeks to explain the development of scientific knowledge by the petty interests of the scientists themselves. Scientists want to elevate their own standings and would do anything to achieve this goal. Latour is often misunderstood as supporting such a view. According to this view, neither Nature nor Society determines economic knowledge. One cannot anticipate who would win the battle over the soul of economics, and the outcomes depend on the personalities involved, their whims, personal ties, and tactics. Cunning and shrewd scientists can, according to this view, manipulate powerful people outside of science and cause them to believe whatever they want. The ANA agrees that personal skills and choices are significant. Skillful practitioners can maneuver and adjust their ideas to correspond to known facts and common beliefs, and if they know how to mobilize allies and align them together they have more chances of convincing their colleagues and other interested actors. But the ANA does not imply that these personal squabbles are the most important factor in determining the course of a scientific discipline. The squabbles are conducted in certain institutional orders, and the choices of the actors are constrained by the conditions under which they act. If they keep denying facts that *seem* obvious or fail to satisfy the demands of society, their organizational skills and smart stratagems may not be enough to sustain their ideas.

Similar but more sensible accounts focus on the interests of the profession as a whole rather than on personal interests. Economists, like other professional groups (Bourdieu 1975, 1988; cf. Abbott 1988), wish to secure their position as a required profession. To accomplish this goal they have to gain monopoly over economic knowledge, and this aspiration to make their knowledge inaccessible for others is the most important variable, for instance, in explaining the history of economic thought since the professionalization of the discipline began in the last decades of the nineteenth century. John Maloney, one of the historians who developed this thesis, raises several professional motives that had led to "the priority which the Marshallian school of economics gave to the development of price theory," that is, marginalism. First, it was "a conscious drive towards a secure professional autonomy." Second, "to belong to an esoteric closed shop selling scarce commodity . . . is gratifying as an end in itself." Third, it is "much less time-consuming . . . to make a professional reputation through theoretical brilliance rather than through dull and dogged factual work" (1985, 233). These three professional interests could have led the Cambridge school to develop price theory, but "neither of these factors," Maloney qualifies his explanation, "will by itself lead to the kind of *accumulative* bias in favor of high theory" (ibid.). The continuing emphasis on abstract theory is attributed by Maloney to the usefulness of such a theory "for grading entrants in terms of general intellectual caliber" (ibid.). This is a fourth professional interest that completes the explanation of the triumph of high theory by the interests of the economic profession.

Alon Kadish (1989) also explains the shaping of economic profession in late-nineteenth-century England, and like Maloney, his explanation hinges on professional interests. But according to Kadish, Marshall concentrated his intellectual efforts on the development of deductive reasoning because he wanted to distinguish economics from the rival discipline of history. Marshall wanted to turn economics into a distinct field of specialization at Cambridge, a specialization that would be required of all those who will deal with economic policy and analysis. At that time history was already an established practice at Cambridge, and Marshall did not want people trained in history but with meager knowledge and understanding in economic theory to deal with economic issues. That is why he pushed forward the exclusive analysis of marginal utility and marginal product, even though he never thought that the study of history was insignificant in economics.

Philip Mirowski is a third historian who explains the development of economics during the last century by referring to the interests of those who were actually involved in producing it. In his opinion, the major drive was the economists' desire to be "scientists." That was their most important professional goal (1989b). The accounts of Maloney, Kadish, Mirowski, and Trachtenberg[7] add an important aspect to our understanding of the evolution of economics. There is no doubt that we must consider the motives of those who actually "make economics." But this explanation leaves open the question of what kind of knowledge is the most conducive for advancing professional interests. As was the case with other types of explanation, there is no given and established tie between a specific interest and substantive knowledge. The ties had to be worked out by rhetorical work of interested economists. Mirowski himself is aware that the economists did not agree on how to realize their goal to be "a science." Two camps, "the advocates and the detractors of statistical-probabilistic work," professed to properly represent "Science," and this dispute was, in his opinion, "indicative of the conflicting and confused images of science in that period."[8] Mirowski, who at least in this respect resembles most other historians of economic thought, is subscribed to the belief that science is typically characterized by consensus. But the comparative study of science by both sociologists and historians shows that "conflicting and confused images of science" are very common in all scientific practices.

Thus we saw in chapter 4 that both institutionalists and neoclassicists wished to turn economics into a science. Both looked up to the methods of successful disciplines, such as physics and biology, and the methods of those fields undoubtedly influenced the choices of economists. But which science to follow, physics (as many neoclassicists did) or biology (that was favored by institutionalists)? Or perhaps medicine, as a few other economists have suggested? What aspect of those sciences have to be noticed by economists? How to adjust the methods of the model science to the special circumstances of economics? Different answers to these questions separated the economists despite their shared desire to be "more scientific." The complexity of society, for example, was recruited by institutionalists to delegitimize the neoclassical enterprise as too simplistic, *and* by neoclassicists to cast doubt on the feasibility of the institutionalists' wish to find laws of behavior.

Thus, even if the economists did wish to bolster their position as a "science," as argued by Kadish, Maloney, Mirowski, and others, it still does not follow that they *had* to adopt marginalism or mathematical economics. In the 1870s, for example, historicist economists thought that their "merchandise" would better satisfy the need for professional prestige. According to Collison Black, "the whole science of political economy" in Britain around 1870 was "being widely attacked and criticized, and Sir Francis Galton had questioned whether Section F [of political economy] merited a place in the British Association [for the advancement of Science] at all" (1983, 55). John Kells Ingram, one of the leaders of the British historical school, suggested historicism as the solution (ibid.; Koot 1987, 62), an offer that entailed an intensified focus on the interface of economics and politics. In contrast, John Cairnes, John Stuart Mill's devoted student, suggested that accentuated political neutrality might be the remedy. That was the reason that many economists, including Jevons and Marshall, preferred the term "economics" over political economy.[9] Eventually, Cairnes's option won more supporters, but again, this is what we have to explain. Perhaps more economists *thought* that it would serve the profession better, but we must understand how they have come to believe so.

An illustration that there is no predetermined strategy for how to promote scientific prestige and autonomy is the fate of mathematical economics prior to its postwar boom. At the time that marginalism was preferred, supposedly to enhance the autonomy of economists, mathematical formulations were rejected. For example, Cluade Ménard argues that the mathematics of Walrasian economics was one of the reasons that Walras's approach *failed* to gain support from his contemporaries, including Marshall (1990, 102–4). The latter knew about Walras's work and consciously ignored it despite his efforts to secure the autonomous and scientific status of economics. This was not only because the economists of the time did not know mathematics. Many of them, including Marshall and Keynes, were much more mathematically proficient than Walras. But contemporary economists did not think that economic theory would benefit from mathematization. This attitude changed after the 1930s. The neo-Walrasian research program succeeded exactly because of the same factor that had thwarted Walras's efforts half a century earlier. "What Walras was looking for, in his relations with mathematicians, was not only help but guarantee: he expected from them an a posteriori legitimation to his program" (ibid., 101). In the last quarter of the nineteenth century mathematics did not have the power to do it. But apparently the circumstances changed, and in the post–World War II era, mathematics did provide legitimation.[10]

The ANA does not isolate one factor as the most crucial in explaining changes in science. What it does is focus on those who produce scientific knowledge, the scientists, in order to watch how they make decisions and how they reach agreements. Facts, logic, social needs, philosophical ideas, political power, personal goals, and professional interests are all part of the big puzzle, but their significance for the ongoing scientific enterprise depends on the way they are *translated* by the scientists who take part in the production of knowledge. All these potential allies are mute; their implications for the question at hand are not objectively given, and the participants have to speak in their behalf (Callon and Latour 1981; see the discussion in chap. 1). That is why the process of science production is so crucial. The outcomes of scientific controversies are never determined by "external" forces or "internal" facts—although they are surely important—but depend also on the acts and rhetoric of the actors (cf. Johnston 1976).

Unlike the Kuhnian and Lakatosian models, the ANA does not provide a neat model with universal and unambiguous analyses of changes in science. On the contrary, its analyses are inherently open to a variety of possible scenarios. This could have been a disadvantage if the other models worked well. But this is not the case. The inadequacies of the Kuhnian model were already agreed upon by many historians of economics with a Lakatosian bent. But the Lakatosian approach is fraught with numerous problems as well. It looks neat and attractive, but the moment it is applied it stops to be so clear and unproblematic. The reality is too rich and open to be encapsulated into the Lakatosian mold. The power of the ANA is not in offering a simple formula to explain how scientific theories emerge and diffuse and to judge their quality, but rather in providing us a framework for catching the multifaceted heterogeneity of science and comprehend all the components that are involved in its incessant movement.

Economics as an Open Network: Did Economics Progress?

The questions why institutionalism emerged as a major trend in interwar economics, why its struggle with "old-fashioned" neoclassical economics has never been concluded, and why both camps have been defeated by postwar mathematical economics are not answered in this book. In the previous section I reviewed several explanations and showed their inadequacy. But by saying that previous accounts were inadequate, I did not mean to say they have taught us nothing. On the contrary, all the accounts mentioned above have identified important variables of the equation. They have generally erred—in addition to overlooking the translation problem—in their efforts to identify one major "cause" and in assuming fixed and everlasting relations between "independent variables" (the "causes," or "allies") and the "dependent variable," economic knowledge in our case. But it was not our aim to claim that they have played no role.

Economic facts, successful prediction, and brilliant theoretical conceptions are brought into the network of economic knowledge-production and participate in determining its future. Similarly, it would be ridiculous to say that major economic events, such as the Great Depression or the high inflation of the late 1970s, had no effect on economic thought. These events were very conspicuous and economists could not discuss their field without some reference to them. It would be equally senseless to think that the production of economic knowledge was not influenced by the prolonged dialogue and rivalry with Marxist scholarship and politics. It is also impossible to think that economists were not inspired by conceptual developments in other intellectual fields. And yes, they, like practitioners in many other academic fields, were unavoidably biased by their own wish to be recognized as the proper authority on the knowledge of the economy.

But none of the above factors can be isolated as "The Cause" of economic knowledge. This claim is not merely a compromise to satisfy all contenders. It is rather an argument that these factors are inextricably tied to each other and therefore it is impossible to estimate their relative weights. It is impossible, for example, to say whether "internal" forces were more or less important than "external" ones in the struggle between institutionalism and neoclassical economics. This conflict was focused on questions of "what is science," the scope and goals of the discipline, and its relevance to social welfare. The answers to these questions are inherently a matter of taste and values and, therefore, cannot remain detached from culture and society. "Images of knowledge," Elkana has written, "are determining factors for problem choice in the body of knowledge. They are the long-sought bridges between the purely social and the body of knowledge" (Elkana 1981, 18), and hence, they are simultaneously "internal" and "external." They are influenced by the surrounding ideologies, and in turn determine what would be considered "important, interesting, worthwhile, risky, symmetrical, beautiful, absurd, [and] harmonious" (ibid.).[11]

Because of this multiplicity of influences, the history of economic knowledge can never be as neat and coherent as typically told by the conventional accounts. In those accounts the development of economics is always stepping in an orderly manner from one stage to another according to a "master plan" of history. It is implied that the discipline is a coherent whole, which, except for the short periods of transformation, is unified by shared beliefs and practices. The reality is much more complex and jumbled. Practitioners come from different countries, different schools, and different professional training. They are exposed to various influences from other disciplines, attend to different issues within the field, and hold many shades of opinions. Researchers who feel close to each other form, or are identified as, a "school," and the schools compete over the definition of the discipline and its character. But it should be remembered that even within each "school" there is a diversity of opinions and preferences.

The diversity and plurality were evident, I hope, in the previous chapters. I, indeed, focused on two major schools, which were the most powerful within academic economics. The full spectrum of economic knowledge included many more approaches, such as socialism of various kinds, followers of classical economics, and various idiosyncratic combinations of ideas from different fields and theories. The frequent reference to "institutionalism" and "neoclassical economics" in this book might have also obscured the internal differences within each camp. But those differences were, I hope, quite evident in the analysis of the arguments. In chapter 4 we saw that the institutionalists differed in their philosophies of science. Some expressed unlimited faith in the ability of science to provide definite answers to very complex questions, while some others were closer to the careful position of neoclassicists and warned that the power of science was limited. In chapter 6, we saw that several institutionalists accepted the market economy as a basis for social action to bring about better results. Others denied any role for the market. Consequently, they differed in their attitude toward neoclassical price theory, which was based on a market economy; some accepted it as a starting point or as a component of a much wider theory, while others wished to get rid of it completely (chap. 3). These differences were reflected in the way the past was interpreted. While most institutionalists accepted as important the contributions of the great economists from Smith to Marshall, others rejected the works of all or some of those economists (chap. 8).

That institutionalists disagreed on many thing is well known, because the rivals of that school used this fact to claim that institutionalism was not a cohesive doctrine that could be a serious alternative for neoclassical economics. But, as we saw in chapter 3, institutionalists disputed that assertion and claimed that they had enough things in common to be regarded as one group. I hope that the readers of this book can appreciate now the justification for this argument as well. Interestingly, the question whether neoclassical economics is unified has been given less attention. The relations between Walras, Menger, and Jevons were discussed in connection with the "marginalist revolution" (see the articles in Black et al. 1973), but it is often assumed that Marshallian economics and current neoclassical practices are unified enough to be treated as coherent schools. In this work, however, we saw that the interwar neoclassicists themselves had substantial differences. Some of them joined with institutionalists in seeing economics as one of the exact sciences; others adhered to a view of economics as a literary discourse, involving both science and art. Some neoclassicists accepted theinstitutionalists' conception of human nature; others insisted that economic science must start from the assumption of rationality. Many neoclassicists accepted that government must play a much bigger role in the economy; others kept resisting any such interference. These differences have not been studied and analyzed because nobody sought to challenge the existence of a "neoclassical" school. Its "enemy," the institutionalists, chose not to challenge the unity of neoclassicism because they preferred to present marginalism as inflexible and stagnant. In general, we can conclude that the identity of scientific schools (or other social entities) and the *perception* of their unity are the result of social negotiation. It is related to the effort of individuals to black box their own contributions and its result can never be predicted. But behind any facade of unity there is always a medley of views originating in the diversity of individual backgrounds, circumstances, and experiences.

It should also be remembered that I dealt only with the American scene. The stories of Italian, Swedish, French, German, Austrian, Indian, and Japanese economics in the same period appear to be quite different. In Britain, there were similar conflicts between advocates of orthodox theory (the Cambridge school) and institutionalist-type economists (economic historians at Oxford and the Fabian socialists at the LSE), but the institutional arena and the alignment of forces were different. At the time that American economics was busy with the struggle between institutionalism and neoclassical theory, new developments were in the making both in the U.S. and Britain, developments that made their impact a decade or two later. Most important for later developments is the simultaneous development of Keynesianism and mathematical economics. Usually, historians speak about the "Keynesian Revolution," of the 1930s, and a few mention also a "Mathematical Revolution" initiated by Samuelson somewhat later. But while the Keynesian movement was moving forward at full steam in the late 1930s, those who were not yet engulfed by its tide did not stop working. It is difficult to imagine that hundreds of economists would convert to a new theory and stop working on the many projects that they had previously been conducting.[12] W. Arthur Lewis, a student at the London School of Economics in the 1930s and the Nobel Prize winner for 1979, recalls that the LSE "had not quite caught up with Keynesianism, which was taught by the young lecturers but denounced by the big names." On the other hand, he says, "the school was in the forefront of the development and worldwide expansion of neoclassical economics" (in Breit and Spencer 1986, 4). The "Keynesian Revolution" is dated 1936, the year *General Theory* was published. Three years later, John Hicks published *Value and Capital*, a book that helped to put the "mathematical revolution in motion." Other schools were not idle in the 1930s. In institutionalism, Adolf A. Berle Jr. and Gardiner C. Means published *The Modern Corporation and Private Property* in 1932, and Commons published *Institutional Economics* two years later. Joan Robinson at Cambridge, and Edward Chamberlin at Harvard, launched the theory of imperfect competition in the early 1930s. Friedrich von Hayek carried the Austrian School forward with *Price and Production* (pub. 1931) and *Profit, Interest and Investment* (pub. 1939). Advocates of socialism and the Austrian economists who abhorred it developed a theoretical examination of planned economies (Lavoie 1985). Ragnar Frisch and Jan Tinbergen tackled fundamental problems in econometrics and made pioneering applications of econometrics in macroeconomics. All these developments took place simultaneously. For sociologists of science, the fact that all these developments took place at the same time does not constitute a problem. It does become a problem only if we adopt a rigid view that conceives disciplines as ruled by one paradigm or research program only. When we think about economics as a network which is connected in various ways with many other networks, we can notice the simultaneity of all these developments: institutionalism, Keynesianism, mathematical economics, econometrics, and new developments within Marshallian theory (e.g., imperfect/monopolistic competition).

The modern sociology of science underlines the diversity of any scientific enterprise. In modern science, when science is practiced in many locations all over the globe, it is difficult to imagine that one school would sweep the whole discipline in a short period. Communication is indeed faster, but the organization is much more complex, and various locales are embedded in different social networks. Susan Leigh Star borrows the concept of an "open system" from information theory to describe this aspect: "Real-world information systems are continuously evolving and decentralized. They require negotiation between distributed parts in order to function and as a result contain arm's-length relationships between components. The internal consistency of an open system cannot be assured because its very character is open and evolving" (1989, 20). In economics, for example, some practitioners drew upon mechanics and calculus; others have built upon evolutionary theories. Some established connection with the Federal Reserve system and other governmental agencies, while others tied their work to a network of radical critique of capitalism. Some cultural elements are more general and widespread (e.g., basic principles of logic, the idea of democracy), while others are limited to specific locales (e.g., econometric techniques, general equilibrium models, Veblen's teachings). The networks themselves are tied to each other in a complex and fluid web of relations (Fujimura 1992; Star and Griesemer 1989). Because of this, "simply keeping up with developments as perspectives are evolving is impossible" (Star 1989, 24), or as Philip Mirowski (1986b, 3) says, "it is by no means a simple matter" to identify the orthodoxy of modern economics, because "orthodoxies have a habit of not standing still." Nor does the opposition to orthodoxy stand still, of course.

The ongoing analysis carries a straightforward implication for the question of whether science progresses smoothly through succession of scientific research programs or dramatically through revolutions. If there are many simultaneous changes, loose connections among individuals, liquid definitions of camps, and shifting alliances, then one can always find some evidence of continuity and some evidence of revolution. Economics provides many examples, of which the case of institutionalism (chap. 8) is quite typical. Institutionalists followed and intensified the use of historical evidence and statistics that were promoted earlier by Marshall and prominent American economists. But they also became more skeptical toward the marginalist approach that unified many economists at the end of the nineteenth century. Most institutionalists preferred the less revolutionary image and presented their approach as the adjustment of past practices to modern economies and advanced science. Few others, however, thought that the revolutionary image was better and more useful and presented institutionalism as a revolutionary solution to the inability of traditional economics to solve economic problems. The opponents of institutionalism also depicted it as revolutionary but for the opposite purpose of depriving it of legitimacy. We can see the same considerations in the way economists presented Keynesianism. Keynes himself presented his view as revolutionary, probably because the Great Depression had hit hard the confidence in preceding theories. But after World War II, many Keynesians sought to describe it as an improvement of earlier teachings, not their replacement.[13] Another example, modern mathematical economics, is presented as a natural development of Marshallian economics despite many fundamental differences in their *weltanschauungen*.

Did economics progress at all in the last century? Did the institutionalists contribute to its progress? Have the postwar economists taken economics forward or have they moved backward? Obviously, the answers to these consequential questions depend on the theoretical perspective of the respondent. But what does progress mean in our constructivist framework? Many of the critics of constructivism think that since constructivists do not accept the existence of any absolute criterion to judge science, there is no meaning to the concept of "progress." Due to the lack of a ruler to measure progress, it is impossible to say that a recent theory is better than an older one. Any claim for an advancement is necessarily partisan and, therefore, has no value.

But this interpretation is grossly imprecise. Indeed, it is impossible to measure the growth of economics with an objective ruler. And indeed, various scholars hold different views concerning the importance of this idea or another for the "progress" of economics. Obviously, the institutionalists thought that their empirical and quantitative studies carried the discipline forward, whereas neoclassical economists were quite skeptical about it. A constructivist sociologist cannot decide who is right. She would say that the decision that would eventually have been accepted, will be the result of resource mobilization of the participants in the discourse. But whatever the decision in the field, *science continues to progress*. The reasoning is the opposite from the one imputed to constructivism by its faultfinders. We cannot say what is better because *all parties* contribute to our knowledge and understanding. Competent and well-trained people, who are motivated by the passion to know and understand or by the desire for glory and fame, will always find something new to add to the stock of knowledge. They could have found more things, or other things, had they employed other methods, but it is the nature of the scientific *practice* that it always produces new knowledge. It is a "practice"; scientists constantly do something, and during these activities they gather data, invent concepts, classify, measure, combine things or break them up, experiment with objects or watch them closely. Some kind of knowledge is always being produced.

The discussion of progress in economics carries us to the last topic of this book. So far we have been concerned with the history of economics and the reasons it has evolved the way it has. But as we often said about the heroes of our story, the view of history is closely connected to methodological choices relevant for current practice. Does our story carry important conclusions for modern economists? It is impossible to end this book without a few thoughts about this question, although my goal would be merely to raise some issues rather than answer them. The discussion will therefore be very brief.

Pride without Arrogance: What Is a Good Science?

Methodologists of economics are concerned with the question of whether economics is a science or not, and what economists should do in order to be "real" scientists. Obviously, these questions preoccupied the inter-war economists as much as they preoccupy their modern successors. The constructivists tell us, however, that there is no one way of doing science. Although there are a multitude of connections between scientific fields, each field has its own properties, partially due to its unique subject matter, and partially due to the historical contingencies in which it has been practiced. According to Daniel Hausman, "the values of economic theorists are distinctive in the weight given to mathematical elegance, in the comparatively small attention given to experimentation, data gathering, and testing, and in the concern for policy relevance" (1992, 84). He then proceeds to examine whether this is compatible with being a "science." But if there is no one, and only one, model of science, how could we assess the quality of this practice? Science is what scientists do; economics is what economists do. If economists prefer mathematical elegance over data gathering, can we fault them for their view of science?

Blaug and Backhouse have criticized recently the constructivist approach exactly on this ground. They say that this approach accepts science as it is, rather then setting values and norms for scientific practice. As a sociological or historical pursuit, description of what scientists actually do is, obviously, an important job. But as Blaug (1994) and Backhouse (1994c, 179) properly grasp, constructivism has direct normative implications. If sciences are practiced in many ways and there is no supreme model of science to be used as a guide for all scientific practices, then we must accept all the choices of scientists and view any scientific strategy as legitimate. Everything goes! In their view this is a very undesirable feature as it prevents the betterment of scientific practices. As an example, Backhouse cites Roy Weintraub's defense of general equilibrium theory (GET; Backhouse 1994c, 179). Weintraub, a general equilibrium theorist himself, is among the few who have adopted a constructivist perspective in economics. GET has been harshly criticized for its detachment from economic realities. The critics used various methodological norms as the basis for their attack, and especially the Popperian insight that demands empirical testing, something GET has never been exposed to. Backhouse thinks that Weintraub's adoption of constructivism is a sheer evasion from any rigorous test. But according to constructivism economists know best how to pursue knowledge in their field. Noneconomists do not know enough to judge them, so it is impossible to criticize them.[14] For Backhouse, this is crooked logic as it put scientists on a privileged level above any doubt; whatever scientists do is good.

Blaug's and Backhouse's critiques are important but miss the mark. Constructivism is certainly not indifferent to normative issues. Its call to follow what scientists actually do does not mean that the constructivists condone everything. They are also interested in judging theories and improving science but they believe that effective critique must be based on understanding actual scientific behavior. Constructivism does not entail that all scientific theories and practices have the same value. On the contrary, from our constructivist approach—as we saw throughout this manuscript—methodological and normative considerations are cardinal elements of scientific practice. Science is permanently engaged in a discourse of which methods are good and which ones are bad (cf. Feyerabend 1975, 1978). If the critiques of Blaug and Backhouse were correct, there would be no point in this discourse, which is surely not my intention here, nor is it entailed by Latour and the other constructivists. Indeed, in order to judge economics, one must know economics. One must be an actor in the discipline. That makes her a "partisan," but there is no reason to be ashamed of it. The debate on methodology and philosophy of economics cannot be divorced from substantive and theoretical discussion. The arguments about the adequacy of the neoclassical and the institutionalist strategies could not be separated from the reasoning about human behavior and social life (chap. 5) and about economic realities (chap. 6). To judge the economics of the 1990s, to evaluate whether current economic theory helps in understanding economic life, one must be proficient in current economic theory and recent economic research.

This, the critics would be quick to point out, leaves us exposed to the danger that scientific disciplines would turn into closed worlds; theory would turn into dogma, and nobody would be able to protest, as those who disagreed would be thrown out before they become qualified and recognized speakers. The insiders would be accomplices and the outsiders would be considered, according to the reasoning above, illegitimate speakers. Such a danger indeed exists. Moreover, this author shares the critiques of Blaug, Backhouse, and many others, that modern economics has made some wrong choices. But since he is not an economist he cannot say anything, or can he?

The solution is to be found in the openness of the network. The world of science is not a feudal system in which each lord has an unconstrained authority over well-defined territory. Science is a complex and mammoth network that includes not only scientists, laboratories, instruments, and theories. It also includes all the "nonscientific" elements that scientists must be in contact with in order to do their works, such as policy-makers and private benefactors who finance science, public-opinion leaders who create a supportive (or nonsupportive) atmosphere for science, university administrators who take care of the immediate workplace of the scientists, and so forth. Boundaries are constantly challenged, contested, and redrawn. To survive, economists must attach their work to the network of government officials, administrators, and benefactors. The fact that the current network of economists includes such people says either that there is something useful for those people in mainstream economic theory and research, or that the economists are such shrewd manipulators that they have been capable of deceiving powerful politicians and business magnates about the relevance of their work.[15]

Critics of mainstream economics, who think that there are more useful strategies (for the goals they deem important), can mobilize actors and resources outside of economics proper and establish their own networks. The conventional explanations of historians of economics make the mistake of overemphasizing the unity and homogeneity of scientific disciplines. The "invisible college" of modern science is assumed to be unified by professional journals, textbooks, and conferences. That is why the Kuhnian story of revolutions is so heroic and too fantastic. The dictatorship of "normal science," like the dictatorship of the Politburo in the USSR, can never be as perfect and inescapable as the control of Big Brother in George Orwell's *1984*. There are always hubs of opposition that are connected to some other powerful interests. Institutionalists managed to survive and produce more knowledge, although they have been kept on the margins of the profession. Hodgson claims that they have recently started to emerge again as an important power in current economics (1994). The same is true about Austrian economics and Marxian economics. Explanations that focus on the success of mathematical neoclassical economics overlook the fact that a good model of science must explain also the endurance of all these schools.

Moreover, economic knowledge can be produced in other locations than economic departments, and by other people than those with Ph.D.s in economics. Political economists located in political science departments, for example, have managed to create an alternative network that ties the analysis of inflation and unemployment to the analysis of power structure in the advanced industrial states (e.g., Lindberg and Maier 1985). Economic sociologists have also managed to secure their own position as competent speakers on questions of economic organization (e.g., Zukin and Dimaggio 1990; Smelser and Swedberg 1994). Departments of organizational behavior, labor relations, management science, and the like also serve as locations for studying subjects that once had been studied in economics departments. Of course, not all the coexistent networks are equally powerful and influential. Central banks and treasury officials are typically connected to mainstream economics. But political scientists, sociologists, and business school researchers survive and even flourish, which means that they have succeeded in connecting their ideas to some ongoing concerns in society.

Traditional methodologists may view this plurality of economic-knowledge producers with some concern. But there is no reason to be worried. We should no longer pursue the ideal of a Unified Science. In a lecture at Harvard, Kuhn himself joined the conclusion of many sociologists of science and offered to abandon "the view of science as a single monolithic enterprise, bound by a unique method." Rather, he continues, "it should be seen as a complex but unsystematic structure of distinct specialties or species, each responsible for a different domain of phenomena" (1992, 18). Kuhn retains his belief in science by arguing that within each scientific specialty scientists produce knowledge "in ways that increase accuracy, . . . consistency with other accepted beliefs . . . breadth of applicability . . . [and] simplicity" (ibid., 13, 18). Accuracy, applicability, and consistency, though, are not objectively observed. As outsiders we cannot testify whether accuracy in economics has been increased or not in the last decades, or whether the loss of accuracy has been offset by a gain in another criteria. All we can say is that the trials of strength within each scientific niche force scientists to defend their ideas, and this fight compels them to consider their views and improve them.

The normative implications of constructivism, as presented in this book, can thus be summarized in one sentence. Practicing economists may be proud and confident about the way they study the economy, but they should not be too arrogant to assume that their success negates the value of other practices. The achievements of mathematical economics since the early years of the 1950s are numerous and impressive. The conceptual and empirical advancements listed by Blaug (1994)—Game theory, linear programming, input-output analysis, national income accounting, the measurement of inequality, welfare economics, econometric models, macroeconomic models—are real and important. The postwar discourse has contributed many new concepts to the social science literature. It is difficult to imagine what this discourse would look like without "human capital," "demand elasticity," "transaction costs," "agency costs," "moral hazard," "Nash equilibrium," "rent-seeking behavior," "price leadership," "adverse selection," "free riders," and many other concepts that have been added by economists in the last half of the century. But the victory of mathematical economics in the institutional level and their manifold achievements do not prove that they have found the best theory and that older approaches had nothing worthwhile pursuing and remembering. Nor should they look down upon less accepted practices within economics or in other disciplines.

Unlike Lakatosian methodologists who expect the springs of innovation to dry up, the constructivist sociology of science predicts that mathematical economics would continue to yield new concepts and insightful models if enough economists pursue it. The issue scientists and methodologists should consider is the "marginal utility" of this line of research in comparison with alternative avenues. McCloskey, who is a staunch supporter of modern economics, is critical only toward the hubris of modern economists that prevents them from recognizing the value of other types of research. She hopes, therefore, that "a rhetorical criticism, like a course of psychoanalysis, might make economists more self-aware, modest, and tolerant, better in person and profession" (1985, 175). Hausman, from a very different perspective, concurs that economists should "be more eclectic, more opportunistic, more willing to gather data, more willing to work with generalizations with narrow scope, and more willing to collaborate with other social scientists" (Hausman 1992, 280). The call of Hutchison, Blaug, and Backhouse to pit economic theory with more empirical findings is in harmony with this spirit, as is the critique of radical economists like Mirowski, Wilber and Jameson (1983), and others. Even the champions of mathematical economics admit that the discipline should be opened to new practices (e.g., Debreu 1991). The constructivist approach cannot tell practicing economists what theory to choose or what methods to use. All it can say is, with McCloskey, Hausman, and many others, that economists should be interested in expanding the horizons of their discipline in order to increase the diversity of economic knowledge and its richness (Callon 1994).

Notes

Chapter One
Introduction: A Sociological Interpretation of the Modern History of Economics

1. Most writers use the terms "institutional school" or "institutional economists" when they refer to this school and its members. I use the adjective "institutionalist" for identifying the ideas, approaches, and economists of that specific American school in order to distinguish between that particular school and various other views that have incorporated institutional elements in their analyses of the economy.

2. This work is focused on the American arena but the support of interventionism had a much wider acceptance. In Germany, the mainstream was always in favor of intervention, and German economic thought and policy had a strong influence in northern and central Europe. In Britain, the pendulum began to pull toward intervention in the last quarter of the nineteenth century with the work of the British historicists (Koot 1987), Nicholson (Maloney 1985, chap. 4), and Hobson (Blaug 1986a, 93–95). But even the dominant Marshallian school was very supportive of modest intervention as discussed at length in the next chapter. The anti-interventionists had their own strongholds, of course, mostly in France (Ménard 1990) and Austria (Streissler 1990, 171–72).

3. Recent historians doubt that the managed economy of World War I was very successful, but at the time it was widely perceived as a great success.

4. See Blaug (1985a, chaps. 2–7); Backhouse (1985, pt. I); Canterbery (1976, chaps. 3–4); Dasgupta (1985, chaps. 2–5); Bladen (1974, bks. I–II); Ekelund and Hébert (1983, pt. 2); Landreth (1976, chaps. 2–5); Niehans (1990, pt. I). Many historians refer, of course, to earlier economic doctrines, from the Bible and the Greek philosophers to the mercantilists of the seventeenth and eighteenth centuries and the French physiocrats who "anticipated" Smith. But it is widely accepted that Smith was the first systematic and comprehensive economic theorist.

5. Blaug (1985a, chaps. 8–15); Backhouse (1985, pt. II); Canterbery (1976, chap. 6); Dasgupta (1985, chaps. 6–7); Bladen (1985, bk. III, chaps. 1–2); Ekelund and Hébert (1983, pt. 4); Landreth (1976, chaps. 6–8); Niehans (1990, pt. II); Black et al. (1973); Hennings and Samuels (1990).

6. Blaug (1985a, chap. 16); Backhouse (1985); Canterbery (1976, chap. 7); Dasgupta (1985, chap. 8); Bladen (1985, bk. III, chap. 3); Ekelund and Hébert (1983, chap. 18); Landreth (1976, chap. 12). It is quite amazing to see how 1936, the year Keynes published *The General Theory of Employment, Interest and Money*, became almost a "magical" date. Virtually everybody agrees that this was a turning point. An exception is Backhouse (1985) who perceives 1939 as the turning point, either because he sees the Second World War as a watershed, or because of Hicks's *Value and Capital* published at that year. The term "Neoclassical Synthesis" appears in the "Family Tree of Economics" on the back cover of

Samuelson's 4th edition of *Economics: An Introductory Analysis* (1958). In later editions, e.g., the 10th (1976), it is replaced by the term "Post-Keynesian Mainstream Economics."

7. This summary is based on Kuhn (1970a). See also Kuhn (1970b) and his "Second Thoughts on Paradigms" in Kuhn (1977). Discussion of Kuhn's model is available in Laudan (1977, chap. 3 and 1984), Barnes (1982), and in many of the papers in Lakatos and Musgrave (1970). Kuhn's "Reflections on My Critics" in that volume (Kuhn 1970c) is quite a sophisticated defense of his approach.

8. See a profile of Kuhn by Horgan (1991). Kuhn had some regrets for using the ambiguous term "paradigm" and suggested instead the term "disciplinary matrix" to convey the same idea (1970a, postscript; 1977, 318–19); see also Hausman (1992, 83–85).

9. My summary is based on Coats (1969); Canterbery (1976); Dillard (1978); Routh (1975); Ward (1972), but see Redman (1991, 96n) for more Kuhnian applications to economics. See also Remenyi (1979, 31).

10. For discussion of the "revolutionariness" of marginal economics, see the papers in Black et al. (1973) in addition to the references mentioned above in note 9.

11. Lowe, for instance, thinks that the "disintegration of orthodox classical system" started with Ricardo's disciples as early as in the 1820s, gained momentum with J. S. Mill's work, and "swept away the old framework in the 'utility revolution' of the 1870s" (1964, 194).

12. Galbraith claims that Keynesianism left *micro*economics untouched, thus leaving the neoclassical edifice intact; whatever Keynes added to the field, its theory has *not* destroyed the "old regime" (1987, 235–36).

13. There are numerous descriptions and applications of Lakatos's model in economics, including Blaug (1975); the articles in Latsis (1976), Remenyi (1979, 31–33); Fulton (1984); Maddock (1984); the articles in De Marchi and Blaug (1991); Redman (1991, chap. 9); Hausman (1992, 85–88); Backhouse (1994a). For more applications, see Redman (1991, 96n).

14. D. F. Gordon (1965) offers a similar view of the history of economic thought, but since he had written before Lakatos was introduced to economists, he had not used the Lakatosian terminology.

15. See Brown et al. (1934) on the rejection of Keynesianism by many Harvard economists; Winch (1989) on the resistance of the Bank of England; Galbraith (1987, 242–43) and Salant (1989, 42) on the opposition of policy-makers in the Roosevelt administration. Frank Knight wrote to his colleague and friend Jacob Viner: "I regard Mr. Keynes' neo-mercantilistic position . . . as essentially taking the side of the man-in-the-street, against the effort of the economic thinker and analyst to get beyond and dispel the short-sighted views and prejudices of the former — as . . . passing the keys of the citadel out of the window to the Philistines hammering at the gates. His work and influence seem to me extremely 'anti-intellectual' . . ." (A letter to Jacob Viner, August 6, 1940. The Viner files, Princeton University).

16. Remenyi's conceptual development of the Lakatosian framework (1979) was an attempt to solve this ambiguity by introducing the concept of demi-core: a hard core of a sort which is subordinate to the main hard core of the discipline.

The model has not been adopted by other students of economics, and it is my feeling that it would complicate rather than solve the conceptual confusion that the SRP model is plunged in.

17. In the next section I focus on a specific family of a constructivist approach: the actor-network analysis. This section summarizes the general principles of all the constructivist perspectives. A selection of reading from these perspectives includes: Collins (1975, 1982, 1983, 1985); Law (1976); Mendelsohn (1977); Pinch (1977, 1986, 1992); Knorr-Cetina (1981, 1982, 1983, 1991, 1992, 1995); Law and Williams (1982); Restivo (1982); Gilbert and Mulkay (1984); Pickering (1984, 1990); Lynch (1985, 1992, 1993); Fujimura (1987, 1988); Wise (1988, 1989); Woolgar (1988); Star (1989); Star and Gerson (1989); Clarke and Gerson (1990); Clarke and Fujimura (1992); MacKenzie and Spinardi (1995). References to the actor-network analysis literature will appear in the next section.

18. This issue has been recently introduced into the methodological discourse in economics under the title of "recovering practice" (Backhouse 1994b, 10–15; Caldwell 1994).

19. "Positivism" is a much-abused term which has many contradictory meanings. What I mean here is positivism as a philosophical view according to which empirical studies can discover the exact and real nature of the world. Constructivism rejects this view but couches its view in thick empirical descriptions.

20. The accusation of self-refutation was made by numerous scholars. See Hands (1994, 91–93) for a recent summary of the accusation. Many such claims in the field of economic methodology are summarized by McCloskey (1994b, chap. 15), who then answers them forcefully and persuasively.

21. Economists who participate in the discourse on method in economics do not distinguish between the project of the rhetoric of economics and the sociology of science (e.g., Backhouse 1994c, 183–84). Although there are some differences in the way rhetoricians and sociologists analyze scientific fields, it is indeed correct that they share many ideas that set them apart from conventional modern methodology in economics.

22. See the critiques on Roth and Barrett (1990) by Pinch (1990) and Pickering (1990, 684, 716–17n).

23. The Edinburgh school of the 1970s might have believed in such "external" determination, although the interpretation of their position is not completely clear. See, for example, Bloor (1976); Barnes (1977); Barnes and Shapin (1979); Barnes and Edge (1982); Shapin (1982). In any case, it seems that during the 1980s, those associated with crude externalism moved toward the constructivist view as in Shapin and Schaffer (1985); Pickering (1989, 1990); Shapin (1992). See also the debate between Collins and Yearly (1992a, 1992b) and Callon and Latour (1992), and Nickles's (1990, 633–34) comment on Roth and Barrett.

24. Mirowski's comment that "the problem of demarcating the Natural and the Social is one of the most active research areas in the Sociology of Scientific Knowledge" (1994, 55) is completely wrong. He himself asserts later that "neither the natural nor the social sciences possess the kind of stability in method or subject-matter which would permit simple one-way evaluations of success or failure of inquiry" (ibid., 57).

25. For a discussion on the principle of symmetry, see Bloor (1976); Latour (1987, 136, 182–96); Callon and Latour (1992).

26. Or of its kin-in-spirit rhetoric which is also grossly misunderstood (Klamer 1990; McCloskey 1994b, pt. 5).

27. It should be clear that this statement does not entail that we have to believe whatever scientists say. As sociologists and historians, our stories and analyses are not aimed at deciding whether the scientists we study are right or wrong. The moment we express a view on the subject matter, we become *de facto* scientists and must undergo trials of strength ourselves. One can ask at this point why we privilege scientists; why do we accept the views of any group of scientists as legitimate and deny nonscientists the same privilege? The answer is that we do not! We can analyze political and artistic struggles the same way we analyze scientific disputes. For applications of the constructivist approach to other social fields, see Becker and McCall (1990).

28. Hands (1994) argues that the Edinburgh school, or the "strong programme" as it is often referred to, is the only distinctive and coherent school in the new sociology of science. This is rather a strange claim to be heard in 1994. Very few sociologists still adhere to that approach while several other "schools" are widely recognized by practitioners in the field, including the Bath school, associated with H. M. Collins, The French, or Paris, school of Latour and Callon, and the symbolic interactionist approach (Clarke and Gerson 1990). See Pickering (1992b); Sismondo (1993); and Knorr-Cetina (1995) for mapping of the various constructivist approaches.

29. This position is not very different from Charles S. Peirce's as elaborated by Hoover (1994). Hoover quotes from Peirce: "When a theory has been broached it is considered to be on probation until this agreement is reached. After it is reached, the question of certainty becomes an idle one, because there is no one left who doubts it" (1994, 306).

30. In daily language, people often say, "Let the facts speak for themselves." For constructivists, the opposite has become a common idiom. Facts never speak for themselves because they are mute. When a scientist or someone else says that a fact speaks for itself, she means that we should prefer one interpretation over another. This is a key issue, and there are numerous examples that demonstrate it. See, for example, Latour (1987); Hacking (1983); Knorr-Cetina (1981, 1992); Collins (1975, 1985). For constructivists and rhetoricians, Truth, with a capital T, is irrelevant because we can never be sure that we reached it (McCloskey 1994b). All we can have is agreements about truth claims; the ontological problem cannot be separated from the epistemological one (Sismondo 1993). I think this is the major point that Mäki (1995) and other critics of constructivism fail to understand.

31. As Boland argued, "whenever one studies rhetoric, one is implicitly . . . studying sociology" (1989, 170). McCloskey also says that "sociology and rhetoric are one" (1994b, 104). More examples of the application of rhetoric to social sciences can be found in Hunter (1990); Nelson et al. (1987).

32. Philip Mirowski is also aware that the quest for the neoclassical and the Marxian hard cores "is notoriously tricky business." Many historians and some methodologists, he says, have tried it "with none too impressive results" (1986b, 4). Mirowski believes that he has solved the problem by finding analogies from physics that, in his view, are basic "gestalt-conceptions" that separate Marxism from neoclassical economics. Marxism is based on an analogy with the materialist

Cartesian theory, and neoclassical theory on an analogy to energy theory (1986b, 4). Yet Mirowski's suggestion is merely one more interpretation. It may capture a crucial dimension of the gap between the two schools, but there might be equally valid criteria to characterize the differences between the two programs, and perhaps some commonalities to identify them as having the same hard core.

33. Stanley Fish's concept of "interpretive community" (Fish 1980) is related to networks. We can assume that members of a tightly knit network would understand given texts (in the wider meaning of "texts") in a similar fashion. As in scientific networks, Fish does not assume that there are clear boundaries between interpretive communities. For an application of Fish to economics, see E. R. Weintraub (1989).

34. Law (1973) distinguishes between three dimensions of specialties that might be applied to the classification of paradigm: techniques or methods, theory, and subject matters. Classification according to these dimensions may yield completely different results. Keynes, for instance, was Marshallian in his methodology, but differed from Marshall in theory, and perhaps in subject matter as well. Modern Keynesians have the same subject matter as Keynes, may have the same theory (but see Leijonhufvud 1968), but they employ very different methodology. Cf. Hutchison (1978, 291–95).

35. For sources on the constructivist approach, see note 17; Sismondo (1993) distinguishes several types of social constructivism, but as he himself says, usually they are employed together and the distinctions are blurred.

36. Latour (1987) and the second part of Latour (1988a) offer general expositions of his approach. See also Latour (1980, 1982, 1983, 1986, 1988b, 1988c, 1992, and 1993). See also Callon (1980a, 1980b, 1986); Callon and Latour (1981); Callon and Law (1989); Latour and Woolgar (1979); Bijker et al. (1987).

37. Unlike Backhouse, I think that methodological discussions in economics have always been an integral practice of the discipline. Backhouse's short list ignores the methodological controversies between the historicists and the deductivists, not only in the German world, but in Britain and the U.S. as well. Also ignored are the methodological disputes that led unsatisfied young American economists to organize and establish the AEA (see next chapter).

38. Or more generally, to any human study if we consider behavior to be a "text" as well. Any human behavior, including speaking and writing, is composed of acts loaded with symbolic value and meaning, and the interpretation of how one behaves is completely parallel to the interpretation of what one writes (Lavoie 1990b).

39. As a matter of fact, I started my analysis with a very different view of the field of economics and was changing my opinions as I read more and more texts.

Chapter Two
The Neoclassical Era (1870–1914) from a Different Angle

1. This kind of analysis has been much more popular among earlier writers on the history of economic thought (e.g., Gide and Rist n.d.; Mitchell 1969; Bladen 1974; Spiegel 1983; Pribram 1983), perhaps because economics was much more pluralistic in those days and discussion of fundamental issues were inescapable.

2. Institutionalists noticed this separation between the marginalist theory and

the practice of most specialized economists and used it as an argument in favor of a more "relevant" theory (Mitchell 1924, 24; Mitchell 1925, 6; Ayres 1938, 69–70).

3. Marshall adds that "the same bent of mind led our lawyers to impose English civil law on the Hindoos." The ethnocentric views that Marshall seems to criticize here plagued the social sciences until quite recently, and it is important to notice that Marshall at the turn of the century was already aware of this dangerous inclination.

4. Marshall (1910, 763) argues that the Ricardian economists "did not see that the poverty of the poor is the chief cause of that weakness and inefficiency which are the causes of their poverty: they had not the faith that modern economists have in the possibility of a vast improvement in the condition of the working classes." In a footnote he analyzes the ideological exploitation of the narrow approach of economists: "As regards wages there were even some logical errors in the conclusions they deduced from their own premises. These errors . . . are little more than careless mode of expression. But they were seized upon eagerly by those who cared little for the scientific study of economics, and cared only to quote its doctrines for the purpose of keeping the working classes in their place" (ibid., 763n). It seems as if this stricture is as relevant today as it was a century ago.

5. Marshall's evolutionary analogies and the similarity between him and Veblen are acknowledged by Backhouse (1985, 104) as well.

6. John Bates Clark poses a similar puzzle for modern economists, who think in terms of dichotomous relations between abstract theory, on the one hand, and institutional and historical research, on the other.

7. Actually Marshall himself relied heavily upon historical statistics in his book, *Money, Credit, and Commerce* (pub. 1923). Furthermore, the *Principles of Economics* itself is copious with historical examples and analyses, a fact that provoked Lionel Robbins's ire (Robbins 1932, 65). It is not my intention to belittle the significance of the controversy between Marshall and his "Cambridge school" and the more historically oriented economists. The nature of economics as a separate discipline was still contested, but no party in this debate doubted the vast importance of historical studies. See Kadish (1982 and 1989); Maloney (1985); and the papers in Kadish and Tribe (1993) for analyses of the main controversies in British economics during the second half of the nineteenth century.

8. Coats (1983b, 4) speaks on "the combined influence of Marshallian hegemony and John Neville Keynes's influential *Scope and Method of Political Economy.*"

9. Keynes mentions Cairnes's lecture at University College, London, in which he "delivered a frontal attack upon *laissez-faire* in general. 'The maxim of *laissez-faire*,' he declared, 'has no scientific basis whatever, but is at best a mere handy rule of practice'" (Keynes 1924, 26). "This," Keynes adds, "for 50 years past, has been the view of all leading economists" (ibid., 26–27).

10. On American economic thought before 1885, see Hudson (1975); Conkin (1980); Kaufman (1982); Galbraith (1987, chap. 13); and, of course, the first two volumes of Dorfman (1949). Ross's dense work on *The Origins of American*

Social Science (1991) is rich in historical details and intriguing in its interpretation even if one disagrees with its main thesis.

11. My account on this and the following stages relies heavily on Joseph Dorfman's magnum opus, *The Economic Mind in American Civilization* (1949, 1959). His work is amazingly comprehensive and detailed, and I would like to use this opportunity to remind historians and economists of this important project which does not seem to enjoy the recognition it certainly deserves.

12. This view, expressed in a public address at Cornell, led one of the benefactors of Cornell University to complain to the authorities "that Adams was undermining civilization." His part time appointment was canceled, but he got a job in Michigan (Dorfman 1949, 3:167; Furner 1975, 135–37).

13. See Bascom's similar view in Dorfman (1949, 3:206). For a more detailed presentation of Adams's views, see Furner (1975, 127–42).

14. Patten also held some beliefs which would be considered very reactionary to many readers. He criticized the "philanthropy" of "democratic ideals" which would give the benefits of civilization to all regardless of the merit or demerit of the individual (Dorfman 1949, 3:186). He went as far as suggesting imprisoning people who sought public support, and he opposed labor legislation and regulation of monopolies. For Patten's life and work, see Fox (1967).

15. Furner's interpretation (1975, chap. 5) is somewhat different: she found a contrast among the founders of the AEA between the more radical Ely and his followers and the moderate group that included J. B. Clark, H. C. Adams, E. J. James, and others. In her opinion, the compromise was achieved by isolating the extremists on both sides—Ely on the left and Sumner on the right. Basically, however, her story is quite similar to Dorfman's.

16. James Laughlin wrote *History of Bimetallism in the United States*; A. T. Hadley was engaged in historical studies in his *Undercurrents in American Politics*, and Charles J. Bullock (1869–1941), a conservative colleague of Taussig at Harvard, coauthored in 1919 "a pioneering and descriptive study especially notable for its attempts to present the history of America's balance of payments" (Dorfman 1959, 4:251). These, of course, are just a few examples of the incorporation of historical studies into the mainstream of American economics.

Chapter Three
Reconstructing the History of Institutionalism

1. To say that the history is "revised" does not mean that this is a conscious and intentional process to present a self-serving picture. The revision is often an unintended consequence of routine practices in the field. As one research program gains prominence, more and more teachers, referees, authors, and editors are being trained according to its principles, while the knowledge developed by rival research programs is not reproduced in daily practices and eventually forgotten.

2. On Veblen's work, see Dorfman (1934); Gruchy (1947, chap. 2); Ayres (1963); Mitchell (1969, chap. 20). A collection of important articles on Veblen appears in Blaug (1992a).

3. On Commons's work, see Gruchy (1947, chap. 3); Chamberlain (1963);

Mitchell (1969, chap. 21); Rutherford (1988, 1990). A collection of important articles on Commons appears in Blaug (1992b).

4. On Mitchell's work, see Gruchy (1947, chap. 4); Kuznets (1963); P. A. Klein (1983). A collection of important articles on Mitchell appears in Blaug (1992b).

5. The course catalog at the University of Michigan included in the mid 1890s one heading for "Political Economy and Sociology" (Brazer 1982, 142–43).

6. Alvin Hansen (1953) identifies Clark as a neoclassical economist, but this is simply wrong. The confusion stems from the fact that Clark saw a role for orthodox theory. Dorfman (1959, 5:461) says that "the great value of his contribution lies in its synthesis of neoclassical economics and institutionalism, its presentation as an integrated whole." Cf. Stoneman (1979). In my view, however, this whole is of a clear institutionalist flavor, and the role of neoclassical value theory is clearly subjected to institutionalist analysis. See Clark (1924; 1947) and his presidential address (1936). In his lectures on the history of economic thought, Mitchell (1969, 2:736) gives J. M. Clark's approach as an example of institutional economics. Blaug also notes that Clark "regarded himself as a follower of Veblen, Mitchell and Commons, in short, an institutionalist" (1986a, 53).

7. This assertion deserves better documentation, which is beyond the scope of this work. Nonetheless, based on extensive reading of the methodological literature of the period, it is my impression that whenever the speakers refer to institutionalist methods, they have statistics in mind. See, for instance, Mills (1928); Robbins (1932, 96, 102–5). Neoclassical economists were not necessarily hostile toward statistical studies, but they were less likely to support changes in curriculum in favor of statistics.

8. For simliar appraisals of institutionalists, see Gordon (1963, 126–27); Ruggles (1952, 427). Interestingly, while Robbins recognizes the power of interwar institutionalists, many present-day institutionalists do not seem interested in challenging the image of institutionalism as a small heterodox movement. One reason—if they are not simply victims of conventional presentations—might be their own perception of themselves as radical alternative for mainstream economics, a position they tend to associate with institutionalism everywhere.

9. This seems to be an accepted fact. James Tobin (in Breit and Spencer 1986, 114), a Nobel laureate, maintains, for instance, that "Harvard was the leading academic center of economics in North America at the time [1935–39]; only Columbia and Chicago were close competitors." Samuelson (in Breit and Spencer 1986, 61) says that in 1935 there were only "a few strong centers for economic research—Harvard, Chicago, Columbia, and a few others." Columbia had also the largest number of Ph.D. candidates. For the period 1904–28, 25.7% of all 2,809 Ph.D. candidates studied at Columbia, 14.7% at Chicago, 10.4% at Wisconsin, and 8.5% at Harvard. For the period 1929–40, the shares of most big schools declined; Columbia to 16%, Chicago to 12.1%, and Wisconsin to 8.2%; Harvard's share slightly increased to 8.9%. In the 1904–28 period, the University of Pennsylvania trained 7.1% of the candidates, and Cornell trained 4.4%. All other schools had less than 3%. In the decade of 1929–40, Pennsylvania had 5.1%, Cornell and Minnesota 3.9% each, Illinois 4.2%, and Ohio 3.4%. The data are from Froman (1942, 818).

The statistics of doctoral degrees granted in 1929–39, however, are very different. Harvard leads with 176 degrees awarded, before Cornell (125); Columbia (104); Wisconsin (99); and Illinois (98). Following are California (78); Pennsylvania (67); Chicago (52); Minnesota (49); and Johns Hopkins (42). The data from Froman (1942, 826) are problematic, especially the low place of Chicago, and the high position of Cornell (which registered 125 degrees awarded, and only 100 candidates).

10. "Columbia—or, more particularly, the NBER, under the dominance of Wesley C. Mitchell, its principal founder, president, and research director—stressed a would-be scientific empiricism, a search for 'the facts' rather than abstract theory of economic behavior" (Silk 1974, 49). Cf. Kenneth Arrow (in Breit and Spencer 1986, 45–46).

11. Columbia and Wisconsin are mentioned as the two centers of institutionalism by Myrdal (1978, 771), who visited Wisconsin in 1930—before he became an advocate of unstitutionalism himself—and sensed "an almost aggressive advance of institutional economics, held together as a rebellion against the conventional neoclassical school."

12. Schumpeter himself supported the expansion of economics by developing economic sociology, similar to the vision of institutionalists. But in contrast to institutionalists who viewed government coordination and regulation as essential for sustaining capitalism, Schumpeter's elitism led him to oppose vehemently any government intervention (e.g., Schumpeter 1934), although, paradoxically, he perceived socialism as unavoidable (Swedberg 1991).

13. The institutionalist presidents were Wesley Mitchell (1925); J. M. Clark (1936); Frederick C. Mills (1941); Sumner H. Slichter (1942); Edwin G. Nourse (1943); and A. B. Wolfe (1944). The neoclassical presidents were Fred M. Taylor (1929); Alvin H. Hansen (1939); and Jacob Viner (1940). Among the sympathizers with institutionalism I include Allyn A. Young (1926) and T. S. Adams (1928), collaborators of Richard T. Ely, the radical economist of the 1880s (see above); the economic historians Edwin F. Gay (1930) and Abbott P. Usher (1934); labor specialists George E. Barnett (1933) and Harry A. Millis (1935), the monetary theorist O.M.W. Sprague (1938); and E. L Boggart (1932). The neoclassical sympathizers were E. W. Kemmerer (1927); an international adviser on monetary issues, Matthew B. Hammond (1931); and, perhaps, Alvin Johnson (1937), one of the most important theoreticians of the interwar period. This classifiaction is based on a content analysis of the presidential addresses of those economists (Yonay 1989).

14. Nourse's resignation was partially motivated by Keyserling's action behind his back. The two economists differed in their mentality and in their perceptions of how much the Council should be active in pushing forward its recommended policy (Sobel 1980), but both of them were clearly institutionalist in their training and theoretical predilections.

15. The fruits of their work appear regularly in the *Journal of Economic Issues*, but can be found also in numerous books. See, for example, Adams (1980a); Ayres (1952 and 1961); Copeland (1958); Dunlop et al. (1949 and 1975); R. A. Gordon (1952 and 1978); W. Gordon (1980a); Gruchy (1977a); Samuels (1979); Tool (1985); Tool and Samuels (1989a, 1989b).

16. McCloskey (1994b, chaps. 10–11) argues that economists have been enamored of proving theorems that have little bearing on economic policy rather than studying quantitatively real effects of economic factors. She even argues that in fifty years, economists may appreciate improvements in measurement techniques more than they appreciate Arrow's magnificent contributions to economic theory. McCloskey is also puzzled by the way philosophers of economics such as Hausman and Rosenberg identify science with theory as if science included no empirical practices (1994b, 221–22).

17. See Blaug (1986a, 30) for a list of Burns's works in which he criticized Keynesian economics.

18. On Milton Friedman's approach, see his account in Silk (1974). On his clash with the ecometricians of the Cowles Comission, see Reder (1982); on Arrow's approach, see interviews with him in Swedberg (1990); Feiwel (1987c, 1987d); Arrow 1992. My evaluation of Mincer's approach is based on an interview I conducted with him at Columbia in June 1993.

19. On Ayres's own teoretical approach, see Breit (1973); Walker (1979).

20. Gruchy said that Veblen was a man "who may be a sociologist but who can hardly be classed as an economist, who is a misguided advocate of technology determinism, and who has never gotten beyond the stage of writing descriptive monographs" (Gruchy as quoted in Liebhafsky 1980, 23).

21. Not to mention the Austrians and the Walrasians, presently considered neoclassical, who offered completely different options that very few American economists adopted at the time.

22. Mirowski (1990) argues that "real" institutionalism, based on Peircian pragmatism, was based on a skeptical view of science and a hermneutic approach to human knowledge in general. I must disagree. Even according to Mirowski, Commons was alone among major institutionalists in following this Peircian view. Veblen adopted a naive belief in science, which was later taken to extremes by Mitchell and Ayres. Although Commons was more reserved than others, the materials I read undoubtedly suggest that most institutionalists hold views that may seem *today* as naive. Peirce undoubtedly anticipated many of the later doubts concerning science, but as Mirowski himself says, Peirce failed to lead the pragmatist movement. It is not an accident that pragmatism enered the American scene through the works of Dewey, Veblen, and Mitchell, who shared the pervasive belief in science.

23. Wilber and Harrison's suggestion that the institutionalist and the neoclassical frameworks be combined (1978, 85) is, therefore, not new, and certainly in line with the way many prominent institutionalists thought during the 1920s and 1930s. On the relations among various economists, see also Ross (1991, 106–22, chap. 6). We will return to this issue when we discuss, in chapter 6, the importance that institutionalists attributed to the neoclassical models of free competition as a benchmark for analyzing more realistic situations, and in chapter 8, where we deal with the way the economists of the 1920s and 1930s presented their relations to the past.

24. Young, together with Thomas Adams, collaborated with the "radical" Richard Ely in writing the most popular textbook (Ely et al. 1923).

25. Some of Young's advices have not lost their validity today. Look, for in-

stance, at his remark on the potential of studying "case-studies" of economic institutions: "I do not see why the economic history of some American town or village should not be written in a way that would make it a contribution of the first importance to our understanding of the development of the economic life of the United States" (Young 1927, 20). Similarly, he says that as economists, the main interest in the history of banking is not necessarily "banking laws and administrative control of banking by public authorities, as it is . . . the actual operations of banks and actual uses of credit, . . . [e.g., by the] careful study of the records of some particular bank" (ibid., 21–22). Or: "There is need for a series of concrete studies of various aspects of the economics development of carefully defined homogeneous regions and communities. There is also need for careful historical studies, not only of industries, but of individual business undertaking, of the careers of successful captains of industry and finance, of particular products or commodities, and of changing modes of consumption as well as of changing forms of production" (Young 1927, 20–21). These lines of research are missing in economics today as they were missing in 1927 but they can still yield important insights.

Chapter Four
The Struggle over the Meaning of Science

1. The common perceptions regarding the prestige of disciplines are discussed in Cole (1983), who nevertheless presents data which undermine these common stereotypes.

2. A similar argument is made by von Neumann and Morgenstern in their famous book on game theory from 1944 as quoted by McCloskey (1994b, 169).

3. According to Hausman (1992, 91–92), Viner follows here the approach of J. S. Mill.

4. The use of these concepts has continued to be pervasive, and hardly any methodological writing since then has failed to make some reference to them. E.g., Hutchison (1938); Friedman (1953); Blaug (1985a, 70). McCloskey (1994b, 128) quotes an early reference to friction made by Walras in 1874. Rosenberg (1976) discusses at length the meaning of "economic laws" and their resemblance to the laws of mechanics. Mirowski (1989a) thoroughly analyzes the parallel between economic theory and Newtonian mechanics. Mäki (1994) is an example of a recent essay in the philosophy of economics that also justifies the common assumptions in economics by analogies with physics, including the case of friction. Another example is the way Gwartney and Stroup (1980) compare economics with astronomy (Madison 1990, 52n).

5. For a neoclassical defense of the law of diminishing returns, see Blaug (1985a, 69–77).

6. Mitchell is often mentioned as a pioneer of statistical research. It is rarely mentioned, however, that Mitchell taught the graduate course on the history of economics as well. His interest in the the history of economic thought, and his comprehensive and fastidious analysis of past theories are in themselves a testimony to the interest of Mitchell in theory.

7. Backhouse, who explains the roots of the failure of Friedman to convince

his opponents, is nonetheless judging him from within the boundaries of current orthodoxy when he argues that "the language [Friedman] uses is frequently imprecise" (1993a, 126), or that "Friedman's [rhetorical] performance was a disaster" (ibid., 128).

8. I am not speaking about advocates of "the systematic hypothesis-testing according to the canons of classical statistical inference," because both institutionalists and mathematical economists adhered to these principles.

9. The denial of the importance of methodological discussion is characteristic of postwar economics. Many methodologists have, therefore, to defend their practice, e.g., Schoeffler (1955, vii); Briefs (1960, 1); Blaug (1980); Coats (1983b, 4); Hands (1993, ix). Many more examples are available.

10. The quote appears in an earlier version of Epstein (1995, p. 22).

Chapter Five
Bringing People and Institutions Back In: The Struggle over the Scope of Economics

1. On Douglas, see Cain (1979); Silk (1974, 68–69); Reder (1982, 3); and his own memoirs (Douglas 1971).

2. Current theorists speak about "psychic income" as an explanation of why people sometimes prefer lower-paying jobs over better paying ones. Yet they use this term to brush away apparently contradictory evidence without really integrating it into theory and studying its ramifications.

3. This line of defense is very different from the present-day tendency in economics to base all arguments on perfect rationality of all economic agents, including the ability to make complex calculations.

4. Today neoclassicists argue that they do not refer to utility, which is a vague and unmeasurable concept. Instead, they speak about marginal substitution of consumption, which is measured by the amount of money that people are willing to pay (Samuelson and Nordhaus 1989, 449–50; Lindbeck 1984, 10). From an institutionalist perspective, this change of words solves nothing. The problem, they would say, is that the amount that people are willing to pay does not reflect how much they really value it.

5. Mitchell said that Marshall had tried to get rid of hedonism and had followed Menger, Walras, and J. B. Clark who had not based their arguments on hedonism. Similar to Marshall were Irving Fisher and Herbert Davenport, who "expressly repudiated hedonism and professed to dispense with psychology altogether by making economics 'the science that treats phenomena from the standpoint of price'" (1924, 16). Mitchell, like Clark, did not consider this view satisfactory: "If Davenport's 'science that treats phenomena from the standpoint of price' helps to explain the behavior of men, that theory is itself a piece of psychologizing, good or bad" (1924, 16–17).

6. Modern economic theory treats expectations very seriously, but since it still seeks to avoid field work and bases its conclusions mostly on deductive reasoning, modern economists assume how people construct expectations and introduce these expectations into their models (Branson 1989, 205–23; Blanchard and Fischer 1989, 571–75).

7. It is to Copeland's credit that he was aware of the weaknesses of this analogy. He hastened to assert "three of the distinguishing features of a biological
organism which [any] social group lacks: (1) definiteness of size, and of structure
or location of parts (2) reproduction of like organisms at roughly regular intervals
of a generation, and death as the end of a fairly definite life-cycle and (3) contigu-
ity of organic parts. With less confidence we may add that the cells, tissues, and
organs of a metazoan organism do not prey upon and conflict with each other
in their functioning . . . the functioning of the parts of society displays less perfect coordination than is to be found in the individual organism" (Copeland
1924, 130).

Chapter Six
The Free Market on Trial: The Struggle over the Gap between
Reality and Theory

1. On welfare economics, see Stigler (1943); Little (1950); Mishan (1969);
Blaug (1985a, 591–92); Nicholson (1990, chap. 13).
2. Modern theory would refer to such practice, and model it, as "rent-seeking
behavior," i.e., "the use of resources to obtain government-created monopoly
profits" (Carlton and Perloff 1994, 889). This concept has been introduced relatively recently in order to rectify one of the flaws of orthodox theory that was
exposed long ago by the institutionalists, but it is still implied that such behavior
is the exception rather than typical of modern capitalist economies, as argued here
by Edie. Alternatively, it is assumed that rent-seeking behavior is the result of the
increasing intervention of the state in the economy; see, for example, Buchanan et
al. (1980); Rowley et al. (1991). Institutionalists believed that rent-seeking behavior was typical of the capitalist system.
3. On the emerging culture of consumerism around the turn of the century, see
Birken (1988).
4. Once again, the modern neoclassical literature discusses at length how to
use economic incentives in order to promote occupational safety and reduce environmental damages (Nicholson 1990, chap. 21). This literature was partially motivated by the institutionalist criticism.
5. This is another topic currently analyzed by modern neoclassical economics;
see Lecomber (1979).
6. The "visible hand" is a concept that A. D. Chandler Jr. introduced in order
to characterize the transition from small-scale family firms to large corporations
and professional management. The ideology behind this "managerial revolution"
is the same as the one behind the logic of institutionalists: the belief in the ability
of "scientific," rational, professional planning to improve the outcomes of an
unpredictable and erratic free market. See Shenhav (1995).
7. It can be said that lack of knowledge is subsumed by irrationality, because
"rational people" should get "perfect knowledge." But in the real world it would
not be "rational" to pursue "perfect knowledge" because the time and the other
resources required for this are limited. This is a *structural* feature of the economic
system, not a personal property. Recent economic literature builds models of information search that can be used to analyze under which circumstances people

would invest in collecting data, and under which circumstances such a search would not be profitable (Carlton and Perloff, chap. 14). This concern, however, does not help us identify the share of economic activity in which the search of information is not profitable. The institutionalists would argue that this share is very large. It is large enough to justify intervention of the state in planning and regulating economic enterprise.

8. This argument may remind modern readers of the signaling mechanism used by economic agents to convey information to other strategic players, either to ensure their cooperation or to mislead them. For example, higher-education credentials can be perceived as signals of workers to potential employers that they are "high-quality" workers (Spence 1973). It should be noticed that Slichter and other institutionalists had been already concerned with the problem of identifying workers skills half a century before Spence wrote his seminal paper. Moreover, it is more than likely that, unlike many present-day theorists, they would emphasize the systematic biases of those credentials and the deviations from optimal solutions caused by these deviations.

9. Modern neoclassical theory copes with the challenge of advertising and offers several explanations that may account for it without breaking the basic assumptions of the theory. The neoclassical treatment is focused on the optimal expenditures of the single firm (Carlton and Perloff 1994, 604–6), although there have been several attempts to examine the overall effects of advertising on welfare. It has been argued that advertising provides information about new brands and lower prices (ibid., 606–10) and leads to a better matching of consumers and brands (ibid., 613). Yet, several analyses have shown that advertising might be excessive and that it might constitute a barrier to entry of new firms (ibid., 610–15). Thus, "the effects of advertising on consumer welfare are generally ambiguous" (ibid., 625). The modern neoclassical analysis takes into account the institutionalist critique but refuses to consider the possibility that advertising creates "false needs" (ibid., 610).

10. Single banks have an interest in maximizing their business by awarding loans as much as they can. When the competition is not regulated, they are driven to keep too small reserves. This was one of the reasons for the numerous bank failures until governments in many countries adopted more active regulation policies. The same dynamics seems to have taken place in the Savings and Loans industry, in which deregulation led to the recent crisis. On the other hand, neoclassical economists argue nowadays that regulation may breed bank troubles as well. For instance, deposit insurance may distort economic activities because individual banks may be tempted to take risks that they would not take otherwise.

11. This is a basic assumption of neoclassical economics. The logic is that the first units are produced by the most productive resources and are therefore less costly. As prices rise, it is worthwhile for the producers to employ less productive resources (Blaug 1985a, 79–80, 425–31).

12. Cases of different cost structures are handled quite extensively by *modern* industrial organization literature. Ricardo's classical rent theory is indeed a theory about differences in cost structures but until the last decades it was treated as an exceptional case, whereas industrial firms were treated as homogeneous, because capital goods, in contrast to land, could be produced, modified, or moved.

Such an assumption was more sensible during the early stages of industrialization when the machinery was relatively simple but it does not fit modern industry.

13. The terms "increasing returns" and "decreasing costs" are equivalent. If the costs of producing one more unit are monotonously decreasing, the net returns for each additional unit must increase.

14. Slichter's "indictment sheet" (1924) was a very thorough document that included a long list of economic problems. The one subject which Slichter did not mention (except for a very minor comment on p. 351) was monopolies. We must conclude that he did not consider monopoly to be a major problem.

15. For institutionalists this was the case *regardless* of monopolies, which is another reason why the existence of monopolies did not occupy a central part in their critique.

16. Lester, an institutionalist labor economist from Princeton, continued Slichter's line after World War II (1946, 1947) but could not stop the advance of mathematical neoclassicism. The exchange between him and Stigler (1947) is one sign of the turning point in modern economics (see chap. 9).

17. See Millar (1980, 117). See also Gruchy's chapter on the views of Gardiner Means (Gruchy 1947); A. B. Wolfe also advocated the development of welfare economics on the basis of the known price economics (1924, 471).

18. Bye responds to the criticism that "the whole concept of margins is artificial, exaggerated, and confused" (Bye 1924, 281–82). This criticism must have been made by people who did not understand anything about the theory. Clark, Mitchell, Commons, and other leading institutionalists cannot be blamed for misunderstanding marginal analysis.

Chapter Seven
The Struggle over Social Relevance and the Place of Values

1. Mäki even says that this is, or should be, the "real" criterion in evaluation of scientific theories and model, as all theories are unrealistic (1994).

2. Nowadays, "value theory" is commonly called "price theory," because mainstream economics measures value according to market prices. During most of the nineteenth century, however, most economists distinguished between "value" and "price." The institutionalists, as we will see in the last part of this chapter, refused to reduce values to prices.

3. The nature of the works done at the NBER, though, has changed quite thoroughly since Mitchell's days.

4. It is somewhat amusing that in the same line with these eternal enigmas of how flexible human nature is, or how deep the various innate motives are, Tugwell lists the problem of finding out whether "real wages [are] rising or . . . falling," and "the question whether we actually have a surplus or actually have a deficit [in international trade]" (1924, 409). Before price indices and national accounts figures were conceived and developed, the problems of measuring the national economy and the level of prices (common practices in our time) and measuring the human psyche—a problem that appears today as elusive as ever— seemed to lie on a par in terms of difficulty and feasibility. But this point is more than just comic relief. It is a good demonstration of the nature of black boxes.

Today GNP, price indices, and trade figures are commonly used by hundreds of social scientists without even thinking twice. The formulae to calculate them were established as black boxes. The way Tugwell considers the problem of measuring these variables should alert us that the apparent simplicity of measuring real wages and GNP could be misleading! It took economists a long time and many disputes before they agreed upon how to build a price index, or how to calculate GNP. Indeed, these black boxes are still being challenged today, and those who are involved in the attempts to fix the formulae or find alternative measures are aware of the inherent problematics of measuring abstract concepts like national income and price level (Desrosiéres 1991; Porter 1995).

5. I think that any study of public rhetoric should not attempt to distinguish between "sincere" and "dishonest" statements. We are rarely in a position to make a good judgment in this regard, and for most purposes of historical analysis, it is not crucially relevant. But more important, often it is impossible to distinguish between "honest" and "dishonest" statements as people tend to believe what they say (cf. Holland and Quinn 1987, 7).

6. "Monographic studies" was a "code name" for institutionalist works, which yielded historical or quantitative descriptions of concrete institutions or events instead of theoretical treatises typical of neoclassical theory.

7. During the last decade or two, economists became less enamored of econometrics (Leamer 1983; Hendry et al. 1990; Hendry 1980; Hands 1993, 144). This disillusionment led many economists to put an even greater emphasis on theory. This stand is most visible among new classical economists such as Lucas and Sargent; see Mayer (1993, chap. 7). See also Hausman (1992, esp. p. 254) for a similar position on a methodological ground.

8. Bye (1924, 284): "The truth is, of course, that there never has been a 'general' rate of interest or of wages. . . . There are *general* principles applicable to all wage and interest rates, perhaps, but that is all. The correct approach to all value and distribution theory seems to the present writer to require a clear recognition of the diversity in the prices of goods and distributive shares as the normal thing; then there should be included in the theory every important factor influencing particular prices, rents, wages, interest rates, or profits. Such an analysis will seem much more real than those now current and *will be much more useful* in explaining the actual facts of the world. *It will not require an overthrow of existing theory, but merely some additions to it, and a slight rearrangement in its presentation*" (emphases mine).

9. This line of argument, however, was quite rare. Even Viner qualified his statement and said that the mathematical analysis of the Lausanne school was too abstract. It was only the postwar mathematical economics that developed neoclassical theory along neo-Walrasian lines (see chap. 9).

10. According to Blaug, it was Nassau William Senior who "hammered away at the fundamental distinction between the 'science' and the 'art' of political economy; or, as we would now say, between positive and normative economics" (1986a, 221). See also Keynes (1955 [1891], 34–35, 46); Maloney (1985, chap. 9). On the attempts of American economists to separate "positive" and "normative" economics, see Ross (1991, 77–79). Copeland (1924, 121) argued that "economists . . . have often held that economic science should confine itself to an

objective description . . . that it was rightfully a pure, positive science." In addition to J. N. Keynes and N. S. Senior, Copeland mentions J. L. Laughlin and H. J. Davenport, two neoclassical American economists around the turn of the century, as supporters of positive economics.

11. As an example he brought the theory of marginal productivity. This theory, he averred, did not justify the relative shares of workers and capitalists. "It is purely a scientific explanation of the forces fixing market shares of income, and not an ethical defense thereof" (Bye 1924, 281).

12. Another sharp and lucid expression of the view Bye holds is available in Lionel Robbins's (1932) famous methodological tract *An Essay on the Nature and Significance of Economic Science.* I focus on Bye's essay because of my concentration on American economics, but it is Robbins's essay, of course, that has gained wide recognition and popularity among later economists.

13. To clarify the point, we can think of a few other examples. If we "clean" the air by paying polluters to stop production, the clean air will become part of our "wealth" as valued by the market. But if a nation has chosen from the beginning to limit production, or has merely failed to industrialize, its clean air will not be considered part of its wealth, and will not be taken into account in evaluating its welfare in those studies that measure standard of living according to GNP per capita. The same is true about safety and security: if we pay for police and private guards, the "produced" security is part of our wealth, but if we have "natural" security, it is not reckoned as part of our welfare. If we have to make a realistic, non-market-based evaluation of welfare, we must find some way to measure cleanliness and safety and other positive properties, and the only way to do it is by using our judgment of what is "really" good for human beings.

14. Modern welfare economics would respond by saying that the society is indeed better-off, because it is possible to divide the income in such a fashion that everybody would be better-off. But the institutionalist perspective maintains that economics should first determine whether such a division of income is indeed possible and likely *institutionally.* It is not enough to say that the national income increased. Economists should study the institutions which determine the distribution of income and investigate likely outcomes and their welfare implications.

15. A few institutionalists alleged that the empirical methods they promoted were the only objective tools in economics. Tugwell exemplifies those economists. Adam Smith, he reasoned, "had none of the tools of research at his disposal which are being developed today, and so he was forced to use his very shrewd—but for all that very faulty . . .—powers of observation." Therefore he saw only what he wanted to see. Modern economists "are in a better position to guard against it now," because they have the possibility of making tentative suggestions and testing them empirically (1924a, 414).

16. Cf. Homan (1928, 354): "As orthodox economists gradually divorced their discipline from precepts of public policy, they tended to set their findings up as a 'positive' science. . . . One criticism of this attitude is of the sort made by [John] Hobson, that in displaying the principle of order which they find in the existing economic system they tend to become apologists for that system."

17. Wolfe's belief in the possibility of a science of ethics was exceptional even among institutionalists. He believed that modern scientific psychology could give

the human race nothing less than scientific guidance to moral life: "Behavioristic psychology, with whatever help it may get from psychoanalysis and social psychology [will be] capable of giving us a really scientific analysis and understanding of human nature." This "should point the way to a fundamental, objectively scientific, ethical norm, or ultimate end of life" (Wolfe 1924, 477–78). Tugwell and Mitchell were less extreme but agreed with Wolfe that things like "real prosperity" (as opposed to mere "economic surplus"), "fair distribution," or "full and free life" could be measured and compared in various economic schemes. Others, like Clark or Hale, doubted the existence of objective criteria to define, measure, and compare social welfare but agreed that economists still had the duty to deal with nonmaterial social goals.

18. Examples of this common view are : Biven (1989, 55, 66); J. M. Clark (1924, 80–81); Gruchy (1947, 1); Leijonhufvud (1976, 75); Silk (1974, 246–7); Ward (1972, 23); Wright (1945, 284). This view is implicit in many accounts of the rise and fall of various economic theories and it is impossible to list all the examples.

Chapter Eight
Evolution or Revolution? The Struggle over the History of the Discipline

1. By speaking about "presentations," the impression is that any group of scientists has a clear program and chooses ways of presentation and representation in order to manipulate outside audiences. But in fact whatever they say is directed at the same time at themselves and defines what they "really" are!

2. Not less virulent is Lionel Robbins's identification of institutionalism and the German historical school (Robbins 1932, 104).

3. Veblen himself was very critical of the German school (e.g., 1948, 217).

4. Cf. Nourse (1943). "We [economists] are Presbyterians at heart. For the Presbyterians lean toward traditional forms, ritualistic services, rigid creeds, and doctrines of predestination and determinism."

5. Allyn Young, who did not belong to the institutionalist camp, also claimed that the classical English political economy "has never put a very heavy burden upon the economic man" (1928, 5).

6. Douglas's critique is distinct, for example, from those of Thomas Edward Cliffe Leslie (1827–82) and Karl Knies (1821–98), two prominent historicist economists. The historicist schools waged a head-on attack on orthodox theory and were probably interested in accentuating the weaknesses of that theory. Douglas, like most institutionalists, was interested in depicting institutionalism as continuing the old classical school and therefore looked for similarities. Veblen, in contrast, was much more aggressive in his criticism of the economic man (1948, 241–74).

7. Abbott Usher was not identified as an institutionalist, but he was a leading economic historian, a young field at the time which emerged as a close ally of institutionalism.

8. Charles Dunbar, a prominent late-nineteenth-century neoclassical economist, also said that the classical economists had not regarded *laissez-faire* as a maxim; old masters such as Smith and Malthus had in fact encouraged state interference in selected cases, while "Mill . . . suggested legislation as the cure for

pretty nearly every evil not deemed positively incurable" (quoted in Furner 1975, 112). Cf. Evensky (1992) who argues that Adam Smith underwent a change of heart after his arrival in London in 1773. Noticing the extent of selfish rent-seeking behavior, he decided that the invisible hand was not enough; moral leadership of the state captains is needed to transform society into the liberal ideal. Muller's cogent interpretation (1993) seems to support the interpretation of Mitchell and Usher.

9. Allyn Young agreed "that English political economy has never been, in any real sense, deductive or *a priori*" (1928, 5) and maintains that the historical element did exist in the writings of the English political economists (ibid., 13). Quantitative studies were going to change concepts and problems, he assured us, but "this new development . . . is not really a revolution. It is wholly consistent with the spirit and method of the older political economy" (ibid. 1928, 8).

10. An extreme version of hermeneutics would argue that there is no sense in searching for an author's "real intention" because the text is an independent object. Even the interpretation of its author should not be privileged. Thus, Gerrard (1991, 1992) says that there is no "real Keynes" to be searched for; just interpretations of Keynes. The actor-network analysis does not deny the existence of a "real Keynes" as it does not deny the existence of real objects out there. The point is that we have no immediate and absolute access to that "real Keynes" and therefore all we have are various interpretations. Practically, this approach and Gerrard's lead to the same practice.

11. See again Veblen (1948, 217).

12. Of course, scholars who study those works can always take part in the controversy over their interpretations, but when they involve themselves in the controversy they stop to be observers and become participants.

13. There are a few institutionalist economists who wrote a different story—e.g., Gruchy (1972); Adams (1980a); Copeland (1958); and P. Klein (1978). In addition, the current institutionalist journal, *Journal for Economic Issues*, has published many articles that tell the history from the institutionalist point of view. The mainstream in the field of the history of economics, however, overlooks most of these works.

Chapter Nine
Epilogue: The Fall of Institutionalism and the Rise of Modern Economics

1. The common view in textbooks on the history of economic thought treats current neoclassical thought as part of the marginalist revolution of the 1870s. Many writers, however, have begun recently to treat postwar economics as a new species of economic thought. For instance, McCloskey (1994b, passim); Feiwel (1987a).

2. In what follows, I use the term "mathematical economics" to include all works that formalized economic theory using any mathematical technique: differential algebra, geometry, game theory, or whatever. I do not use it to include the employment of statistical procedures, although the term was widely used during the 1930s (see below), 1940s, and 1950s to include statistical studies as well. From the late 1950s this term is kept only to the development of mathematical

models, and it is explicitly distinguished from econometric works. Nowadays it is used even more narrowly to include only those studies that rely heavily on sophisticated mathematics, such as general equilibrium analysis. The use of simple differential equations in macroeconomic theory (of the vintage of the 1950s and 1960s) is, however, also a part of the same trend of formalizing economic theory.

3. When I wrote this statement in 1991, it ran against common knowledge, although several writers had previously argued so. Since then it became accepted by most modern interpreters of Keynes. For superb interpretations of Keynes's philosophy, methodology, and ideology, see Carabelli 1988, 1992; Fitzgibbons 1988, 1992; Hillard 1992; Rothheim 1992. Gerrard (1991 and 1992) criticizes this "fundamentalism" from the point of view of hermeneutics. Clarke (1988) provides many details on the development of Keynes's thought that led to the *General Theory*.

4. A similar fortune befell imperfect competition theory, which was another product of Cambridge. For the Cambridge economists, the development of large corporations and the consequent decline of competition were additional reasons—in addition to the forces elucidated by Keynes—why modern economies called for some degree of collective planning and coordination. The mathematical economists, however, have sterilized the radical elements in this view and incorporated the models of monopolistic competition as an exceptional case that could be taken care of within the capitalistic-competitive economy (Shackle 1967; Hicks 1939, 83–85; Silk 1974, 28, 101–2; Blaug 1986a, 48; Kaldor in Kregel 1988, 14–15; Fox 1967, 170).

5. I refer to a generation of economists who were born in the 1910s and reached graduate school in the late 1930s and 1940s. There were other individuals who were born in Europe, got their professional training there, and contributed to the mathematical revolution in the United States in its early stages (e.g., Abraham Wald, Oskar Lange, Nicholas Georgescu-Roegen, Kenneth Ewart Boulding, Tibor Scitovsky, Gerard Debreu). The separate development of mathematical economics in France by Maurice F. C. Allais, François Perroux, and other is beyond the scope of this book (but see Allais 1992). On the British contributors, see below.

6. This brief story is based on personal accounts of Kenneth Arrow, Paul Samuelson, Milton Friedman, George Stigler, and James Tobin in Breit and Spencer (1986), and on similar accounts of John Hicks, Nicholas Kaldor, and Sidney Weintraub in Kregel (1988). On Arrow, see also Feiwel (1987a, 1987b). Of course, such a comprehensive summary of the modern history of economics has to be argued at length and much more methodically, but such a presentation is far beyond the goals of this book.

7. In the main British journals (*Economic Journal* and *Economica*) such articles started to appear only a few years later toward the end of the 1950s. *Econometrica*, the journal that served as the vehicle of the new mathematical economics, included such articles since the 1930s.

8. See Niehans (1990, chaps. 28, 30, 32, 35); Feiwel (1982). Lindbeck (1984), Baumol (1984), and Weizsäcker (1984) summarize the works of Samuelson, Hicks, and Arrow—three leaders of the movement—respectively, and thereby provide good description of the nature of mathematical economics in its early

years. The textbooks in price theory (or microeconomics) since the 1960s have incorporated the collective results of mathematical economics. Samuelson's successive editions of *Economics: An Introductory Analysis* are perhaps the best way to follow chronologically the development of mathematical economics (the first edition was published in 1948; the 11th in 1980).

9. Some writers do not see such a fundamental gap between Marshall and Walras. See, for instance, Schumpeter (1954, 952); Backhouse (1985, 95–96). These writers base their view on Appendix XXI in Marshall's *Principles of Economics* (1920, 703–4n). Cf. Blaug (1985a, 570–80).

10. The most authoritative historical accounts on general equilibrium theory are given by Weintraub (1979; 1985; 1991b). Good accounts can be found also in Kim (1988, chap. 1); Hands (1984; 1985a); and Arthur Diamond (1988). Simple and short descriptions are provided by Lindbeck (1984) and Weizsäcker (1984).

11. On the Commission, see Christ (1952, 1994); Hildreth (1985); accounts of the history of the Cowles Commission and econometrics are also given by Kenneth Arrow, Gerard Debreu, Edmond Malinvaud, and Robert Solow in a special publication for the fiftieth anniversary of the Commission. See Cowles Commission (1991). The personal memoirs of Arrow, James Tobin, and Lawrence Klein (Breit and Spencer 1986) are also helpful sources on the Cowles Commission.

12. The whole exchange is reprinted in the American Economic Association (1965, 186–230). The importance of that exchange as a battle between two camps is reflected in the frequent references to it more than forty years after it took place. See, for instance, Malinvaud (1991, 66–68); Solow (1991, 84–85); Niehans (1990, 414); Mirowski (1989b, 221).

13. Don Lavoie (1990b) claims that Maclup's position has been misunderstood. Machlup defended marginal utility but he did not reject the necessity to study live economic actors to make theory better, as argued by institutionalists. Machlup, a student of the Austrian school, belonged to the "old-fashioned" neoclassicists and differed from the contemporary mathematical economists who have rejected field methods as inappropriate.

14. The Austrian school was originally, like the Marshallian tradition, antimathematical. It differed from the Cambridge school in narrowly focusing on decision-making of rational individuals. The two schools thus supported the development of a theory of decisions, but differed in the role assigned to that theory. For the Austrians, that was all; the economists should not do anything else. For Marshallians, Frank Knight included, pure theory was a heuristic device which could help in understanding economic behavior. But it was not supposed to be the only tool (cf. Streissler 1973; Alter 1982; Lachmann 1990).

15. Popper himself exempted economic theory from the principle of refutability. See Redman (1990, chap. 8).

16. Blaug (1975, 399) says that "Friedman is simply Popper-with-a-twist applied to economics." McCloskey, in contrast, contends that Friedman's approach is basically pragmatist and not Popperian, but insists that the way Friedman was interpreted—the view that became a "black box"— was Popperian (1985, 10). See also McCloskey (1994b, 4) on the gap between Friedman's methodological approach and the way it has been used later by mathematical economists. Backhouse (1994c) elaborates much more on the deep methodological gaps be-

tween Friedman and mainstream economics. Like the gap between Keynesian economics and the economics of Keynes (see below), the gap between "Friedmanian methodology and the methodology of Friedman" shows that the views of a scholar can be very different from the way she is black-boxed and routinely used by her colleagues.

17. The empiricist camp has tried once in a while to push economics to a more empirically oriented path but without visible success. The banner of this camp has been persistently carried by Hutchison, (e.g., 1976, 1977, 1981). See also Coats's essay (1983b) on Hutchison's work. Mark Blaug also seems to prefer more emphasis on empirical work (1985a, 702–5; 1994). Lakatos's view of science was suggested as methodological guidance for economists (Latsis 1976). First it had been accepted with enthusiasm as a solution for the methodological contradictions within the official Friedmanian methodology, but many doubts have since been expressed. See the articles in Latsis (1976); Hands (1984; 1985a; 1985b); Diamond (1988); Redman (1990, chap. 9).

18. While the above writers emphasize the continuity between Marshall and Keynes, the more common view perceives Keynesianism as a profound revolution as discussed in the Introduction.

19. In this respect Keynes seems to be influenced by the Austrian school, as expressed in Robbins's 1932 essay, although his substantive opinion on the nature of business cycles and how to treat them is diametrically opposed to the position of that school. Keynes's view is also in clear opposition to the attitude of institutionalists who developed national income statistics and entertained many hopes of building a theory on the basis of such data.

20. The *IS* is a curve of all the equilibrium combinations of national income and interest rate. Similarly, the *LM* curve depicts the equilibrium combinations in the market for money. The intersection of these two curves is the point of equilibrium of the economy as a whole. That was how Hicks translated Keynes's theory into mathematics. He used this presentation to show that the possibility of unemployment equilibrium depended on the assumptions made concerning the slopes of these two curves (Blaug 1985b, 92). Such an elaboration is facilitated by mathematical representation but at the same time it draws attention from the historical and institutional arguments in Keynes's book.

21. L. R. Klein (1947) is one of the first books that mathematically formalized Keynesian theory, although the mathematical formalization is still kept for a special "Technical Appendix." Patinkin's *Money, Interest, and Prices* (pub. 1956), and numerous articles by James Tobin, Franco Modigiliani, Milton Friedman, and others continued the formalization of macroeconomic theory in the second half of the 1950s.

22. See Young (1927, 17). On Moore, see Schumpeter (1954, 876); Blaug (1986a, 171–72). On Henry Schultz, see Schumpeter (1954, 962). On the early works of Leontief, Koopmans, and Tinbergen which changed the nature of statistical practice in economics, see, respectively, Silk (1974, 154); Blaug (1985b, 157); and Tinbergen (1988, 76).

23. Ayres (1951, 47; 1952, 132–34) also believed that Keynes was approaching the institutionalist position. See also Copeland (1958); Millar (1980, 116).

Blaug (1986a, 55) and Alvin Hansen (1953, 11) perceive J. M. Clark as a precursor of Keynes, and Landreth says the same about Mitchell (1976, 338). The fact that Patinkin does not mention institutionalism in his erudite *Anticipations of the General Theory* (1982) is an indication of the new mathematical direction taken by Patinkin and mainstream macroeconomics after Keynes's death. Later institutionalists disavowed Keynesianism probably because of this transformation of Keynesianism (Gruchy 1977a, 3, 8; Philip Klein 1980, 48–49).

24. The title of Axel Leijonhufvud's book, *Keynesian Economics and the Economics of Keynes* (1968), reflects this contrast, although Leijonhufvud refers to substantive theoretical differences and not to methodological and philosophical differences. Hutchison's "Keynes *versus* the Keynesians" (1981, chap. 4), which argues that Keynesians turned Keynes's theory into a dogma, implies that the fault of postwar economists was their zeal in adopting Keynes, whereas I think that the difference lies in the way they used Keynesian analysis to advance goals other than his.

25. During the 1970s and 1980s the discipline of economics underwent several important changes (e.g., the rise of monetarism, the development of rational expectations theory; proliferation of game theory models) but it is questionable whether these changes constitute a transformation of economics, or whether they are merely variations and elaborations of the mainstream economics of the 1960s.

26. This is well expressed in personal interviews with Friedman and Samuelson in Blaug (1990b). See also Friedman (1974, 62). The same conclusion can be reached if one reads the other articles in Robert Gordon's *Milton Friedman's Monetary Framework* (1974) which are written by critics of monetarism. Their criticisms notwithstanding, they speak the same "language" as Friedman. Leijonhufvud, however, claims that monetarists and Keynesians have different hard cores (1976, 71).

27. This fact has been surprisingly overlooked by many historians of economic thought who treat current neoclassical economics as a refinement of late-nineteenth-century neoclassical economics (e.g., Boland 1994, 169; but see Caldwell 1994, 145). Interested readers would find Henry Briefs (1960) an excellent analysis of the differences between what I call "old-fashioned" neoclassical economics and mathematical neoclassicism. Don Lavoie, who analyzed Machlup's defense of neoclassical theory in 1946, also noticed that "the 'neoclassicism' that Machlup defended from Lester is not the same thing as the one that dominates the profession today" (Lavoie 1990b, 178). Some current philosophers of economics—Hausman (1992) is the most notable example—advocate a return to the prewar approach of "old-fashioned" neoclassicists.

28. Samuelson (in Breit and Spencer 1986, 59) also claims that economics prior to the mathematical revolution "was strewn with rusty monstrosities of logic inherited from the past, its soil generated few stalks of vigorous new science, and the correspondence between the terrain of the real world and the maps of economics textbooks and treatises was neither smooth nor even one-to-one."

29. Myrdal, a Nobel laureate and an institutional economist, says that he had supported Marshallian theory before World War II and became an institutionalist only when economic theory embarked on a mathematical course. He does not agree that this course has advanced economics: "It was only after World War II

that conventional economists narrowed and hardened their isolation from the other social sciences" (Myrdal 1978, 773). On the way Marshall conceived of his own static models, see A. K. Dasgupta (1985, 100–104).

D. P. O'Brien (1974, 16–17) also identifies a radical shift from Marshallian to mathematical economics. But he claims that economics got "on to this wrong track" with Joan Robinson's work on imperfect competition in Cambridge of the 1930s. I think that this is wrong. Robinson did try to build more rigorous models, but she and most of the Cambridge economists were steeped in the Marshallian tradition and used very simple mathematics, if any. The comment of von Neumann that Robinson's work, judged by her mathematics, "would probably be dated as an early precursor of Newton" (O'Brien 1974, 17) is a criticism by a leading mathematical economist of the "primitivity" of Robinson's mathematics. It is not a praise of its rigor, as O'Brien seems to think.

30. Stigler's position needs clarification. Stigler and Friedman who studied at Chicago were very influenced by Frank Knight and Jacob Viner, two leading "old-fashioned" neoclassicists. Although they played an important role in the mathematical revolution, the meaning that they gave to that revolution was somewhat different from the way that Samuelson, Hicks, Robbins, and most other mathematical economists conceived of it. Friedman, for example, was more supportive of the NBER methods and objected to the approach of the Cowles Commission. Both Stigler and Friedman appear to be less enchanted with mathematical sophistication per se and more tolerant of nonmathematical arguments.

The "Chicago school," which has coalesced after Stigler and Friedman had returned there as faculty members, was politically more conservative than both the "old-fashioned" neoclassical economics and the emerging mathematical economics. The Chicagoans objected to Keynes and to imperfect-competition theory. These two developments had come out of the Marshallian center at Cambridge, and the fact that Chicago did not follow suit might be one of the factors in the decline of the Marshallian methodology which had been supported by many Chicagoans for a long time.

31. This is another indication of the unique position of the emerging Chicago school as noted in note 30.

32. Similar data is provided by George Stigler (1965, chap. 3). Stigler counted the articles which used mathematics in intervals of ten years in five American journals. He found that the rate of articles which used calculus or more sophisticated mathematics increased from 2% in 1922–23, to 10% in 1932–33, to 21% in 1942–43, to 31% in 1952–53, and 46% in 1962–63. Stigler's inclusion of *Econometrica* in his sample is somewhat misleading, because in the 1930s and 1940s *Econometrica* represented only a small rebellious group. I replicated Stigler's study and found that in the three general journals in the United States (*AER, JPE, QJE*), the proportion of articles which included any mathematics at all was 7–10% in 1925–38; it increased to 23–29% in 1942–55, and leveled off in the range of 34–48% during the period of 1955–65. The percentage of econometric articles was in the range of 1–6% from 1925 to 1955. It increased to 14% in 1957 and rose gradually to 32% in 1965.

McCloskey provides data on *AER* from 1981 to 1983, which demonstrate the continuation of the trend: "Of the 159 full-length papers published in the *Ameri-*

can Economic Review . . . only 6 used words alone and only 4 added to their words tabular statistics alone. . . . Fully two-thirds of the papers used mathematics explicitly, and most of the others were speaking in a mathematics-saturated environment. . . . Nearly half of the papers used diagrams. . . . Nearly a third of the papers used regression analysis, often in quite elaborate ways. Over a tenth used explicit simulation. . . . Mathematical analysis illustrated by diagrams . . . was used in 60 of the 159" (McCloskey 1985, 4).

33. The neglect of institutions has somewhat been rectified in the last decade by what is commonly called "neo-institutionalism." Neoinstitutionalists have introduced institutions into mathematical models of microeconomic behavior, but they should not be confused with the institutionalists of the interwar period. Although they refer to institutions, their general approach and their methodology are the same as in the mathematical postwar version of neoclassical economics (Mirowski 1981; Hodgson 1994, 68–70). Unfortunately, the postwar followers of interwar institutionalists—economists such as Gruchy, Ayres, Wendell Gordon, and others—are also referred to as neoinstitutionalists by those who know of their existence (Gruchy 1969; W. Gordon 1980b; Liebhafsky 1980), a situation that may cause confusion and misunderstanding.

34. It must be repeated: the claims in this last paragraph are very sweeping and are supported by anecdotal evidence only. It is impossible to say much more in the confines of this book. Yet it is important to include this part in order to complete the alternative history recounted in this book. For a similar perception of the state of economics, although from a different point of view, see McCloskey (1994b, 28).

Chapter Ten
Conclusions: The Evolution of Economic Analysis

1. DiMaggio does not discuss methodology explicitly in his paper, but he asserts that there is no reason to believe that all the cultural constructs "are implicated in any particular causal, constitutive, or regulatory relationship, or that all pull in the same direction in any empirical instance" (1994, 47). This argument implies that actual behavior has to be observed. On the coexistence of three different modes of explanations, see the excellent analysis of Briefs (1960).

2. Allies, we remember, include concepts, ideas, experiments, etc., as well as people. So the loss of an ally may mean, for instance, that a specific fact, which has been considered certain, loses its certainty as a consequence of a new discovery or a new convincing experiment.

3. For a modern attempt to reconcile the high and persistent unemployment of the Great Depression with the assumption of equilibrium, see the discussion of Roy Weintraub (1991b, 282–83).

4. Star's book (1989) is one of the best works that documents such a process. See also Fujimura (1987, 1988); Latour (1988a); and Clarke and Gerson (1990).

5. Ross offers this explanation in addition to her previous one that focused on cultural images of scientific knowledge.

6. But see the discussion of Weir and Skocpol (1985); Weir (1989).

7. Marc Trachtenberg (1983) attributes the triumph of Keynesianism and the

defeat of institutionalism to yet another professional interest. In his opinion, Keynesianism provided economists with an easily manipulated device to control the economy, whereas institutionalism offered general and vague principles only.

8. He explains that "recourse to explicit stochastic models was regarded in some quarters as a backsliding repudiation of scientific determinism, whereas in other quarters the mere fact a technique was used by astronomers was good enough to earn it the scientific stamp of approval" (Mirowski 1989b, 222).

9. On Jevons's position, see Black (1983, 56). Jevons also suggested narrow specialization as another remedy (ibid., 57). Yet the institutionalists in the interwar period suggested interdisciplinary work as a way out of a crisis that they perceived, and this suggestion can be heard again nowadays (e.g., Leontief 1971, 4; Tinbergen 1988, 90–91). Ironically, suggestions were made recently to reinstate the name "political economy," instead of "economics," to regain the interest of those that thought that economics was too dry and irrelevant (Black 1983, 57; Wade 1983).

10. A similar example is provided by Latour's account on the Pasteurization of France. Latour explains that the simplicity of the contagion theory was first a barrier that impeded the rise of bacteriology. Before Pasteur's success, hygienists attributed diseases to a variety of causes: water, food, soil, air, etc. It therefore appeared derisory to attribute them to one formerly unknown cause. The success of Pasteur and his collaborators is, *inter alia*, due to their ability to turn this simplicity into an asset. See Latour (1988a, 19–20).

11. A similar conclusion can be reached from Kuhn's explanation of the way new paradigms are chosen. According to Kuhn (1970a, 155), some of the arguments made in favor of a new paradigm "are the arguments . . . that appeal to the individual's sense of the appropriate or the aesthetic—the theory is said to be 'neater,' 'more suitable,' or 'simpler' than the old." But according to Elkana (1981), values like neatness, simplicity, and appropriateness, as well as their relative importance, vary from society to society and from time to time.

12. Kuhn describes mainly the scientific practice of pre-twentieth-century science. In those days, the number of practicing scientists was minuscule, and the production of new knowledge took much more time. Thus, the chance for simultaneous important discoveries was low. Nowadays there are hundreds, if not thousands, of scientists in each field, and they are often engaged in complex research projects. It is not a simple thing to change such complex networks, even if a very dramatic event takes place somewhere else in the discipline.

13. Samuelson once wrote that "there are minds that by temperament will define away every proposed revolution. . . . Newton is just a guy getting too much credit for the accretion of knowledge that covered centuries. A mountain is just a high hill; a hill, merely a bulging plain" (1971, 335–36). Samuelson's sarcasm notwithstanding, a mountain is indeed just a high hill. The decision of how to define "a bulging plain" reflects personal temperaments, as well as professional and cognitive interests, especially when the mountain is invisible and extremely abstract.

14. Economic methodologists who have been trained in economic theory and practiced it may know economics well enough, but they can be said not to be objective. And if they specialize in methodology, they can be perceived as incom-

petent theorists or researchers. These judgments, I must emphasize, are common ones, not my own. I, like the constructivists in general, do not think that we should police who should say what. But in practice, those who do not know the theory well will find it hard to convince practitioners to listen to them.

15. For constructivist sociologists of science the question is how economists have convinced those interests that they are relevant and useful for them, whatever one thinks about the genuineness of the claim. As a political sociologist who is interested in the distribution of power, especially the power of professional groups, I do have a personal view about the claim. See Yonay and Robbins (1994).

Bibliography

Abbott, Andrew Delano. 1988. *The System of Professions: An Essay on the Division of Expert Labor.* Chicago: University of Chicago Press.

Adams, John, ed. 1980a. Institutional Economics: Contributions to the Development of Holistic Economics. Boston: Martinus Nijhoff.

———. 1980b. "The Writing of Allan G. Gruchy." In John Adams, ed., *Institutional Economics: Contributions to the Development of Holistic Economics,* 3–18. Boston: Martinus Nijhoff.

Adams, T. S. 1928. "Ideals and Idealism in Taxation." *American Economic Review* 8(1): 1–8.

Allais, Maurice. 1992. "The Passion for Research." In Michael Szenberg, ed., *Eminent Economists: Their Life Philosophies.* Cambridge: Cambridge University Press.

Almond, Gabriel A. 1966. "Political Thought and Political Science." *American Political Science Review* 60(4): 869–79.

Alter, Max. 1982. "Carl Menger and Homo Economicus: Some Thoughts on Austrian Theory and Methodology." *Journal of Economic Issues* 16(1): 149–60.

Amann, Klaus, and Karin Knorr-Cetina. 1989. "Thinking Through Talk: An Ethnographic Study of Molecular Biology Laboratory." In Lowell Hargens, Robert Alun Jones, and Andrew Pickering, eds., *Knowledge and Society: Studies in the Sociology of Culture Past and Present: A Research Annual* 8, 3–26. Greenwich, CT: JAI Press.

American Economic Association. 1961–65. *Index of Economic Journals,* vols. 2–6. Homewood, IL: Richard D. Irwin.

———. 1965. *Readings in Business Cycles.* Homewood, IL: Richard D. Irwin.

Arrow, Kenneth J. 1991. "Cowles in the History of Economic Thought." In *Cowles Fiftieth Anniversary: Four Essays and an Index of Publications,* 1–24. New Haven, CT: The Cowles Foundation for Research in Economics at Yale University.

———. 1992. "I Know a Kawk from a Handsaw." In Michael Szenberg, ed., *Eminent Economists: Their Life Philosophies.* Cambridge: Cambridge University Press.

Ayres, Clarence Edwin. 1938. *The Problem of Economic Order.* New York: Farrar & Rinehart.

———. 1951. "The Co-Ordinates of Institutionalism." *American Economic Review* 41 (May): 47–55.

———. 1952. *The Industrial Economy.* Boston: Houghton Mifflin.

———. 1957. "A New Look at Institutionalism: Discussion." *American Economic Review* 47 (May): 26–27.

———. 1961. *Toward a Reasonable Society.* Austin: University of Texas Press.

———. 1963. "The Legacy of Thorstein Veblen." In *Institutional Economics:*

Veblen, Commons, and Mitchell Reconsidered. A series of lectures by Joseph Dorfman, C. E. Ayres, Neil W. Chamberlain, Simon Kuznets, R. A. Gordon. Berkeley: University of California Press, 45–62.

Backhouse, Roger. 1985. *A History of Modern Economic Analysis.* Oxford: Basil Blackwell.

———. 1993a. "The Debate over Milton Friedman's Theoretical Framework: An Economist's View." In Willie Henderson, Roger Backhouse, and Tony Dudley-Evans, eds., *Economics and Language,* 103–31. London: Routledge.

——— ed. 1994a. *New Directions in Economic Methodology.* London: Routledge.

———. 1994b. "Introduction: New Directions in Economic Methodology." In Backhouse, ed., *New Directions in Economic Methodology,* 1–24. London: Routledge.

———. 1994c. "Scientific Thinking Without Scientific Method: Two Views of Popper." In Backhouse, ed., *New Directions in Economic Methodology,* 173–91. London: Routledge.

Backhouse, Roger, Tony Dudley-Evans, and Willie Henderson. 1993. "Exploring the Language and Rhetoric of Economics." In Willie Henderson, Tony Dudley-Evans, and Roger Backhouse, eds., *Economics and Language,* 1–20. London: Routledge.

Barber, William J. 1985. *From New Era to New Deal: Herbert Hoover, the Economists, and American Economic Policy, 1921–1933.* Cambridge: Cambridge University Press.

Barnes, Barry. 1977. *Interests and the Growth of Knowledge.* London: Routledge & Kegan Paul.

———. 1982. *T. S. Kuhn and Social Science.* New York: Columbia University Press.

Barnes, Barry, and David Edge, eds. 1982. *Science in Context.* Cambridge, Mass.: MIT Press.

Barnes, Barry, and Steven Shapin, eds. 1979. *Natural Order: Historical Studies of Scientific Cultures.* Beverly Hills: Sage.

Baumberger, Jörg. 1977. "No Kuhnian Revolutions in Economics." *Journal for Economic Issues* 11(1): 1–20.

Baumol, William. 1984. "Baumol on Hicks." In Henry W. Spiegel and Warren J. Samuels, eds., *Contemporary Economists in Perspective,* 37–64. Greenwich, CT: JAI Press.

Becker, Howard S., and Michal McCall, eds. 1990. *Symbolic Interactionism and Cultural Studies.* Chicago: University of Chicago Press.

Bijker, Wiebe E., Thomas P. Hughes, and Trevor Pinch, eds. 1987. *The Social Construction of Technological Systems: New Directions in the Sociology and History of Technology.* Cambridge: MIT Press.

Birken, Lawrence. 1988. "From Macroeconomics to Microeconomics: The Marginalist Revolution in Socio-Cultural Perspective." *History of Political Economy* 20: 251–74.

Biven, W. Carl. 1989. *Who Killed John Maynard Keynes? Conflicts in the Evolution of Economic Policy.* Homewood, IL: Dow Jones-Irwin.

Black, R. D. Collison. 1973. "W. S. Jevons and the Foundation of Modern Economics." In R. D. Collison Black et al., eds., *The Marginal Revolution in Economics*, 98–112. Durham: Duke University Press.

———. 1983. "The Present Position and Prospects of Political Economy," in A. W. Coats, ed., *Methodological Controversy in Economics*, 55–70.

Black, R. D. Collison, A. W. Coats, and Craufurd D. W. Goodwin, eds. 1973. *The Marginal Revolution in Economics*. Durham: Duke University Press.

Bladen, Vincent. 1974. *From Adam Smith to Maynard Keynes*. Toronto: University of Toronto Press.

Blanchard, Olivier Jean, and Stanley Fischer. 1989. *Lectures on Macroeconomics*. Cambridge: MIT Press.

Blaug, Mark. 1973. "Was There a Marginal revolution?" In R. D. Collison Black et al., eds., *The Marginal Revolution in Economics*, 3–14. Durham: Duke University Press.

———. 1974. *The Cambridge Revolution: Success or Failure?* London: The Institute of Economic Affairs.

———. 1975. "Kuhn versus Lakatos, or Paradigms versus Research Programmes in the History of Economics." *History of Political Economy* 7(4): 399–433.

———. 1980. "Economic Methodology in One Easy Lesson." *British Review of Economic Issues*.

———. 1985a. *Economic Theory in Retrospect*. 4th ed. Cambridge: Cambridge University Press.

———. 1985b. *Great Economists Since Keynes*. Cambridge: Cambridge University Press.

———. 1986a. *Great Economists Before Keynes*. Cambridge: Cambridge University Press.

———. 1986b. *Who's Who in Economics: A Biographical Dictionary of Major Economists, 1700–1986*. 2d ed. Cambridge, MA: MIT Press.

———. 1990a. *Economic Theories, True or False*. Aldershot, Hants: Edward Elgar.

———. 1990b. *John Manard Keynes: Life, Ideas, Legacy*. London: Macmillan.

———. 1991. "Afterward." In Neil De Marchi and Mark Blaug, eds., *Appraising Modern Economics: Studies in the Methodology of Scientific Research Programmes*. Aldershot, Hants: Edward Elgar.

———, ed. 1992a. *Thorstein Veblen (1874–1948), John Commons (1862–1945), Clarence Ayres (1891–1972)*. Aldershot, Hants: Edward Elgar.

———, ed. 1992b. *Wesley Mitchell (1857–1929), John Commons (1862–1945), Clarence Ayres (1891–1972)*. Aldershot, Hants: Edward Elgar.

———. 1994. "Why I Am Not a Constructivist: Confessions of an Unrepentant Popperian." In Roger Backhouse, ed., *New Directions in Economic Methodology*, 109–36. London: Routledge.

Blaug Mark, and Paul Sturges, eds. 1983. *Who's Who in Economics: A Biographical Dictionary of Major Economists, 1700–1981*. Brighton, Sussex: Wheatsheaf Books.

Bloor, David. 1976. *Knowledge and Social Imagery*. London: Routledge & Kegan Paul.

Boland, Lawrence A. 1989. *The Methodology of Economic Model Building: Methodology after Samuelson*. London: Routledge.

Boland, Lawrence A. 1994. "Scientific Thinking Without Scientific Method: Two Views of Popper." In Roger Backhouse, ed., *New Directions in Economic Methodology*, 154–72. London: Routledge.

Boulding, Kenneth E. 1957. A New Look at Institutionalism. *American Economic Review* 47 (May): 1–12.

Bourdieu, Pierre. 1975. "The Specificity of the Scientific Field and the Social Conditions of the Progress of Reason." *Social Science Information* 14: 19–47.

———. 1988. *Homo Academicus*. Stanford: Stanford University Press.

Brandis, Royall. 1985. "Distribution Theory: Scientific Analysis or Moral Philosophy?" *Journal for Economic Issues* 19(4): 867–78.

Branson, William H. 1989. *Macroeconomic Theory and Policy*. 3d ed. New York: Harper & Row.

Brazer, Marjorie C. 1982. "The Economics Department of the University of Michigan: A Centennial Retrospective." In Saul H. Hymans, ed., *Economics and the World Around It*, 133–275. Ann Arbor: University of Michigan Press.

Breit, William, 1973. "The Development of Clarence Aires' Methodological Institutionalism." *Social Science Quarterly* 54(2): 244–57.

Breit, William, and Roger W. Spencer. 1986. *Lives of the Laureates: Seven Nobel Economists*. Cambridge, MA: MIT Press.

Briefs, Henry W. 1960. *Three Views of Method in Economics*. Washington, D.C.: Georgetown University Press.

Bronfenbrenner, Martin. 1971. The "Structure of Revolutions." in Economic Thought. *History of Political Economy* 3(1): 136–51.

Brown, Douglass V. et al., eds. 1934. *The Economics of the Recovery Program*. New York: Whittlesey House.

Brown, Vivienne. 1993. "Decanonizing Discourses: Textual Analysis and the History of Economic Thought." In Roger Backhouse, Tony Dudley-Evans, and Willie Henderson, eds., *Economics and Language*, 64–84. London: Routledge.

Buchanan, James M., Robert D. Tollison, and Gordon Tullock. 1980. *Toward a Theory of the Rent-Seeking Society*. College Station: Texas A & M University Press.

Burns, Arthur F. 1985. "An Economist's Perspective Over 60 Years." Interview. *Challenge* 27(January/February): 17–25.

Bye, Raymond T. 1924. "Some Recent Developments of Economic Theory." In Rexford Guy Tugwell, ed., *The Trend of Economics*, 269–300. New York: Alfred A. Knopf.

———. 1925. "Problems of Economic Theory." *American Economic Review* 15(1): 58–61.

Cain, Glen G. 1979. "Paul H. Douglas." In David L. Sills, ed., *The International Encyclopedia of the Social Sciences*, 153–57. New York: The Free Press.

Caldwell, Bruce J. 1994. "Two Proposals For the Recovery of Economic Practice." In Roger Backhouse, ed., *New Directions in Economic Methodology*, 137–53. London: Routledge.

Callon, Michel. 1980a. "The State and Technological Innovation: A Case Study of the Electrical Vehicle in France." *Research Policy* 9: 358–76.

———. 1980b. "Struggles and Negotiations to Define What is Problematic and What is Not: The Sociologic Translation," in Karin D. Knorr et al., eds., *The Social Process of Scientific Investigation*: 197–220.

———. 1986. "Some Elements of a Sociology of Translation: Domestication of the Scallops and the Fishermen of St. Brieuc's Bay." In J. Law, ed., *Power, Action and Belief: A New Sociology of Knowledge*, 196–229.

———. 1994. "Is Science a Public Good? Fifth Mullins Lecture, Virginia Polytechnic Institute, 23 March 1993."

Callon, Michel, and Bruno Latour. 1981. "Unscrewing the Big Leviathan: How Actors Macro-Structure Reality and How Sociologists Help Them to Do So." In Karin Knorr-Cetina and Aaron V. Cicourel, eds., *Advances in Social Theory and Methodology*. Boston: Routledge

———. 1992. "Don't Throw the Baby Out with the Bath School! A Reply to Collins and Yearley." In Andrew Pickering, ed., *Science as Practice and Culture*, 343–68. Chicago: University of Chicago Press.

Callon, Michel, and John Law. 1989. "On the Construction of Sociotechnical Networks: Content and Context Revisited." In Lowell Hargens, Robert Alun Jones, and Andrew Pickering, eds., *Knowledge and Society: Studies in the Sociology of Culture Past and Present: A Research Annual*, vol. 8, 57–83. Greenwich, CT.: JAI Press.

Camic, Charles. 1991. "Reputation and Predecessor Selection: Parsons and the Institutionalists." Talk at the Sociology Departmental Colloquium, Northwestern University.

———. 1992. "Reputation and Predecessor Selection: Parsons and the Institutionalists. *American Sociological Review* 57(4): 421–45.

Canterbery, E. Ray. 1976. *The Making of Economics*. Belmont, CA: Wadsworth Publishing Company.

Carabelli, A. 1988. *On Keynes's Method*. London: Macmillan.

———. 1992. "Organic Interdependence and Keynes's Choice of Units in the *General Theory*." In Bill Gerrard and John Hillard, eds., *The Philosophy and Economics of J. M. Keynes*, 3–31. Aldershot, Hants: Edward Elgar.

Carlton, Dennis W., and Jeffrey M. Perloff. 1994. *Modern Industrial Organization*. 2d ed. Harper Collins College Publishers.

Cartwright, Nancy. 1991. "Replicability, Reproducibility, and Robustness: Comments on Harry Collins." *History of Political Economy* 23(1): 143–55.

Chamberlain, Neil W. 1963. "The Institutional Economics of John R. Commons." In *Institutional Economics: Veblen, Commons, and Mitchell Reconsidered*. A series of lectures by Joseph Dorfman, C. E. Ayres, Neil W. Chamberlain, Simon Kuznets, R. A. Gordon. Berkeley: University of California Press, 63–94.

Chandler, A. D. Jr. 1977. The Visible Hand: The Managerial Revolution in American Business. Cambridge: Harvard University Press.

Christ, Carl F. 1952. "History of the Cowles Commission." In Economic Theory and Measurement: A Twenty Year Report, 1932–1952. Chicago: Cowles Commission for Research in Economics.

———. 1994. "The Cowles Commission's Contributions to Econometrics at Chicago, 1939–1955." *Journal for Economic Literature* 32(1): 30–59.

Clark, John Bates. 1968 [1907]. *Essentials for Economic Theory as Applied to Modern Problems of Industry and Public Policy*. Reprinted ed. New York: Augustus M. Kelly.

Clark, John Maurice. 1924. "The Socializing of Theoretical Economics." In Rexford Guy Tugwell, ed., *The Trend of Economics*, 71–102. New York: Alfred A. Knopf.

———. 1925. "Problems of Economic Theory." *American Economic Review* 15(1): 56–58.

———. 1936. "Past Accomplishments and Present Prospects." *American Economic Review* 26(1): 1–11.

———. 1947. "Some Current Cleavages Among Economists." *American Economic Review* 37(Supp.): 1–11.

Clarke, Adele E., and Elihu M. Gerson. 1990. "Symbolic Interactionism in Social Studies of Science." In Howard S. Becker and Michal McCall, eds., *Symbolic Interactionism and Cultural Studies*. Chicago: University of Chicago Press.

Clarke, Adele E., and Joan H. Fujimura, eds. 1992. *The Right Tools for the Job: At Work in Twentieth-Century Life Sciences*. Princeton University Press.

Clarke, Peter. 1988. *The Keynesian Revolution in the Making, 1924–1936*. Oxford: Clarendon Press.

Coats, A. W. 1969. "Is There a 'Structure of Scientific Revolutions' in Economics?" *Kyklos* 22(2): 289–95.

———. 1973. "The Economic and Social Context of the Marginal revolution of the 1870's." In R. D. Collison Black et al., eds., *The Marginal Revolution in Economics*, 37–58. Durham: Duke University Press.

———. 1983a. *Methodological Controversy in Economics*. Greenwich: JAI Press.

———. 1983b. "Half a Century of Methodological Controversy in Economics." In Coats, ed., *Methodological Controversy in Economics*, 1–42.

———. 1984. "The Sociology of Knowledge and the History of Economics." In *Research in the History of Economic Thought and Methodology* 2: 211–34.

Cobb, John Candler. 1926. "Quantitative Analysis and the Evolution of Economic Science." *American Economic Review* 16 (3): 426–33.

———. 1928. "The Significance and Use of Data in the Social Sciences." *Economic Journal* 38(1): 63–75.

Cole, Stephen. 1983. "The Hierarchy of the Sciences." *American Journal of Sociology* 89(1): 111–39.

Collins, Harry M. 1975. "The Seven Sexes: A Study in the Sociology of a Phenomenon, or the Replication of Experiments in Physics." *Sociology* 9(2): 205–24.

———. 1982. "Tacit Knowledge." In Barnes and Edge, eds., *Science in Context*, 44–64.

———. 1983. "The Sociology of Scientific Knowledge: Studies of Contemporary Science." *Annual Review of Sociology* 9: 265–85.

———. 1985. *Changing Order: Replication and Induction in Scientific Practice*. London: Sage.

———. 1991a. "History and Sociology of Science and History and Methodology of Economics." In Neil de Marchi and Mark Blaug, eds., *Appraising Economic Theories*, 492–98. Aldershot, Hants: Edward Elgar.

———. 1991b. "The Meaning of Replication and the Science of Economics." *History of Political Economy* 23(1): 123–42.

Collins, Harry M., and Steven Yearley. 1992a. "Epistemological Chicken." In Andrew Pickering, ed., *Science as Practice and Culture*, 301–26. Chicago: University of Chicago Press.

————. 1992b. "Journey Into Space." In Andrew Pickering, ed., *Science as Practice and Culture*, 369–89. Chicago: University of Chicago Press.

Collins, Robert M. 1981. *The Business Response to Keynes, 1929–1964*. New York: Columbia University Press.

Commons, John R. 1931. "Institutional Economics." *American Economic Review* 21(4, December): 648–57.

————. 1990 [1934]. *Institutional Economics: Its Place in Political Economy*. New Brunswick: Transaction Publishers.

Conkin, Paul K. 1980. *Prophets of Prosperity: America's First Political Economists*. Bloomington: Indiana University Press.

Copeland, Morris A. 1924. "Communities of Economic Interest and the Price System." In 103–50. New York: Alfred A. Knopf.

————. 1931. "Economic Theory and the Natural Science Point of View." *American Economic Review* 21: 67–79.

————. 1958. *Fact and Theory in Economics: The Testament of an Institutionalist*. Ed. Chandler Morse. Ithaca, NY: Cornell University Press.

Cowles Commission. 1991. *Cowles Fiftieth Anniversary: Four Essays and an Index of Publications*. New Haven, CT: The Cowles Foundation for Research in Economics at Yale University.

Cyert, Richard M. 1988. *The Economic Theory of Organization and the Firm*. New York: Harvester, Wheatsheaf.

Dasgupta, A. K. 1985. *Epochs of Economic Thought*. Oxford: Basil Blackwell.

Davis, J. Ronnie. 1971. *The New Economics and the Old Economists*. Ames: Iowa State University Press.

Dean, John. 1979. "Controversy over Classification: A Case Study from the History of Botany." In Barnes and Shapin, eds., *Natural Order*, 211–30. Beverly Hills: Sage.

Deane, Phylis. 1978. *The Evolution of Economic Ideas*. Cambridge: Cambridge University Press.

Debreu, Gerard. 1991. The Mathematization of Economic Theory. *American Economic Review* 81(1): 1–7.

De Marchi, Neil. 1991. "Introduction: Re-Thinking Lakatos." In De Marchi and Mark Blaug, eds., *Appraising Modern Economics: Studies in the Methodology of Scientific Research Programmes*, 1–30. Aldershot, Hants: Edward Elgar.

De Marchi, Neil, and Mark Blaug, eds. 1991. *Appraising Modern Economics: Studies in the Methodology of Scientific Research Programmes*. Aldershot, Hants: Edward Elgar.

De Vroey, Michel. 1975. "The Transition from Classical to Neoclassical Economics: A Scientific Revolution." *Journal of Economic Issues* 9: 415–40.

Desrosiéres, Alain. 1991. "How to Make Things Which Hold Together: Social Science, Statistics and the State." In P. Wagner, B. Wittrock, and R. Whitley, eds., *Discourses on Society: The Shaping of the Social Science Discourses*, 195–218. Dordrecht: Kluwer.

Dewey, John. 1963 [1938]. *Experience & Education*. The Kappa Delta Pi Lecture Series. New York: Collier Books.

Diamond, Arthur M., Jr. 1988. "The Empirical Progressiveness of the General Equilibrium Research Program." *History of Political Economy* 20(1): 119–35.

Dillard, D. 1978. "Revolutions in Economic Theory." *Southern Economic Journal* 44: 705–24.

DiMaggio, Paul. 1994. "Culture and Economy." In Neil J. Smelser and Richard Swedberg, eds., *The Handbook of Economic Sociology*, chap. 2, pp. 27–57. Princeton and New York: Princeton University Press and Russell Sage Foundation.

Dorfman, Joseph. 1934. *Thorstein Veblen and His America*. New York: Viking Press.

———. 1949. *The Economic Mind in American Civilization*, vol. 3, *1865–1918*. New York: Viking Press. Reprinted 1969 by Augustus M. Kelley, New York.

———. 1955. "The Role of the German Historical School in American Economic Thought." *American Economic Review* 45(Supp., May): 17–28.

———. 1959. *The Economic Mind in American Civilization*, vols. 4–5, *1918–1933*. New York: Viking Press.

———. 1963. "The Background of Institutional Economics." In *Institutional Economics: Veblen, Commons, and Mitchell Reconsidered*. A series of lectures by Joseph Dorfman, C. E. Ayres, Neil W. Chamberlain, Simon Kuznets, R. A. Gordon. Berkeley: University of California Press, 1–44.

Douglas, Paul H. 1924. "The Reality of Non-Commercial Incentives in Economic Life." In Rexford Guy Tugwell, ed., *The Trend of Economics*, 151–88. New York: Alfred A. Knopf.

———. 1971. *In the Fullest of Time: The Memoirs of Paul H. Douglas*. New York: Harcourt Brace Jovanovich.

Dudley-Evans, Tony. 1993. "The Debate over Milton Friedman's Theoretical Framework: An Applied Linguist's View." In Willie Henderson, Roger Backhouse, and Tony Dudley-Evans, eds., *Economics and Language*, 132–52. London: Routledge.

Dunlop, John T., and James J. Healy. *Collective Bargaining: Principles and Cases*. 1949. Homewood, IL: Richard D. Irwin.

Dunlop, John T., Frederick H. Harbison, Clark Kerr, and Charles A. Myers. 1975. *Industrialism And Industrial Man Reconsidered: Some Perspectives on a Study over Two Decades of the Problems of Labor and Management in Economic Growth*. Princeton: The Inter-University Study of Human Resources in National Development.

Edie, Lionel D. 1927. "The Positive Contribution of the Institutional Concept." *Quarterly Journal of Economics* 41 (3): 405–40.

Ekelund, R. E., and R. F. Hébert. 1983. *A History of Economic Theory and Method*. 2d ed. New York: McGraw-Hill.

Elkana, Yehuda. 1981. "A Programmatic Attempt at an Anthropology of Knowledge." In Everett Mendelsohn and Elkana, eds., *Science and Culture*. 1–76. Dordrecht: D. Reidel and Company.

Ely, Richard T., Thomas S. Adams, Max Lorenz, and Allyn A. Young. 1923. *Outlines of Economics*. 4th rev. ed. New York: Macmillan.

Epstein, Steven. 1995. "The Construction of Lay Expertise: AIDS Activism and the Forging of Credibility in the Reform of Clinical Trials." *Science Technology and Human Values* 20 (4): 408–37.

Evensky, Jerry. 1992. "Ethics and the Classical Liberal Tradition in Economics." *History of Political Economy* 24 (1): 61–77.

Feinstein, Alvan R. 1983. "An Additional Basic Science for Clinical Medicine: I. The Constraining Fundamental Paradigms." *Annals of Internal Medicine* 99: 544–50.

Feiwel, George R., ed. 1982. *Samuelson and Neoclassical Economics*. Boston: Kluwer Nijhoff.

———, ed. 1987a. *Arrow and the Ascent of Modern Economics*. Basingstoke: Macmillan.

———, ed. 1987b. *Arrow and the Foundations of the Theory of Economic Policy*. New York: New York University Press.

———. 1987c. "Oral History I: An Interview [with] Kenneth J. Arrow." In Feiwel, ed., *Arrow and the Ascent of Modern Economics*, 191–242. Basingstoke: Macmillan.

———. 1987d. "The Many Dimensions of Kenneth J. Arrow." In Feiwel, ed., *Arrow and the Foundations of the Theory of Economic Policy*, 1–115. New York: New York University Press.

Fetter, Frank A. 1925. The Economists and the Public. *American Economic Review* 15(1): 13–25.

Feyerabend, Paul K. 1975. *Against Method*. London: New Left Books.

———. 1978. *Science in a Free Society*. London: New Left Books.

Fish, Stanley. 1980. *Is there a Text in This Class?* Cambridge: Harvard University Press.

Fitzgibbons, Athol. 1988. *Keynes's Vision: A New Political Economy*. Oxford: Clarendon.

———. 1992. "The Political Economy of New Keynesian Fundamentalism." In Bill Gerrard and John Hillard, eds., *The Philosophy and Economics of J. M. Keynes*, 96–104. Aldershot, Hants: Edward Elgar.

Fox, Daniel M. 1967. *The Discovery of Abundance: Simon N. Patten and the Transformation of Social Theory*. Ithaca: Cornell University Press.

Friedman, Milton. 1953. "The Methodology of Positive Economics." In Friedman, *Essays in Positive Economics*, 3–43. Chicago: University of Chicago Press.

———. 1974. "A Theoretical Framework for Monetary Analysis," and "Comments on the Critics," in Robert Gordon, ed., *Milton Friedman's Monetary Framework*. Chicago: University of Chicago Press.

Froman, Lewis A. 1942. "Graduate Students in Economics, 1904–1940." *American Economic Review* 32(4): 817–26.

Fujimura, Joan H. 1987. "Constructing 'Do-able' Problems in Cancer Research: Articulating Alignment," *Social Studies of Science* 17(2): 257–93.

———. 1988. "The Molecular Biological Bandwagon in Cancer Research: Where Social Worlds Meet." *Social Problems* 35(3): 261–83.

———. 1992. "Crafting Science: Standardized Packages, Boundary Objects, and 'Translation.' " In Andrew Pickering, ed., *Science as Practice and Culture*, 168–211.

Fuller, Steve. 1990. "They Shoot Dead Horses, Don't They?: Philosophical Fear and Sociological Loathing in St. Louis." *Social Studies of Science* 20: 664–81.

Fulton, G. 1984. "Research Programmes in Economics." *History of Political Economy* 16: 187–206.

Furner, Mary O. 1975. *Advocacy and Objectivity: A Crisis in the Professionalization of American Social Science, 1865–1905.* Lexington: University of Kentucky Press.

Furner, Mary O., and Barry Supple. 1990. "Ideas, Institutions, and State in the United States and Britain: An Introduction." In Furner and Supple, eds., *The State and Economic Knowledge: The American and British Experiences*, 3–39. Cambridge: Woodrow Wilson International Center for Scholars and Cambridge University Press.

Galbraith, John Kenneth. 1987. *History of Economic Thought.* Boston: Houghton Mifflin.

Gambs, John S. 1975. *John Kenneth Galbraith.* Twayne Publishers.

———. 1980. "Allan Gruchy and the Association for Evolutionary Economics." In William Breit and Roger W. Spencer, eds., *Institutional Economics: Contributions to the Development of Holistic Economics*, 26–30. Boston: Martinus Nijhoff.

Gay, Edwin F. 1930. "Historical Records." *American Economic Review* 20: 1–8.

Gerrard, Bill. 1991. "Keynes's *General Theory*: Interpreting the Interpretations." *Economic Journal* 101(2): 276–87.

———. 1992. "From *A Treatise on Probability* to the *General Theory*: Continuity or Change in Keynes's Thought?" In Gerrard and John Hillard, eds., *The Philosophy and Economics of J. M. Keynes*, 80–95. Aldershot, Hants: Edward Elgar.

———. 1993. "The Significance of Interpretation in Economics." In Willie Henderson, Roger Backhouse, and Tony Dudley-Evans, eds., *Economics and Language*, 51–63. London: Routledge.

Gide, Charles, and Charles Rist, N.d. *A History of Economic Doctrines.* Authorized translation from the 2d rev. and augmented ed. of 1913. Boston: D. C. Heath & Co.

Gieryn, Thomas F. 1995. "Boundaries of Science." In Shila Jasanoff, Jerald Markel, James C. Petterson, and Trevor Pinch, eds., *Handbook of Science and Technology Studies*, 393–443. Los Angeles: Sage.

Gilbert, G. Nigel, and Michael Mulkay. 1984. *Opening Pandora's Box.* Cambridge: Cambridge University Press.

Goodrich, Carter. 1932a. "Hoxie, Robert Franklin." In the *Encyclopedia of the Social Sciences*. London: Macmillan.

———. 1932b. "Parker, Carleton, Hubbell." In the *Encyclopedia of the Social Sciences*, 579. London: Macmillan.

Gordon, Donald F. 1965. "The Role of the History of Economic Thought in the Understanding of Modern Economic Theory." *American Economic Review* 55(2, May): 119–27.

Gordon, Robert Aaron. 1952. *Business Fluctuations.* New York: Harper & Brothers.

———. 1963. "Institutional Elements in Contemporary Economics." In *Institutional Economics: Veblen, Commons, and Mitchell Reconsidered.* A series of lectures by Joseph Dorfman, C. E. Ayres, Neil W. Chamberlain, Simon Kuznets, R. A. Gordon. Berkeley: University of California Press, 123–47.

Gordon, Robert Aaron. 1978. *The Need to Disaggregate the Full Employment Goal*. A Special Report of the National Commission for Manpower Policy, Special Report No. 17.

Gordon, Robert J., ed. 1974. *Milton Friedman's Monetary Framework*. Chicago: University of Chicago Press.

Gordon, Wendel. 1980a. *Institutional Economics: The Changing System*. Austin: University of Texas Press.

———. 1980b. "Neoinstitutionalists and the Economics of Dissent." In John Adams, ed., *Institutional Economics: Contributions to the Development of Holistic Economics*, 33–44. Boston: Martinus Nijhoff.

Grether, D., and C. Plott. 1979. "Economic Theory of Choice and the Preference Reversal Phenomenon." *American Economic Review* 69: 623–38.

Groenewegen, Peter. 1990. "Neoclassical Value and Distribution Theory: The English-Speaking Pioneers." In Klaus Hennings and Warren J. Samuels, eds., *Neoclassical Economic Theory, 1870 to 1930*, 13–51. Boston: Kluwer Academic Publishers.

Gruchy, Allan G. 1947. *Modern Economic Thought*. New York: Prentice-Hall.

———. 1957. "A New Look at Institutionalism: Discussion." *American Economic Review* 47 (May): 13–15.

———. 1969. "Neoinstitutionalists and the Economics of Dissent." *Journal for Economic Issues* 3 (March): 3–17.

———. 1972. *Contemporary Economic Thought*. Clifton, NJ: Augustus M. Kelley.

———. 1977a. *Comparative Economic Systems*. 2d ed. Boston: Houghton Mifflin.

———. 1977b. "Institutionalism, Planning, and the Current Crisis." *Journal for Economic Issues* 11 (June): 431–48.

Gwartney, James D., and Richard Stroup. 1980. *Economics: Private and Public Choice*. 2d ed. New York: Academic Press.

Hacking, Ian. 1983. *Representing and Inventing: Introductory Topics in the Philosophy of Natural Science*. Cambridge: Cambridge University Press.

Hahn, Frank, and Robert Solow. 1995. *A Critical Essay on Modern Macroeconomic Theory*. Cambridge: MIT Press.

Hale, Robert Lee. 1924. "Economic Theory and the Statesman." In Rexford Guy Tugwell, ed., *The Trend of Economics*, 189–226. New York: Alfred A. Knopf.

Hall, Peter A., ed. 1989. *The Political Power of Economic Ideas: Keynesianism across Nations*. Princeton: Princeton University Press.

Hands, Douglas Wade. 1984. "The Role of Crucial Counterexamples in the Growth of Economic Knowledge: Two Case Studies in the Recent History of Economic Thought." *History of Political Economy* 16(1): 59–67.

———. 1985a. "Karl Popper and Economic Methodology: A New Look." *Economics and Philosophy* 1: 83–99.

———. 1985b. "Second Thoughts on Lakatos." *History of Political Economy* 17(1): 1–16.

———. 1993. *Testing, Rationality, and Progress: Essays on the Popperian Tradition in Economic Methodology*. Lanham, MD: Rowman and Littlefield.

Hands, Douglas Wade. 1994. "The Sociology of Scientific Knowledge: Some Thoughts on the Possibilities." In Roger Backhouse, ed., *New Directions in Economic Methodology*, 75–106. London: Routledge.

Hansen, Alvin H. 1953. *A Guide to Keynes*. New York: McGraw-Hill.

Harcourt, Geoffrey C. 1987. "Theoretical Methods and Unfinished Business." In David Reese, ed., *The Legacy of Keynes*, 1–22.

Harris, Abram L. 1932. "Types of institutionalism." *Journal of Political Economy* 40(6): 721–49.

Harvey, Bill. 1980. "The Effects of Social Context on the Process of Scientific Investigation: Experimental Tests of Quantum Mechanics." In Karin D. Knorr et al., eds., *The Social Process of Scientific Investigation*, 139–64.

Harwood, Jonathan. 1979. "Heredity, Environment, and the Legitimation of Social Policy." In Barnes and Shapin, eds., *Natural Order*, 231–51. Beverly Hills: Sage.

Hausman, Daniel M. 1989. "Economic Methodology in a Nutshell." *Journal of Economic Perspectives* 3(Spring), 115–27.

———. 1992. *The Inexact and Separate Science of Economics*. Cambridge: Cambridge University Press.

———. 1994. "Kuhn, Lakatos and the Character of Economics." In Roger Backhouse, ed., *New Directions in Economic Methodology*, 195–215. London: Routledge.

Heilbroner, Robert L. 1972. *The Worldly Philosophers: The Lives, Times and Ideas of the Great Economic Thinkers*. 4th ed., newly revised. New York: Simon and Schuster.

Hendry, David. 1980. "Econometrics—Alchemy or Science?" *Economica* 47: 387–406.

Hendry, D., E. Leamer, and D. Poirier. 1990. "A Conversation on Econometric Methodology." *Econometric Theory* 6: 171–261.

Hennings, Klaus, and Warren J. Samuels, eds. 1990. *Neoclassical Economic Theory, 1870 to 1930*. Boston: Kluwer Academic Publishers.

Henry, John F. 1982. "The Transformation of John Bates Clark: An Essay in Interpretation." *History of Political Economy* 14(2): 166–77.

Hicks, J. R. 1939. *Value and Capital*. Oxford: Clarendon Press.

Hildreth, Clifford. 1985. The Cowles Commission in Chicago, 1939–1955. Discussion Paper No. 225, October 1985. Minneapolis: Center for Economic Research at the University of Minnesota.

Hill, Forest G. 1957. "A New Look at Institutionalism: Discussion." *American Economic Review* 47 (May): 15–18.

Hillard, John. 1992. "Keynes, Orthodoxy and Uncertainty." In Bill Gerrard and Hillard, eds., *The Philosophy and Economics of J. M. Keynes*, 59–79. Aldershot, Hants: Edward Elgar.

Hirsch, Paul, Stuart Michaels, and Ray Friedman. 1987. " 'Dirty hands' versus 'clean models.' " *Theory and Society* 16:317–26.

Hodgson, Geoffrey M. 1994. "The Return of Institutional Economics." In Neil J. Smelser and Richard Swedberg, eds., *The Handbook of Economic Sociology*, chap. 3, pp. 58–76. Princeton and New York: Princeton University Press and Russell Sage Foundation.

Holland, Dorothy, and Naomi Quinn. 1987. *Cultural Models in Language and Thought*. Cambridge: Cambridge University Press.

Homan, Paul T. 1928. "Issues in Economic Theory: An Attempt to Clarify." *Quarterly Journal of Economics* 42(3): 333–65.

———. 1931. "Economic Theory—Institutionalism: What It Is and What It Hopes to Become." *American Economic Review* 21 (March): 134–41.

Hoover, Kevin D. 1994. "Pragmatism, Pragmaticism and Economic Method." In Roger Backhouse, ed., *New Directions in Economic Methodology*, 286–315. London: Routledge.

Horgan, John. 1991. "Profile: Reluctant Revolutionary" in *Scientific American*, May 1991, 40–49.

Howey, Richard S. 1973. "The Origins of Marginalism." In R. D. Collison Black et al., eds., *The Marginal Revolution in Economics*, 15–36. Durham: Duke University Press.

Hudson, Michael. 1975. *Economics and Technology in 19th Century American Thought*. New York: Garland Publishing.

Humphries, Sally C. 1969. "History, Economics, and Anthropology: The Work of Karl Polanyi." *History and Theory* 8.

Hunter, Albert, ed. 1990. *The Rhetoric of Social Research Understood and Believed*. New Brunswick: Rutgers University Press.

Hutchison, Terence Wilmot. 1938. *The Significance and Basic Postulates of Economics*. London: Macmillan.

———. 1941. "Reply to Prof. Knight." *Journal of Political Economy* 49: 732–50.

———. 1956. "Reply to Machlup." *Southern Journal of Economics* 22: 476–83.

———. 1976. "On the History and Philosophy of Science and Economics." In Spiro J. Latsis, ed., *Method and Appraisal in Economics*, 181–206. Cambridge: Cambridge University Press.

———. 1977. *Knowledge and Ignorance in Economics*. Oxford: Basil Blackwell.

———. 1978. *On Revolutions and Progress in Economic Knowledge*. Cambridge: Cambridge University Press.

———. 1981. *The Politics and Philosophy of Economics*. Oxford: Blackwell.

Jaffé, William. 1973. "Lèon Walras's Role in the 'Marginal Revolution' of the 1870s." In *The Marginal Revolution in Economics*, ed. R. D. Collison Black et al., 113–39. Durham: Duke University Press.

———. 1976. "Menger, Jevons, and Walras De-homogenized." *Economic Inquiry* 14: 511–24.

Jalladeau, Joël. 1975. "The Methodological Conversion of John Bates Clark." *History of Political Economy* 7(2): 209–26.

Jensen, Hans E. 1983. "J. M. Keynes as a Marshallian." *Journal for Economic Issues* 17(1): 67–94.

Jha, Marmadeshwar. 1973. *The Age of Marshall: Aspects of British Economic Thought*, 1890–1915. 2d ed. London: Frank Cass.

Johnson, Alvin S. 1922. *Introduction to Economics*. Rev. ed. Reissued in 1971. Port Washington, NY: Kennikat Press.

Johnson, Jim [Bruno Latour]. 1988. "Mixing Humans and Nonhumans Together: The Sociology of a Door-Closer." *Social Problems* 35(3): 298–310.

Johnston, R. 1976. "Contextual Knowledge: A Model for the Overthrow of the

Internal/External Dichotomy in Science." *Australia and New-Zealand Journal of Sociology* 12:193–203.

Kadish, Alon. 1982. *The Oxford Economists in the Late Nineteenth Century.* Oxford: Clarendon Press.

Kadish, Alon. 1989. *Historians, Economists, and Economic History.* London: Routledge.

———. 1993a. "Marshall and the Cambridge Economics Tripos." In Alon Kadish and Keith Tribe, eds., *The Market for Political Economy: The Advent of Economics in British University Culture, 1850–1905,* 227–50. London: Routledge.

———. 1993b. "The City, the Fabians and the Foundation of the London School of Economics." In Alon Kadish and Keith Tribe, eds., *The Market for Political Economy: The Advent of Economics in British University Culture, 1850–1905,* 137–61. London: Routledge.

Kadish, Alon, and Keith Tribe, eds. 1993. *The Market for Political Economy: The Advent of Economics in British University Culture, 1850–1905.* London: Routledge.

Kaufman, Allen. 1982. *Capitalism, Slavery, and Republican Values: Antebellum Political Economists, 1819–1848.* Austin: University of Texas Press.

Keynes, John Maynard. 1924. *The End of Laissez-Faire.* London: Leonard & Virginia Woolf at The Hogarth Press.

———. 1939. "Professor Tinbergen's Method" *Economic Journal* 49: 558–68.

———. 1963. *Essays in Persuasion.* New York: W. W. Norton.

———. 1964 [1936]. *The General Theory of Employment, Interest, and Money.* San Diego: First Harvest/HBJ.

———. 1988 [1919]. *The Economic Consequences of the Peace.* New York: Penguin Books.

Keynes, John Neville. 1955. *The Scope and Method of Political Economy.* 4th ed. New York: Kelly & Millman.

Kim, Kyun. 1988. *Equilibrium Business Cycle Theory in Historical Perspective.* Cambridge: Cambridge University Press.

Klamer, Arjo. 1987. "As if Economists and Their Subjects Were Rational," in Nelson, John S., Allan Megill, and Donald N. McCloskey, eds., *The Rhetoric of the Human Sciences.* Madison: University of Wisconsin Press.

———. 1989. "An Accountant Among Economists: Conversation with Sir John R. Hicks," *Journal for Economic Perspectives* 3(4): 167–80.

———. 1990. "Towards the Native's Point of View: The Difficulty of Changing the Conversation." In Don Lavoie, ed., *Economics and Hermeneutics,* 19–33. London: Routledge.

Klamer, Arjo, and David Colander. 1990. *The Making of an Economist.* Boulder: Westview Press.

Klamer, Arjo, Donald N. McCloskey, and Robert M. Solow, eds. 1988. *The Consequences of Economic Rhetoric.* Cambridge: Cambridge University Press.

Klein, Lawrence R. 1947. *The Keynesian Revolution.* 2d ed. New York: Macmillan.

———. 1985. *Economic Theory and Econometrics.* Essays of Lawrence R. Klein. Ed. Jaime Marquez. Philadelphia: University of Pennsylvania Press.

Klein, Philip A. 1978. "American Institutionalism: Premature Death, Permanent Resurrection." *Journal for Economic Issues* 12(2): 251–76.

———. 1980. "A Reconsideration of Holistic Economics." In John Adams, ed., *Institutional Economics: Contributions to the Development of Holistic Economics*, 45–58. Boston: Martinus Nijhoff.

———. 1983. "The Neglected Institutionalism of Wesley Clair Mitchell: The Theoretical Basis for Business Cycle Indicators." *Journal for Economic Issues* 17(4): 867–99.

Knapp, Joseph G. 1979. *Edwin G. Nourse—Economist for the People*. Danville, IL: Interstate Printers and Publishers.

Knight, Frank H. 1924. "The Limitation of Scientific Method in Economics." In Rexford Guy Tugwell, ed., *The Trend of Economics*, 227–68. New York: Alfred A. Knopf.

———. 1928. "Fact and Metaphysics in Economic psychology." *American Economic Review* 18(2): 247–66.

———. 1940. "Review of the Significance and Basic Postulates of Economics, by Terence W. Hutchison." *Journal of Political Economy* 48.

———. 1941. "A Rejoinder." *Journal of Political Economy* 49: 750–53.

———. 1946. *Freedom and Reform: Essays in Economics and Social Philosophy*. Indianapolis: Liberty Press.

———. 1952. "Institutionalism and Empiricism in Economics." *American Economic Review* 42 (May): 45–55.

———. 1957. "A New Look at Institutionalism: Discussion." *American Economic Review* 47 (May): 18–21.

Knorr-Cetina, Karin D. 1980. "The Scientist as an Analogical Reasoner: A Critique of the Metaphor Theory of Innovation." In Knorr-Cetina, Karin D., Roger Krohn, and Richard Whitley, eds., *The Social Process of Scientific Investigation*, 25–52.

———. 1981. *The Manufacture of Knowledge*. Oxford: Pergamon Press.

———. 1982. "Scientific Communities or Transepistemic Arenas of Research? A Critique of Quasi-Economic Models of Science." *Social Studies of Science* 12: 101–30.

———. 1983. "The Ethnographic Study of Scientific Work: Towards a Constructivist Interpretation of Science." In Knorr-Cetina and Mulkay, *The Social Process of Scientific Investigation*.

———. 1991. "Epistemic Cultures: Forms of Reason in Science." *History of Political Economy* 23(1): 105–22.

———. 1992. "The Couch, the Cathedral, and the Laboratory: On the Relationship between Experiment and Laboratory in Science." In Andrew Pickering, ed., *Science as Practice and Culture*, 113–38.

———. 1995. "Laboratory Studies: The Cultural Approach to the Study of Science." In Shila Jasanoff, Jerald Markel, James C. Petterson, and Trevor Pinch, eds., *Handbook of Science and Technology Studies*, 140–66. Los Angeles: Sage.

Koopmans, Tjalling C. 1957. *Three Essays on the State of Economic Science*. New York: McGraw-Hill.

Koot, Gerard M. 1987. *English Historical Economics, 1870–1926*. Cambridge: Cambridge University Press.

Kregel, J. A., ed. 1988. *Recollections of Eminent Economists*, vol. 1. Houndmills, Basingstoke, Hampshire: Macmillan.

Kuhn, Thomas S. 1970a. *The Structure of Scientific Revolutions*. 2d ed. Chicago: University of Chicago Press. (Originally published 1962.)

————. 1970b. "Logic of Discovery or Psychology of Research." In Imre Lakatos and Alan Musgrave, eds., *Criticism and the Growth of Knowledge*, 1–24. Cambridge: Cambridge University Press.

————. 1970c. "Reflections on My Critics." In Imre Lakatos and Alan Musgrave, eds., *Criticism and the Growth of Knowledge*, 231–78. Cambridge: Cambridge University Press.

————. 1977. *The Essential Tension: Selected Studies in Scientific Tradition and Change*. Chicago: University of Chicago Press.

————. 1992. *The Trouble with the Historical Philosophy of Science: Robert and Maurine Rothschild Distinguished Lecture*. Cambridge: Department of the History of Science, Harvard University.

Kuznets, Simon. 1963. "The Contribution of Wesley C. Mitchell." In *Institutional Economics: Veblen, Commons, and Mitchell Reconsidered*. A series of lectures by Joseph Dorfman, C. E. Ayres, Neil W. Chamberlain, Simon Kuznets, and R. A. Gordon. Berkeley: University of California Press, 95–122.

Lachmann, Ludwig M. 1990. "Austrian Economics: A Hermeneutical Approach." In Don Lavoie, ed., *Economics and Hermeneutics*, 134–46. London: Routledge.

Lakatos, Imre, and Alan Musgrave, eds. 1970. *Criticism and the Growth of Knowledge*. Cambridge: Cambridge University Press. (Proceeding of the International Colloquium in the Philosophy of Science, London 1965, vol. 4.)

Landreth, Harry. 1976. *History of Economic Theory: Scope, Method, and Content*. Boston: Houghton Mifflin.

Latour, Bruno. 1980. "Is It Possible to Reconstruct the Research Process? Sociology of the Brain Peptide." In Knorr-Cetina, Karin D., Roger Krohn, and Richard Whitley, eds., *The Social Process of Scientific Investigation*, 53–73.

————. 1982. "The Cycle of Credibility." In Barnes and Edge, eds., *Science in Context*, 35–43.

————. 1983. "Give Me a Laboratory and I Will Raise the World." In Karin Knorr-Cetina and Michael Mulkey, eds., *Science Observed: Perspectives on the Social Studies of Science*, 143–70.

————. 1986. "Visualization and Cognition: Thinking with Eyes and Hands." In *Knowledge and Society: Studies in the Sociology of Culture Past and Present*, vol. 6, 1–40.

————. 1987. Science in Action. Cambridge: Harvard University Press.

————. 1988a. *The Pasteurization of France*. Cambridge: Harvard University Press.

————. 1988b. "A Relativistic Account of Einstein's Relativity." *Social Studies of Science* 18: 3–44.

————. 1988c. "The Politics of Explanation." In Steve Woolgar, ed., *Knowledge and Reflexivity: New Frontiers in the Sociology of Knowledge*, 155–76. Beverly Hills: Sage.

Latour, Bruno. 1992. "One More Turn After the Social Turn." In Ernam McMullin, ed., *The Social Dimension of Science*, 272–94. Notre Dame: Notre Dame University Press.

———. 1993. *We Have Never Been Modern*. New York: Harvester Wheatsheaf.

Latour, Bruno, and Steve Woolgar. 1979. *Laboratory Life*. Princeton: Princeton University Press.

Latsis, Spiro J. 1976. *Method and Appraisal in Economics*. Cambridge: Cambridge University Press.

Laudan, Larry. 1977. *Progress and Its Problems: Towards a Theory of Scientific Growth*. Berkeley: University of California Press.

———. 1982. "Two Puzzles about Science: Reflections on Some Crises in the Philosophy and Sociology of Science." *Minerva* 20: 253–68.

———. 1984. *Science and Values*. Berkeley: University of California Press.

———. 1990. *Science and Relativism: Some Key Controversies in the Philosophy. of Science* Chicago: University of Chicago Press.

Lavoie, Don. 1985. *Rivalry and Central Planning: The Socialist Calculation Debate Reconsidered*. Cambridge: Cambridge University Press.

———. 1990a. "Introduction." In Lavoie, ed., *Economics and Hermeneutics*, 1–15. London: Routledge.

———. 1990b. "Hermeneutics, Subjectivity, and the Lester/Machlup Debate: Toward a More Anthropological Approach to Empirical Economics." In Warren J. Samuels, ed., *Economics as a Discourse: An Analysis of the Language of Economists*, 167–87. Boston: Kluwer Academic Publishers.

Law, John. 1973. "The Development of Specialties in Science: The Case of X-ray Protein Crystallography." *Science Studies* 3: 275–303.

———. 1976. "Theories and Methods in the Sociology of Science: An Interpretive Approach." *Social Science Information* 13(4/5): 163–72.

Law, John, and R. J. Williams. 1982. "Putting Facts Together: A Study of Scientific Persuasion," *Social Studies of Science* 12: 535–58.

Lawson, T. 1994. "A Realist Theory for Economics." In Roger Backhouse, ed., *New Directions in Economic Methodology*, 257–85. London: Routledge.

Leamer, Edward. 1983. "Let's Take the Con Out of Econometrics." *American Economic Review* 73: 31–43.

Lecomber, Richard. 1979. *The Economics of Natural Resources*. New York: John Wiley & Sons.

Lee, Bradford A. 1989. "The Miscarriage of Necessity and Invention: Proto-Keynesianism and Democratic States in the 1930s." In Peter A. Hall, ed., *The Political Power of Economic Ideas: Keynesianism across Nations*, 129–70. Princeton: Princeton University Press.

Leijonhufvud, Axel. 1968. *On Keynesian Economics and Economics of Keynes*. Oxford: Oxford University Press.

———. 1976. "Schools, 'Revolutions,' and Research Programmes in Economic Theory." In Spiro J. Latsis, ed., *Method and Appraisal in Economics*, 65–107. Cambridge: Cambridge University Press.

Lekachman, Robert. 1966. *The Age of Keynes*. New York: Random House.

Leontief, Wassily. 1971. "Theoretical Assumptions and Nonobserved Facts." *American Economic Review* 61(1): 1–7.

Lester, Richard A. 1946. "Shortcomings of Marginal Analysis for Wage-Employment Problems." *American Economic Review* 36 (March): 63–82.

———. 1947. "Marginalism, Minimum Wages, and Labor Markets." *American Economic Review* 37 (March): 135–48.

Liebhafsky, H. H. 1980. "Allan Gruchy, Neoinstitutionalist." In John Adams, ed., *Institutional Economics: Contributions to the Development of Holistic Economics*, 19–25. Boston: Martinus Nijhoff.

Lind, Hans. 1992. "A Case Study of Normal Research in Theoretical Economics." *Economics and Philosophy* 8: 86–103.

———. 1993. "The Myth of Institutionalist Method." *Journal for Economic Issues* 27: 1–17.

Lindbeck, Assar. 1984. "Lindbeck on Samuelson." In Henry W. Spiegel and Warren J. Samuels, eds., *Contemporary Economists in Perspective*, 5–18. Greenwich, CT: JAI Press.

Lindberg, Leon N., and Charles S. Maier, eds. 1985. *The Politics of Inflation and Economic Stagnation*. Washington: Brookings Institution.

Little, Ian Malcolm David. 1950. *A Critique of Welfare Economics*. Oxford: Oxford University Press.

Lowe, Adolph. 1964. *On Economic Knowledge: Toward a Science of Political Economics*. New York: Harper & Row.

Lynch, Michael. 1985. *Art and Artifact in Laboratory Science*. London: Routledge & Kegan Paul.

———. 1992. "Extending Wittgenstein: The Pivotal Move from Epistemology to the Sociology of Science." In Andrew Pickering, ed., *Science as Practice and Culture*, 215–65.

———. 1993. *Scientific Practice and Ordinary Action: Ethnomethodology and Social Studies of Science*. Cambridge: Cambridge University Press.

Machlup, Fritz. 1946. "Marginal Analysis and Empirical Research." *American Economic Review* 36 (Sept.): 519–54.

———. 1947. "Rejoinder to an Antimarginalist." *American Economic Review* 37 (March): 148–54.

———. 1955. "The Problem of Verification in Economics." *The Southern Economic Journal* 22(1): 1–21.

———. 1956. "Rejoinder to a Reluctant Ultra-Empiricist." *The Southern Economic Journal* 22 (4): 483–93.

MacKenzie, Donald, and Barry Barnes. 1979. "Scientific Judgment: The Biometry-Mendelism Controversy." In Barnes and Shapin, eds., *Natural Order*, 191–210. Beverly Hills: Sage.

MacKenzie, Donald, and Graham Spinardi. 1995. "Tacit Knowledge, Weapon Design, and the Uninvention of Nuclear Weapons." *American Journal of Sociology* 101(1): 44–99.

Maddock, Rodney. 1984. "Rational Expectations Macrotheory: A Lakatosian Case Study in Program Adjustment. *History of Political Economy* 16: 291–310.

Madison, G. B. 1990. "Getting beyond Objectivism: The Philosophical Hermeneutics of Gadamer and Ricoeur." In Don Lavoie, ed., *Economics and Hermeneutics*, 34–58. London: Routledge.

Mäki, Uskali. 1994. "Reorienting the Assumptions Issue." In Roger Backhouse, ed., *New Directions in Economic Methodology*, 236–56. London: Routledge.

———. 1995. "Diagnosing McCloskey." *Journal for Economic Literature* 33: 1300–1318.

Malinvaud, Edmond. 1991. "Econometric Methodology at the Cowles Commission: Rise and Maturity." In *Cowles Fiftieth Anniversary: Four Essays and an Index of Publications*, 49–80. New Haven, CT: The Cowles Foundation for Research in Economics at Yale University.

Maloney, John. 1985. *Marshall, Orthodoxy, and the Professionalization of Economics*. Cambridge: Cambridge University Press.

Marks, H. M. 1987. Ideas and Reforms: Therapeutic Experiments and Medical Practice, 1900–1980. Doctoral Dissertation, MIT.

Marshall, Alfred. 1910. *Principles of Economics*. 6th ed. London: Macmillan.

———. 1920. *Principles of Economics*. 8th ed. Philadelphia: Porcupine Press.

Mayer, Thomas 1980. "Economics as a Hard Science: Realistic Goal or Wishful Thinking?" *Economic Inquiry* 18: 165–87.

———. 1993. *Truth Versus Precision in Economics*. Aldershot, Hants: Edward Elgar.

McCloskey, Donald N. 1985. *The Rhetoric of Economics*. Madison: University of Wisconsin Press.

———. 1988a. "Two Replies and a Dialogue on the Rhetoric of Economics: Mäki, Rappaport, and Rosenberg." *Economics and Philosophy* 4: 150–66.

———. 1988b. "Thick and Thin Methodologies in the History of Economic Thought." In Neil de Marchi, ed., *The Popperian Legacy In Economics*, 245–57. Cambridge: Cambridge University Press.

———. 1990a. *If You're So Smart: The Narrative of Economic Expertise*. Chicago: University of Chicago Press.

———. 1990b. "Storytelling in Economics." In Don Lavoie, ed., *Economics and Hermeneutics*, 61–75. London: Routledge.

———. 1994a. "How to Do a Rhetorical Analysis, and Why." In Roger Backhouse, ed., *New Directions in Economic Methodology*, 319–42. London: Routledge.

———. 1994b. *Knowledge and Persuasion in Economics*. Cambridge: Cambridge University Press.

———. 1995. "Modern Epistemology Against Analytic Philosophy: A reply to Mäki." *Journal for Economic Literature* 32(4): 33: 1319–23.

Mead, George Herbert. 1962 [1934]. *Mind, Self, & Society: From the Standpoint of a Social Behaviorist*. Works of George Herbert Mead, vol. 1. Ed. and with an Introduction by Charles W. Morris. Chicago: University of Chicago Press.

Mehta, Judith. 1993. "Meaning in the Context of Bargaining Games—Narratives in Opposition." In Willie Henderson, Roger Backhouse, and Tony Dudley-Evans, eds., *Economics and Language*, 85–99. London: Routledge.

Ménard, Claude. 1990. "The Lausanne Tradition: Walras and Pareto." In Klaus Hennings and Warren J. Samuels, eds., *Neoclassical Economic Theory, 1870 to 1930*, 95–137. Boston: Kluwer Academic Publishers.

Mendel, Marguerite, and Daniel Salée. 1991. *The Legacy of Karl Polanyi: Mar-*

ket, State and Society at the End of the Twentieth Century. New York: St. Martin Press.

Mendelsohn, Everett. 1974. "Revolution and Reduction: The Sociology of Methodological and Philosophical Concerns in Nineteenth Century Biology." In Y. Elkana, ed., *The Interaction between Science and Philosophy,* 407–26. Atlantic Highlands, NJ: Humanities Press.

———. 1977. "The Social Construction of Scientific Knowledge." In Everett Mendelsohn, Peter Weingart, and Richard Whitley, eds., *The Social Production of Scientific Knowledge.* Dordrecht: D. Reidel and Company.

Millar, James R. 1980. "Institutionalism from a Natural Science Point of View: An Intellectual Profile of Morris A. Copeland." In John Adams, ed., *Institutional Economics: Contributions to the Development of Holistic Economics,* 105–24. Boston: Martinus Nijhoff.

Mills, Frederick C. 1924. "On Measurement in Economics." In Rexford Guy Tugwell, ed., *The Trend of Economics,* 35–70. New York: Alfred A. Knopf.

———. 1928. "The Present Status and Future Prospects of Quantitative Economics." Round Table Discussion, *American Economic Review* 18(1): 28–45.

Minsky, Hyman P. 1988. "Beginnings." In J. A. Kregel, ed., *Recollections of Eminent Economists,* vol. 1, 169–80. Houndmills, Basingstoke, Hampshire: Macmillan.

Mirowski, Philip. 1981. "Is There a Mathematical Neoinstitutional Economics?" *Journal of Economic Issues* 15(3): 593–613.

———, ed. 1986a. *The Reconstruction of Economic Theory,* Boston: Kluwer Nijhoff.

———. 1986b. "Introduction: Paradigms, Hard Cores, and Fuglemen in Modern Economic Theory." In Mirowski, ed., *The Reconstruction of Economic Theory:* 1–11.

———. 1989a. *More Heat than Light: Economics as Social Physics, Physics as Nature's Economics.* Cambridge: Cambridge University Press.

———. 1989b. "The Probabilistic Counter-Revolution, or How Stochastic Concepts Came to Neoclassical Economic Theory." In Neil De Marchi and Christopher Gilbert, eds., *History and Methodology of Economics,* 217–35. Oxford: Clarendon Press.

———. 1990. "The Philosophical Bases of Institutionalist Economics." In Don Lavoie, ed., *Economics and Hermeneutics,* 76–112. London: Routledge.

———. 1994. "What Are the Questions?" In Roger Backhouse, ed., *New Directions in Economic Methodology,* 50–74. London: Routledge.

Mishan, E. J. 1969. *Welfare Economics: Ten Introductory Essays.* 2d ed. New York: Random House.

Mitchell, Wesley C. 1924. "The Prospects of Economics." In Rexford Guy Tugwell, ed., *The Trend of Economics,* 1–34. New York: Alfred A. Knopf.

———. 1925. "Quantitative Analysis in Economic Theory." *American Economic Review* 15(1): 1–12.

———. 1967. *Types of Economic Theory from Mercantilism to Institutionalism,* vol. 1. New York: Augustus M. Kelly.

———. 1969. *Types of Economic Theory from Mercantilism to Institutionalism,* vol. 2. New York: Augustus M. Kelly.

Moore, Geoffrey H. 1979. "Arthur F. Burns." In David L. Sills, ed., *The International Encyclopedia of the Social Sciences*, 81–86. New York: The Free Press.

Morse, Chandler. 1958. "Introduction: The Meaning of the Institutionalist Approach." In *Fact and Theory in Economics: The Testament of an Institutionalist*. Ithaca, NY: Cornell University Press, v–xiv.

Mulkay, Michael J. 1975. "Three Models of Scientific Development. *The Sociological Review* 23 (3): 509–26.

Muller, Jerry Z. 1993. *Adam Smith in His Time and Ours: Designing the Decent Society*. New York: The Free Press.

Myler, Jack C. 1956. *German Historicism and American Economics: A Study of the Influence of the German Historical School on American Economic Thought*. A Dissertation presented to the Faculty of Princeton University.

Myrdal, Gunner. 1978. "Institutionalist Economics." *Journal for Economic Issues* 12 (December): 771–83.

Napoleoni, Claudio. 1972. *Economic Thought in the Twentieth Century*. London: Martin Robertson.

Neale, Walter C. 1990. "Karl Polanyi and American Institutionalism: A Strange Case of Convergence." In Kari Polanyi-Levitt, ed., *The Life and Work of Karl Polanyi: A Celebration*, 145–51. Montreal: Black Rose Books.

Nelson, John S., Allan Megill, and Donald N. McCloskey, eds. 1987. *The Rhetoric of the Human Sciences*. Madison: University of Wisconsin Press.

Nelson, Richard R. 1994. "Evolutionary Theorizing about Economic Change." In Neil J. Smelser and Richard Swedberg, eds., *The Handbook of Economic Sociology*, chap. 3, pp. 108–36. Princeton and New York: Princeton University Press and Russell Sage Foundation.

Nicholson, Walter. 1990. *Intermediate Microeconomics and Its Application*. 5th ed. Chicago: The Dryden Press.

Nickles, Thomas. 1990. "How to Talk with Sociologists (or Philosophers)." *Social Studies of Science* 20: 633–38.

Niehans, Jürg. 1990. *A History of Economic Theory: Classic Contributions, 1720–1980*. Baltimore: Johns Hopkins University Press.

Nourse, Edwin. 1943. "Collective Bargaining and the Common Interest." *American Economic Review* 33(1): 1–20.

O'Brien, D. P. 1974. *Whither Economics?* An Inaugural Lecture by Professor D. P. O'Brien. University of Durham.

——— 1981. "A. Marshall, 1842–1924." In D. P. O'Brien and John R. Presley, eds., *Pioneers of Modern Economics in Britain*, 36–71. Totowa, NJ: Barnes & Noble.

Oser, Jacob. 1970. *The Evolution of Economic Thought*. 2d ed. New York: Harcourt, Brace & World.

Patinkin, Don. 1976. "Keynes and Econometrics: On the Interaction between the Macroeconomic Revolutions of the Interwar Period." *Econometrica* 44(6): 1091–1123.

———. 1982. *Anticipations of the General Theory? And Other Essays on Keynes*. Chicago: University of Chicago Press.

Perrin, C. E. 1987. "Revolution or Reform?: The Chemical Revolution and Eighteenth Century Concepts of Scientific Change." *History of Science* 25: 395–423.

Pheby, J. 1988. *Methodology and Economics: A Critical Introduction.* London: Macmillan.

Phillips, Ronnie J. 1989. "Is There a Texas School of Economics?" *Journal for Economic Issues* 23(3): 863–72.

Pickering, Andrew. 1984. *Constructing Quarks: A Sociological History of Particle Physics.* Chicago: University of Chicago Press.

———. 1989. "Living in the Material World: On Realism and Experimental Practice." In David Gooding, Trevor Pinch, and Simon Schaffer, eds., *The Uses of Experiments,* 257–97. Cambridge: Cambridge University Press.

———. 1990. "Knowledge, Practice, and Mere Construction." *Social Studies of Science* 20: 682–729.

———. 1992a. "From Science as Knowledge to Science as Practice." In Pickering, ed., *Science as Practice and Culture,* 1–26.

———, ed. 1992b. *Science as Practice and Culture.* Chicago: University of Chicago Press.

Pinch, Trevor J. 1977. "What Does a Proof Do If It Does Not Prove?" In Mendelsohn et al., *The Social Production of Scientific Knowledge.*

———. 1986. *Confronting Nature: The Sociology of Solar-Neutrino Detection.* Dordrecht: Reidel.

———. 1990. "Deconstructing Roth and Barrett." *Social Studies of Science* 20: 658–63.

———. 1992. "Opening Black Boxes: Science, Technology and Society." *Social Studies of Science* 22: 487–510.

Porter, Theodore M. 1995. *Trust in Numbers: The Pursuit of Objectivity in Science and Public Life.* Princeton University Press.

Pribram, K. 1983. *A History of Economic Reasoning.* Baltimore: Johns Hopkins University Press.

Proctor, Robert N. 1991. *Value-Free Science: Purity and Power in Modern Knowledge.* Cambridge: Harvard University Press.

Ramstaad, Yngve. 1986. "A Pragmatist's quest of Holistic Knowledge." *Journal for Economic Issues* 20: 1067–1106.

Reder, Melvin W. 1982. "Chicago Economics: Permanence and Change." *Journal for Economic Literature* 20:1–38.

Redman, Deborah A. 1991. *Economics and the Philosophy of Science.* Oxford: Oxford University Press.

Reisman, David. 1981. "The Dissenting Economist: J. K. Galbraith." In J. R. Shackleton and Gareth Locksley, eds., *Twelve Contemporary Economists,* 72–86. London: Macmillan Press.

Remenyi, J. V. 1979. "Core-Demi-Core Interaction: Towards a General Theory of Disciplinary and Subdisciplinary Growth." *History of Political Economy* 11: 30–63.

Restivo, Sal. 1982. "The Myth of the Kuhnian Revolution." *Sociological Theory* 1. New York: Jossey-Bass, 293–305.

Rima, Ingrid H. 1977. "Neoclassicism and Dissent: 1890–1930." In Sidney Weintraub, ed., *Modern Economic Thought,* 7–21. Philadelphia: University of Pennsylvania Press.

Robbins, Lionel. 1932. *An Essay on the Nature and Significance of Economic Science*. London: St. Martin Press.

Rorty, Richard. 1989. *Contingency, Irony and Solidarity*. Cambridge: Cambridge University Press.

Rosenberg, Alexander. 1976. *Microeconomic Laws: A Philosophical Analysis*. Pittsburgh: University of Pittsburgh Press.

Ross, Dorothy. 1991. *The Origins of American Social Science*. Cambridge: Cambridge University Press.

Roth, Paul A., and Robert Barrett. 1990. "Deconstructing Quarks." *Social Studies of Science* 20: 579–632.

Rotheim, Roy J. 1992. "Interdependence and the Cambridge Economic Tradition." In Bill Gerrard and John Hillard, eds., *The Philosophy and Economics of J. M. Keynes*, 32–58. Aldershot, Hants: Edward Elgar.

Routh, Guy. 1975. *The Origin of Economic Ideas*. London: Macmillan.

Rowley, Charles K., Robert D. Tollison, and Gordon Tullock. 1991. *The Political Economy of Rent-Seeking*. Boston: Kluwer Academic Publishers.

Ruggles, Richard. 1952. "Methodological Developments." In B. F. Haley, ed., *Survey of Contemporary Economics*, vol. 2, 408–53. Homewood, IL: Irwin.

Rutherford, Malcolm. 1988 [1983]. "J. R. Commons' Institutional Economics." *Journal for Economic Issues* 17(3). Reprinted in Warren J. Samuels, ed., *Institutional Economics*, 265–88. Aldershot, Hants: Edward Elgar.

———. 1990. "Introduction to the Transactions Voice." In John R. Commons, *Institutional Economics: Its Place in Political Economy*. New Brunswick, NJ: Transaction Publishers.

Salant, Walter S. 1989. "The Spread of Keynesian Doctrines and Practices in the United States." In Peter A. Hall, ed., *The Political Power of Economic Ideas: Keynesianism across Nations*, 27–51. Princeton: Princeton University Press.

Samuels, Warren J., ed. 1979. *The Economy As a System of Power: Papers from the Journal for Economic Issues. Vol. 1: Corporate Systems*.

Samuelson, Paul A. 1955. *Economics: An Introductory Analysis*. 3d ed. New York: McGraw-Hill.

———. 1958. *Economics: An Introductory Analysis*. 4th ed. New York: McGraw-Hill.

———. 1966. *The Collected Papers of Paul A. Samuelson*. Ed. Joseph E. Stiglitz. Cambridge: MIT Press.

———. 1970. "Economics in a Golden Age: A Personal Memoir." In Gerald Holton, ed. *The Twentieth Century Sciences: Studies in the Biography of Ideas*. New York: W. W. Norton.

———. 1971. "The Monopolistic Competition Revolution." In Edwin Mansfield, ed., *Microeconomics: Selected Readings*, 325–36. New York: W. W. Norton.

———. 1976. *Economics: An Introductory Analysis*. 10th ed. New York: McGraw-Hill.

Samuelson, Paul A., and William D. Nordhaus. 1989. *Economics*. 13th ed. New York: McGraw-Hill.

Schoeffler, Sidney. 1955. *The Failures of Economics: A Diagnostic Study*. Cambridge: Harvard University Press.

Schumpeter, Joseph A. 1934. "Depressions." In *The Economics of the Recovery Program*, ed. Douglass V. Brown et al., 1–21. New York: Whittlesey House.

———. 1954. *History of Economic Analysis*. Oxford: Oxford University Press.

Shackle, G.L.S. 1967. *The Years of High Theory: Invention and Tradition in Economic Theory*. Cambridge: Cambridge University Press.

Shapin, Steven. 1982. "History of Science and Its Sociological Reconstructions." *History of Science* 20: 157–211.

———. 1992. "Discipline and Bounding: The History and Sociology of Science as Seen Through the Externalism-Internalism Debate." *History of Science* 30: 333–69.

Shapin, Steven, and Simon Schaffer. 1985. *Leviathan and the Air-Pump: Hobbes, Boyle, and the Experimental Life*. Princeton: Princeton University Press.

Shenhav, Yehuda. 1995. "From Chaos to Systems: The Engineering Foundations of Organization Theory, 1879–1932." *Administrative Science Quarterly* 40: 557–85.

Silk, Leonard. 1974. *The Economists*. New York: Basic Books.

Simon, Herbert. 1979. "Rational Decision Making in Business Organization." *American Economic Review* 69: 493–513.

Sismondo, Sergio. 1993. "Some Social Constructions: Finding the Limits of the Constructivist Metaphor." *Social Studies of Science* 23: 515–53.

Slichter, Sumner H. 1924. "The Organization and Control of Economic Activity." In Rexford Guy Tugwell, ed., *The Trend of Economics*, 301–56. New York: Alfred A. Knopf.

Smelser, Neil J., and Richard Swedberg, eds. 1994. *The Handbook of Economic Sociology*. Princeton and New York: Princeton University Press and Russell Sage Foundation.

Smith, Adam. 1961 [1776]. *An Inquiry into the Nature and Causes of the Wealth of Nations: Representative Selections*. Ed. by Bruce Mazlish. The Library of Liberal Arts. Indianapolis: Bobbs-Merrill.

Smith, Barbara Herrnstein. 1988. *Contingencies of Value: Alternative Perspectives for Critical Theory*. Cambridge: Harvard University Press.

———. 1993. "Unloading the Self-Refutation Charge." Paper delivered at the Davis Center Seminar, Princeton University, April 30, 1993.

Snow, C. P. 1964. *The Two Cultures: And A Second Look*. Cambridge: Cambridge University Press.

Sobel, Robert. 1980. *The Worldly Economists*. New York: The Free Press.

Solow, Robert M. 1991. "Cowles and the Tradition of Macroeconomics." In *Cowles Fiftieth Anniversary: Four Essays and an Index of Publications*, 81–108. New Haven, CT: The Cowles Foundation for Research in Economics at Yale University.

Soule, George. 1924. "Economics—Science and Art." In Rexford Guy Tugwell, ed., *The Trend of Economics*, 357–68. New York: Alfred A. Knopf.

Spector, Malcolm, and John Kitsuse. 1987. *Constructing Social Problems*. New York: Aldine de Gruyter.

Spence, Michael. 1973. "Job Market Signaling." *Quarterly Journal of Economics* 87: 355–74.

Spiegel, Henry William. 1983. *The Growth of Economic Theory*. 2d ed. Durham: Duke University Press.

Stanfield, James Ronald. 1974. "Kuhnian Revolutions and the Keynesian Revolution." *Journal for Economic Issues* 8: 97–109.

―――. 1986. *The Economic Thought of Karl Polanyi: Lives and Livelihood.* Houndsmills, Basingstoke, Hampshire: Macmillan.

Star, Susan Leigh. 1989. *Regions of the Mind: Brain Research and the Quest for Scientific Certainty.* Stanford: Stanford University Press.

Star, Susan Leigh, and Elihu M. Gerson. 1987. "The Management and Dynamics of Anomalies in Scientific Work." *Sociological Quarterly* 28: 147–69.

Star, Susan Leigh, and R. Griesemer. 1989. "Institutional Ecology, 'Translation,' and Boundary Objects: Amateurs and Professionals in Berkeley's Museum of Vertebrate Zoology." *Social Studies of Science* 19: 387–420.

Stigler, George J. 1943. "The New Welfare Economics." *American Economic Review* 33: 355–59.

―――. 1946. "The Economics of Minimum Wage Legislation." *American Economic Review* 36: 360–65.

―――. 1947. "Professor Lester and Marginalism." *American Economic Review* 37(3): 154–57.

―――. 1965. *Essays in the History of Economics.* Chicago: University of Chicago Press.

―――. 1973. "The Adoption of the Marginal Utility Theory." In R. D. Collison Black et al., eds., *The Marginal Revolution in Economics,* 305–20. Durham: Duke University Press.

Stigler, George J., and Gary S. Becker. 1977. "De Gustibus Non Est Disputandum." *American Economic Review* 67(2): 76–90.

Stoneman, William E. 1979. *A History of the Economic Analysis of the Great Depression in America.* New York: Garlend Publishing.

Streissler, E. 1973. "To What Extent Was the Austrian School Marginalist?" In R. D. Collison Black et al., eds., *The Marginal Revolution in Economics,* 160–75. Durham: Duke University Press.

―――. 1990. "Menger, Böhm-Bawerk, and Wieser: The Origins of the Austrian School." In Klaus Hennings and Warren J. Samuels, eds., *Neoclassical Economic Theory, 1870 to 1930,* 151–89. Boston: Kluwer Academic Publishers.

Swedberg, Richard. 1990. *Economics and Sociology.* Princeton: Princeton University Press.

―――. 1991. *Joseph A. Schumpeter: His Life and Work.* Cambridge: Polity.

Taussig, F. W. 1939. *Principles of Economics.* 4th ed. New York: Macmillan.

Taylor, Horace. 1928. *Making Goods and Making Money.* New York: Macmillan.

Tinbergen, Jan. 1988. "Recollections of Professional Experiences." In J. A. Kregel, ed., *Recollections of Eminent Economists,"* vol. 1, 67–96. Houndmills, Basingstoke, Hampshire: Macmillan.

Tool, Marc R. 1985. *The Discretionary Economy: A Normative Theory of Political Economy.* 2d ed. Boulder: Westview.

Tool, Marc R., and Warren J. Samuels, eds. 1989a. *The Economy as a System of Power.* 2d rev. ed. New Brunswick, NJ: Transaction Books.

―――. 1989b. *State, Society, and Corporate Power.* 2d rev. ed. New Brunswick, NJ: Transaction Books.

Trachtenberg, Marc. 1983. "Keynes Triumphant: A Study of the Social History of

Economic Ideas." In Jones and Kuklick, eds., *Current Perspectives on the History of the Social Sciences*, 17–86.

Tugwell, Rexford Guy. 1924a. "Experimental Economics." In Tugwell, ed., *The Trend of Economics*, 369–422. New York: Alfred A. Knopf.

——— ed. 1924b. *The Trend of Economics*. New York: Alfred A. Knopf.

Usher, Abbott Payson. 1934. "The Liberal Theory of Constructive Statecraft," *American Economic Review* 24(1): 1–10.

Veblen, Thorstein. 1925. "Economic Theory in the Calculable Future." *American Economic Review* 15(1): 48–56.

———. 1948. "Why Is Economics Not an Evolutionary Science?" In *The Portable Veblen*, ed. Max Lerner, 215–40.

Wade, Larry L. 1983. "Political Economy: Problems with Paradigms." In *Political Economy: Recent Views*, ed. Larry L. Wade, 1–26. Boston: Kluwer-Nijhoff.

Walker, Donald A. 1979. "The Institutionalist Economic Theories of Clarence Ayres." *Economic Inquiry* 17(4): 519–38.

Ward, Benjamin. 1972. *What's Wrong with Economics*. New York: Basic Books.

Watson-Verran, Helen, and David Turnbull. 1995. "Science and Other Indigenous Knowledge Systems." In Shila Jasanoff, Jerald Markel, James C. Petterson, and Trevor Pinch, eds., *Handbook of Science and Technology Studies*, 115–39. Los Angeles: Sage.

Weimer, Walter B., and David S. Palermo. 1973. "Paradigms and Normal Science in Psychology." *Science Studies* 3: 211–44.

Weintraub, E. Roy. 1979. *Microfoundation: The Compatibility of Microeconomics and Macroeconomics*. Cambridge: Cambridge University Press.

———. 1985. *General Equilibrium Analysis: Studies and Appraisal*. Cambridge: Cambridge University Press.

———. 1989. "Methodology Doesn't Matter, but the History of Thought Might." *Scandinavian Journal of Economics*. Reprinted in S. Honkapohja, ed., *The State of Macroeconomics*, 263–79. Oxford: Basil Blackwell.

———. 1991a. "Minisymposium: Reconstructing Economic Knowledge: Editor's Introduction." *History of Political Economy* 23(1): 101–3.

———. 1991b. *Stabilizing Dynamics: Constructing Economic Knowledge*. Cambridge: Cambridge University Press.

Weintraub, Sidney. 1977a. "Hicksian Keynesianism: Dominance and Decline." In S. Weintraub, ed., *Modern Economic Thought*, 45–66. Philadelphia: University of Pennsylvania Press.

———, ed. 1977b. *Modern Economic Thought*. Philadelphia: University of Pennsylvania Press.

———. 1988. "A Jevonian seditionist: a mutiny to enhance the economic bounty." In J. A. Kregel, ed., *Recollections of Eminent Economists*, vol. 1, 37–56. Houndmills, Basingstoke, Hampshire: Macmillan.

Weir, Margaret. 1989. "Ideas and Politics: The Acceptance of Keynesianism in Britain and the United States." In Peter A. Hall, ed., *The Political Power of Economic Ideas: Keynesianism across Nations*, 53–86. Princeton: Princeton University Press.

Weir, Margaret and Theda Skocpol. 1985. "State Structure and the Possibilities for 'Keynesian' Responses to the Great Depression in Sweden, Britain, and the

United States." In Evans et al., eds., *Bringing the State Back In*. Cambridge: Cambridge University Press.

Weizsäcker, Carl Christian von. 1984. "Weizsäcker on Arrow." In Henry W. Spiegel and Warren J. Samuels, eds., *Contemporary Economists in Perspective*, 65–81. Greenwich, CT: JAI Press.

Weld, William Ernest. 1924. "Regional Comparison and Economic Progress." In Rexford Guy Tugwell, ed., *The Trend of Economics*, 423–42. New York: Alfred A. Knopf.

White. Hayden. 1973. *Metahistory: The Historical Imagination in Nineteenth-Century Europe*. Baltimore: Johns Hopkins University Press.

———. 1987. *The Content of the Form: Narrative Discourses and Historical Representation*. Baltimore: Johns Hopkins University Press.

Whitley, Richard. 1984. *The Intellectual and Social Organization of Sciences*. Oxford: Clarendon Press.

Wilber, Charles K., and Robert S. Harrison. 1978. "The Methodological Basis of Institutional Economics: Pattern Model, Storytelling, and Holism." *Journal for Economic Issues* 12 (March): 61–89.

Wilber, Charles K., and Kenneth P. Jameson. 1983. *An Inquiry into the Poverty of Economics*. Notre Dame, IN: University of Notre Dame Press.

Wiley, Norbert F. 1979. "The Rise and Fall of Dominating Theories in American Sociology." In William E. Snizek et al., eds., *Contemporary Issues in Theory and Research*. Westport, CT: Greenwood Press.

———. 1983. "The Congruence of Weber and Keynes." In Randall Collins, ed., *Sociological Theory*, 30–57. San Francisco: Jossey-Bass.

Winch, Donald. 1989. "Keynes, Keynesianism, and State Intervention." In Peter A. Hall (ed.), *The Political Power of Economic Ideas: Keynesianism across Nations*, 107–27. Princeton: Princeton University Press.

Wise, M. Norton. 1988. "Mediating Machines." *Science in Context* 2: 77–113.

———. (With the collaboration of Crosbie Smith), 1989. "Work and Waste: Political Economy and Natural Philosophy in Nineteenth Century Britain." *History of Science* 27: 263–301, 391–449; 28: 221–61.

Wolfe, Albert Benedict. 1924. "Functional Economics." In Rexford Guy Tugwell, ed., *The Trend of Economics*, 443–82. New York: Alfred A. Knopf.

Woolgar, Steve. 1988. *Science: The Very Idea*. London and New York: Ellis Horwood/Tavistock.

Working, Helbrook. 1927. "The Use of the Quantitative Method in the Study of Economic Theory." Round Table Discussion, *American Economic Review* 17(1): 18–24.

Wright, David McCord. 1945. "The Future of Keynesian Economics." *American Economic Review* 35: 284–307.

Yonay, Yuval P. 1989. "Collective Amnesia and Scientific Progress: The Distorted Presentation of the Institutionalist School by the Conventional Historiography of Economics and Its Bearings on the Kuhnian-Lakatosian Debate. A paper presented at the 84th Annual Meeting of the American Sociological Association, San Francisco, August 1989.

———. 1991. "When Black Boxes Clash: The Struggle Over the Soul of Economics." Ph.D. Dissertation. Northwestern University.

Yonay, Yuval P. 1992. "From Marshall to Samuelson: The Great Watershed in Economic Science." A Paper given at the Institute for Advanced Study, Princeton, NJ, December 10, 1992.

———. 1993. "The Institutionalist School Revisited: Beyond Veblen, Commons, and Mitchell." Unpublished paper. The Institute for Advanced Study, Princeton, NJ.

Yonay, Yuval P., and Joyce T. Robbins. 1994. "The Symbiosis of Theory and Applied Research: True Science And/Or a Self-legitimating Myth?" A Paper presented at the Israeli Sociological Association, Acre, March 1994 (Hebrew). An English version was presented at the École des mines, Paris, October 6, 1995.

Young, Allyn A. 1927. "Economics as a Field of Research." *Quarterly Journal of Economics* 42(1): 1–25.

———. 1928. "English Political Economy." *Economica* 8(1): 1–15.

Zukin, Sharon, and Paul Dimaggio, eds. 1990. *Structures of Capital: The Social Organization of the Economy*. Cambridge: Cambridge University Press.

Index

Abbott, Andrew Delano, 208
actor-network analysis (ANA), 4, 13, 20–26, 201, 202, 208, 211, 241n.10
Adams, Henry C., 37, 39, 151, 229n.12
Adams, John, 69–70, 182
Adams, Thomas Sewell, 74–75, 231n.13, 232n.24
administrative economics, 110
advertising, 120–22, 141, 236n.9
Aftalion, Albert, 47
AIDS research, 99
Alchian, Armen, 186
Allais, Maurice F. C., 242n.5
allies, definition of, 22, 247n.2
Almond, Gabriel A., 9
Altmeyer, Arthur J., 53
Amann, Klaus, 14
American Economic Association (AEA): establishment of, 35–46; *Index of Economic Articles*, 27; post–World War II skirmishes in, 194; presidents of, 36, 57–58, 88, 173, 178, 194, 231n.13; revolutionary ideas of founders of, 36–37, 41, 134, 151
American Economic Review (AER), 31, 186, 194, 246–47n.32
ANA. *See* actor-network analysis
anomalies, 5, 8, 200–202
anthropology, economic, 59
Arrow, Kenneth J., 36, 56, 65, 68, 186, 192, 205
Association for Evolutionary Economics, 59
Austrian school, 7, 39, 42, 47, 150, 189, 215, 220, 232n.21, 243n.14
Ayres, Clarence E., 58, 72, 95, 176, 182, 247n.33; institutionalist thought of, 66–67, 69

Backhouse, Roger, 11–13, 19, 23, 27, 32, 53, 62, 66, 97, 218–19, 222, 223n.6, 227n.37, 233n.7
Bagehot, Walter, 34
banks, 125, 236n.10
Barber, William J., 13, 58
Barnes, Barry, 9, 79, 162, 183

Barnett, George E., 231n.13
Bath school, 226n.28
Baumberger, Jörg, 9
Becker, Gary S., 104
Bentham, Jeremy, 105, 191
Bergson, Abram, 186
Berle, Adolph A., Jr., 53; *The Modern Corporation and Private Property* (with Means), 215
big business: institutionalism and, 56, 126–27. *See also* capitalism
biology, 17, 33, 34, 78, 79, 98, 162, 183, 209–10
Birken, Lawrence, 9
Black, John D., 87–88, 165–66
Black, R. D. Collison, 41, 151, 210, 214
black boxes: agreement needed for creation of, 21; definition of, 20, 127; examples of, 24–25, 50, 70, 78, 79, 99, 112–13, 115, 122, 124, 127–29, 148, 154, 176, 180, 237–38n.4
Bladen, Vincent, 187
Blaug, Mark, 4, 9, 10, 12–14, 23, 36, 40, 43, 53, 62–64, 66, 69, 79, 119, 128, 145, 146, 175, 200, 203, 204, 221, 222; critique of constructivism by, 218–19; on institutionalism, 61–62; on Marshall, 32–34
Boggart, E. L., 231n.13
Böhm-Bawerk, Eugen, 148
Boland, Lawrence A., 226n.31
botany, taxonomy in, 98, 161
Boulding, Kenneth E., 36, 53, 242n.5; on institutionalism, 60–63, 66, 189
Bourdieu, Pierre, 208
Bowley, Arthur, 33, 129, 145
Boyle, Robert, 16–17
Brandis, Royall, 40
Briefs, Henry W., 94, 192, 245n.27
Britain, 214–15; historical school in, 39, 210, 223n.2; institutionalists in, 214, 223n.2
Bronfenbrenner, Martin, 9
Brown, D. V., 201
Brown, Vivienne, 163, 198
Bullock, Charles J., 229n.16

Burns, Arthur F., 53, 58, 72, 205, 207; *Measuring Business Cycles* (with Mitchell), 58, 188; pragmatism of, 63–64

business cycles, 47, 109; early work on, 47; Mitchell's study of, 51, 58, 61, 62. *See also* real business cycle theory

business men: as human calculators, 103–4; Veblen on nature of, 115

Bye, Raymond, 54–55, 84, 85, 87, 151; classicists denounced by, 179; on developments in theory, 147–48; on economics and ethics, 152, 155; on empirical research, 146, 178; on institutionalists as extreme revolutionaries, 165, 168; neoclassical defense by, 132–34; on scope of economics, 106–8, 110

Cairnes, John, 34, 169, 210, 228n.9

Callon, Michel, 18, 20, 25–26, 196, 201, 211, 222

Cambridge school, 6, 30, 35, 42, 47, 185, 214, 242n.4, 246n.29

Camic, Charles, 57

Canterbery, E. Ray, 11, 62

capitalism: basic conflict of interest in, 128; J. B. Clark's ideas on, 40; in Commons's studies, 51; influence on theories by, 204–6. *See also* big business

capitalists, Keynes originally opposed by, 206

Carabelli, A., 191

Carey, Henry, 134, 181

Cartwright, Nancy, 14

Carver, Thomas Nixon, 44, 45, 57, 133, 148

case-studies, 232–33n.25

Cassel, Carl Gustav, 133, 148

ceteris paribus, 93, 170

Chamberlin, Edward, 127, 215

Chandler, A. D., Jr., 235n.6

Chicago, University of, 56, 57, 65, 230–31n.9

Clapham, John, 33, 147, 149

Clark, John Bates, 7, 10, 36, 45, 48, 150, 172, 203, 228n.6; *The Distribution of Wealth*, 40; marginal analysis in, 39–40, 204–5; *The Philosophy of Wealth*, 40

Clark, John Maurice, 11, 27, 38, 54, 56, 57, 62, 67, 72, 89, 105, 141, 171, 176, 182; on accuracy in science, 92–93, 95; AEA Presidential Address of, 36, 39; on classical economics, 174–75; collectivist ap-

proach of, 110–11; on economic man, 108; on economics and ethics, 152–53, 240n.17; on firing workers in recessions, 121; institutionalist thought of, 53, 65, 230n.6; Keynes and, 191, 192; neoclassical theory evaluated by, 131; "social economics" of, 110; *Studies in the Economics of Overhead Costs*, 121

classical economics: meaning of term, 180. *See also* Cairnes, John; Malthus, Thomas; Mill, John Stuart; Ricardo, David; Senior, Nassau William; Smith, Adam

Coats, A. W., 10, 26, 204, 228n.8

Cobb, John Candler, 81, 89, 109, 142, 168, 169

Colander, David, 195

collective economics, 110

collectivist approach, 110–12

Collins, Harry M., 14, 15

Collins, R. M., 206

Columbia University, 52, 56, 57, 59, 145, 197, 230–31nn.9–11

Commons, John R., 3, 46, 53, 56, 60, 61, 67, 68, 71, 89, 145, 176, 181, 182, 192, 197, 232n.22; classical theory and, 72, 131; "collective economics" of, 110; *Institutional Economics*, 88, 215; as institutionalist, 51–52, 63, 64–65, 88

competition: cutthroat, 126; monopolistic (imperfect), 126–27; as source of waste, 124–27. *See also* perfect competition

conspicuous consumption, 153

constructivist approach, 4–6, 13–20, 61, 67–70; actor-network analysis (ANA) in, 4, 13, 20–26; concept of progress in, 217; normative issues in, 218–19, 221; principle of symmetry in, 17–18, 49; on variation in scientific cultures, 78

consumption (consumers): advertising and, 120; conspicuous, 153; knowledge and, 123–24; marginal analysis of, 107; marginal substitution of, 234n.4; power of business over, 129–30; production separated from, 106

Cooley, Charles H., 46, 52, 155

Copeland, Morris, 53, 58, 72, 93–94, 120, 121, 153, 155, 176, 177; on classical theory, 131–32; on prices and value, 119; on socialist critique, 118; on society as an organism, 111, 235n.7

core beliefs, 23–24, 226n.32

Cornell University, 75, 230–31n.9

corporations. *See* big business
cost structures, 125–26, 236n.12
Council of Economic Advisers, 58, 63–64
Cournot, Antoine Augustin, 9
Cowles Commission, 185, 188, 243n.11
Cyert, Richard M., 127

Darwin, Charles, 48, 78, 89
Dasgupta, A. K., 62, 187
Davenport, Herbert, 36, 44, 133, 148, 152
Davies, J. Ronnie, 13
Dean, John, 24, 98, 161
Deane, Phylis, 11, 62, 191
Debreu, Gerard, 194–95, 222, 242n.5
deductive method: *ceteris paribus* in, 93,
    170; inductive method combined with,
    89, 91; institutionalist criticism of, 52,
    83; neoclassicists and, 32, 80–81, 180;
    personal preferences ruled out by, 204; in
    physics, 87; "probability theory" com-
    pared to, 144
deficit budgets, 10
De Marchi, Neil, 14, 198, 200
Descartes, René, 78
De Vroey, Michel, 9
Dewey, John, 104, 105, 232n.22
DiMaggio, Paul, 104, 199, 220, 247n.1
diminishing returns, law of, 85
disutility, 132, 133
Dorfman, Joseph, 36–45, 47, 52, 53, 56–
    58, 61, 63, 65, 73–75, 134, 141, 149,
    181, 229n.11; on critique of value theory,
    138; *The Economic Mind in American
    Civilization*, 229n.11
Dorfman, Robert, 186
Douglas, Paul, 27, 57, 129; on human
    nature, 102, 103, 171–72; on work,
    105
Dudley-Evans, Tony, 17
Dunbar, Charles E., 42, 169, 240n.8
Dunlop, John, 58

Econometrica, 187, 246n.32
econometrics, 185, 187–90, 215; Keynes's
    opposition to, 185, 191–92
Econometric Society, 187–88
Economica, 242n.7
economic freedom, idea of, 38
Economic Journal, 35, 146, 242n.7
economic knowledge: changes in, 199–
    211, 212–13; plurality of producers of,
    221

economic man, 100–110; J. M. Clark on
    changing nature of, 108; institutionalists
    and, 101–6, 170–71; rationality of, 103–
    4, 106–7
economic policy: institutionalist emphasis
    on, 63–65; neoclassicists' differences on,
    71; "old-fashioned" neoclassicists on,
    193–94
economics: "applied," 145–47; case-studies
    in, 232–33n.25; empirical papers in, 17
—history of: conventional version, 7–14,
    49, 196–97; struggle over, 163–83
    natural sciences compared to, 83–87; not
    always in accord with facts, 83; pantheon
    of, 31, 194; pre-Keynesian, 3–4; psychol-
    ogy in. *See* psychology; scope of, struggle
    over, 100–110; sociology of, 14, 15; text-
    books of, 55–56, 62; three divisions of,
    145–46; Tugwell on academization of,
    175; whether positive or normative sci-
    ence, 150–52, 155; whether there is prog-
    ress in, 211–17
economic schools: as arbitrary designations,
    6; definition of, 22–23; diversity within,
    213; perception of unity of, 214; rise and
    fall of, 160–61, 200
economic theory: approximation of reality,
    116–18, 132; continuing evolution of,
    147–48; divergent perceptions of, 92–94,
    96; economists' emphasis on, 62, 64–65;
    empirical research and, 87–92; of institu-
    tionalists, 93–94, 96; as key to powerful
    policies, 147–50; as not abstract enough,
    149; statistical tests of, 90, 144; whether
    present in institutionalism, 67–68, 132.
    See also value theory
economists: constructivist recommenda-
    tions to, 222; professional interests of,
    207–11
Edgeworth, Francis Y., 145
Edie, Lionel D., 55, 81, 83, 89, 104–6, 109,
    119–21, 129, 130, 166, 168, 169, 172;
    optimism about empiricism by, 142–43;
    on social change and institutions, 111
Edinburgh school, 225n.23, 226n.28
efficiency, 152–53
Einstein, Albert, 78
Ekelund, R. E., 35, 57, 62, 63, 66, 127
Elkana, Yehuda, 18, 212, 248n.11
Ely, Richard T., 36–38, 45, 48, 51, 169,
    181, 232n.24; *Outline of Economics*, 39;
    on what ought to be in the future, 151

empirical research (quantitative research), 51–55, 74, 230n.7; institutionalist emphasis on, 80–81, 137–38, 140–43; of mathematical economics, 185; monographic studies in, 142, 238n.6
—neoclassical attitude toward, 79, 90, 144; doubts about, 143–47; appropriation, 178–79; strong praise, 61
place of theory in, 87–91. *See also* National Bureau of Economic Research; statistics
environmental problems, 120–22
epistemic cultures, 17
equilibrium theory, 23, 30, 149, 184, 187, 243n.10; in international trade, 194; Weintraub's defense of, 218–19
ethics, economics and, 150–57, 239–40n.17; mathematical economics and, 194
evolution: Bye on, 165, 167; institutionalism as, 177; Usher on, 174. *See also* Darwin, Charles
expectations, 8, 185, 234n.6
experimentalism, Boyle's, 16–17
externalities, 121–22, 153

"Family Tree of Economics" (Samuelson), 194
fashion, 153
Feinstein, Alan, 98
Fetter, Frank, 36, 38, 44
Feyerabend, Paul K., 219
Fish, Stanley, 16, 227n.33
Fisher, Irving, 44, 45, 71, 148, 185
Ford, Gerald, 58
Foster, Fagg, 59
Fourier, Charles, 176, 177
Fowles, John, *Aristos*, 3, 196
Franklin, Benjamin, 89
free enterprise, 115–35. See also: *laissez-faire*; perfect competition
French school, 226n.28
Freud, Sigmund, 52, 183
Friedman, Milton, 57, 96–97, 185, 186, 194, 233–34n.7, 243n.16; *Essays in Positive Economics*, 189–90; mathematical economics and, 193, 205, 245n.26; statistical research by, 65
Frisch, Ragnar, 188, 215
Fujimura, Joan H., 162, 216
Fuller, Steve, 15
Furner, Mary O., 38, 40, 42, 229n.15

Galbraith, John Kenneth, 11, 58, 59, 62, 96, 191, 224nn.12, 15
Galton, Francis, 210
Gambs, John S., 59, 189
game theory models, 245n.25
Gay, Edwin F., 167, 231n.13
George, Henry, 181
Georgescu-Roegen, Nicholas, 242n.5
Germany: Americans who studied in, 36; historical school in, 39, 42, 47, 91, 166–67, 176, 180–81, 240nn.2, 3; institutionalist school in, 223n.2
Gerrard, Bill, 18, 27, 29, 163, 241n.10
Gerson, Elihu M., 201
Gieryn, Thomas F., 97
Giffen, Robert, 169
Gilbert, G. Nigel, 23
Goodrich, Carter, 52
Gordon, D. F., 11, 224n.14
Gordon, Robert A., 58, 72
Gordon, Wendell, 59, 247n.33
Gossen, Hermann Heinrich, 9
government (the State): early AEA attitude to, 36–42; externalities and, 122; Fisher's attitude to, 45; institutional economists in, 56, 58; institutionalist support of, 172–73; Knight opposes intervention by, 134; neoclassical support of, 35
—planning by: institutionalism and, 127; socialist-sponsored debate on, 215; World War I experience, 140–41
Taussig's attitude to, 44
Great Depression, 212; institutionalist perception of, 201; Keynesian economics and, 4, 7, 12, 201; neoclassical explanation of, 201–2
Grether, D., 96
Griesemer, R., 216
Groenewegen, Peter, 32
Gruchy, Allan G., 59, 62, 175, 189, 110, 182, 191, 245n.23, 247n.33; institutionalist thought of, 66–67, 69

Haberler, *Theory of International Trade*, 194
Hadley, Arthur T., 36, 42, 44, 229n.16
Hahn, Frank, 162
Hale, Robert Lee, 83, 126, 240n.17
Hall, Peter A., 4
Hamilton, Walton Hale, 53, 89
Hammond, Matthew B., 231n.13
Hands, Douglas Wade, 13, 99, 226n.28

Hansen, Alvin H., 36, 53, 129, 231n.13
Harcourt, Geoffrey C., 10, 32
harmony of interests, 175
Harris, Abram L., 50
Harrison, Robert S., 93, 95
Harvard University, 42, 56, 57, 230–31n.9
Harvey, Bill, 201
Harwood, Jonathan, 78–79
Hausman, Daniel M., 13, 23, 65, 95, 96, 190, 218, 222, 245n.27
Hayek, Friedrich von, 47; *Price and Production*, 215; *Profit, Interest and Investment*, 215
Hébert, R. F., 35, 57, 62, 63, 66, 127
hedonism, 101–3, 106–7, 112–13, 153, 170, 191
Heilbroner, Robert L., 4
Henry, John F., 40, 41
Hicks, John R., 186, 223n.6; Keynes mathematized by, 192, 244n.20; *Value and Capital*, 215
Hill, Forest, 62
Hirsch, Paul, 198
historical school: in AEA, 36; in Britain, 39, 210, 223n.2; in Germany, 39, 42, 47, 91, 166–67, 176, 180–81, 240nn.2, 3; inductive method of, 32; Marshall and, 32–34, 228n.7; orthodox theory opposed by, 240n.6
historical studies, neoclassicists on, 145–46
Hobbes, Thomas, 16–17
Hobson, John Atkinson, 223n.2, 230n.16
Hodgson, Geoffrey M., 65, 69, 220
holistic economics, 62, 110
Hollander, Jacob, 178
Homan, Paul T., 155, 239n.16
Hoover, C. B., 58
Hoover, Kevin D., 16
Hotelling, Harold, 185
Howey, Richard S., 10
Hoxie, Robert F., 46; *Trade Unionism in the United States*, 52
human nature: changing concepts of, 112–14; economic models of, 198–99; Knight on, 134; in struggle over scope, 100–110. *See also* economic man; psychology
Humphries, Sally C., 59
Hutchison, Terence, 204, 222; *The Significance and Basic Postulates of Economics*, 189

Illinois, University of, 230–31n.9
imperfect competition, 215, 242n.4
increasing returns, 126
individualistic approach of neoclassicists, 104–5, 110–11
inductive method, 180; deductive method combined with, 89, 91; of historical school, 32; institutionalism and, 32, 80–81, 83
industry, coordination of, 127, 141
Ingram, John Kells, 210
institutionalism: author's use of term, 6–7, 27, 223n.1; centers of teaching of, 52; combining neoclassicism and, 232n.23; concept of science in, 93; constructivist approach to, 197; contemporary, 182–83, 220, 245n.23, 247n.33; contributions to economics by, 60–65, 135; deductive method criticized by, 52, 83; diversity of thought within, 213–14; econometrics' battle with, 188; on externalities, 122; general principles of, 52, 69; as guardian of tradition, 168–75; history of, 49–60, 75–76; 1890–1914, 50–53; in interwar period, 5, 53–58, 160–61, 181–82, 184, 197, 205; after World War II, 58–59, 161, 184, 189; inductive method and, 32, 80–81, 83; Keynesian Revolution supported by, 191; Marshall and, 32, 169
—name of: alternative names, 62, 110; originally only applied to Veblen, 71, 110; origin of name, 110
new type of theory developed by, 93–94, 96; promises and successes of, 140–43; as radical alternative to mainstream economics, 230n.8
—struggle between neoclassicists and, 3–4, 24–26, 57, 70–75; basic differences, 71–72; over history, 163–83; human nature and institutions, 100–114; institutionalists as extreme revolutionaries, 165–67; relevance and values, 136–62; right method, 79–80
unorthodox sources for, 176–78, 181; whether there is doctrine of, 65–70, 213.
invisible hand, 117, 122, 173
iron law of wages, 148
irrationality, 104, 106, 116, 235n.7

Jaffé, William, 10, 41
Jalladeau, Joël, 40
James, Edmund Janes, 37
James, J. S., 77
Jameson, Kenneth P., 222
Jensen, Arthur, 79
Jevons, William S., 7, 10, 30, 39, 41, 90, 93, 106, 107, 145, 149, 186, 191, 210; on empirical verification, 169, 170
Jha, Marmadeshwar, 35
Johns Hopkins University, 231n.9
Johnson, Alvin S., 75, 231n.13
Johnston, R., 211
Jones, Richard, 176
Journal for Economic Issues, 59, 241n.13
Journal of Political Economy (JPE), 44, 186, 246n.32

Kadish, Alon, 32, 33, 186, 209, 210
Kaldor, Nicholas, 184
Kemmerer, E. W., 231n.13
Keynes, John Maynard: Austrian school opposed by, 47; econometrics opposed by, 185, 191–92; *The Economic Consequences of the Peace*, 191; *General Theory of Employment, Interest and Money*, 11, 63, 190–92, 215, 223n.6; Great Depression and, 4, 7, 12, 201–2; on money-motive, 100; New Deal and, 63; resistance to, 10–11, 12–13, 160, 206, 224n.15; "Revolution" of, 10–12, 190–91, 214–15; *Treatise on Money*, 11, 192
Keynes, John Neville, 169, 171; *Scope and Method of Political Economy*, 34, 228n.8
Keynesian-neoclassical synthesis, 8, 161, 162, 185, 193–95, 223n.6; mathematical models in, 192–93, 197, 244n.21; and thought of Keynes, 192, 245nn.24, 26
Keyserling, Leon, 54, 56, 58, 63, 231n.14
Kitsuse, John, 207
Klamer, Arjo, 15, 22, 186, 195, 198
Klein, Lawrence R., 188, 192, 205, 244n.21
Klein, Philip, 59, 245n.23
Knapp, Joseph G., 58
Knies, Karl, 40, 181, 240n.6
Knight, Frank, 27, 57, 66, 71, 133, 147, 148, 189, 224n.15; on divisions of economics, 145–46; on economics and physics, 82, 84–86; government intervention and, 134; on institutionalist research, 144, 162; on separation of goals and means, 157; on Veblen, 166, 240n.3

Knorr-Cetina, Karin, 14, 17, 19, 78
knowledge: lack of, 122–24; perfect, 116, 119, 122–24, 235n.7. *See also* economic knowledge; scientific knowledge
Koopmans, Tjalling C., 96, 188
Koot, Gerard M., 210
Kuhn, Thomas S., 4–5, 23, 29, 31, 49, 224nn.7, 8, 248n.12; on history of science, 163; model of, 8–10, 47, 195, 200–202, 211, 220, 224n.10; on new vs. established paradigms, 158; *Structure of Scientific Revolutions*, 29, 136, 163; unified science rejected by, 221
Kuznets, Simon, 53, 58, 61

labor unions (trade unions): AEA founders' attitude to, 37, 39–41; Hoxie's book on, 52; neoclassical ideas on, 35, 128. *See also* workers
laissez-faire: classical economists and, 173–74; early AEA opposition to, 36–38, 42; Keynes's undermining of, 10; mathematical economists and, 195; neoclassical school and, 7, 34–35, 173, 180, 228n.9; pre-Keynesian attacks on, 3, 4; Walras and, 46. *See also* free enterprise; perfect competition
Lakatos, Imre, model of, 4–5, 8, 11–14, 23, 31, 47, 63, 195, 198, 200, 202, 211, 222, 224n.16, 244n.17
Lamarck, Chevalier, 89
Land Economics, 197
Landreth, Harry, 60, 62, 65, 66, 175
Lange, Oskar, 57, 194, 242n.5
Laplace, Pierre-Simon de, 89
Latour, Bruno, 5, 6, 15, 16, 18, 49, 76, 78, 120, 164, 203, 208, 211, 219; actor-network analysis (ANA) of, 4, 13, 20–26, 201, 202, 208, 211, 241n.10; on Pasteurization, 248n.10; *Science in Action*, 49
Laudan, Larry, 202
Laughlin, J. Laurence, 42, 45, 229n.16
Lausanne school, 7, 149, 238n.9
Lavoie, Don, 27, 199, 215, 243n.13, 245n.27
Law, John, 162, 227n.34
Lawson, T., 100
Lee, Bradford A., 12
Leijonhufvud, Axel, 8, 23, 206, 245n.26; *Keynesian Economics and the Economics of Keynes*, 245n.24
Lekachman, Robert, 4

Leland, Simeon, 57
Lescohier, Don D., 53
Leslie, Thomas, 34, 240n.6
Lester, Richard A., 188–89, 237n.16
Lewis, W. Arthur, 215
Lindberg, Leon N., 220
List, Frederick, 134
Little, I.M.D., 194
London School of Economics (LSE), 47,
    186, 189, 214, 215
Lowe, Adolph, 34, 151, 224n.11

Machlup, Fritz, 188–89, 243n.13
MacKenzie, Donald, 79, 162, 183
Madison, G. B., 139
Maier, Charles S., 220
Mäki, Uskali, 18, 23, 84, 96, 226n.30
Malinvaud, Edmond, 188
Maloney, John, 32, 33, 208–10
Malthus, Thomas, 7, 173
marginal analysis, 7, 9, 11, 34; in AEA his-
    tory, 38–39, 42; capitalism supported by,
    204; classical economics is attacked by,
    42; J. B. Clark's use of, 40–41; Machlup-
    Stigler defense of, 188–89; reasons for
    rise of, 202–4, 208–9; said to be Ricar-
    dian, 149–50; statistics and, 93;
    Tugwell's critique of, 85; as unique tool
    of economists, 33; Walrasian version of,
    46
marginal productivity theory, 40, 41, 44,
    73, 148, 239n.11; wages in, 128–29,
    133, 156
marginal utility theory, 30–31, 106–8,
    148
Marks, H. M., 99
Marshall, Alfred, 10, 23, 45, 48, 70, 78,
    148, 172, 210; abolition of poverty
    sought by, 173; conflicting interpreta-
    tions of, 179–80; on economic laws as
    tendencies, 169; general discussion of,
    30–35; hedonism and rationalism re-
    jected by, 107, 234n.5; Keynes and, 11,
    34, 190, 191; laissez-faire and, 4, 34–35,
    134; marginal analysis in, 7, 31, 41, 208–
    9; markets treated separately by, 187;
    mathematical economics and, 183, 196,
    210; Money, Credit, and Commerce,
    228n.7; New Economics critique of, 193,
    194; Principles of Economics, 31, 33, 43,
    74, 193, 228n.7; quantitative research
    and, 90, 168–70; letter on statistics, 144

unmeasurability of assumptions of, 93;
    Walras's approach rejected by, 210
Marx, Karl, 47, 107, 177, 183
Marxism, 212, 220, 226n.32; Veblenian
    analysis compared to, 50
mathematical economics, 56, 97, 162;
    achievements of, 221–22; author's use of
    term, 241–42n.2; econometrics allied
    with, 187–90; Hicks's contribution to,
    215; Keynes's attitude to, 191–92;
    Keynesian system converted to, 192–93,
    244nn.20, 21; Marshall's work and, 183,
    196, 210; rise of, 185–87, 204; triumph
    of, 193–95, 197–98
Mayo-Smith, Richard, 151
McCloskey, Deirdre N., 13, 15, 17–19, 22,
    28, 98, 117, 190, 226n.31, 232n.16,
    243n.16; on hubris of modern econo-
    mists, 222; study of AER by, 246–47n.32
McDougall, William, 52
Mead, George Herbert, 104
Means, Gardner, 53, 62; "administrative
    economics" of, 110; The Modern Corpo-
    ration and Private Property (with Berle),
    215
medical research, 98–99
Mehta, Judith, 198
Ménard, Claude, 46, 48, 187, 210
Mendel, Marguerite, 59
Mendelsohn, Everett, 164
Menger, Carl, 7, 10, 30, 39–41, 47, 149
Michigan, University of, 52, 230n.5
Mill, James, 180
Mill, John Stuart, 34, 35, 38, 107, 172,
    177, 224n.11
Millis, Harry A., 57, 231n.13
Mills, Frederick C., 53, 55, 83, 89–91, 101,
    169, 178, 231n.13
Mincer, Jacob, 65, 72–73
minimum-wage statute, 128
Minnesota, University of, 230–31n.9
Minsky, Hyman P., 57
Mirowski, Philip, 7, 17, 18, 49, 53, 63, 65,
    95, 97, 182, 204, 216, 222, 225n.24,
    226n.32, 232n.22; on economists as "sci-
    entists," 209; on neoclassicists and statis-
    tics, 144–45
Mises, Ludwig von, 148
Mitchell, Wesley C., 27, 53, 56, 58, 60, 62,
    67, 71, 101, 109, 120, 121, 144, 145,
    175, 176, 182, 231n.10, 240n.17;
    Blaug's critique of, 61; on business cycles,

Mitchell, Wesley C. (*cont.*)
51, 58, 61, 62, 109; distinguished career
of, 57, 141, 197, 231n.13; falsely associated with German historicism, 166–67,
181; Friedman on, 65; on human nature,
100, 105; on industrial coordination,
127, 141; institutionalist thought of, 51–
52, 68; on Marshall, 168–69; *Measuring
Business Cycles* (with Burns), 58, 188; on
orthodox economists, 172, 173, 177; as
pragmatist, 104, 232n.22; on theory, 72,
88, 90–91, 93, 138, 149–50, 165–66,
233n.6; *Types of Economic Theory*, 88,
100; on World War I and economics,
140–41
monetarism, 8, 185, 206, 245n.25; as part
of dominant coalition, 192–93
monographic studies, 142, 238n.6
monopolistic competition, 126–27
Moore, Geoffrey H., 64
Moore, Henry L., 93, 144, 145
Morse, Chandler, 96
Moulton, Harold, 54
Mulkay, Michael J., 23, 202
Myler, Jack, *German Historicism and
American Economics*, 180–81
Myrdal, Gunnar, 59, 245n.29

Napoleoni, Claudio, 62
National Bureau of Economic Research
(NBER), 51–53, 58, 61, 71, 141, 145,
197, 231n.10, 237n.3; NBER method
discarded, 188
national income data, Keynes's opposition
to, 191, 244n.19
natural resources, overutilization of, 121,
122
natural sciences: economics compared to,
83–87; social sciences as different from,
157. *See also* biology; physics
Neale, Walter C., 59
Nelson, Richard R., 199
neoclassical school, 29–48; author's use of
term, 6–7; combining institutionalism
and, 232n.23; in constructivist approach,
23–24; diversity of thought within, 205,
214; empiricism defended by, 178–79;
explanations for decline of, 5; individualistic approach of, 104–5
—institutionalists and: basic differences,
71–72; institutionalists' partial support,
131–32. *See also:* institutionalism—strug-

gle between neoclassicists and
Keynes and, 8, 11, 223n.6; as metaphysical, 81; as name for two antagonistic
schools, 4, 245n.27.; passage of time
missing from, 148 perfect competition in,
116–18
—theory and: continual development of
theory, 147–50, 167; orthodox theory
supported, 90–92. *See also* economic theory; value theory
whether classical school similar to, 149–
50. *See also* "old-fashioned" neoclassical
economics
neoinstitutionalists, 247n.33
network: concept of, 22–23, 199, 216, 219–
20; economics as, 215–16, 219–21; when
allies are lost by a, 201. *See also* actor-
network analysis
Newcomb, Simon, 42
New Deal, institutionalism and, 4, 58, 63,
64, 160, 184, 197
New Economics, 193–95. *See also* Keynesian-neoclassical synthesis
New School for Social Research, 51, 197
Newton, Isaac, 17–18, 78, 84, 89
Nicholson, Joseph Shield, 223n.2
Nicholson, Walter, 122
Niehans, Jürg, 31, 62
Nordhaus, William D., 116, 128
Nourse, Edwin, 54, 58, 231nn.13, 14,
240n.4

O'Brien, D. P., 32, 190, 246n.29
Ohio, University of, 230n.9
"old-fashioned" neoclassical economics, 70–75, 144, 184, 193–95, 205,
211, 245n.27. *See also* neoclassical economics: as name for two antagonistic
schools
Oser, Jacob, 11, 31, 62, 191
Owen, Robert, 176
Oxford University, 214

Palermo, David S., 9
paradigms: classification of, 227n.34; debates about, 136; in Kuhn's model of science, 8–9, 158, 224n.8, 248n.11; in Latourian scheme, 23; reasons for lost dominance by, 201
Pareto, Vilfredo, 7, 46, 149, 168, 186
Paris school, 226n.28
Parker, Carleton H., 46, 52

Pasteur, Louis, 78, 89, 248n.10
Patinkin, Don, 191; *Anticipations of the General Theory*, 245n.23
Patten, Simon Nelson, 36–38, 169, 229n.14
Peirce, Charles S., 77, 226n.29, 232n.22
Pennsylvania, University of, 230–31n.9
perfect competition, 116–24
Perlman, Mark, 72
Perlman, Selig, 53, 72
Perrin, C. E., 164
Perroux, François, 242n.5
Pheby, J., 96
Phillips, Ronnie J., 58
physics, 17, 78, 79, 82–87, 98, 100, 209–10, 233n.4
Pickering, Andrew, 6, 16
Pigou, Arthur, 148, 190
Pinch, Trevor J., 164
planning. *See* government—planning by
Plott, C., 96
Polanyi, Karl, 59
political economy, as former name for economics, 150–51, 210, 248n.9
politics, victory of an economic approach not due to, 205–6
pollution, 120–22
Popper, Karl, 189, 218, 243n.15
positivism, 15, 225n.19
poverty, 35, 228n.4
pragmatism, 104, 232n.22
predictions: as a criterion for theory evaluation, 19, 189–90
preferences: advertising as shaping of, 120; neoclassicists and, 109
price, elasticity of, statistical measurement of, 93
price indices, Keynes's opposition to, 191
price theory: in mathematical economics, 186. *See also* value theory
Priestley, Joseph, 89
probability theory, 143–45, 191
Proctor, Robert N., 204
production: consumption separated from, 106; in Veblen, 50, 51, 115, 118–19
psychic income, 234n.2
psychology: similarity to institutionalism, 98; neoclassicists and, 106–9, 113–14; in Parker's economics, 52; proposed research in, 92, 141; scientific ethics and, 239n.17; Taussig's interest in, 43. *See also* human nature

qualitative research, 78–81, 87–88
Quarterly Journal of Economics (QJE), 43, 172, 186, 246n.32

Ramstaad, Yngve, 60, 92
rational expectations theory, 8, 185, 245n.25
rationality: of advertisers, 120; classicists' attitude to, 171; of economic man, 103–4, 106–7, 112, 119, 170; in present-day economics, 195, 234n.3
real business cycle theory, 8, 185
recovering practice, 225n.18
Reder, Melvin, 56, 57
Redman, Deborah A., 9, 12
relevance, validity and, 136–62
Remenyi, J. V., 224n.16
rent-seeking behavior, 235n.2
rent theory, Ricardo's, 236n.12
revolution, in Kuhn's model, 8–10, 220, 224n.10
revolutionaries, institutionalists as, 165–67, 175, 177, 182
Ricardo, David, 7, 8, 38, 149–50, 169, 173, 236n.12; Jones's criticism of, 176; Marshall's criticism of, 32–33, 228n.4
Rima, Ingrid H., 31
Robbins, Lionel, 47, 56, 186, 202, 204; *An Essay on the Nature and Significance of Economic Science*, 189, 190, 239n.12; on Marshall, 193
Robinson, Joan, 127, 215, 246n.29
Robinson Crusoe story, 138–39
Rorty, Richard, 15
Roscher, Wilhelm, 177
Ross, Dorothy, 39, 42, 53, 151, 228n.10; on marginalist success, 202–3; *The Origins of American Social Science*, 228n.10
Routh, Guy, 11, 62, 191
Rutherford, Malcolm, 181

Saint-Simon, Comte de, 176
Salée, Daniel, 59
salesmanship, 120, 121
Samuelson, Paul A., 11, 31, 53, 63, 116, 127, 128, 185–86, 205, 223n.7, 248n.13; critique of Galbraith by, 96; *Economics: An Introductory Analysis*, 31, 194, 243n.8; on institutionalism, 56; Marshall criticized by, 193; "Mathematical Revolution" of, 193, 214; "old-fashioned"

Samuelson, Paul A. (*cont.*)
  neoclassical economics criticized by,
  245n.28
Say's Law, 190
Schaffer, Simon, 16, 17, 19, 78
Schumpeter, Joseph, 47, 57, 62, 148, 162,
  109, 201, 231n.12
science: claims of truth in, 21–22, 226n.30;
  competing valid approaches in, 136–37;
  construction of knowledge in, 14–19;
  constructivist approach to. *See* constructivist approach; diversity and plurality of, 17, 20, 29, 77, 79, 213; empirical
  evidence in, 15–16
—history of: bias, 29; continuity vs. revolution, 216; struggle of scientists over,
  163–83
  how to package innovations in, 164–
  65; internalist and externalist explanations of, 16, 202–3, 211; "invisible
  college" of, 220; lack of unity of, 29,
  218, 223; meaning of, 77–99; methodological disputes in, 98, 161; normal,
  8; one field as exemplar of, 78; as one
  of two cultures, 78; as open network,
  215–16, 219–21; refutability in, 189,
  190, 243n.15; simplicity in, 96–97;
  whether absolute accuracy needed in, 92–
  93. *See also* deductive method; inductive
  method
scientific knowledge: construction of, 14–
  19. *See also* knowledge
scientific method, 17–18, 77–78, 98
scientific research program. *See* SRP
Scitovsky, Tibor, 242n.5
Seligman, E.R.A., 36, 37
Senior, Nassau William, 238n.10; *An Outline of the Science of Political Economy*,
  171
Serres, Michael, 25
Shackle, G.L.S., 10, 127
Shapin, Steven, 16, 17, 19, 78
Sidgwick, Henry, 35, 172
Silk, Leonard, 134
Simon, Herbert, 66, 124
Sismondi, Jean Charles de, 176, 177
Sismondo, Sergio, 227n.35
Slichter, Sumner, 54, 81, 118, 120, 121,
  176, 231n.13; on economic man, 103–4;
  on economic theory, 111–12, 138, 139,
  146–47, 170; on free enterprise, 131; on
  lack of knowledge, 122–24; on labor and

capital, 128–30; on waste of competition,
  124–25, 127
Smelser, Neil J., 220
Smith, Adam, 7–9, 107, 112, 131, 173,
  223n.4, 239n.15; J. M. Clark's praise of,
  174–75; on individual in society, 115; the
  invisible hand, 117, 122, 173; state intervention and, 240–41n.8; Tugwell's attack on, 175; *The Wealth of Nations*, 7,
  9, 48, 115
Smith, Barbara Herrnstein, 15, 16, 18, 180
Snow, C. P., 78
Sobel, Robert, 58, 63, 64, 141
social constructivism, 16
social economics, 110
Social Harmony, dogma of, 35
socialism, 36–37, 40, 118, 176
social problems, definition of, as outcome of
  social negotiation, 207
society: institutionalism and, 110–12, 210;
  organic concept of, 37, 111, 235n.7;
  pragmatists' view of, 104; Smith on action of individual in, 115
sociology, 98, 183; of science, 4–5, 14–15,
  215, 222. *See also* constructivist approach
Solow, Robert, 162
Soule, George, 56, 81, 84, 138, 141, 142,
  160; on 19th-century statistics, 169–70;
  on whether economic phenomena are inevitable, 155–56
Spector, Malcolm, 207
Spence, Michael, 236n.8
Spengler, Joseph, 58, 146
Spiegel, Henry William, 62
Spiethoff, Arthur, 47
Sprague, O.M.W., 231n.13
Sraffa, Piero, 127
SRP (scientific research program), 5, 8, 11–
  14, 26, 224n.16
stagflation (1970s), 201
Stanfield, James Ronald, 10, 59
Star, Susan Leigh, 201, 215–16
State, the. *See* government
statistics: economists' use of, 55–56, 65, 71,
  90, 209, 248n.8; Moore's, 93; neoclassi-
  cal approach to, 144–45, 149; neoclassi-
  cism tested by, 90, 144; 19th-century
  economists' and, 169–70. *See also* econometrics; empirical research
Stigler, George J., 9, 31, 104, 128, 186–89,
  201, 205; *Essays in the History of Eco-*

nomics, 136; on mathematical economics and ethics, 194; study of journals by, 246n.32
stochastic models, 248n.8
Stockholm school, 47
Stocking, George, 58
Stoneman, William E., 36, 53
Streissler, E., 47
Sturges, Paul, 43
Sumner, William Graham, 42
Supple, Barry, 38, 42
Swedberg, Richard, 57, 220
symbolic interactionists, 104, 226n.28
symmetry, principle of, 17–18, 49

tariffs, 134
Taussig, Frank W., 36, 42–44, 45, 56, 57, 71, 148, 151, 193; institutionalists supported by, 172; *Principles of Economics*, 43; on quantitative research, 149, 178
taxonomy, 98, 161
Taylor, Fred Manville, 44–45, 231n.13
Taylor, Horace, 118, 119, 139, 170, 174
Texas, University of, in Austin, 58
textbooks of economics, 55–56, 62
texts, interpretation of, 16, 27–28, 227n.33, 241nn.10, 12
Thompson, William, 176
Thorndike, Edward L., 52, 104
Tinbergen, Jan, 188, 191, 215
Tobin, James, 11, 188, 205
Tool, Marc, 59
Toynbee, Arnold, 34
Trachtenberg, Marc, 209, 247n.7
trade unions. *See* labor unions
translation, process of, 25–26
Tugwell, Rexford, 27, 54–56, 58, 63, 72, 89, 101, 102, 150, 154, 181, 204, 240n.17; critique of classical economics by, 85, 138, 139–40, 182; on empirical methods, 239n.15; optimism about science by, 141–42; *The Trend of Economics*, 45, 132, 152, 171
Turnbull, David, 17

underconsumption, in free enterprise, 124
unemployment: of Great Depression, 247n.3; neoclassical ideas on, 35; as "social problem," 207
usefulness, criterion of, 136, 160, 237n.1
Usher, Abbott P., 173–74, 231n.13, 240n.7

utilitarianism, 101
utility, 234n.4. *See also* marginal utility theory

validity, relevance and, 157–62
value theory: Bye on, 238n.8; criticisms of, 131, 132, 136; now called price theory, 237n.2; overstressed by neoclassicists, 138–40; whether basic to economics, 150–57
Veblen, Thorstein, 3, 46, 68, 89, 182, 199, 232n.22; falsely identified with German historicism, 166, 181, 240n.3; Gruchy's description of, 232n.20; institutionalism originally only applied to, 71, 110; as institutionalist, 50–52, 54–55, 60–62, 67, 69; orthodox theory opposed by, 72, 175–76; profit-production polarity of, 50, 51, 115, 118–19; *The Vested Interest and the Common Man*, 115
Viner, Jacob, 57, 149, 166–68, 224n.15, 231n.13; institutionalism criticized by, 83, 86, 87, 90–91, 143–44, 162, 177; *Studies in the Theory of International Trade*, 194
Vining, Rutledge, 188

wages: iron law of, 148; persistence of low, 154, 156; in marginal productivity theory, 128–29, 133, 156; minimum, 128; physical productivity and, 129
Wald, Abraham, 145, 242n.5
Walker, Charles Swan, 37
Walker, Francis A., 169
Walras, Léon, 7, 10, 30, 31, 39, 41, 46, 145, 149, 186, 187, 232n.21, 238n.9; recent prominence of ideas of, 194, 210–11
Ward, Benjamin, 206
Washington, University of, 52
waste: competition as source of, 124–27; economists' ability to prevent, 141; persistence of, 154
Watson-Verran, Helen, 17
wealth: desire for, as universal, 171; neoclassical attitude to, 154, 156–57
Webb, Sidney, 186
Weber, Max, 183
Weimer, Walter B., 9
Weintraub, E. Roy, 13, 14, 16, 17, 23, 30, 98, 194, 247n.3; on equilibrium theory, 218–19
Weintraub, Sidney, 11, 192

Weir, Margaret, 12
Weld, William, 55, 56, 139, 168, 170
welfare economics, mathematical, 194
welfare state, Commons and, 63
welfare theory, 153–54, 156
White, Hayden, 29
Whitley, Richard, 161
Wicksell, Knut, 148
Wilber, Charles K., 93, 95, 222
Wiley, Norbert F., 9, 160
Wisconsin, University of, 37, 51–53, 56, 59, 74, 145, 197, 230–31nn.9, 11
Witte, Edwin, 53
Wolfe, Albert B., 77, 81, 111, 120, 138, 152, 231n.13; on concept of economic man, 101–2; on economics and ethics, 154–56, 239–40n.17; "Psychological Data in Scientific Economics," 108–9
Woolgar, Steve, 6, 15, 78
work, nature of, 105–6

workers: conflict between employers and, 131; employers' power over, 128–30; immobility of, 129; Malthus against reforms for, 173; in neoclassical model, 130; qualifications of, 122–23, 236n.8; rational choice by, 123; recession firing of, 121, 122; safety of, 121. See also labor unions; wages
Working, Holbrook, 88
World War I: economics changed by, 140–41; managed economy of, 4, 160, 223n.3; Taussig in, 43–44; War Industries Board in, 158, 207
Wright, Carroll D., 57

Yale University, 42, 74, 99
Young, Allyn A., 73–74, 167, 174, 186, 231n.13, 232nn.24, 25, 241n.9

Zukin, Sharon, 220